CSCS® STUDY GUIDE 2025-2026:

4 Practice Exams and
CSCS® Prep Book
[9th Edition]

Jeremy Downs

Copyright © 2025 by Ascencia Test Prep

ISBN-13: 9781637989241

ALL RIGHTS RESERVED. By purchase of this book, you have been licensed one copy for personal use only. No part of this work may be reproduced, redistributed, or used in any form or by any means without prior written permission of the publisher and copyright owner. Ascencia Test Prep; Trivium Test Prep; Accepted, Inc.; and Cirrus Test Prep are all imprints of Trivium Test Prep, LLC.

*CSCS® and Certified Strength and Conditioning Specialist® are registered trademarks of the National Strength and Conditioning Association. Neither this publication nor the publisher have any affiliation with, or any recognition, sponsorship, or endorsement by, the NSCA.

Image(s) used under license from Shutterstock.com

Table of Contents

Introduction i

Online Resources ix

1 Exercise Science 1
Basic Anatomy Concepts 1
The Skeletal System 4
The Muscular System 10
The Cardiovascular System 20
The Nervous System 26
The Endocrine System 30
The Digestive System 35
Biomechanics 38
Bioenergetics 46
Training Differences Among Athletes 49

2 Nutrition 57
Basic Nutrition Concepts 57
Applications of Nutrition Concepts 77
Performance-Enhancing Substances 86

3 Assessment 91
Basic Assessment Concepts 91
Types of Assessments 94
Administering Assessments 124
Assessments in Special Populations 129

4 Exercise Technique 133
Fundamentals of Exercise Technique 133
Warm-Up and Cooldown Protocols 136
Flexibility and Stretching Exercises 139
Resistance Training 151
Core Stability and Balance Training 169
Speed, Agility, and Quickness 177
Plyometric Training 181
Aerobic or Cardiorespiratory Endurance Training 189

5 Program Design 195
Fundamentals of Exercise Program Design 195
Designing an Exercise Program 210
Aerobic Endurance Training 235
Special Populations 239

6 Client Relations and Coaching 245
Building Professional Relationships 245
Effective Coaching Communication 249
Motivation 254

Setting Goals and Managing Expectations 264
Client Privacy 268

7 Safety and Risk Management 273
Professional Liability 273
Risk Management 277
Medical Clearance 281
Overtraining and Abnormal Responses to Exercise 285
Injuries and Medical Emergencies 288

8 Professional Development and Responsibility 293
Scope of Practice 293
Professional Standards and Codes of Conduct 296
Professional Development 299

9 Practice Test 303
Answer Key 327

INTRODUCTION

What is a Personal Trainer?

The world of personal training is vast and growing in many ways. A personal trainer is an educated exercise professional who possesses the knowledge and skill set to create and instruct others in various fitness-related settings. Personal trainers must strive to achieve a base of knowledge and to acquire the skills to properly design and implement research-based training programs that are safe and effective for their clientele. It is up to the certified personal trainer to ensure the client receives the highest quality training experience through appropriate goal setting, needs analysis, exercise prescriptions, and health and fitness education. Additionally, it is the certified personal trainer's responsibility to develop and employ these methods within his or her scope of practice. There are a variety of different career paths a certified personal trainer can pursue based on his or her interests and abilities.

Personal trainers can be productive in many different settings and businesses. The most common settings in which personal trainers work are the large, well-known gym chains and smaller, privately owned fitness centers that are common in the United States. These facilities are generally open to hiring newly trained, certified fitness professionals and are a good starting point for anyone looking to advance within a specific company.

However, there are a number of other settings in which certified personal trainers can utilize their health and fitness knowledge. For example, personal trainers can work in clinical settings, corporate training, in-home private settings, sports camps, and more. Working in a clinical setting as a personal trainer often involves administering exercise stress tests with a team supervised by a physician or medical practitioner. Corporate trainers tend to work at the private fitness centers of corporations in an office building. Some clientele prefer a more personalized workout within the privacy of their own home; the certified personal trainer will travel to the client's house with his or her equipment. Depending on the fitness professional's background, it may be preferable to work as a sports-specific strength and conditioning coach. There are many career paths available, but one key component of the personal training world is the certification.

Getting Certified

BENEFITS OF CERTIFICATION

Earning a certification through a nationally recognized fitness organization is one of the most important accomplishments for a fitness professional aiming to further his or her career. Certification is important for several reasons. First, fitness certifications require the acquisition of a substantial amount of valuable expertise and knowledge to pass the examination. Second, maintenance of most certifications requires continuing education through conventions, seminars, or other educational opportunities, so professionals keep their knowledge current and stay abreast of trends in the field. Finally, certification through major organizations demonstrates credibility to peers and clientele. The examination process requires adequate preparation to ensure successful candidates become personal trainers.

Fitness certification exams test individuals on a wide variety of exercise-science-based concepts. The concepts tested include, but are not limited to: exercise physiology, biomechanics, exercise psychology, anatomy and physiology, exercise prescription and program design, fitness facility organization and management, fitness programs for various populations, and more. Various fitness organizations provide test preparation materials such as study guides, review books, and practice tests that provide individuals with an idea of what they should expect on the exam. Fitness professionals seeking to become certified must prepare themselves for the exam by studying and being able to apply the knowledge in the materials. The certification exams are intentionally difficult in order to adequately prepare the candidates to work as competent professionals in the field of exercise science. This ensures the certified personal trainer will provide clients with safe and effective fitness programs.

Maintaining a fitness certification through the major organizations requires continued educational pursuits among the various topics in exercise science. This can be achieved through many avenues such as fitness conventions, web seminars, informational sessions with accompanying tests, and additional certifications. The purpose of continuing education credits for certifications is to ensure that the certified personal trainer maintains current knowledge and relevant expertise. Ever-improving scientific testing protocols, procedures, and equipment optimize the data that fitness professionals use to create ideal programs for clients. Studying the most up-to-date material ensures that the client is provided the most efficient method for obtaining their goals, but it is up to the trainer to guide them in the correct direction.

Credibility among trainers is ensured through the aforementioned certification process. Clientele and employers who are seeking the most qualified candidate can be assured they have a professional trainer by the certification the trainer holds. Based on the strenuous testing protocol and ongoing education requirements, certification makes it easier to determine whether a trainer is ready for a gig. High-profile employers will often require elite certifications of their training staff. For instance, professional sports teams often insist on a specific certification before considering an applicant. This requirement is often common at the collegiate level of fitness professionals as well. It shows the employers that the trainer has taken the time to understand the information relevant to providing the most effective program for their athletes.

It is highly important for individuals seeking any employment in the fitness industry to acquire certification through the major exercise organizations. The rigorous testing protocols require fitness professionals to achieve significant expertise in a variety of topics, which enhances their ability to create effective exercise programs. The major fitness organizations ensure fitness professionals keep their knowledge and expertise current. Certification supplies the employer and clients with an understanding of a fitness professional's level of credibility and competency in the field. In preparation for this great achievement, the fitness professional must first select which certification best fits his or her goals.

The following list provides information on some of the advantages and disadvantages for various major fitness certifications:

AMERICAN COUNCIL ON EXERCISE (ACE) CERTIFICATION

Advantages: The ACE certifications undergo accreditation through the National Commission for Certifying Agencies (NCCA), which ensures a program's certifications are evaluated for high-quality outcomes for their professionals. There are a variety of different certification specializations that can be obtained, which provides fitness professionals with different fields of expertise to study. ACE has an agreement for guaranteed interviews with several major fitness clubs that are found throughout the United States, enhancing the ability to find potential jobs. ACE certifications do not require a college-level degree to sit for the exam. All research utilized to develop the study material is scientifically evidence-based to ensure its effectiveness.

Disadvantages: The study materials and test can be expensive, totaling over $600 for the Personal Trainers Certification alone without specializations. Higher-profile training jobs, such as professional and collegiate strength coaches, typically require certification through other organizations such as ACSM or NSCA®.

NATIONAL ACADEMY OF SPORTS MEDICINE (NASM) CERTIFICATION

Advantages: The NASM certifications are also accredited through the NCCA like ACE, ensuring credibility. NASM certifications also do not require a bachelor's degree to sit for examination. NASM offers a money-back guarantee in finding employment in the field within ninety days. The certification exams are difficult, but the material effectively prepares candidates for the test if studied adequately. There are a variety of different specializations to choose from, including corrective exercise, sports performance, youth training, and more. Many colleges and universities have partnered with NASM to supply certifications through classes offered at the schools.

Disadvantages: The study materials and exams are also expensive, ranging from $699 to $1,299 depending on what program is selected. The certifications do not require continuing education to maintain certification, which could potentially cause information to become obsolete.

NATIONAL STRENGTH AND CONDITIONING ASSOCIATION® (NSCA®)—CERTIFIED STRENGTH AND CONDITIONING SPECIALIST® (CSCS®)

Advantages: The NSCA® is accredited through the NCCA® like the previous two certifying organizations. The NSCA®—Certified Strength and Conditioning Specialist® exam is very well known nationally and with professional athletic organizations as one of the top fitness certifications. The CSCS® certification is specifically designed for preparing exercise programs for athletes and improving sports performance. Another advantage is that there are numerous study sources for the exam, including a textbook, practice exams, online and classroom clinics, and test prep materials. Also, becoming a member of the organization reduces the cost of the exam itself, and the exam is slightly cheaper than the aforementioned certifications. The textbook is thorough and excellent preparation for the exam.

Disadvantages: The NSCA®—CSCS® certification exam is difficult and contains a large amount of information and requires a lot of preparation time. Furthermore, this specific certification requires that candidates either be currently enrolled as a senior or hold a bachelor's degree in exercise science. Finally, the study materials can become pricey if more than a textbook is required.

American College of Sports Medicine (ACSM) Certification

Advantages: Like the aforementioned certifications, the ACSM certifications are accredited through the NCCA. Also, like the NSCA®, the ACSM is a highly recognized certifying fitness organization. There are multiple certifications available for those with backgrounds in exercise science (e.g., ACSM—Certified Exercise Physiologist) and those without (e.g., ACSM—Certified Personal Trainer). These certifications are designed to adequately prepare the fitness professional for exercise program design for general and special populations. The certification is excellent at teaching how to manage and stratify risks with new clientele. There are various modes of test preparation supplies similar to that of the NSCA®.

Disadvantages: Some ACSM exams require a bachelor's degree in exercise science or a related field. They have a high degree of difficulty and the preparation materials and services can be expensive. Furthermore, employers may prefer other certifications depending on the type of clientele they work with. For example, although the ACSM is considered as a gold standard in fitness, professional athletic teams may seek NSCA®—CSCS® certified trainers because they specialize in sports performance.

It is in the best interest of the fitness professional to do as much research on the various certifications as possible. This includes researching the type of environment in which the fitness professional wants to advance their career. Selecting the right certification for a specified career path in fitness can help to save a lot of money and time in the long run. It may be necessary to look into specific employers to determine which type of training certification will improve the chances for success. Additionally, researching the testing procedures and requirements will help educate the fitness professional on the level of commitment required to become a certified trainer.

National Strength and Conditioning Association® (NSCA®)–Certified Strength and Conditioning Specialist® (CSCS®)

The **National Strength and Conditioning Association®** (**NSCA®**) is one of the oldest accredited certifying fitness organizations dedicated to improving the health and fitness industry. The organization formed in 1978 as a convention for strength coaches throughout the country and has expanded to one of the leading organizations in fitness. The NSCA® has a solid foundation in exercise for improved sports performance and fitness and has developed additional certifications in tactical strength and conditioning and fitness for special populations. Current certifications include the Certified Strength and Conditioning Specialist® (CSCS®), Certified Personal Trainer® (CPT®), Tactical Strength and Conditioning Facilitator® (TSAC-F®), and Certified Special Populations Specialist® (CSPS®). The organization produced decades of peer-reviewed research journals and magazines aimed at providing fitness professionals with evidence-based strength and conditioning guidelines. NSCA® certifications are highly recognized in the fitness industry and generally very well respected. The main goal of the NSCA® is to supply the health and fitness world with the best research-based information on fitness and sports performance for the benefit of all fitness professionals.

NSCA®–CSCS® Test Details

The NSCA®—CSCS® exam is a computer-based, multiple-choice exam separated into two sections, each of which is further split into domains. The two sections include a scientific foundations section and a practical application section. Both sections include an additional fifteen questions that are unscored and regarded as potential examination questions for the future. These are not indicated on the test and are mixed in with the rest of the scored questions, so you must answer all the questions on the exam.

What's on the NSCA®–CSCS®?

Section 1: Scientific Foundations

Domain	Number of Questions	Percentage of Test
Exercise Science	59	74%
Nutrition	21	26%
Total:	95 total questions (including 15 unscored)	1 hour and 30 minutes

Section 2: Practical/Applied

Domain	Number of Questions	Percentage of Test
Exercise Technique	38	35%
Program Design	39	35%
Organization and Administration	13	12%
Testing and Evaluation	20	18%
Total:	125 total questions (including 15 unscored)	2 hours and 30 minutes

The first section, Scientific Foundations, covers exercise science and nutrition. Candidates will be tested on anatomy, exercise physiology as it relates to the major body systems, biomechanics, nutrition, hydration, and weight management, among other topics. Candidates have one and a half hours to complete this portion of the CSCS® exam.

The second section, Practical/Applied, is split into four domains and includes various videos and pictures relating to different exercise techniques, exercise testing, and functional anatomy. Review your knowledge of performing and interpreting the results of subjective assessments, physical assessments, and body composition assessments. Expect questions on training methods; periodization; the principles of specificity, overload, and variation; program design for special populations; and other issues. There may also be questions about proper cueing techniques, safe training and spotting practices, and signs of contraindications. Like Section 1, this section contains fifteen unscored questions. They are interspersed throughout the exam and are not indicated, so you must answer every question. Candidates are afforded two and a half hours to complete this portion of the exam.

To take the exam, a candidate must have a bachelor's degree or be currently enrolled as a college senior at an accredited institution. He or she must also have certification in CPR and AED. The exam is administered by Pearson VUE and offered at testing centers throughout the nation. Candidates should see the NSCA® for the most up-to-date information on fees and to register. There is a discount for NSCA® members. On test day, candidates must bring a valid photo ID and registration information.

Online Resources

To help you fully prepare for your CSCS® exam, Ascencia includes online resources with the purchase of this study guide.

Practice Tests

In addition to the practice test included in this book, we also offer three online exams. Since many exams today are computer based, getting to practice your test-taking skills on the computer is a great way to prepare.

Flash Cards

A convenient supplement to this study guide, Ascencia's flash cards enable you to review important terms easily on your computer or smartphone.

Cheat Sheets

Review the core skills you need to master with easy-to-read Cheat Sheets.

From Stress to Success

Watch *From Stress to Success*, a brief but insightful YouTube video that offers the tips, tricks, and secrets experts use to score higher on the exam.

Feedback

Let us know what you think!

Access these materials at:

ascenciatestprep.com/cscs-online-resources

ONE: EXERCISE SCIENCE

Basic Anatomy Concepts

THE BIOLOGICAL HIERARCHY

In order to understand the principles of exercise science, it is important that one understands the basic concepts of anatomy and physiology. The biological hierarchy is a systematic breakdown of the structures of the human body and is typically organized from smallest to largest or largest to smallest. The human body is made up of small units called **cells**. A cell is a microscopic, self-replicating, structural and functional unit of the body that performs many different jobs. The cell is made up of many smaller units that are sometimes considered as part of the biological hierarchy, including: cytoplasm, organelles, nuclei, and a membrane that separates the cell contents from its surroundings.

Tissues comprise the next largest structures in the body and are a collection of cells that all perform a similar function. To simplify, the human body has four basic types of tissue: connective, epithelial, muscular, and nervous. In exercise science, it is important to understand the different functions of the tissues and how they are utilized during exercise. Connective tissues include things like bones, ligaments, and cartilage and are one of the basic types of tissues in the human body that have an unstructured cellular arrangement. Connective tissues function to support, separate, or connect the body's various organs and tissues.

Epithelial cells are found in the skin, blood vessels, and many organs. Muscular tissues are found in the digestive system and heart and contain contractile units that pull on connective tissues to create movement. Muscular tissues are further broken down into smooth, skeletal, and cardiac muscle. Finally, nervous tissue makes up the peripheral nervous systems that transmit impulses throughout the body.

After tissues, the next largest structure on the biological hierarchy are **organs**. Organs are a collection of tissues within the body that share a similar function. For instance, the esophagus is an organ with the primary function of carrying food and liquids from the mouth to the stomach.

The esophagus is part of the digestive **organ system**. Organ systems rank above organs as the largest structure on the biological hierarchy and are a group of organs that work together to perform a similar function. The digestive organ system is the entire group of organs in the body that processes food from start to finish.

Finally, an **organism** is the total collection of all the parts of the biological hierarchy working together to form a living being and is the largest structure in the biological hierarchy.

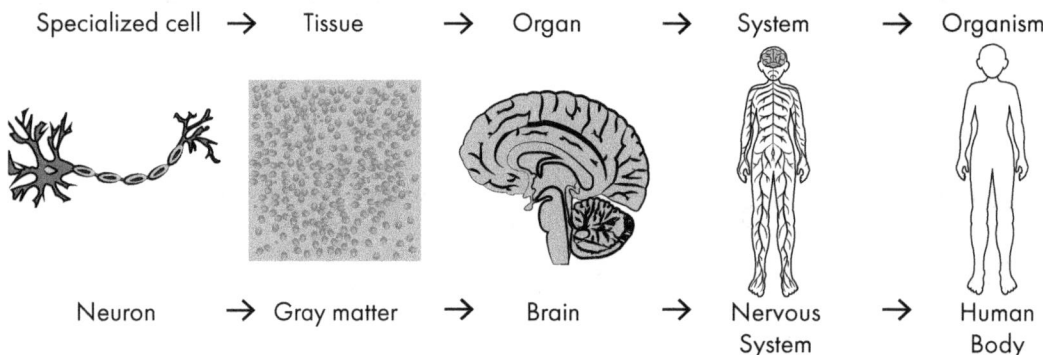

Figure 1.1. Biological Hierarchy and Levels of Organization

DIRECTIONAL TERMINOLOGY

In the field of exercise science, it is important for the professional to have an understanding of anatomical terminology associated with directions. These terms are often applied to describe the anatomical position of body parts, muscle groups, and important anatomical structures and landmarks on the body.

> When learning the anatomical directions, it is helpful to create 3 × 5 flashcards with the direction on one side and the definition on the other for quick studying. This method can be done with **bold** terms and their definitions for improved memorization.

Defined directional terms include the following:
- **inferior**: toward the bottom of the body
- **superior**: toward the top of the body
- **anterior**: toward the front
- **posterior**: toward the back
- **dorsal**: toward the back
- **ventral**: toward the front
- **medial**: toward the midline of the body
- **lateral**: further from the midline of the body
- **proximal**: closer to the axial skeleton
- **distal**: further from the axial skeleton

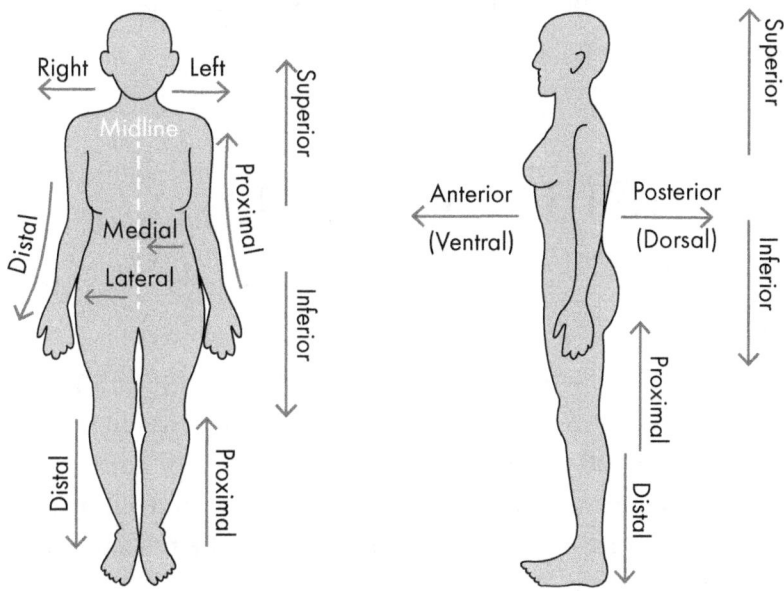

Figure 1.2. Directional Terminology

PRACTICE QUESTIONS

1. The biological hierarchy from the largest structure to the smallest structure is:
    - **A)** organism, organ, organ system, tissue, cell.
    - **B)** organism, organ system, organ, tissue, cell.
    - **C)** organ system, organism, tissue, organ, cell.
    - **D)** cell, tissue, organ, organ system, organism.

    Answers:
    - A) Incorrect. *Organ systems* are larger than *organs*.
    - **B) Correct.** This answer correctly lists the structures from largest to smallest.
    - C) Incorrect. The *organ system* is smaller than *organism,* and *tissue* is smaller than *organ*.
    - D) Incorrect. This is the biological hierarchy from smallest to largest.

2. The heart is
    - **A)** a cell.
    - **B)** a tissue.
    - **C)** an organ system.
    - **D)** an organ.

    Answers:
    - A) Incorrect. The heart is larger than just a cell.
    - B) Incorrect. The heart is larger than just a tissue.

C) Incorrect. The heart is a smaller part of an organ system.

D) **Correct.** The heart is an organ.

The Skeletal System

STRUCTURE AND FORM OF THE SKELETAL SYSTEM

Major Bones

Knowledge of the anatomical structures of the body can help fitness professionals understand the important roles they play in exercise science. The skeletal system is made up of over 200 different **bones**. Bones are a stiff connective tissue in the human body with many functions, including: protecting internal organs, synthesizing blood cells, storing necessary minerals, and providing the muscular system with leverage to create movement.

These hundreds of bones make up the human **skeleton**. The skeleton is a collection of interconnected bones joined by various connective tissues that provide a framework of structural integrity to the body's numerous biological systems. **Ligaments** are a type of rigid, yet flexible connective tissue that adheres bone to bone. **Cartilage** is also an important connective tissue that is closely related to the skeleton. Cartilage is a type of dense connective tissue that is found in various parts of the body and in multiple varieties, including: hyaline, elastic, and fibrocartilage. It performs multiple functions, such as providing a cushion for the bones in joints and structural integrity for many of the body's orifices. The following figure describes the location of the various major bones of the human body:

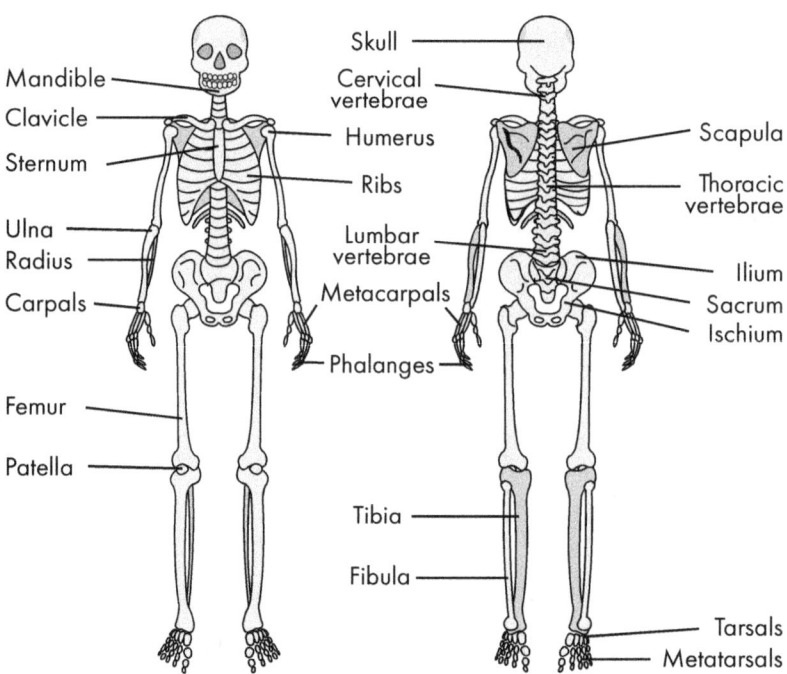

Figure 1.3. Major Bones of the Human Body

4 CSCS Study Guide

Several conditions can have adverse effects on the human skeletal system. For example, **rheumatoid arthritis** can cause significant joint damage, compromising the connective tissues that provide support to the skeletal system. Rheumatoid arthritis is a type of inflammation at the joint caused by chronic autoimmune disorder, which can lead to excessive joint degradation. The immune system attacks healthy joint tissue, making the joints stiff and causing the cartilage and bone to deteriorate.

> The skull of a fetus contains holes between the bones called "fontanelles" that are covered by a membranous connective tissue.

Osteoporosis is another condition that has a deleterious effect on the skeletal system. Osteoporosis refers to poor bone mineral density due to the loss or lack of the production of calcium content and bone cells, which leads to bone brittleness. Calcium supplementation and weight-bearing activity can help to improve bone mineral density in these individuals. It is important for fitness professionals to understand the consequences of conditions that have a negative effect on the skeletal system so that they can take the necessary steps to create appropriate exercise plans.

Joint Classifications

The sections at which two bones are conjoined via connective tissue that allows for human movement are called **joints**. There are several different kinds of joints in the human body with various functions. A **hinge joint** allows for human movement through one plane of motion as **flexion** and **extension**. Flexion occurs when a joint decreases in joint angle due to muscular contraction, whereas extension is when a joint increases in joint angle due to muscular contraction. Examples of hinge joints include the elbows, knees, and most fingers.

A **ball-and-socket** joint allows for range of motion through multiple planes and is typically comprised of a round bone end and a flat or cup-shaped surface. The hip and shoulder joint are both examples of ball-and-socket joints. They allow for many degrees of freedom through multiple planes of motion. The hip joint is made up of the femoral head (ball) and the acetabulum of the pelvis (socket). A **saddle joint** has surfaces that are convex on one bone and concave on the other and articulate through multiple ranges of motion, excluding rotation. The joint in the hand that comprises the thumb is a saddle joint. It allows for movement through many planes of motion, but cannot rotate about an axis.

Joints can be subdivided into categories such as **uniaxial**, **biaxial**, and **multiaxial**. Uniaxial joints allow for movement through one plane of motion; biaxial joints allow for movement through two perpendicular planes of motion; and multiaxial joints allow for movement through many planes of motion.

Joint articulations occur in various directions through different planes of motion. The types of movement can be described using specific terminology for further classification. As previously mentioned, joint flexion and extension occur when the joint angle is decreased and increased, respectively. **Supination** occurs at the forearm when the palm is rotated to face upward, whereas **pronation** occurs as the palm is turned over to face downward. They are also able to supinate and pronate, but these terms are often interchanged with inversion and eversion, respectively.

> Are there any joints that allow for a small degree of hyperextension?

Abduction refers to the contraction of muscle to move the legs or arms away from the midline of the body. Conversely, **adduction** refers to the contraction of muscle to move the legs or arms toward the midline of the body. Additionally, ball-and-socket joints can perform an action called **circumduction**. Circumduction is a circular movement of the limb as a combination of the four basic joint motions: flexion, extension, adduction, and abduction. Finally, **hyperextension** is extension of a joint beyond the joints' typical range of motion. This list of muscular actions is not by any means exhaustive but covers the basics of human movement found in many of the exercises used in training programs.

The Spine

The spine is part of the axial skeleton, which is made up of a total of twenty-nine bones called vertebrae. Starting from the base of the skull there are seven cervical vertebrae, twelve thoracic vertebrae, five lumbar vertebrae, and five sacral vertebrae. The coccyx is found at the very end of the spine, just below the sacrum.

One very important feature of the spine is the natural S-shaped curve that these vertebrae follow. The cervical vertebrae follow an anterior curve. The thoracic vertebrae begin to curve back posteriorly. Finally, another anterior curve is found at the lumbar vertebrae.

Postural deviations that cause excessive curvatures can have painful ramifications on the human body. Several common spinal deviations can be determined via simple visual examinations. **Lordosis** is an excessive anterior curvature of the natural S-shape of the spine and is most commonly found in the lumbar vertebrae. This condition is often caused by muscular imbalances that occur due to unilateral training programs, a sedentary lifestyle, and poor posture. **Kyphosis** is an excessive posterior curvature of the natural S shape of the spine and is commonly found in the thoracic vertebrae.

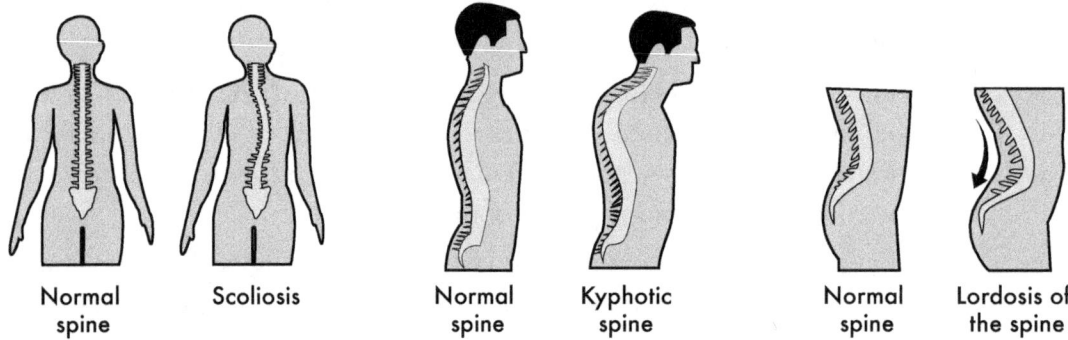

Figure 1.4. Common Spinal Deviations

Similar to lordosis, kyphosis can be caused by a tightening of the chest and anterior shoulder muscles and a general weakening of the muscles that retract the shoulders. An excessive lateral curvature of the spine is referred to as **scoliosis**. This condition is predominantly idiopathic and often arises in childhood.

Center of Gravity and Base of Support

A fundamental concept of exercise science is understanding center of gravity and how it relates to base of support. Understanding proper spinal posture in addition to these two concepts lends insight into how stability is developed. **Center of gravity** refers to the imaginary point on the body at which body weight is completely and evenly distributed in relation to the ground. **Base of support** refers to the contact points on the ground and surface between those contact points where the body is placed. For example, a person may be standing on two feet placed directly next to each other. This means that the individual's base of support is only the area under the feet. However, if that person's feet spread out, then the base of support would include the space between the feet.

 How might football players increase their stability at the line of scrimmage?

Typically, a wider base of support and contact area will provide greater stability. Additionally, the closer the center of gravity is to the ground, the greater a person's stability. When a body's center of gravity is kept within the base of support, less effort is required by the muscles for balance. Shifting the center of gravity forces the body to compensate by contracting muscles to rebalance. The body's natural posture and spinal curvature place the least stress on the muscles and joints, preventing postural deviations like lordosis and kyphosis from occurring. As it relates to spinal posture, excessive curvatures of the spine can place the center of gravity out of position, causing a decrease in stability. For instance, an excessive kyphosis of the thoracic spine will force an individual's torso to lean forward, shifting the center of gravity forward. This places the center of gravity outside of the base of support and causes a decrease in stability. Therefore, proper spinal alignment contributes to better stability.

PRACTICE QUESTIONS

1. What is the difference between kyphosis and lordosis of the spine?

    A) Kyphosis refers to excessive posterior curvature of the spine; lordosis is anterior.

    B) Kyphosis refers to excessive anterior curvature of the spine; lordosis is posterior.

    C) Kyphosis refers to excessive lateral curvature of the spine; lordosis is anterior.

    D) The two terms are interchangeable.

Answers:

A) **Correct.** Kyphosis is excessive posterior curvature of the spine, while lordosis is anterior.

B) Incorrect. Kyphosis and lordosis have opposite meanings of what is expressed in the question.

C) Incorrect. Lateral curvature refers to scoliosis.

D) Incorrect. The two terms have opposite meanings and are not interchangeable.

2. Which joint allows for the most freedom of movement?
   A) biaxial joints
   B) hinge joints
   C) saddle joints
   D) ball-and-socket joints

Answers:

A) Incorrect. Biaxial joints only allow for freedom of movement in two planes of motion.

B) Incorrect. Hinge joints typically only allow for freedom of movement in one plane of motion.

C) Incorrect. A saddle joint has range of motion through multiple planes of motion; however, they do not allow for rotation around an axis.

D) **Correct.** Ball-and-socket joints allow for the most freedom of movement.

Effects of Exercise on the Skeletal System

Exercise has a positive effect on the skeletal system. Specifically, axial loading of the skeleton has been shown to slightly improve and maintain bone mineral density. This benefit is crucial in delaying the onset of osteoporosis in old age and can help to prevent falls due to broken bones. Bone mineral density refers to the strength of bone as it relates to the contents of calcium and other minerals. Denser bones equate to stronger bones. The types of exercise used to improve bone mineral density involve those that place stress on the bone through impact. Jumping, high impact exercise, weight training, and higher intensity activities have more of a beneficial result on improving bone mass. Additionally, age and gender considerations can vary the effects of exercise on bone mass and strength.

Bone development occurs at different rates based on age. Bones grow more quickly during childhood but begin to slow down as a person gets older. Adults can continue to develop bone mineral density and reduce the effects of bone loss with age; however, the rate of bone growth is much quicker in children. Therefore, resistance training and higher intensity exercise involving impact should be started at an early age to help induce more significant gains in bone mineral density at a young age. Exercises involving impact should be continued throughout life to make sure the skeletal system stays healthy and strong over the course of a person's lifetime. Although increases in bone mineral density significantly decrease with age, continuation of axial loading in training programs will help to mitigate the rate of density loss, decreasing risk of injury. The onset of osteoporosis typically occurs later in life and can be determined by bone mineral density scans at a physician's office. Prevalence of osteoporosis and its precursor, osteopenia, are higher in women over the age of fifty and increase the risk of bone fractures of major bones such as the pelvis and spinal vertebrae. These individuals should continue to participate in resistance training programs that emphasize improved stability, posture, and the ability to perform daily tasks.

PRACTICE QUESTIONS

1. Bone mineral density is developed more easily at what point in life?

- **A)** adulthood
- **B)** childhood
- **C)** any age
- **D)** advanced age

Answers:

- A) Incorrect. Bone mineral density develops more easily during childhood.
- **B) Correct.** Bone mineral density develops more easily during childhood.
- C) Incorrect. Though exercise does help to improve bone density later in life, it is developed more easily during childhood.
- D) Incorrect. Bone mineral density declines and the potential for osteoporosis increases in the elderly.

2. The precursor to osteoporosis is called

- **A)** bone mineral density.
- **B)** lordosis.
- **C)** scoliosis.
- **D)** osteopenia.

Answers:

- A) Incorrect. This is what is affected by osteoporosis.
- B) Incorrect. Lordosis is excessive anterior curvature of the lumbar spine.
- C) Incorrect. Scoliosis is excessive lateral curvature of the spine.
- **D) Correct.** Osteopenia is the precursor to osteoporosis.

CONTINUE

The Muscular System

Muscle Cell Structure

The muscular system is integral in human movement and exercise science. It provides the force necessary to propel the human skeleton through space. Learning about the structural and functional processes behind muscle can help us to better understand the important role the muscular system plays in fitness. Of equal importance is the ability to understand the relationships behind the nervous and muscular systems and how their constant interaction influences the body.

Muscle cells consist of a number of important structural components. The smallest of these components are the contractile units called **sarcomeres**. A sarcomere is a contractile unit found in striated muscle that is bound end to end and shortens upon muscular contractions. Sarcomeres have an end-to-end arrangement the length of a **myofibril**. Myofibrils refer to bands of muscle tissue bound together within skeletal muscle fibers that contain the sarcomeres.

Within the sarcomere are two distinct contractile proteins that play a major role in how a muscle shortens to move joints through their range of motion. These proteins are known as **actin** and **myosin**. Actin is a thin protein found in the sarcomeres of muscles that provides a surface to which myosin can attach in order for muscular contraction to occur. Myosin is a thick protein found in the sarcomeres of muscles containing the head that binds with actin during muscular contraction. These two myofilament proteins form a cross-bridging effect integral to the **sliding filament theory**. The sliding filament theory states that the proteins in the muscles, actin and myosin, form a connection to pull the thin actin filaments over the myosin. This causes a shortening of the sarcomeres and the concomitant shortening of the muscles known as muscular contraction. The actin filaments have a layer that sits above a portion of the myosin. Muscle fibers

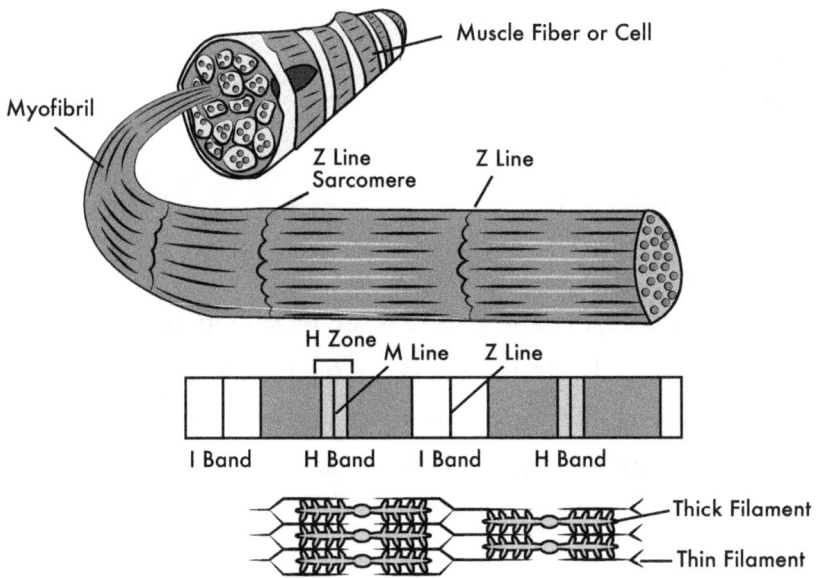

Figure 1.5. Diagram of Actin and Myosin

at resting length form a certain layer of overlap that allows for crossbridging of the myofilaments to occur. Figure 1.5 shows a diagram of actin and myosin.

The sarcomere can be broken down into certain zones that contain portions of certain filaments. The **A-band** is the area of the sarcomere in which thick myosin filaments are found and does not shorten during muscular contraction. The actin filaments slide over the A-band during muscular contraction. The A-band will contain some overlap of filaments during muscular contraction. The **Z-band** separates the sarcomeres: a single sarcomere is the distance between two Z-bands containing both the thin and thick filaments. The Z-bands come closer together during muscular contraction as the actin filaments are attached to the Z-bands and pulled by the myosin filaments. The **I-band** is the area in a sarcomere between the thick myosin filaments in which only thin actin filament is found. This area shortens upon muscular contraction. Finally, the **H-zone** is found between the actin filaments, in which only thick myosin filament is found.

The structures listed above are all part of what is called a **motor unit**. Motor units consist of the single neuron and its associated skeletal muscle fibers that are innervated by that neuron. The neuron that innervates the muscle fiber of a motor unit is referred to as a **motor neuron**. These motor neurons are located within the spinal cord and branch out to the muscles to send the nervous impulses for muscular contraction. The **neuromuscular junction** is the site at which the motor neuron and muscle fibers are joined to form a chemical synapse for nervous transmission to muscle. Motor units are essential for producing the muscular **twitch** that elicits the contraction of muscle fibers. A twitch refers to the stimulation of a muscle via **action potentials** such that the activation threshold of the muscle is reached and a contraction occurs. An action potential is a nervous stimulus produced to initiate the shortening of a sarcomere and muscular contraction. The activation threshold requires that many action potentials be sent to the muscle in order for contraction to occur. If the activation threshold is not breached, muscular contraction will not occur even if a stimulus is sent.

Muscles have unique mechanisms that provide the body with feedback based on the stimuli received. To achieve this, **proprioceptors**, such as **muscle spindle fibers** and **Golgi tendon organs**, provide sensory information to the nervous system. Proprioceptors are sensory receptors that provide the body with kinesthetic awareness of its surroundings via stimuli. The mechanisms behind these proprioceptors help to protect the body from injury and provide a sense of coordination in space.

Muscle spindle fibers are a proprioceptor found in the large area of the muscle that sense a stretch in the muscle and subsequent neuromotor response that causes a muscular contraction of the **agonist** muscle and a reciprocal inhibition of the **antagonist** muscle. Agonists are the primary muscles that are performing the contraction, whereas antagonists are the muscles that contract in the opposing direction of the agonist muscles. For example, when the doctor taps on the quadriceps tendon below a person's patella from a seated position, the leg kicks out lightly. This is an example of the muscle spindle fiber sensing a rapid stretching of the muscle attached to that tendon and sending a signal to contract the quadriceps to protect it.

Golgi tendon organs are a proprioceptor found within the musculotendinous junction that sense the amount of force being placed on the muscle and function to prevent excessive forceful contractions of the muscle via autogenic inhibition. An example of this can be seen in static stretching when a person begins a standing hamstring stretch in an attempt to touch the toes. First, the muscle spindle fibers sense a rapid stretching of the hamstrings and contract to protect them, and the person is still unable to reach. Reciprocal inhibition occurs at the quadriceps. After holding the stretch for a brief period of time, the Golgi tendon organs send a message to the nervous system to deactivate muscular contraction of the stretching muscle allowing further range of motion in the stretch. Autogenic inhibition occurs at the hamstrings due to the Golgi tendon organ, and the person's toes can eventually (maybe) be reached.

In exercise science, distinguishing between the different muscular adaptations and characteristics can make or break a training program. Training requires knowledge of which type of muscle fiber is more beneficial to the event or sport. Types of muscle fibers are typically delineated into either **type I** or **type II** fibers. Type I and type II fibers are found in skeletal muscles and can be developed for performance using specific energy requirements of the muscle. Type I muscle fibers are often referred to as **slow- twitch**, whereas, type II muscle fibers are referred to as **fast-twitch**. Slow-twitch muscle fibers are characterized by their abilities in sustained performance over long durations, aerobic capacity, mitochondrial density, and early muscular recruitment.

> ✏️ Write down a list of ten different sports, and try to name which type of muscle fiber type will most benefit the athletes of each sport. For more of a challenge, add the differences between positions of those sports!

These fibers benefit endurance athletes, such as triathletes, marathoners, etc. Training for muscular endurance with light loads and high repetitions helps to increase the capability of slow-twitch, type I muscle fibers. Fast-twitch muscle fibers are characterized by their ability to perform powerful movements requiring a lot of force; however, they fatigue rapidly. They are further broken down into oxidative glycolytic (IIa) and glycolytic (IIb) which derive energy in a different manner. Type IIa fibers are more toward the middle of the spectrum of muscle fibers in terms of their oxidative capacity, mitochondrial density, and endurance. Type IIb fibers are at the opposite extreme of the scale as type I fibers. They have low mitochondrial density and utilize the muscle glycogen stores as well as create phosphate stores for energy. Muscular recruitment of these fibers is generally only during high intensity activities that require significant force production. Individuals who benefit most from developing their type II, fast-twitch muscle fibers participate in sports or events that require short sprints, agility, and power with intermittent rest and recovery. For example, ice hockey, football, baseball, tennis, and basketball all require well-developed fast-twitch muscles.

PRACTICE QUESTIONS

1. A sarcomere is
   - **A)** a myofibril.
   - **B)** a type IIb muscle fiber.
   - **C)** a site at which the motor neuron and muscle fibers are joined to form a chemical synapse.
   - **D)** a contractile unit found in striated muscle that is connected end-to-end along myofibrils.

   Answers:
   - A) Incorrect. Myofibrils contain sarcomeres.
   - B) Incorrect. This is a type of fast-twitch muscle fiber.
   - C) Incorrect. This is the neuromuscular junction.
   - **D) Correct.** This is the definition of a sarcomere.

2. Examples of proprioceptors include
   - **A)** Golgi tendon organs and slow-twitch muscle fibers.
   - **B)** Golgi tendon organs and type I muscle fibers.
   - **C)** muscle spindle fibers and Golgi tendon organs.
   - **D)** muscle spindle fibers and striated muscle.

   Answers:
   - A) Incorrect. Slow-twitch muscle fibers are not proprioceptors.
   - B) Incorrect. Type I muscle fibers are not proprioceptors.
   - **C) Correct.** These are two examples of proprioceptors.
   - D) Incorrect. Striated muscle is not a proprioceptor.

SKELETAL MUSCLES

Fitness professionals should have an in-depth understanding of the major skeletal muscles and their primary actions. Knowledge of muscular functions and actions helps to determine exercise selection when training clients and can prevent muscular imbalance or unilateral training programs. The following is a table listing some of the major muscles of the body, their primary muscular action, and the plane of motion in which those actions occur:

Table 1.1. Major Muscles of the Body, Their Primary Muscle Action, and Plane of Motion

Muscle	Action	Plane of Motion
trapezius	scapular elevation, upward rotation	frontal
pectoralis major	shoulder horizontal adduction, internal rotation, shoulder flexion	transverse, sagittal
latissimus dorsi	shoulder adduction, scapular depression, shoulder extension, shoulder internal rotation	frontal, sagittal, transverse
biceps	elbow flexion, forearm supination	sagittal, transverse
triceps	elbow extension	sagittal
rectus abdominis	spinal flexion, pelvic stabilization	sagittal
internal and external obliques	spinal flexion, rotation, and lateral flexion	sagittal, transverse, and frontal
erector spinae	spinal extension, torso ipsilateral rotation, lateral flexion, anterior tilt of pelvis	sagittal, transverse, and frontal
gluteus maximus	hip extension, external rotation	sagittal, transverse
quadriceps	knee extension, hip flexion	sagittal
hamstrings	hip extension, knee flexion	sagittal
adductors	adduct the thigh	frontal
abductors	abduct the thigh	frontal
gastrocnemius	plantar flexion of ankle	sagittal

This table is by no means exhaustive, and the fitness professional should make it a point to understand the various actions and associate them to particular exercises to create well-rounded fitness programs.

Skeletal Muscle Function

Skeletal muscle is the striated muscle that helps to aid in bodily movement. In order to move the body, skeletal muscle goes through phases of muscular contraction and relaxation. The **contraction phase** is a phase during the neuromuscular stimulation process that involves myosin crossbridges attaching and pulling actin filaments closer together, resulting in a shortening of the sarcomeres and subsequent muscle fibers. Calcium ions are discharged from a network of webbing—called the sarcoplasmic reticulum—into the sarcomeres. This results in the release of a blockade of filaments known as troponin and tropomyosin and exposes the actin filament for crossbridging from the myosin heads. The muscular twitch mentioned previously stimulates this contraction phase. Once muscular contraction is stopped, a **relaxation phase** occurs. During the relaxation phase, the muscle returns to its resting state due to a return of the calcium ions to the sarcoplasmic reticulum, while the troponin and tropomyosin return to supporting the prevention of crossbridging. In addition to contraction and relaxation, there is a phase that allows time for muscular recovery. This phase in neuromuscular stimulation—the **recharge phase**—allows for replenishment of the muscles' primary energy source, adenosine triphosphate (ATP), to maintain the muscle action spectrum of the bound actin-myosin crossbridges.

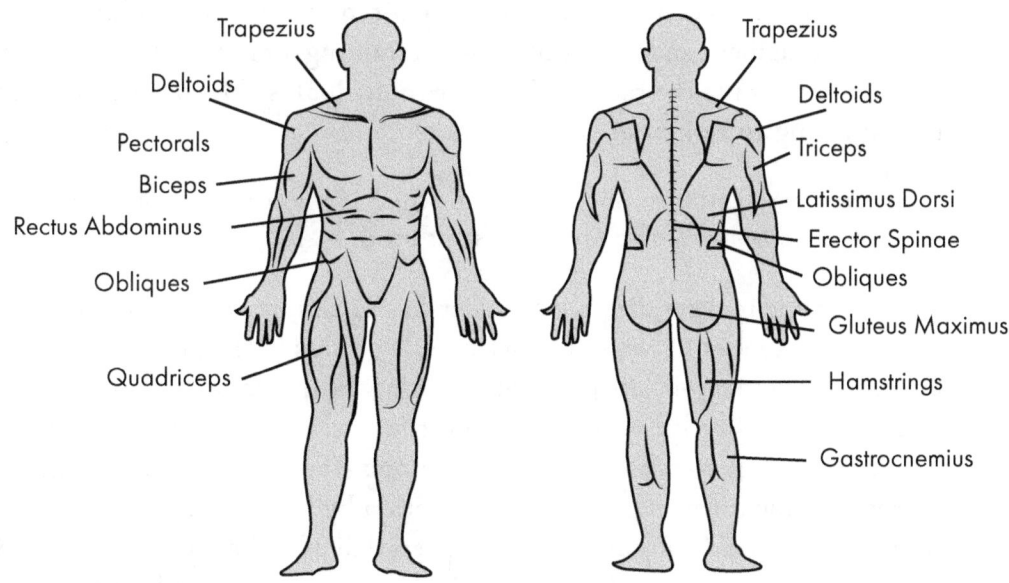

Figure 1.6. Major Muscles of the Body

Muscle Actions

Understanding the anatomical actions that muscles perform helps the fitness professional create exercise programs that are well balanced, specific, and effective. It is also important for fitness professionals to understand which muscles are utilized during these actions. Muscular contractions occur in many ways: **concentric, eccentric, isometric, isotonic,** and **isokinetic.** Concentric refers to a muscular contraction in which the length of the muscle is shortening to lift the resistance. For example, the biceps are concentrically contracting during the upward movement of a bicep curl exercise. In contrast, this occurs in biceps in the downward movement of a lat pulldown exercise. Eccentric refers to a muscular contraction in which the muscle is resisting a force as it lengthens. Using the same example of a bicep curl, the bicep muscle is eccentrically contracting as the weight is lowered toward the floor. Again in contrast, during the lat pulldown, the biceps are eccentrically contracting during the upward movement as the arms lengthen. So, it is not as simple as saying the *downward* or *upward* movement is concentric or eccentric as it depends greatly on the exercise being performed and the muscle groups being used.

Isometric refers to a muscular contraction in which the resistance and force are even and no movement is taking place. This type of contraction takes place in exercises such as the wall sit or plank. The muscles are holding the body in place, and there is no concentric or eccentric muscular action. The sarcomeres stay at a static length; however, muscular contraction is occurring. Isotonic refers to a muscular contraction that is being performed at the same force throughout range of motion. Essentially, isotonic resistance training is the most common method where the resistance remains the same throughout the exercise. Isokinetic refers to a muscular contraction in which the rate of force application remains constant. This is more often seen in a rehabilitative setting using expensive equipment and is least common in training for muscular fitness. An isokinetic dynamometer limits the rate at which the individual is able to apply force to the resistance, creating an isokinetic contraction.

 Perform exercises, and determine which portion of each exercise is concentric and eccentric based on the muscles used.

The prime movers discussed earlier in the chapter as agonist or antagonist are assisted in a number of ways by other muscle groups in the body. For example, people performing a box step-up are primarily utilizing the quadriceps, hamstrings, and gluteus maximus muscles to lift themselves onto the box. However, they are also using their gluteus medius as a **stabilizer** during the box step-up. A stabilizer muscle helps to control movement throughout range of motion by isometrically contracting to steady the joints and body during exercise. Stabilizers will often have other associated muscular actions they perform. In this example, the gluteus medius also helps in hip abduction. The gluteus medius is assisted in hip abduction by muscular **synergists**. Muscular synergists assist the agonist muscles in performing a movement. This can also be seen during the squat exercise with the quadriceps and hamstrings working as synergists. Similar to stabilizer muscles, the body also utilizes muscles as **neutralizers** during human movement. These muscles contract to prevent any additional compensatory movement caused by the prime movers throughout the range of motion. During the squat exercise, for example, the abductors of the outer thigh are often recruited to subdue firing of the adductor muscles to prevent medial collapse of the knee joint throughout range of motion. The abductors neutralize the compensatory movement at the knee during the squat.

Compensatory movements during exercise are common in untrained individuals or those recovering from an injury stemming from overuse. That is why it is important for fitness professionals to understand the concepts of appropriate **force-couple** and **length-tension relationships** between muscle groups. A force-couple relationship refers to the concomitant contraction of various muscle groups that produce movement of the human body. In short, these are muscles that contract, not necessarily in the same direction, but together in order to produce a specific movement. For instance, a common force-couple at the hip occurs as the iliopsoas muscles connect to the vertebrae and contract to produce an anterior pelvic tilt from the front, while the erector spinae in the back contract to perform the same anterior pelvic tilt. Exaggeration of this force-couple can lead to postural deviations caused by inappropriate length-tension relationships of the aforementioned musculature. Length-tension relationships refer to the optimal muscular length at the level of the sarcomere for maximum force potential of the muscle. Shortened, tight muscles will have too much overlap of actin on myosin to produce optimum force through full range of motion, whereas lengthened, overstretched muscles will lack the crossbridges to pull through full range of motion. This often leads to compensatory movement, poor posture, and overuse injury.

PRACTICE QUESTIONS

1. Length-tension relationships refer to
    A) the amount of actin-myosin crossbridges that occur within the sarcomeres, giving the muscle its range of motion.
    B) muscles working together to perform a particular body movement.
    C) muscles contracting in opposite directions to produce force around the same rotational axis.
    D) muscles contracting to move a joint beyond its typical range of motion.

    Answers:
    A) **Correct.** This is the definition of a length-tension relationship in muscle.
    B) Incorrect. This refers to muscular synergists.
    C) Incorrect. This refers to force-couple relationships.
    D) Incorrect. This refers to hyperextension.

2. What happens to calcium ions during the relaxation phase of muscular contraction?
    A) They release the blockade of troponin and tropomyosin to allow for actin-myosin crossbridging.
    B) They return to the sarcoplasmic reticulum, allowing the blockade of troponin and tropomyosin to prevent crossbridging of actin and myosin.
    C) They are buffered by the muscle.
    D) Nothing happens to the calcium ions during the relaxation phase.

    Answers:
    A) Incorrect. This occurs during the contraction phase.
    B) **Correct.** The calcium returns to the sarcoplasmic reticulum, and crossbridging is again prevented.
    C) Incorrect. Buffering does not occur.

D) Incorrect. Calcium ions play an important role throughout the process.

Exercise and the Muscular System

Exercise has a profound effect on the muscles of the body. The physiological adaptations to the muscular system are influenced by the implementation of resistance training, flexibility training, and endurance training. Resistance training specifically causes an increase in the size of the muscle known as muscular **hypertrophy**. There are two types of hypertrophy developed through resistance training: sarcoplasmic and myofibrillar hypertrophy. Sarcoplasmic hypertrophy occurs as the sarcoplasmic reticulum, and muscle glycogen stores are increased. This type of hypertrophy does not necessarily result in increased force production of the muscle. Myofibrillar hypertrophy is an increase in the overall size of the muscle fibers and results in improved muscle cross-sectional area as well as improved strength. Muscular strength improvements can be developed without an obligatory increase in muscle size; however, the larger the muscle, the more potential strength it can obtain. In contrast, muscular **atrophy** is a decrease in muscle size and strength due to detraining or lack of use. This occurs as a result of a sedentary lifestyle, injury, or musculoskeletal disorders. Additionally, muscular **hyperplasia** refers to an increase in the number of muscle fibers. This process is not fully understood and is less common than hypertrophy as it relates to strength improvements with training.

Improvements to muscular size and strength come at the cost of minor damage caused by training. As a result, **delayed onset muscle soreness (DOMS)** is a side effect of performing training that overloads the muscles. DOMS is the post-exercise muscular soreness caused by micro-tears in the muscle fibers as a result of resistance training or other exercise. Peak muscular soreness due to resistance training can last for several days following a workout but is typically at its most painful one to two days following the workout. Resistance training is often the culprit of this side effect; however, endurance training can elicit the same effect. The micro-tears caused by training provoke a response from the body to adapt and become stronger, preventing future soreness at similar intensities. Soreness from DOMS should only last for a few days, and then subsequent workouts at the same intensity should have less of a response.

 DOMS is primarily associated with micro-tears in muscle fibers caused by the *eccentric* muscular contraction of exercises.

Flexibility training can be used to influence muscle length if performed consistently. Muscle flexibility improves the range of motion of joints, prevents compensatory movements due to tight muscles, and improves muscle elasticity for activity. To improve muscle flexibility, dynamic and static stretching can be performed.

 More than just static and dynamic stretching exists. Two other methods of flexibility include: Proprioceptive Neuromuscular Facilitation (PNF) stretching and ballistic stretching. PNF stretches require a partner to perform, and ballistic stretches are rapid and can be dangerous if performed improperly.

Dynamic stretching should be used to prepare the muscles for activity by increasing blood flow to the muscles, increasing muscle elasticity, and decreasing joint stiffness. This mode of flexibility training does not necessarily improve long-term range of motion but better prepares individuals for exercise. Static stretching can help to elongate muscle fibers and improve joint range of motion over time. This mode of flexibility training can help to improve muscle length-tension relationships by preventing inadequate sarcomere crossbridging caused by excessive actin overlap of myosin. Flexibility allows for appropriate sarcomere resting length, which promotes optimal length-tension relationships for force production of muscles.

PRACTICE QUESTIONS

1. DOMS stands for
   - **A)** Dynamic Onset Muscle Soreness.
   - **B)** Dynamic Onset Muscle Strength.
   - **C)** Delayed Onset Muscle Soreness.
   - **D)** Delayed Onset Muscle Strength.

   Answers:
   - A) Incorrect. The use of the word *dynamic* is not correct.
   - B) Incorrect. The use of the words *dynamic* and *strength* are not correct.
   - **C) Correct.** DOMS stands for Delayed Onset Muscle Soreness.
   - D) Incorrect. The use of the word *strength* is not correct.

2. The primary benefit of resistance training for muscles is to elicit the effect of muscle
   - **A)** hypertrophy.
   - **B)** atrophy.
   - **C)** hyperplasia.
   - **D)** fatigue.

   Answers:
   - **A) Correct.** Resistance training elicits muscular hypertrophy and, subsequently, increased strength.
   - B) Incorrect. Resistance training prevents muscular atrophy.
   - C) Incorrect. Although hyperplasia may be a benefit, it is not well understood as the primary benefit of resistance training.
   - D) Incorrect. Muscular fatigue does occur as a result of resistance training, but it is not the primary benefit.

The Cardiovascular System

The cardiovascular system is made up of the **heart, lungs, veins,** and **arteries**. The heart is a four-chambered muscular pump that forces blood to the entire body. It has several protective layers that help prevent outside environmental factors from disrupting its rhythm and function. The **pericardia** are the outermost two layers of the heart that act as protective layers and contain a lubricative liquid. The **epicardium** is a layer of tissue on the outside of the heart that is the deep part of the pericardia. Finally, the **endocardium** is the innermost, smooth layer of the heart walls.

The lungs are organs of the body with a vast network of branching airways that involve the intake of oxygen from the environment for the blood supply and gas exchange of oxygen and carbon dioxide. Veins carry deoxygenated blood away from the tissues and organs of the body, whereas arteries carry oxygenated blood from the heart to the tissues and organs. These tubes start larger in diameter close to the heart and lungs and become smaller as they reach toward the tissues and organs. Arteries become **arterioles**—smaller branching portions of the artery that allow blood to flow into the **capillaries**. The capillaries are the smallest branch of the circulatory system in which gas exchange from blood to tissues occurs. The deoxygenated blood from the tissues travels back to the heart through veins.

Structure and Form of the Cardiovascular System

The cardiovascular system plays a vital role in human physiological function. The heart and lungs work in conjunction with each other to provide the body with an adequate supply of oxygenated **blood** to sustain life. Blood is a viscous liquid medium that supports the transport of oxygen to the tissues of the body and the removal of waste products, like carbon dioxide, from the tissues of the body.

The top two chambers of the heart are referred to individually as **atrium**. The right atrium is fed deoxygenated blood by two major veins: the **superior vena cava** and the **inferior vena cava**. The superior vena cava transports deoxygenated blood from the upper part of the body to the right atrium, and the inferior vena cava transports deoxygenated blood from the lower part of the body. The bottom two chambers of the heart are the **ventricles**.

Separating the atrium and ventricles are valves made of connective tissue that prevent the backflow of blood. Valves also separate the chambers from the various tubes that carry blood to the rest of the body. The **mitral valve** separates the left atrium and ventricle, preventing backflow of oxygenated blood into the atrium. The **tricuspid valve** separates the right atrium from the right ventricle, preventing backflow of deoxygenated blood to the atrium.

Additionally, valves separating the heart from blood flow to the rest of the body include the **aortic valve** and **pulmonary valve**. The aortic valve separates the left ventricle from the **aorta**, allowing for oxygenated blood from the left ventricle to be pumped through to the aorta. The aorta is the main artery for oxygenated blood transport to the majority of the human body. The pulmonary valve separates the right ventricle from the **pulmonary artery**, preventing the backflow of deoxygenated blood from the pulmonary artery from entering the right ventricle. The pulmonary artery carries deoxygenated blood from the heart to the **lungs** for gas exchange. In contrast, the **pulmonary vein** carries oxygenated blood from the lungs back to the heart for transport to the rest of the body.

Figure 1.7. shows the path of blood flow through the heart.

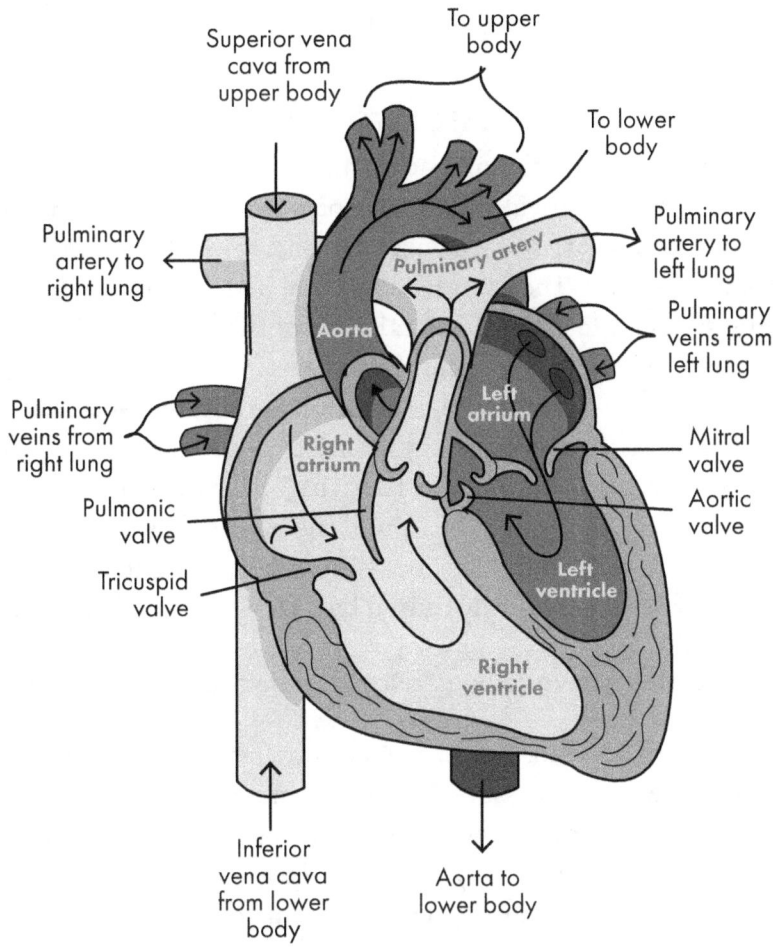

Figure 1.7. The Path of Blood Flow through the Heart

> ? Describe the direction of blood flow through the heart. Can you explain it using proper terminology?

The lungs are an organ with a branching system of airways that allow the blood to be oxygenated. Air is inhaled through the mouth and nose and carried down the trachea to the **bronchi**. The bronchi bifurcate toward each lung, branching to carry air to either side. From here, the bronchioles further branch and carry air to the **alveoli**. The alveoli are tiny air sacs in the lungs that allow for the exchange of oxygen and carbon dioxide with the blood.

The **red blood cells** contain **hemoglobin** for the transport of oxygen through the bloodstream to the tissues. Hemoglobin is a protein found in red blood cells that contains elements that help bind oxygen for transport. Blood also contains a substance known as **platelets**. Platelets are the element of blood that assists in forming clots. In order for the lungs to draw in air from the environment, a muscle called the **diaphragm** is constantly contracting. The diaphragm is a muscle that helps to create a pressure differential in the abdomen and chest which allows air to flow into and out of the lungs when contracting and relaxing, respectively. The heart and lungs work simultaneously to keep consistent flow of oxygenated blood to the tissues.

Pathologies of the Cardiorespiratory System

There are numerous pathologies that affect the cardiorespiratory system that should be a concern to an individual's fitness program. Disorders that affect heart rhythm, blood flow to heart tissue, the arteries and veins, lung function, and more can be impacted by exercise. The heart has electrical nodes that help determine a healthy heart rate. The **sinus node** is the electrical node of the heart that helps determine the heart rate, located in the right atrium of the heart. Disorders affecting the heart's normal rhythm, causing an abnormal heart rhythm, are referred to as **arrhythmias**. Sometimes arrhythmias can be determined by a device called an **electrocardiogram**. An electrocardiogram measures the electrical activity of the heart through a device using nodes placed on the surface of the skin around the heart. These can also be used to determine if something more serious, like a **heart attack**, is going to occur. Heart attacks are the death of heart tissue, typically caused by a lack of blood flow from blockage.

 Another name for a heart attack is a *myocardial infarction*.

A common cause for concern when starting an exercise program is an individual's **blood pressure**. Blood pressure (BP) is the amount of pressure placed on the walls of the blood vessels by the body's blood flow. It is measured in millimeters of mercury (mmHg) and determined using a sphygmomanometer. The number is read as **systolic blood pressure** over **diastolic blood pressure**, and a healthy guideline is 120 over 80 mmHg.

Systolic blood pressure is the top number of a blood pressure reading indicating the maximal amount of pressure placed on the arteries following contraction of the left ventricle. Diastolic blood pressure is the bottom number of a blood pressure reading that indicates the lowest amount of pressure placed on the arteries as the ventricles of the heart relax. To improve consistency with blood pressure readings, the process should be performed from a seated position and on the right arm each time. When checking clients' BP readings while they are sitting, one must ensure that the clients' feet are not crossed as this can artificially increase BP readings.

A common concern about blood pressure among fitness professionals is when it is too high or too low. This can lead to medical emergencies and is sometimes exacerbated by exercise. **Hypertension** is increased blood pressure, whereas **hypotension** is decreased blood pressure. Hypertension is indicated as blood pressure above 140/80 mmHg, and hypotension is indicated as blood pressure below 90/60 mmHg. Clients presenting either of these concerns prior to starting an exercise program should seek a physician for exercise clearance. Sometimes, diseases such as **atherosclerosis** can increase the risk of having a severe cardiovascular event like a heart attack or stroke. Atherosclerosis is a disease which is characterized by hardening or narrowing of the arteries due to plaque deposits. A physician's clearance should always be obtained prior to starting a program with clients suffering from these conditions, and the trainer should make sure to monitor for signs of a stroke or heart attack during sessions.

Pathologies affecting the lungs are also a high risk for fitness professionals. One of the most common conditions exacerbated by exercise is **asthma**. Asthma is a chronic disease affecting breathing and is due to inflammation of the respiratory airways of the body. Some clients suffer from exercise-induced asthma and may require a physician-prescribed inhaler during exercise sessions. These individuals should be informed to bring the inhaler with them to all workouts to prevent any severe events, and their breathing should be monitored.

Other clients may suffer from more severe conditions, like **chronic obstructive pulmonary disease (COPD)** or **emphysema**. COPD is a broad definition of many diseases causing chronic obstruction of airflow to the lungs, including: emphysema, asthma, and bronchitis. Clients with severe COPD may struggle during the most simple of exercise efforts, but exercise can nonetheless help to improve their condition. Emphysema is a chronic obstructive pulmonary disease characterized by damage to the alveoli and subsequent entrapment of air and eventual breaking of the air sacs. This disease can increase the **residual capacity** of an individual. Residual capacity is the air that remains in the lungs following an expiration or exhaling. The remaining air becomes stale and makes it difficult to breathe. These chronic pulmonary conditions are often the result of smoking or exposure to pollution and chemicals that can damage the airways.

PRACTICE QUESTIONS

1. The pulmonary artery carries

    A) deoxygenated blood from the heart to the lungs.

    B) oxygenated blood from the lungs to the heart.

    C) oxygenated blood from the heart to the lungs.

    D) deoxygenated blood from the right atrium to the right ventricle.

    Answers:

    A) **Correct.** The pulmonary artery is the artery that transports blood from the heart to the lungs for oxygen collection.

    B) Incorrect. This refers to the pulmonary vein.

    C) Incorrect. This pathway does not make sense as the blood is already oxygenated.

    D) Incorrect. There is no artery carrying blood from heart chamber to heart chamber.

2. Blood pressure is determined using

    A) an electrocardiogram.

    B) heart rate and ventilation rate.

    C) a sphygmomanometer.

    D) a pulse.

Answers:

    A) Incorrect. This device is used for measuring the heart's electrical signal.

    B) Incorrect. Blood pressure cannot be determined this way.

    C) **Correct.** The device to determine blood pressure is a sphygmomanometer.

    D) Incorrect. This is used to determine heart rate.

Effects of Exercise on the Cardiovascular System

The cardiovascular and respiratory systems can be improved through regular participation in an exercise program. Aerobic or cardiovascular exercise in a healthy client will have standard short-term responses that the fitness professional should expect during workouts. An increased heart rate and **hyperventilation** are common acute responses as exercise rises in intensity. These rates should return to normal resting levels following cessation of exercise. Hyperventilation refers to increased breathing rate. This is due to the body requiring a larger supply of oxygen to produce energy in the form of ATP required for exercise. Additionally, the heart must pump faster to supply the blood that carries the oxygen to the muscles. An increase in systolic blood pressure is also a normal acute response to cardiovascular exercise. However, there is very little change to diastolic blood pressure. Additional acute cardiovascular responses to exercise include increased cardiac output by the heart and the shunting of blood to working musculature and away from the areas that are less utilized, like the digestive tract.

The long-term cardiovascular physiological adaptations to aerobic exercise include improved heart efficiency, increased heart size, increased capillary density, decreased blood pressure, and increased blood volume. These factors all contribute to a more efficient cardiovascular system. The increase in heart efficiency is due to the improved stroke volume, which means the heart pumps more blood to the body in one beat than pre-training levels. The increased stroke volume improves cardiac output of the heart, increasing the rate and amount at which blood is pumped to the working tissues. This allows the heart to function at a lower resting heart rate and permits reduced efforts at submaximal exercise levels. The heart muscle also hypertrophies like skeletal muscle, adding to the increase in stroke volume. The increase in capillary density and efficiency allows for more optimal gas exchange at the level of the vessels. More oxygen is provided to the working muscles while carbon dioxide and waste is removed more easily.

Blood pressure reduction is an important chronic effect of cardiovascular exercise because it can help prevent dangerous conditions, like hypertension. It can also help reduce blood pressure in clients already suffering from pre-hypertensive and hypertensive conditions. Finally, a rise in blood volume associated with increased blood plasma, platelets for clotting, and red blood cells all benefit cardiovascular health.

An interesting phenomenon occurs in blood pressure due to postural changes. Blood pressure can vary based on whether the client is lying, sitting, or standing. This is important to understand because it can directly affect the blood pressure reading during a fitness assessment. If the client is transitioning from a lying to standing posture, the blood pressure first dips slightly and then increases dramatically to compensate for the change in body position. The body must respond to the assistance of gravity in transporting blood to the brain by having to pump the blood upward while standing. This can sometimes take a while to occur and dizziness is associated with the change in blood pressure. The drop in blood pressure is commonly referred to as orthostatic hypotension. In most cases, this is due to dehydration and is more frequent in older adults than in younger individuals. It is important for the trainer to understand why this is happening because it is common during workouts to go from prone or supine to standing positions.

PRACTICE QUESTIONS

1. Orthostatic hypotension is commonly caused by
    A) height.
    B) training status.
    C) a change in blood pressure due to postural position.
    D) high blood pressure.

    Answers:
    A) Incorrect. Height is not the common cause of orthostatic hypotension.
    B) Incorrect. Training status does not cause orthostatic hypotension.
    C) **Correct.** Orthostatic hypotension is caused by a change in blood pressure due to postural position.
    D) Incorrect. High blood pressure is not the common cause for orthostatic hypotension.

2. Hyperventilation refers to
    A) increased breathing rate.
    B) increased blood pressure.
    C) increased sweating.
    D) decreased breathing rate.

Answers:

A) Correct. This is the definition of hyperventilation.

B) Incorrect. This is hypertension.

C) Incorrect. This is a common reaction to increased exercise intensity.

D) Incorrect. This is hypoventilation.

The Nervous System

STRUCTURE AND FORM OF THE NERVOUS SYSTEM

The nervous system is typically broken down into two parts: the central nervous system (CNS) and the peripheral nervous system (PNS). The CNS is made up of the **brain** and **spinal cord**. The brain is an organ of the central nervous system made up of nervous tissue that is responsible for nearly all thought processes and actions of the human body. The spinal cord is responsible for the relaying of information to and from the rest of the body to the brain. The spinal cord is protected by the vertebral column: a structure of bones that enclose the delicate nervous tissue. **Nerve cells**, or **neurons**, are involved in the transmission of electrical impulses through conductivity and input from internal and external stimuli. Neurons have a nucleus and transmit these electrical impulses through their **axons** and **dendrites**. The axon is a stem-like structure, often covered in myelin, found on neurons that carry information to other neurons throughout the body. Dendrites, which receive the information from other neurons, are the branching system on the neuron's body. Below is a figure showing the structures of a neuron:

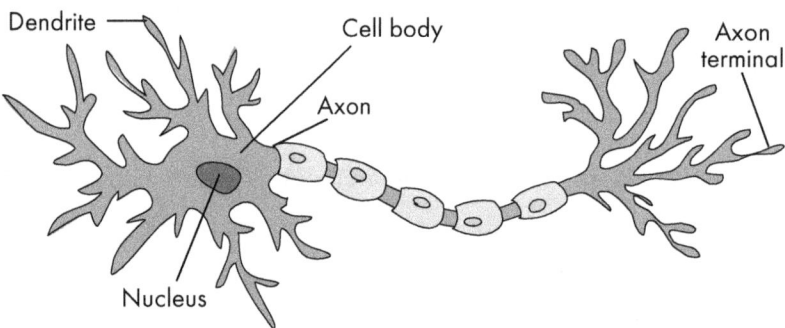

Figure 1.8. The Structures of a Neuron

> When coming across diagrams you find particularly helpful in explaining anatomical structure, draw a simple version of the same diagram and label the parts for practice and memorization.

The functions of the nervous system of the body can be broken down into the **autonomic nervous system** and the **somatic nervous system**. The autonomic nervous system is part of the nervous system that controls involuntary actions that occur in the body, such as respiration, heartbeat, digestive processes, and more. The somatic nervous system is associated with the body's ability to control skeletal muscle and voluntary movement as well as the involuntary reflexes associated with skeletal muscles.

Additionally, the autonomic nervous system breaks down even further into sympathetic and parasympathetic nervous systems that have differing functions. The sympathetic nervous system is responsible for the body's reaction to stress and induces a "fight-or-flight" response to stimuli. For instance, if an individual is frightened by something, the sympathetic nervous system is provoked and there are increases in the person's heart rate, blood pressure, etc. The individual will either stay and go on the defensive or react by getting away from the threat as fast as possible. The body responds by preparing a person for this reaction.

In contrast, the parasympathetic nervous system is stimulated by the body's need for rest or recovery. The parasympathetic nervous system responds by decreasing heart rate, blood pressure, and muscular activation when a person is getting ready to sleep, digesting food, etc. The body reacts to eating a large meal by activating the parasympathetic nervous system, which is why people feel sluggish after eating a large meal.

Pathologies of the Nervous System

Like the cardiovascular and musculoskeletal systems, the nervous system can have pathologies that may affect the body while exercising. Some of these pathologies can occur at any stage of life, while others are more common in older adults. **Epilepsy**, for example, can occur at all stages of life. Epilepsy is a chronic disease involving episodic seizures due to disruption of the CNS. There are a number of different kinds of epileptic diseases that are defined by the type of seizure, age of the person, and other factors, like the location of the brain that is affected. The diagnosis is usually given when the person suffers more than one seizure separated by at least a day.

A number of causes can induce the seizures that are involved in epileptic syndromes, including: strokes, autism, traumatic brain injury, genetic disorders, developmental disorders, and even **Alzheimer's disease**. Alzheimer's disease is characterized by the loss of memory and deteriorating cognitive function, usually later in life, due to the degeneration of neurons in the brain. The disease is a form of dementia that progresses gradually and has no known cure. Onset usually occurs past age sixty, but can also occur as early as forty years old. These individuals have trouble retaining newly acquired information to the point where everyday tasks and life are negatively affected. Significant details, such as people, places, and more are forgotten.

Another significant nervous system disorder is known as **multiple sclerosis (MS)**. MS involves the gradual breakdown and scarring of the myelin sheaths surrounding axons due to immune system attacks in a neuron, causing disruption of nervous transmission of impulses. The myelin sheaths surrounding the axon help speed up the process of nervous electrical transmission; when they are damaged, transmission is negatively impacted. The nerve damage associated with MS causes vision trouble, difficulty walking, fatigue, pain, involuntary spasms, and numerous other symptoms.

This disease is thought to be genetic, and there is no known cure. However, treatments are available to slow the disease's progression.

PRACTICE QUESTIONS

1. The autonomic nervous system breaks down further into
   - **A)** the peripheral nervous system and the central nervous system.
   - **B)** the somatic nervous system and the parasympathetic nervous system.
   - **C)** the parasympathetic nervous system and the sympathetic nervous system.
   - **D)** the sympathetic nervous system and the central nervous system.

   Answers:
   - A) Incorrect. These are the larger hierarchical nervous systems.
   - B) Incorrect. The somatic nervous system is incorrect.
   - **C) Correct.** These are the two branches of the autonomic nervous system.
   - D) Incorrect. The central nervous system is incorrect.

2. Where is the myelin sheath located?
   - **A)** on the dendrites
   - **B)** on the brain
   - **C)** on the heart
   - **D)** on the axons

   Answers:
   - A) Incorrect. It is not found on the dendrites.
   - B) Incorrect. It is not found on the brain.
   - C) Incorrect. It is not found on the heart.
   - **D) Correct.** It is found on the axons.

EFFECTS OF EXERCISE ON THE NERVOUS SYSTEM

As previously mentioned, the nervous system plays a vital role in the optimal function of the human body. Therefore, it is important for the fitness professional to understand how exercise affects the nervous system. Exercise helps to improve the efficiency of the nervous system's connection to the muscles. A significant neuromuscular adaptation to exercise can be seen as a result of performing resistance training exercises regularly. The muscles are placed under excessive levels of stress, and the nervous system adapts by recruiting more motor units to perform the same movement. The result is an increase in strength within the first several weeks of resistance training. The neuromuscular strength gains are usually significantly noticeable among new clients and require that the muscles be placed in a state of overload to elicit a response. Conduction of a nervous impulse to muscle creates the muscular contractions that assist in human movement.

Exercise helps to make this conduction of impulses more efficient. The pattern of nerve conduction follows these steps:

1. An impulse travels from the brain to the end of the axon at the synapse with a muscle cell.
2. The neurotransmitter, acetylcholine, is released into the synaptic cleft.
3. The acetylcholine is received by the sarcolemma of muscle.
4. Action potential in muscle is triggered.
5. Action potential initiates the release of calcium from the sarcoplasmic reticulum of a muscle cell.
6. Calcium exposes the thin actin filaments of muscle to the thick myosin filament heads for attachment.
7. Myosin crossbridging occurs.
8. Muscular contraction results from crossbridging and flexion of myosin heads on actin.

The force of a muscular contraction is determined by the nervous system's stimulation of either more motor units or its consistent stimulation of a muscle. The process of stimulating more motor units is known as motor unit recruitment. Individual motor units are recruited via a nervous stimulus to perform a particular action. If a load is too heavy, more motor units are stimulated by the nervous system to induce a stronger contraction of the muscles. For instance, the body will require less motor units to lift a coffee mug to the mouth than to perform a bicep curl with a twenty-five pound dumbbell. A stimulus of a significant amount is achieved, and more motor units are recruited with the dumbbell. Summation involves the nervous system sending an impulse for muscular twitch and then immediately sending another impulse to the same motor unit before it has time to relax. The resultant continuous stimuli occur until a condition called tetanus is reached and the muscle ceases to relax. A frequency of stimuli has been reached so that the muscle does not regress to a relaxed state. In both instances, an insignificant stimulus will result in no contraction of muscle at all.

When resistance training exercise is performed properly and on a consistent basis, the body makes neuromuscular adaptations that improve strength. Motor unit recruitment becomes more efficient, allowing the body to lift heavier loads. This adaptation occurs as a result of the amount of force being placed on the muscles. The nervous system will first recruit type I muscle fibers. However, if these fibers are not sufficient to move the force, type II fibers will be recruited to assist. The body responds to varying types of exercise by developing musculature based on how the person is training. The fitness professional should understand how specific training mechanisms influence the neuromuscular system and how it adapts to different types of exercise.

PRACTICE QUESTIONS

1. Motor unit recruitment refers to

    A) the constant stimulus of a motor unit to produce a continuous contraction of muscle.

    B) the process of stimulating more motor units to overcome a force.

    C) the impulse sent for muscular contraction.

    D) type I muscle fibers.

    Answers:

    A) Incorrect. This refers to summation.

    B) Correct. This is the definition of motor unit recruitment.

    C) Incorrect. This is nerve transmission to muscle.

    D) Incorrect. This is a type of muscle fiber.

2. What occurs at the end of the axon?

    A) a stimulus

    B) the sarcolemma

    C) actin and myosin

    D) the synapse

    Answers:

    A) Incorrect. This is what creates an impulse.

    B) Incorrect. This is found in the muscle fiber.

    C) Incorrect. This is found at the level of the sarcomere.

    D) Correct. The synapse occurs at the end of an axon.

The Endocrine System

STRUCTURE AND FORM OF THE ENDOCRINE SYSTEM

The endocrine system is made up of a varietal system of **glands** with the purpose of regulating numerous processes throughout the body via secretion of **hormones**. A gland is an organ associated with controlling the release of chemical substances, known as hormones, for the regulation of metabolic processes, growth and development, sexual reproduction, and other bodily functions. Hormones are the chemical substances used for controlling different bodily and cellular processes released by the glands.

There are many glands found throughout the body with different important functions. For instance, the **hypothalamus** is a gland found in the brain that is responsible for the control of the autonomic nervous system's function and the connection between the body's central nervous system and the endocrine system. It is important because of its control of the body's life-sustaining processes that are regulated by the autonomic nervous system. Along with the hypothalamus, the brain houses the **pituitary** and **pineal** glands. The pituitary gland is found at the base of the brain and is responsible for the release of hormones that regulate human growth and development. The pineal gland regulates the body's sleep processes through the release of the hormone melatonin.

Additional glands found throughout the body help with other important bodily processes. The **parathyroid gland** is located near the thyroid gland and stores and secretes parathyroid hormones that are responsible for the regulation of the body's calcium levels. It is important for the fitness professional to understand how the body regulates calcium levels as they determine things like bone mineral density. The **adrenal glands** are located superior to the kidneys and produce **epinephrine**, norepinephrine, **cortisol**, and aldosterone. Epinephrine is a hormone that is responsible for the regulation of heart rate, blood pressure, and more due to autonomic responses to stimuli. Cortisol is a hormone produced and secreted by the adrenal glands and is responsible for the regulation of processes when stress is placed on the body. It increases blood sugar, macronutrient metabolism, and more during times of stress. These glands are responsible for many exercise-induced hormonal responses as well as the "fight-or-flight" response associated with stressful environmental factors.

Another important organ associated with the endocrine system is the **pancreas**. The pancreas is found in the abdomen and is responsible for the secretion of a digestive substance into the duodenum of the small intestine as well as the regulation of **insulin** and other hormones. The regulation of insulin is important because it is how the body controls blood sugar levels. During exercise, the body utilizes the glycogen stores in the muscles, which results in a drop in blood glucose levels. The fitness professional should understand how exercise affects individuals who suffer from conditions that create issues with blood sugar regulation, like diabetes type I and II.

Additional organs associated with the endocrine system include the male and female reproductive organs. The **testes** are a reproductive organ in males that produce sperm and androgens for reproduction. In contrast, the **ovaries** are a female reproductive organ found produce ova and female hormones for reproduction. The endocrine system is responsible for determining which type of sexual organs will be developed throughout the early stages of life and adolescence. For example, the hormone **testosterone** is responsible for the development of male reproductive organs while fetal development is occurring. The endocrine system is responsible for the release of this hormone. Testosterone is a hormone secreted mainly by the testes in males that regulates the growth of muscle mass, body hair, bone mass, and more. It is not absent in females but occurs in much smaller quantities and can be found in the ovaries. The absence of this hormone in sufficient quantities to produce male sex organs will result in female reproductive organ development.

> Create a chart with a list of endocrine glands in the first column. In the second column, try to list the hormone that each gland secretes. In a third column, try to list the function of the gland and its hormones.

In addition to gender determination, the endocrine system is also responsible for the development of the **placenta** in women who are pregnant. The placenta is a part of the uterus during pregnancy that passes nutrition and nourishment to the fetus from the mother via the umbilicus. It also produces and develops several hormones responsible for fetal growth and preparatory hormones for motherhood, such as lactogen for breastfeeding. The chart below indicates the location of the various endocrine glands as they vary between male and female:

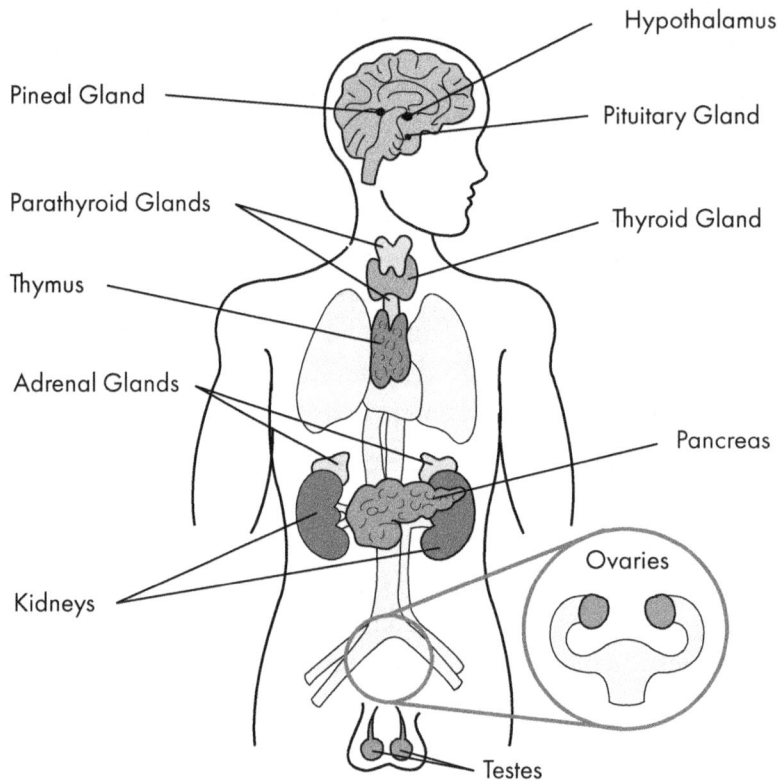

Figure 1.9. The Location of Male and Female Endocrine Glands

Many of the important hormones associated with exercise science can be broken down into either **anabolic hormones** or **catabolic hormones**. Anabolic hormones are associated with the regulation of growth and development, such as testosterone, estrogen, insulin, and **human growth hormone**. Human growth hormone is released by the pituitary gland, which regulates muscle and bone development. Another example of an anabolic hormone is an **insulin-like growth factor (IGF)**. An IGF is a hormone synthesized in the liver that aids in tissue growth and many other functions.

Catabolic hormones are associated with the regulation of breaking down substances in the body into smaller molecules. For example, the breakdown of muscle glycogen for energy via the release of glucagon is a catabolic process. Anabolic hormones are often discussed in the field of exercise science as a means of performance enhancement in sports. The body naturally releases many of the anabolic hormones as a result of exercise, and the hormones help to produce muscular protein synthesis. However, the use of supplemental forms of anabolic steroids is a controversial method for enhancing this process. Anabolic steroids can increase the rate and size of muscle mass production, but with significant and dangerous side effects. The abuse of anabolic steroids can cause negative effects on reproductive organ function, psychological side effects (like depression and mood swings), and severe damage to the liver. Fitness professionals should be able to answer questions regarding the abuse of anabolic steroids in order to be able to inform their clientele of the risks.

PRACTICE QUESTIONS

1. The endocrine system is made up of glands that
    - **A)** secrete hormones for various functions.
    - **B)** provide structural support for organs.
    - **C)** produce forces for movement.
    - **D)** have limited or no function.

   Answers:
    - **A) Correct.** The glands of the endocrine system secrete hormones for various bodily functions.
    - B) Incorrect. The muscles and connective tissues support the organs.
    - C) Incorrect. The muscles produce forces for movement.
    - D) Incorrect. The glands have many various functions.

2. Testosterone is
    - **A)** a gland.
    - **B)** a catabolic hormone.
    - **C)** an anabolic hormone.
    - **D)** an organ.

   Answers:
    - A) Incorrect. Testosterone is a hormone secreted by a gland.
    - B) Incorrect. Testosterone is an anabolic hormone.
    - **C) Correct.** Testosterone is an anabolic hormone.
    - D) Incorrect. Testosterone is not an organ.

EFFECTS OF EXERCISE ON THE ENDOCRINE SYSTEM

Exercise induces specific endocrine responses in human beings that play an important role in improving client fitness. The neuroendocrine response is essentially how the body responds to high intensity exercise with the release of specific hormones that elicit performance gains. This response also occurs as a sort of "fight-or-flight" mechanism in stressful situations. Specifically, when the body is placed under stress, the endocrine system releases cortisol to stimulate production of epinephrine and norepinephrine in response. These hormones help the body take action quickly.

Additionally, the neuroendocrine response to working larger muscle groups, like in a barbell back squat exercise, provokes a release of anabolic hormones associated with increased muscular hypertrophy and muscular strength. These hormones include: human growth hormone, insulin-like growth factor 1 (IGF-1), testosterone, and catecholamines. Human growth hormone plays an important role in muscular development and lipolysis. IGF-1 helps maintain and repair muscle, and increased testosterone helps to improve muscular strength as well as the muscles' ability to maintain peak strength output. Finally, catecholamines also assist in muscular strength output and improve muscle energy stores and the rate of muscular contraction. Improvements to the neuroendocrine response to exercise require a progression of exercise intensity involving large muscle groups and high-intensity exercise.

PRACTICE QUESTIONS

1. What does the release of cortisol by the endocrine system stimulate?
    - **A)** production of insulin
    - **B)** production of melatonin
    - **C)** production of epinephrine and norepinephrine
    - **D)** production of parathyroid hormone

    Answers:
    - A) Incorrect. The pancreas is responsible for insulin production.
    - B) Incorrect. The pineal gland is responsible for melatonin production.
    - **C) Correct.** Cortisol release stimulates the production of epinephrine and norepinephrine.
    - D) Incorrect. The parathyroid is responsible for parathyroid hormone production.

2. Which exercise would likely induce the neuroendocrine response?
    - **A)** biceps curls
    - **B)** seated calf raises
    - **C)** wrist extensions
    - **D)** back squats

    Answers:
    - A) Incorrect. This exercise works smaller muscle groups and likely will not influence the neuroendocrine response.
    - B) Incorrect. This exercise works smaller muscle groups and likely will not influence the neuroendocrine response.
    - C) Incorrect. This exercise works smaller muscle groups and likely will not influence the neuroendocrine response.

D) Correct. Back squats work large muscle groups throughout the body and will likely stimulate the neuroendocrine response to exercise.

The Digestive System

Structure and Form of the Digestive System

The digestive system is a tube that extends through the body used for the breakdown of food and the absorption of nutrients. Digestion and absorption of nutrients provide the body with the fuel to maintain homeostasis and produce human movement. The digestive system starts at the **mouth**. The mouth allows for the consumption and mastication of nutrients via an opening in the face. It contains the **tongue** and uses a substance called **saliva** to assist in the first processes of breaking down food. The tongue is a large muscle located in the mouth for the movement of food for mastication by the teeth, and contains taste sensory organs. Saliva is the liquid solution secreted by the salivary glands to assist in the digestion of food through salivary enzymes.

The chewed and lubricated food then travels to the **esophagus**. The esophagus is part of the digestive tract leading from the mouth to the **stomach** that transports food via peristalsis. Peristalsis is the contraction of smooth muscle found in the digestive tract for moving food. The stomach is an organ of the digestive tract found in the abdominal cavity that mixes food with powerful acidic liquid for further digestion. Once the stomach has created an acidic bolus of digested food known as *chyme*, it travels to the **small intestine** where a significant amount of nutrient absorption takes place. The small intestine is a tube-like structure of the digestive tract containing millions of finger-like projections known as villi and microvilli to increase surface area for the absorption of nutrients found in food. The small intestine then transports food to the **large intestine**. The large intestine is similarly tube-like but larger in diameter than the small intestine to assist in further nutrient absorption, water absorption, waste collection, and the production of feces for excretion.

At the end of the large intestine are the **rectum** and **anus**, which are responsible for the storage of feces and removal of feces, respectively. The anus is the opening at the opposite end of the digestive tract as the mouth.

Along the digestive tract are several muscular rings, known as **sphincters**, and additional organs to aid in digestion. The muscular rings help to regulate the movement of digested food through the digestive tract. The anus is the sphincter between the rectum and the outside of the body. There are also sphincters between the mouth and esophagus (upper esophageal sphincter), between the esophagus and the stomach (lower esophageal sphincter), between the stomach and first portion of the small intestine (pyloric sphincter), and between the small intestine and large intestine (ileocecal sphincter).

> Follow the flow of food through the digestive system and list the order in which it travels through. This will help in understanding the process through which food travels and will aid in remembering the organs associated with the digestive tract.

Additionally, the acidic bolus of food created by the stomach's digestive juices is buffered by a substance called **bile**. Bile is created by the **liver** and stored in the **gallbladder**. The liver is an organ located in the abdomen involved in many processes of the body, including: the cleansing of blood, the creation of bile for digestion, the processing of toxins in the body, and more. The gallbladder stores and distributes bile to be released into the small intestine to mitigate the acidic pH of the chyme.

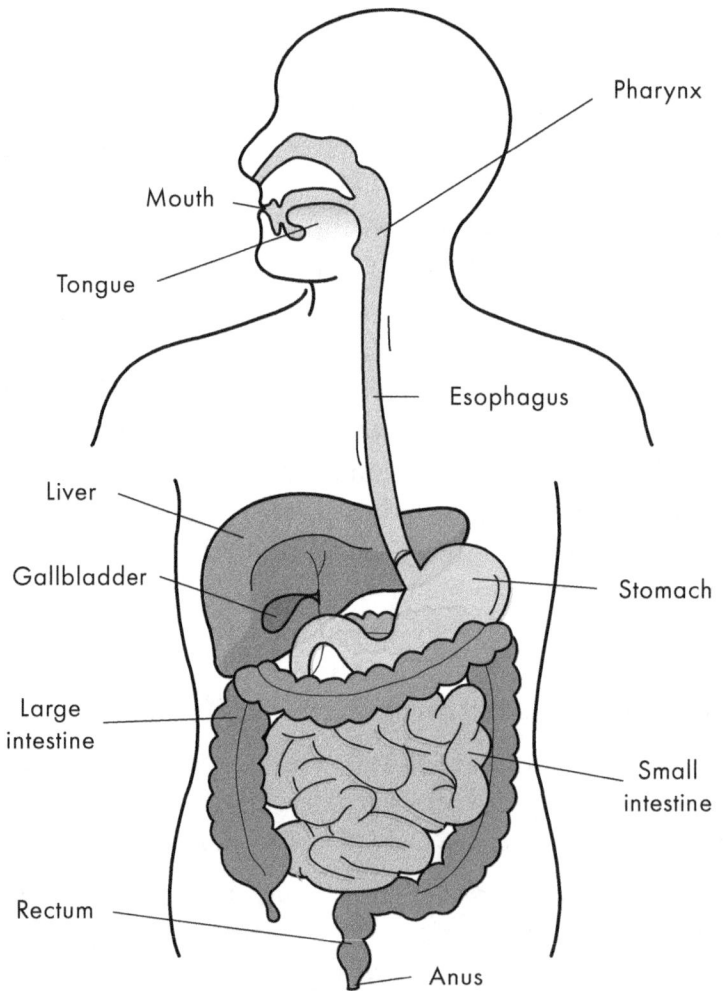

Figure 1.10. The Digestive System

Finally, the **pancreas** aids in the production of enzymes utilized in the digestive process. The pancreas also develops insulin that regulates blood sugar, which is an important factor to monitor during exercise as drops and spikes in blood sugar can be dangerous. Exercise can cause significant fluctuations in blood sugar in those who suffer from diseases that affect the pancreas, like diabetes. These fluctuations can result in the individual feeling light-headed or dizzy, faint, overheated, and more dangerous scenarios.

Figure 1.10 is a diagram of the digestive system, including the various aforementioned organs and where they are generally located.

The absorption of nutrients during the digestive processes primarily takes place in the small intestine. The mouth and stomach are responsible for the breakdown of food that make the digestive process easier. Only certain things are absorbed by the stomach, one of which is alcohol. The walls of the small intestine are lined with the millions of villi and microvilli discussed earlier, because it is the site of absorption for all macronutrients and most everything else. The increased surface area allows for optimal exposure to the walls of the small intestine for absorption. Some water and minerals are passed through to the large intestine where they continue to be absorbed back into the bloodstream.

PRACTICE QUESTIONS

1. What are the muscular rings that allow for the movement of food through the digestive tract?
    - **A)** the small intestine
    - **B)** the rectum
    - **C)** the stomach
    - **D)** the sphincter

    Answers:
    - A) Incorrect. This is a tube-like structure for nutrient absorption.
    - B) Incorrect. This is for the storage of feces before waste excretion.
    - C) Incorrect. This is for the breakdown of food using acidic liquid.
    - D) **Correct.** Sphincters are found throughout the digestive tract and are muscular rings that regulate food movement.

2. How does the pancreas affect those who are exercising?
    - **A)** It regulates blood pressure.
    - **B)** It regulates blood sugar.
    - **C)** It regulates heart rate
    - **D)** It regulates hydration status.

    Answers:
    - A) Incorrect. It does not regulate blood pressure.
    - B) **Correct.** It secretes insulin for blood sugar regulation.
    - C) Incorrect. It does not regulate heart rate.
    - D) Incorrect. It does not regulate hydration status.

Biomechanics

Human Kinetics and Lever Systems

To move, the body creates a system of **levers** out of the components of the musculoskeletal system. A lever is the arrangement of resistance, force, and the fulcrum around which movement is achieved. In exercise science, the resistance is typically the weight being lifted, the force is muscular contraction, and the fulcrum is the joint around which movement is created. Essentially, the muscles pull on the tendons that are attached to the bones to create **torque** around a joint, where torque is the rotational force created when the limb is moved through its range of motion to move a resistance.

Lever systems in human movement consist of three key components: the **fulcrum** (axis), **lever arm**, muscle or **muscular force**, and resistance or **resistive force**. The fulcrum refers to the point around which movement is created in a lever system. In the body, the fulcrum is typically the joint around which resistance and muscular contraction are applied. The lever arm is the hard, unbending surface that typically sits on the fulcrum and to which the resistance and force are applied. The muscular force is the point on the lever arm on which the muscle is exerting force on the tendon to pull the joint through its range of motion. Finally, the resistive force is the point at which the resistance is placed on the lever arm in a lever system.

Levers work on a system of **mechanical advantage** to provide certain types of movement. Mechanical advantage refers to the efficiency of the lever based on where the forces are being applied. Some of the body's lever systems operate such that they provide the ability to lift a larger load over a shorter distance more slowly or a smaller load over a much larger distance more quickly. Those operating under the ability to lift larger loads over a shorter distance are said to have more of a mechanical advantage because the muscle force required per the amount of resistance is minimal. However, those operating under the ability to provide speed of movement are said to have a mechanical disadvantage because the muscle force they require per the amount of resistance is greater. For example, the calf raise exercise is an example of the first type of mechanical advantage, allowing for the advantage of strength. When the resistive force is placed at the opposite end of the lever arm as the fulcrum, and the muscular force is placed in the middle, like in a biceps curl, the lever system is said to have a mechanical advantage

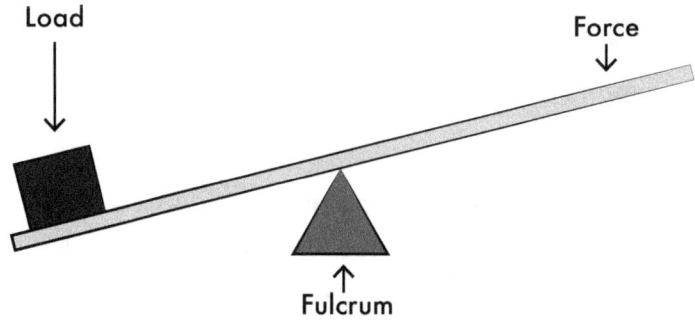

Figure 1.11. Lever

for speed. The type of lever often determines what mechanical advantage the joint will have when exercising. Figure 1.11 demonstrates how a lever system works.

There are three principal types of levers found in the human body. They are typically described as first-class, second-class, and third-class levers. Fitness professionals benefit from understanding how these levers work and how they relate to different human movements. Understanding the biomechanical physics behind the body's lever systems allows the trainer to decide how to manipulate force to adjust exercise intensity and determine what is safe. **First-class levers** refer to a lever system in which the muscle force and resistive force are at opposite sides of the fulcrum. As an example, the head resting on the first vertebrae depicts a first-class lever system: the skull is the resistive force in front of the axis, the fulcrum is the C1 cervical vertebrae, and the muscles of the back of the neck are the muscle force. A diagram of this can be seen in Figure 1.12.

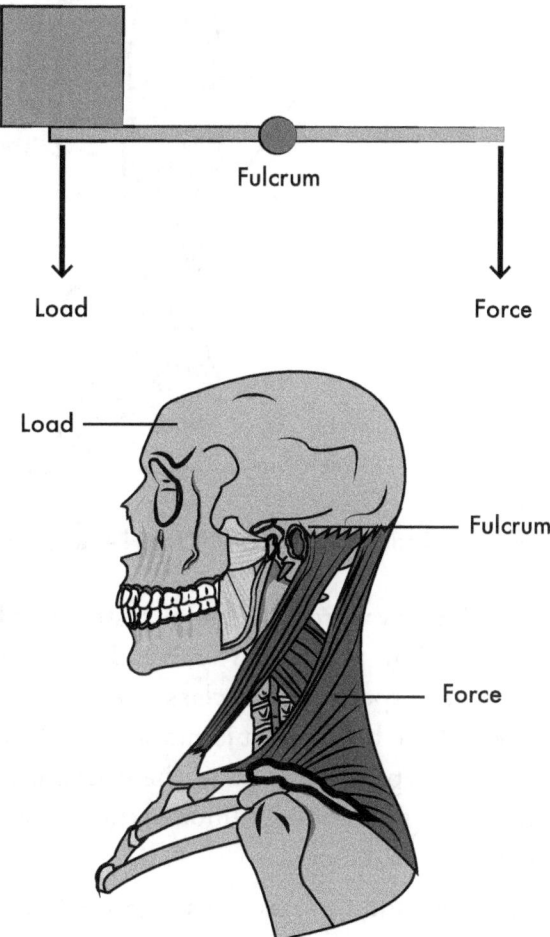

Figure 1.12. First-Class Lever System

Second-class levers refer to a lever system in which the muscle force is placed further from the fulcrum than the resistive force. This type of lever system provides the mechanical advantage of strength. An example of a second-class lever system in the body is found at the ankle joint. The fulcrum is the ball of the foot, the muscular force is the gastrocnemius and soleus muscles, and the resistive force is the body weight and additional weight being lifted. An example of this can be seen below:

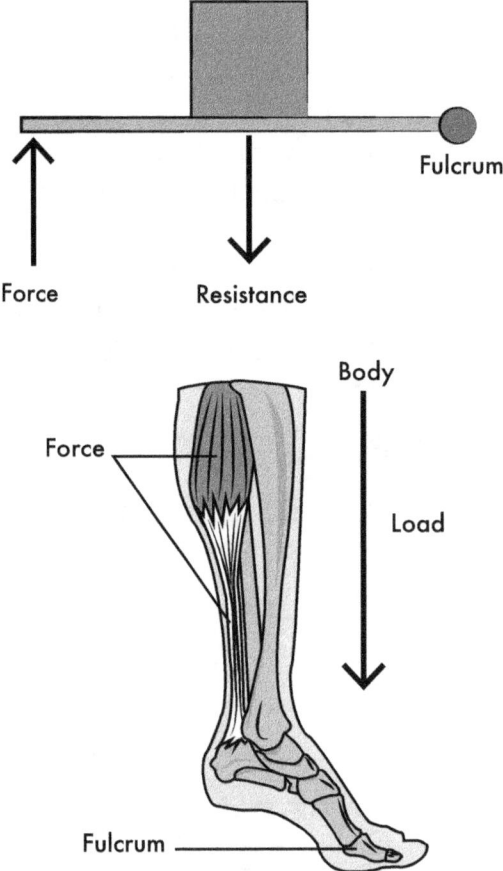

Figure 1.13. Second-Class Lever System

Finally, **third-class levers** refer to a lever system in which the muscle force is placed closer to the fulcrum than the resistive force. This type of lever system provides the mechanical advantage of speed. Third- class levers are the most common lever systems found in the body and can be found at joints such as the knee (flexed by hamstrings) or the elbow (flexed by biceps). At the knee, the fulcrum is the knee joint, the muscular forces are the hamstrings and its tendinous attachment, and the resistive force is the lower portion of the leg and foot.

A thorough understanding of lever systems and human kinetics provides the fitness professional with a knowledge base for how human movement is created. Applying these lever systems to the basic principles of physics is important information to understand in explaining the biomechanics of the human body.

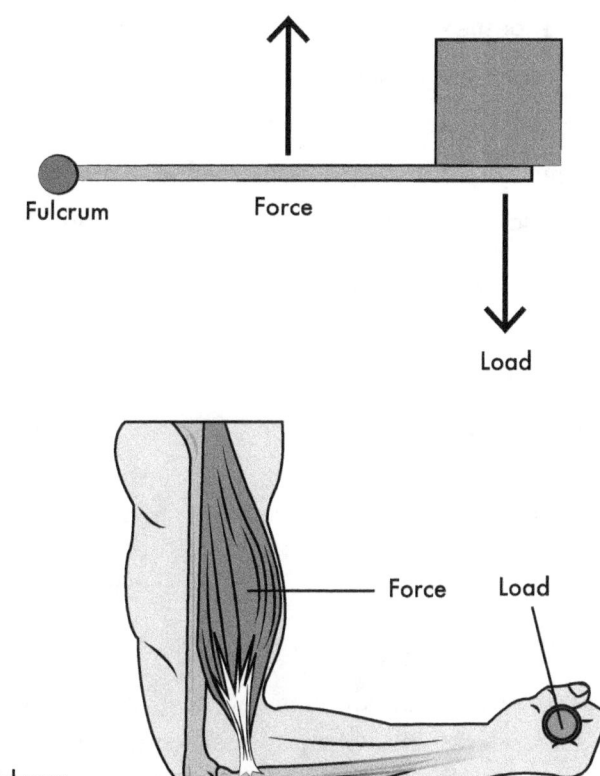

Figure 1.14. Third-Class Lever System

PRACTICE QUESTIONS

1. The best anatomical structure to be described as a fulcrum in the human body is
    - **A)** a joint.
    - **B)** a bone.
    - **C)** a muscle.
    - **D)** an organ.

Answers:

- **A) Correct.** Joints can be described as the fulcrum of a lever system in the human body.
- B) Incorrect. Bones are better described as the lever arms in a lever system.
- C) Incorrect. Muscles are better described as the muscular force used to lift the resistance.
- D) Incorrect. Organs are a structure of the biological hierarchy of the human body.

2. Which is the best example of a first-class lever in the human body?

- **A)** the quadriceps muscle and knee
- **B)** the biceps muscle and elbow
- **C)** the muscles on the back of the neck and the skull on the first vertebrae
- **D)** the muscles of the calf and the joint at the toes and ball of the foot

Answers:

- A) Incorrect. This is a third-class lever.
- B) Incorrect. This is a third-class lever.
- **C) Correct.** This is one of the only first-class levers on the body where the skull meets the C1 vertebrae.
- D) Incorrect. This is one of the only examples of a second-class lever of the body.

STRENGTH AND POWER

Basic concepts of physics explain many of the ideas that exercise science is derived from. Developing a knowledge base of these basic concepts will help the fitness professional to understand biomechanics and human kinetics in more detail. For instance, **mass** and **force** are common terminology used in the description of various fitness topics. Mass refers to the amount of matter that any particular object is made up of and is typically measured in kilograms. Mass is often utilized in body composition analysis and sometimes in weightlifting. Force is the mass of an object times its **acceleration**, where acceleration is the rate of increase in **velocity**. Velocity is the rate at which an object is traveling, including its direction and magnitude. Another way to describe velocity is the rate at which an object travels a specific distance. These concepts are the fundamentals of **Newton's laws of motion.**

Isaac Newton created three laws of motion that describe the physics surrounding objects that are moving. The first law of motion states that objects in motion will either remain in a state of motion or state of rest until acted on by outside forces. This concept can be applied to human motion as seen when the kicker in football is setting up for a kickoff. The ball remains at rest on the ground until the player provides an outside force to move it by kicking it. The ball will continue moving until it is stopped by the ground or another player catches it to stop it. This is a very basic explanation, and there are other forces at play. However, this concept explains the change from resting to motion by an outside force.

The second law of motion states that the mass of the object determines the amount of force required for acceleration of that object. This is where the equation *Force = Mass × Acceleration* was derived. In exercise, this example explains the fundamental concept of resistance training. The force is provided by the muscles, the mass is the weight, and the acceleration is the rate of the moving weight. Masses that are much greater will require more force to move at the same rate of acceleration, whereas lighter masses will require less force to move at the same rate of acceleration.

Finally, the third law of motion states that when an action occurs, there are reactions that are equal yet opposite. This law is demonstrated in many sports. For instance, when tennis players strike a tennis ball with their racket, the force that is applied to the ball by the racket will receive a reactive force of the same magnitude which will be applied to the racket by the ball in the opposite direction.

During exercise, **work** is being performed to lift weights when a force is applied to an object to move it over a distance. Additionally, **power** is the ability to perform work divided by the time it takes to perform that work. Other concepts, such as **momentum** and **impulse**, are used in athletics to determine the forces of objects in contact sports. Such concepts also help in the creation of protective equipment. Momentum refers to the mass of an object times the velocity it is traveling. Impulse refers to the amount of force multiplied by the time the force is applied.

The human body produces forces through arcing ranges of motion. These forces are rotational and can be associated with the aforementioned *work* and *power* equations. **Rotational work** is the amount of muscular force (force) needed to move an object through a joint's angular range of motion (distance). Additionally, **rotational power** refers to the amount of work being done by the muscles (work) at a joint divided by the rate at which they are applied (time). Finally, **angular velocity** refers to the rate at which a muscle produces movement through full range of motion at a joint. Understanding these concepts is important because they apply to human movement as well. For example, knowing the relationship between force as it applies to distance can allow the fitness professional to understand that larger ranges of motion will require more effort on the part of the client. Exercises with large ranges of motion will require more energy and force to be used.

Listed below are some important physics equations that relate to the principles of biomechanics:
- **force** = mass × acceleration
- **acceleration** = change in velocity/change in time
- **velocity** = distance/time
- **work** = force × distance
- **power** = work/time
- **momentum** = mass × velocity
- **impulse** = force × time

Strength is an objective that is often utilized in the field of exercise science. It is measured by a muscle's ability to apply force to an object. Unlike *power*, strength does not have a time component and is simply the all-out effort from the muscle. Strength is often measured in exercise via a one-repetition maximum (1RM) test, which is the ability to complete one full repetition without compensation to determine strength in a particular movement.

Certain relationships should be kept in mind that help determine the amount of force that can be applied. For example, the relationship of force and velocity can be described by the **force-velocity curve**. The force-velocity curve refers to the inversely proportional relationship between the amount of force required to move an object at a specific rate and the rate at which the object moves (velocity). As the amount of force from the muscle increases, the velocity of the movement will decrease and vice versa. This can be applied to fitness programs that are designed to emphasize key traits. For instance, athletes seeking to improve single-repetition maximum strength will train with little emphasis on the velocity of the movement. Their program is geared more toward heavy loads and strength. Athletes looking to improve sprint speed, however, will focus more on improvement to velocity at lighter loads. A basic version of the force-velocity curve as it pertains to training programs can be seen in Figure 1.15.

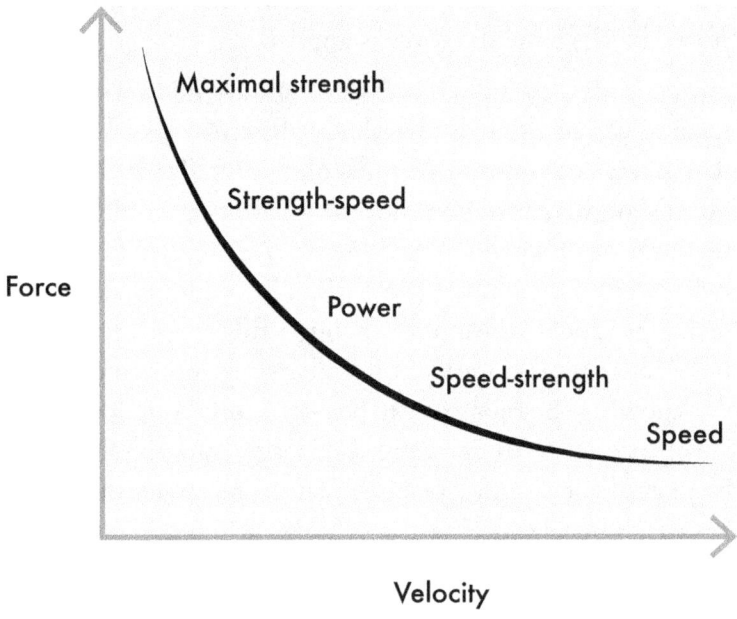

Figure 1.15. Basic Force-Velocity Curve

Additionally, there is a similar curve to describe force and time called the **force-time curve**. The force-time curve represents the time it takes to reach peak force output by the muscles. In other words, the force-time curve shows the time it takes for the body to recruit enough muscle fibers to perform at a certain force output. Force starts off at a minimal amount, and over the course of several milliseconds, it begins to elevate to its peak amount. An example of a force-time curve can be seen in Figure 1.16.

A force-time curve for isometric muscular contraction is shown. The isometric muscular contraction on this force-time curve peaks and then stabilizes since isometric exercises are not a single effort, but rather are typically held for a period of time.

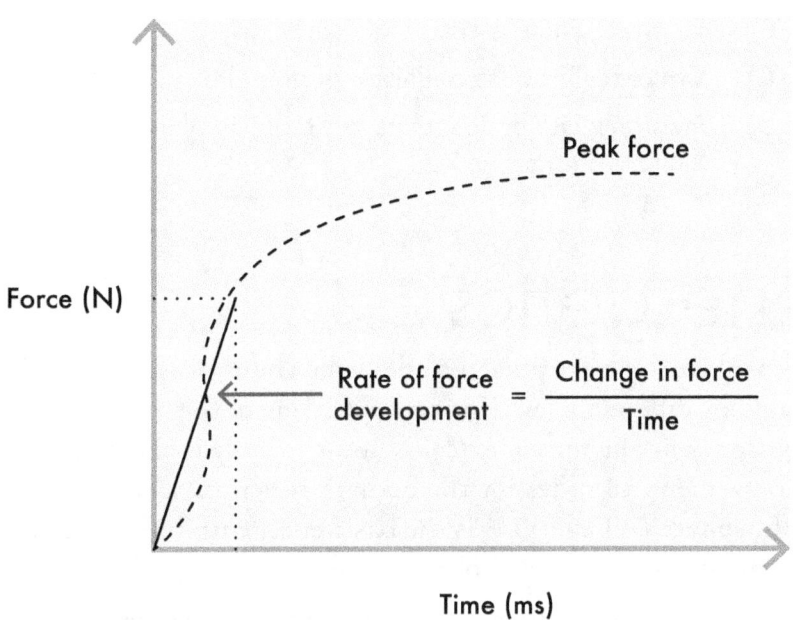

Figure 1.16. Force-Time Curve

PRACTICE QUESTIONS

1. As time increases, the amount of force one can apply

    A) does not matter because the two components are unrelated.

    B) increases.

    C) stays the same.

    D) decreases.

    Answers:

    A) Incorrect. The two components impact one another.

    B) Incorrect. Force decreases as time increases.

    C) Incorrect. There is a change to force with a concurrent change in time.

    D) Correct. The force-time curve indicates that applied force decreases over time.

2. Which of the following describes the amount of weight lifted in a single repetition, regardless of velocity?

    A) power

    B) force

    C) strength

    D) endurance

    Answers:

    A) Incorrect. Power is the application of force × velocity, where velocity is necessary.

B) Incorrect. Force is mass × acceleration.

C) Correct. This is the definition of strength.

D) Incorrect. Endurance refers to the ability of the muscle to apply force for multiple efforts.

Bioenergetics

Bioenergetics is a term used to describe the processes by which the body converts energy for different uses. This concept is one of the most important characteristics in exercise science because it explains how the body is able to utilize various fuel sources for movement. In order for the body to function, it must create units of **adenosine triphosphate (ATP)**. ATP is the basic energy unit required by the body to perform movement and other metabolic processes.

The term **metabolism** is often used to describe the chemical reactions that build and break down the various tissues of the body to sustain life. There are two types of metabolic processes: **anabolism** and **catabolism**. Anabolism refers to the metabolic processes that require energy to build up molecules, whereas catabolism refers to the metabolic processes that break down or burn larger molecules into smaller ones.

The human body relies primarily on two major energy systems for exercise. The **aerobic energy system** refers to the ability of the human body to convert macronutrients into ATP through multiple metabolic processes in the presence of oxygen for sustained durations. This energy system is primarily relied upon for longer-duration activities, such as cycling, running, and swimming. The **anaerobic energy system** refers to the ability of the body to produce ATP via creatine phosphate or muscle glycogen stores found in the body. This energy system is primarily utilized for activities that are shorter in duration, such as weightlifting, sprinting, and jumping. These energy systems derive ATP from metabolic processes that catabolize macronutrients.

The Krebs cycle and **electron transport chain (ETC)** are where the body creates its ATP for energy. The Krebs cycle is an aerobic metabolic breakdown of macronutrients in the body by mitochondria to form carbon dioxide and ATP. **Glycolysis** occurs in the body to create a coenzyme called acetyl coenzyme A (acetyl CoA) that is used in the Krebs cycle. Glycolysis refers to the ability of the body to break down blood **glucose** and muscle **glycogen** stores for the creation of ATP. Glucose refers to sugars found in the body and bloodstream, and glycogen refers to a glucose-based energy supply that is typically synthesized and stored in the liver and skeletal muscle of the human body. The previously mentioned acetyl CoA enters the Krebs cycle to produce a number of byproducts:

- two molecules of ATP
- four molecules of carbon dioxide
- six molecules of **nicotinamide adenine dinucleotide (NADH)**
- two $FADH_2$ molecules

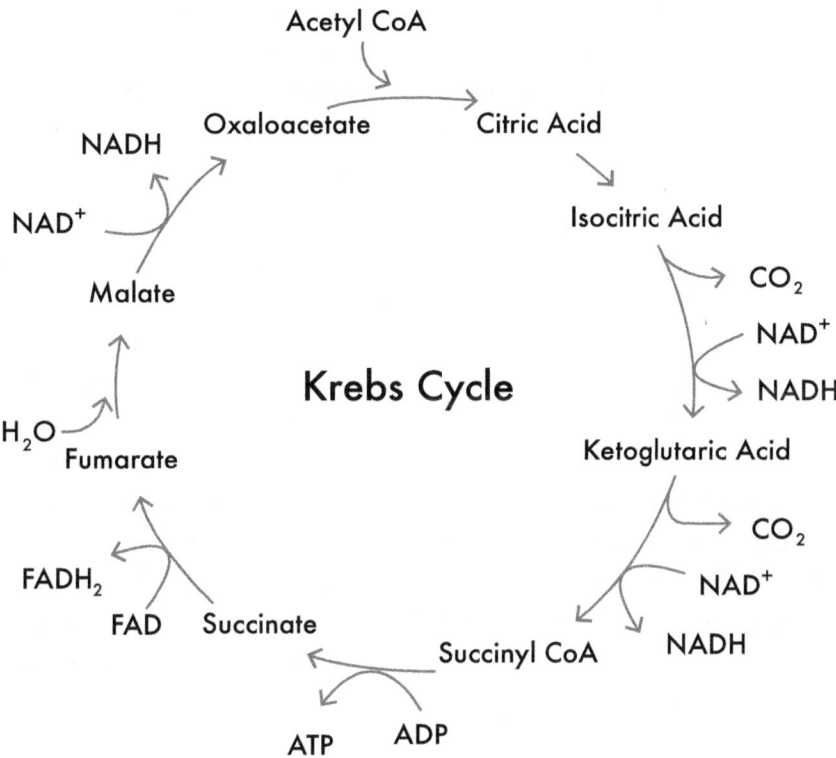

Figure 1.17. The Krebs Cycle

The two molecules of ATP are utilized to fuel the body, and the carbon dioxide molecules are released through respiration. The molecules of NADH and $FADH_2$ are sent through the ETC to produce additional ATP. The ETC is a portion of the aerobic metabolic process of the Krebs cycle in which NADH and $FADH_2$ are used to transfer hydrogen ions to oxygen, forming water and releasing energy in the form of ADP. The ADP is converted to ATP, supplying additional energy to the body. NADH is a niacin-based coenzyme that is vital in electron transfer during the Krebs cycle and ETC. The electron transport chain can produce an additional 34 ATP as a result of the Krebs cycle metabolizing acetyl CoA, which is also an aerobic metabolic process. The body can also produce ATP through anaerobic processes more rapidly.

Anaerobic production of ATP is another method the body uses as an energy supply. **Creatine phosphate** is utilized to synthesize ATP rapidly. Creatine phosphate is an energy source used by the body in the first seconds of exercise. The phosphate group in creatine phosphate supplies adenosine diphosphate (ADP) with the additional phosphate to create ATP and supply more energy for movement. The **phosphagen system** takes advantage of this to produce ATP for high intensity exercise at short durations of ten seconds or less. Bouts of intense exercise using the phosphagen system tend to create byproducts that hinder performance at this intensity for long durations. One such byproduct is called **lactic acid**. Lactic acid builds up in the bloodstream when anaerobic glycolysis produces hydrogen ions in the bloodstream due to lack of oxygen uptake to meet the needs of the exercising muscle. The hydrogen ions decrease the pH of the blood in the muscles, causing an intense burning sensation that limits performance.

EXERCISE SCIENCE

Training at high intensities helps to mitigate the onset of lactic acid buildup, thereby improving the client's **lactate threshold**. The lactate threshold refers to the maximal rate at which lactic acid due to exercise can be buffered from the bloodstream. Highly trained athletes have a higher lactate threshold and are able to withstand higher intensities of exercise for longer durations.

Training can also help to improve an individual's **oxygen uptake**, which is the ability of the body to consume and utilize oxygen. At the start of exercise, the body undergoes an **oxygen deficit** and will start to ventilate more quickly to catch up to demands. The oxygen deficit is the necessitation of anaerobic processes to supply energy at the start of an exercise session until the oxygen uptake reaches a steady state. **Oxygen debt** occurs immediately following exercise and is the excessive consumption of oxygen to return the body to a resting state. Metabolism following a bout of intense exercise remains at elevated rates for a short period of time. **Excess post-exercise oxygen consumption (EPOC)** is one of the metabolic processes of bioenergetics that occurs following exercise. EPOC is similar to oxygen debt and refers to the body's continued consumption of oxygen following exercise for a full return to homeostasis. This continued oxygen consumption results in more energy expenditure even at rest and is a highly beneficial side effect of exercise for weight loss.

PRACTICE QUESTIONS

1. The anaerobic energy system requires
    - **A)** oxygen for the creation of ATP molecules.
    - **B)** creatine phosphate for the creation of ATP molecules.
    - **C)** lactic acid for energy production.
    - **D)** acetyl CoA for ATP production.

    Answers:
    - A) Incorrect. Oxygen is used to form ATP in the aerobic energy system.
    - **B) Correct.** Creatine phosphate is used to create ATP molecules in the anaerobic energy system.
    - C) Incorrect. Lactic acid is a byproduct of anaerobic exercise.
    - D) Incorrect. Acetyl CoA forms ATP in the presence of oxygen in the Krebs cycle.

2. Anabolism is
    - **A)** the breakdown of molecules through metabolism.
    - **B)** adenosine triphosphate.
    - **C)** the building up of molecules through metabolism.
    - **D)** the ability of the body to consume and use oxygen.

Answers:
A) Incorrect. This is referring to catabolism.
B) Incorrect. This is the body's energy source, ATP.
C) Correct. Anabolism is a metabolic process in which molecules are built up.
D) Incorrect. This is referring to oxygen uptake.

Training Differences Among Athletes

Fitness professionals should be aware of the common anatomical and physiological differences among individuals of different ages, genders, and training status. As young athletes age, their bodies will go through rapid growth spurts that may have an effect on their coordination and body development. Oftentimes in sports, children will be placed into an age bracket that includes athletes who are multiple years older. This puts the younger athletes at a disadvantage as they may not have developed certain skills yet. The fitness professional should be aware of the athlete's age and consider exercise modification for younger clients if they are struggling to keep up with their teammates. As a result, these athletes will see more benefits from being able to perform the exercise properly and will have less risk of injury.

Differences in gender should also be considered when developing an exercise plan. Males tend to develop upper body strength more easily when compared to females, whereas females tend to develop lower body strength more easily. Also, female adolescent development occurs at an earlier age, and they may grow more quickly than their male counterparts. Differences in anatomical structure are also relevant to sport. For example, females tend to develop a knock-knee more often than males due to the anatomical difference in pelvis width compared to knee location. The wider pelvis places more medial stress on the knee when performing squats or landing from a jump. With this in mind, it is important for the fitness professional to look for technique flaws during specific movements in sports.

Athletes will often have already developed some basic strength and coordination through their sport or conditioning at practice and will respond differently to exercise. Differences will also occur between sports as to what muscular or cardiovascular progress an individual has made. For instance, individuals who have participated in gymnastics since they were very young will often have a great deal of flexibility when compared to those who played baseball. Another example may be the difference in upper body versus lower body muscular development between a figure skater and rock climber. Athletes who have been training for a longer period of their life will require a more challenging fitness program to meet their needs and elicit performance gains.

CHILDREN

The fitness professional should also be aware of the differences involved in training children compared to training adults. It is a common myth that resistance training in children is unsafe. Children can perform resistance training safely, however, they require more supervision and lower intensities. The exercises should be performed in an effort to learn and develop technique and coordination rather than focus on increasing resistance and strength. Training children should also incorporate a well-rounded program that includes all the major muscle groups of the body in multiple planes of motion. Additionally, cardiovascular activity should be performed through a variety of activities as this will help prevent any long-term overuse through specialization in sport. Encouraging kids to try many different forms of exercise will benefit them more in the long-term.

Physiological differences in children are important to think about when starting a youth exercise program as well. Prior to adolescence, children will not develop muscle quite as rapidly, their coordination will not be as well developed, and they will have difficulty regulating body temperature. Their coordination will struggle due to the changing width of their base of support and the height of their center of gravity. To combat poor thermoregulation in children, the fitness professional should encourage taking water breaks often and try to educate young clients to drink plenty of fluids prior to beginning their workouts. The increased fluid intake will help keep them hydrated and avoid heat-related traumatic events.

PRACTICE QUESTIONS

1. When training children, the fitness professional should focus primarily on
    - **A)** increasing the amount of weight lifted.
    - **B)** improving strength.
    - **C)** improving technique and teaching proper form.
    - **D)** improving power.

Answers:

- A) Incorrect. Weights should be kept light for children so they can work on technique.
- B) Incorrect. While strength is not the primary focus, it is one of the benefits of training children.
- **C) Correct.** Improving technique and emphasizing form is most important when training children.
- D) Incorrect. Power is an advanced benefit of exercise and should not be the primary emphasis of a child's training routine.

2. Athletes will generally have

- **A)** more coordination than untrained individuals.
- **B)** less strength when starting a fitness program.
- **C)** less coordination when starting a fitness program.
- **D)** more fatigue than untrained individuals.

Answers:

- **A) Correct.** Athletes tend to have more strength and coordination when starting a fitness program.
- B) Incorrect. Athletes tend to have more strength when starting a fitness program.
- C) Incorrect. Athletes tend to have more coordination when starting a fitness program.
- D) Incorrect. Untrained individuals tend to fatigue faster.

FEMALE ATHLETES

There are a number of differences between female and male clientele in terms of health and fitness. Trainers should understand these differences in order to make the necessary adjustments to avoid additional risks that come with training different populations. Additional physiological and biomechanical considerations should be taken into account when developing a training program for female athletes, specifically as concerns the physiological side effects of overtraining with female athletes and the biomechanical differences among the genders. Trainers should take the time to analyze the sport, the athlete, and emphasize proper fitness protocols in terms of training variables, nutrition, and recovery methods.

Training female athletes also requires knowledge of the appropriate physiological adaptations that occur with a fitness program. An understanding of **the female athlete triad** can help the trainer and the athlete avoid a potentially dangerous situation while participating in a training program. The female athlete triad refers to the deleterious effects of over-exercising among female athletes and consists of three signs and symptoms: amenorrhea, early osteoporosis, and disordered eating habits. Typically this cycle begins with a lack of proper nutritional intake brought about by a desire to look different or a restrictive diet in order to cut weight with the assumption that it will improve performance. The trainer should develop and discuss an appropriate caloric intake to help prevent the female athlete from falling into a pattern of disordered eating if calories are being restricted. Disordered eating, like anorexia or bulimia, can bring about further potential dangers, leading to the other two indicators of the triad. Amenorrhea refers to a cessation of the menstrual cycle over a three-month period. This is due to the dramatically insufficient caloric intake and a drop in estrogen levels of the athlete. These low estrogen levels lead to the third and final point of the triad: decreased bone mineral density and early onset osteoporosis. Estrogen is a hormone that helps to keep bones strong in females, and the additional lack of nutrients from the disordered eating habits creates serious problems for bone health.

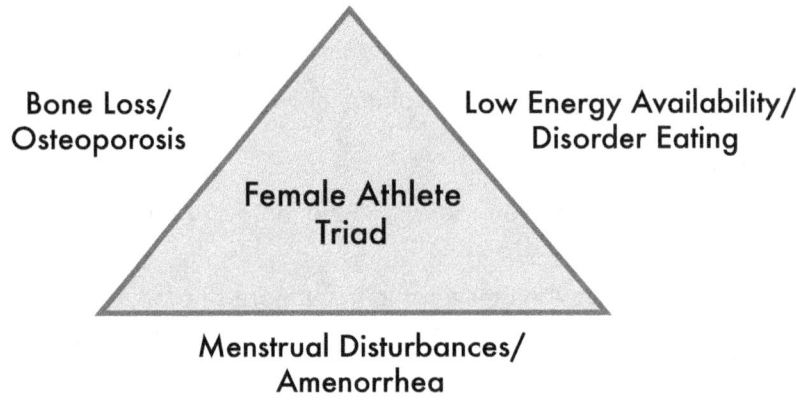

Figure 1.18. The Female Athlete Triad

Biomechanical variations between genders make a difference in how fitness programs should be implemented. Generally, the female body tends to carry more of its muscle mass in the lower body than the male body. The female body also carries extra adipose tissue—necessary for a healthy body composition—and has a wider pelvis and subsequent difference in hip and knee biomechanics. Due to differences in muscle mass development, it is not uncommon for females to lift significantly less resistance during certain upper body exercises. Healthy guidelines for female athlete body composition should be followed to avoid potentially harmful effects, like the female athlete triad. Female athletes should be instructed not to decrease caloric intake too dramatically and should keep in mind a healthy body fat composition for females is around twenty percent. Every athlete is different and not everyone will have the same exact body composition for the same performance level.

> **?** What sports, other than basketball and volleyball, might cause problems for women with a wide Q angle?

A wider pelvis in females comes with a subsequent biomechanical difference in the Q angle at the hip joint. This is important because wider Q angles can lead to more pressure on the medial aspect of the knee joint in females. Female athletes who participate in sports that require constant jumping, such as volleyball and basketball, are at a higher risk of knee injuries due to this biomechanical disadvantage. The trainer must take this difference into consideration and inform the female athlete of proper jumping and landing mechanics. Additionally, the trainer should make arrangements to evenly strengthen the musculature of the legs in order to prevent further exacerbating this increased medial knee stress upon landing. Analyzing the sport will help to determine if additional biomechanical assessment of jumping and landing techniques may be necessary. The female pelvis width creates a larger Q angle and can negatively affect the ligaments of the knee if added force is applied medially. The picture below shows a visual representation of how to determine a Q angle.

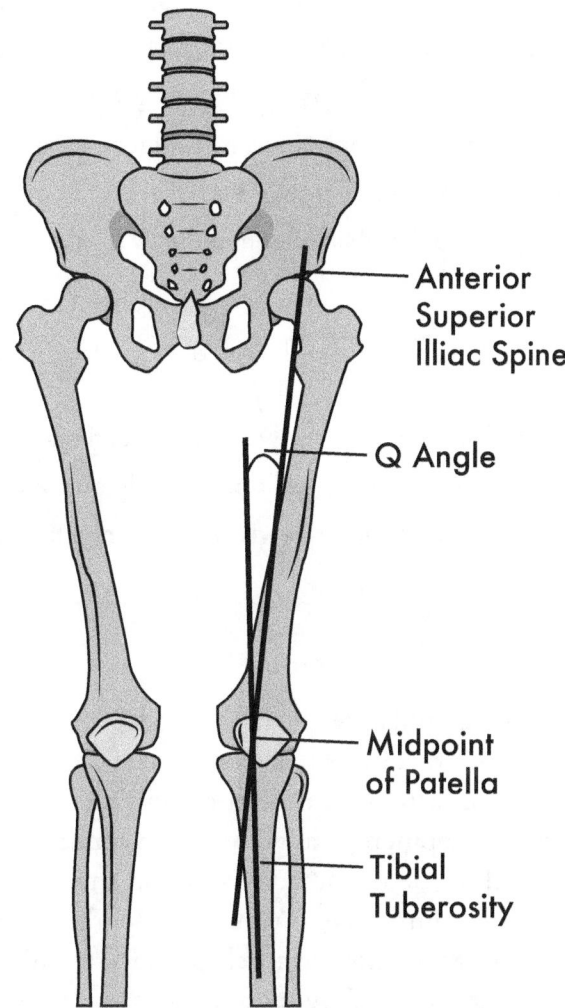

Figure 1.19. Determining a Q Angle

PRACTICE QUESTIONS

1. The female athlete triad is made up of which three below?
    A) amenorrhea, nutrition, and osteoporosis
    B) amenorrhea, osteoporosis, and exercise
    C) exercise, nutrition, and recovery
    D) amenorrhea, disordered eating, and osteoporosis

    Answers:
    A) Incorrect. Nutrition is not an aspect of the triad.
    B) Incorrect. Exercise is not an aspect of the triad.
    C) Incorrect. None of these three are correct.
    D) Correct. The female athlete triad consists of amenorrhea, disordered eating, and osteoporosis.

2. In the diagram above, which describes how to calculate a client's Q angle, how will a smaller pelvis influence the Q angle?

- **A)** If the client has a small pelvis, then the Q angle will be small.
- **B)** The size of a client's pelvis will not influence the Q angle.
- **C)** If the client has a small pelvis, then the Q angle will be large.
- **D)** Only a large pelvis will influence the Q angle.

Answers:

- **A) Correct.** A small pelvis will typically create a small Q angle, as typically seen in males.
- B) Incorrect. The size of the pelvis can affect the size of the Q angle.
- C) Incorrect. A small pelvis will not typically create a large Q angle.
- D) Incorrect. The size of the pelvis will influence the Q angle no matter how large or small.

Older Adults

Fitness professionals should take special consideration when working with older adults. The human body goes through physiological changes that can impact its reaction to exercise. A number of factors result in these physiological changes, including lifestyle habits, injury, the development of adverse health conditions, and more. Physiologically, changes occur at all of the major body systems and can directly affect how training programs should be administered. A trainer must take into account the effect that aging has on the body prior to developing a well-rounded training program. Prior to starting a fitness program, the trainer should implement an assessment process that includes a *Physical Activity Readiness Questionnaire* as well as a thorough medical history to identify any concerns that should be addressed by a client's physician.

The musculoskeletal system changes throughout life. As children, bones and muscles are more flexible and recover more quickly. Older adults are subject to developing arthritis, osteoporosis, and other musculoskeletal disorders that may negatively impact their ability to perform certain tasks and increase risk of injury. Additionally, muscles become less flexible as we age due to sedentary career choices and lifestyle changes. Taking this into consideration, training older adults should include more time spent warming up the muscles to make them more pliable and ready for activity. Training programs for older adults should also include an increased focus on developing stability to reduce the risk of falls. Changes to posture are common among older adults, which can have a negative influence on balance and increase the risk of a fall. Older adults suffering from severe arthritis in the joints of the legs may have difficulty with walking, sitting, and standing. Training these biomechanically compromised individuals may require the implementation of exercises to improve their ability to perform the activities of daily living.

Aging also influences the cardiovascular and nervous systems. As people grow older, their maximal heart rate decreases, making it necessary to adjust target heart rates during exercise. It is also important to determine whether the individual is healthy enough for exercise prior to starting a cardiovascular training program. Potentially risky conditions of the cardiovascular system are more common in older adults than in younger populations. For example, atherosclerosis is developed over years of plaque buildup in the arteries and generally occurs more often in older adults. This can directly impact the ability of the individual to perform higher intensity exercises and should be taken into consideration by the trainer. Like the muscular system, the nervous system also goes through stages of atrophy with older adults. This means that training may require reiterating certain techniques over the course of a training program. Older individuals may require more attention throughout their sessions to keep them focused on controlling their body position.

 Falls in older adults often occur due to breaks that happen *before* they hit the ground due to loss of bone mineral density.

Although programming for older adults may require numerous exercise modifications, the benefits of an exercise program are worthwhile. Resistance training and exercises that involve impact can help to subdue the onset of osteoporosis in older adults as well as help to improve balance. Although flexibility diminishes significantly as people age, it can help to reduce common postural and biomechanical deviations that cause aches and pains. Cardiovascular training also benefits older adults as it strengthens their heart and lungs and helps to reduce the risk of heart attack or stroke. Caution should be taken to reduce the risk of injury while training older adults, however the benefits of training outweigh the risks of a sedentary lifestyle, even in older populations.

PRACTICE QUESTIONS

1. What effect does age have on the cardiovascular system?
   - **A)** The cardiovascular system stays the same with age.
   - **B)** Maximal heart rate increases with age.
   - **C)** Maximal heart rate decreases with age.
   - **D)** The risk of atherosclerosis decreases with age.

Answers:
   - A) Incorrect. The cardiovascular system changes with age.
   - B) Incorrect. Maximal heart rate does not increase with age.
   - **C) Correct.** Maximal heart rate decreases with age.
   - D) Incorrect. The risk of atherosclerosis increases with age.

2. Due to an increased fall risk with older adults, what might the trainer include in an older adult's exercise program?

- **A)** high intensity aerobic training
- **B)** swimming
- **C)** exercises to improve maximal strength in the upper body
- **D)** exercises for improved balance during activities of daily living

Answers:

- A) Incorrect. High intensity aerobic training will not necessarily decrease the risk of a fall.
- B) Incorrect. Swimming requires little balance but is a great low impact joint exercise.
- C) Incorrect. Improved maximal upper body strength will not necessarily decrease the risk of a fall.
- **D) Correct.** Exercises to improve balance during activities of daily living, such as box step-ups, will help to reduce the risk of a fall in older adults.

TWO: NUTRITION

Basic Nutrition Concepts

Macronutrients and Micronutrients

Macronutrients are nutrients that are required in large quantities, typically in the range of tens to hundreds of grams (g) per day. They are divided into **carbohydrates**, **proteins**, and **fats**. Carbohydrates are composed of carbon, hydrogen, and oxygen, and usually have a hydrogen to oxygen (H:O) ratio of two to one as is the case with water (H_2O)—hence the term *hydrate*. **Sugars** are sweet crystalline simple carbohydrates and comprise monosaccharides, such as glucose, fructose, galactose, and disaccharides (two simple sugars linked together—like sucrose, lactose, and maltose). Carbohydrates also occur as long chains that can be branched, such as starches and soluble and insoluble fiber. Fiber is indigestible and therefore provides no calories. All other carbohydrates provide 4 kilocalories per gram of energy.

Although fiber contains no calories, it does have health benefits. It can cause a feeling of fullness and decreased appetite. Soluble fiber binds dietary cholesterol and can help reduce blood LDL (low-density lipoproteins) cholesterol—the bad cholesterol. Soluble fiber can also help slow the breakdown and absorption of carbohydrates, which can help control blood sugar. Insoluble fiber helps speed the passage of stools and can relieve constipation. All fiber is found in plant foods. Soluble fiber is found in oatmeal, beans, and fruits. Insoluble fiber is found in whole wheat, brown rice, and seeds.

> 🔍 The energy derived from food or expended as exercise may be measured in **calories, kilocalories** (kcal) or in **Calories**. A calorie is the energy needed to raise the temperature of one gram of water one degree Celsius. Kcal and Calories with a large C are the equivalent of 1,000 calories with a small c.

Carbohydrates provide fuel for energy. The six-carbon sugar—glucose—is the main substrate for energy metabolism, although fructose is also used. Glucose is the primary sugar circulating in the blood, and its levels are controlled by hormones, such as insulin, glucagon, norepinephrine, epinephrine, and cortisol in response to diet, energy expenditure, and stress. Glucose can be derived from simple sugars—such as sucrose—as well as from starches.

Energy is first extracted from glucose anaerobically through glycolysis, which produces the three-carbon molecule *pyruvate*. Pyruvate can be converted to lactate or can enter the mitochondria where it is broken down aerobically in the tricarboxylic acid cycle (TCA), or citric acid cycle. The TCA cycle produces carbon dioxide (CO_2) as well as nicotinamide adenine dinucleotide plus hydrogen (NADH). The final phase of aerobic energy production is oxidative phosphorylation, which also occurs in the mitochondria. During oxidative phosphorylation, energy from the oxidation of NADH drives the conversion of adenosine diphosphate (ADP) to the energy compound adenosine tri phosphate (ATP), and oxygen reacts with hydrogen to form water.

Glucose is stored in the polymer glycogen in muscle, liver, and other tissues for easy access when energy is needed. Skeletal muscle is the most significant site of glycogen storage in the body.

The five-carbon sugar *ribose* is a component of the metabolic cofactors ATP, NADH, and flavin adenine dinucleotide plus hydrogen (FADH). Deoxyribose is a component of deoxyribonucleic acid (DNA).

Proteins are chains of building blocks called amino acids. Amino acids have the general formula RCHCOOH. NH_2 is a basic amino group attached to the alpha (a)-carbon of a carboxylic acid—hence the name *amino acid*. Amino acids are bound together in proteins by peptide bonds.

Although proteins are long chains, they fold into characteristic complex three-dimensional structures that are influenced by the *R* groups. There are twenty amino acids important in human metabolism, with eight to ten of them considered essential in that they are required in the diet. Arginine and histidine are not always included in the total, since they are only essential under certain conditions, such as periods of fast growth. Animal products, including meat, fish, eggs, and dairy contain complete protein in that all of the essential amino acids are provided. Plant foods contain incomplete protein, which is why vegetarians and especially vegans need to eat a wide variety of plant foods in order to meet their protein needs.

> 🔍 A mnemonic for the ten essential amino acids is Private Tim Hall, abbreviated PVT TIM HALL: phenylalanine, valine, threonine, tryptophan, isoleucine, methionine, histidine, arginine, leucine, and lysine with the caveat that arginine and histidine be considered conditionally essential as they are only necessary during periods of rapid growth and some other conditions.

Proteins and amino acids serve multiple functions, including structural (bone, cartilage, muscles, organs); regulatory (hormones, neurotransmitters, and cellular receptors); enzymes (which carry out metabolic, synthetic, and regulatory reactions); and blood proteins (e.g., albumin—which regulates fluid balance—and thrombin, which is involved in clotting). Protein can also serve as an energy source when other sources are depleted. In particular, the branched chain amino acids—leucine, isoleucine, and valine—are plentiful in muscle and can be used as fuel during intense exercise. As a fuel, protein provides 4 kcal per gram of energy.

Lipids, which include fats and their derivatives as well as other water-insoluble compounds—such as sterols—supply fuel as well as play important structural and regulatory roles. Fats make up cell membranes and are precursors to local signaling molecules called eicosanoids, which modulate inflammation. Fat pads, or adipose tissue, provide energy stores and protect the body and its organs. Dietary fat provides 9 kcal of energy per gram.

The simplest type of lipid is the fatty acid, which is a long hydrocarbon chain with a carboxylic acid (COOH) group at the end. The hydrocarbon chain may be saturated (have no double bonds), monounsaturated (have one double bond), or polyunsaturated (have multiple double bonds). Unsaturation produces kinks in fat molecules that improve fluidity and are protective against cardiovascular disease. Synthetic trans-unsaturated fats are not kinked and are thought to be detrimental to health.

Omega-3 and omega-6 fatty acids have double bonds beginning with three carbons or six carbons respectively from the non-carboxylic acid end of the fatty acid. They are essential in the diet as humans lack the enzymes required to do omega-3 and omega-6 desaturations. Plant foods, especially nuts and seeds, are sources of linoleic and alpha-linolenic acid (eighteen carbon omega-6 and omega-3 fatty acids respectively). These fatty acids can be elongated by the body to form arachidonic acid and eicosapentaenoic acid (EPA)—the twenty-carbon precursors to eicosanoids. The twenty-two-carbon omega-3 fatty acid, docosahexaenoic acid (DHA), is important for the brain and vision. Arachidonic acid is plentiful in meat, and EPA and DHA can be found in abundance in seafood.

The body packages stored fat into triglycerides, in which three fatty acids form ester bonds with glycerol. Intramuscular triglycerides are an important fuel during exercise. Fat is the most significant store of energy in the body, with muscle glycogen being second. High levels of triglycerides in the blood are a risk for cardiovascular disease.

In phospholipids, two fatty acids form ester bonds with glycerol, and the third carbon of glycerol is bonded to a negatively charged phosphate group. In water phospholipids, bilayers are formed with the hydrophobic fatty acid tails facing inward while the hydrophilic phosphate groups are attracted to water. Cell membranes are phospholipid bilayers that have proteins and cholesterol interspersed in them. Sterols are fat-soluble complex ringed molecules and include cholesterol and steroid hormones.

Fatty acids are converted to energy through an aerobic process called beta-oxidation, which occurs in the mitochondria. Beta-oxidation breaks down the fatty acid two carbons at a time. In order for these two carbon units to be completely oxidized, oxaloacetate—an intermediate from carbohydrate metabolism—is required. With insufficient carbohydrate intake, these two carbon units form keto acids, which can be toxic.

Alcohol is not a nutrient, although it is a source of empty calories (i.e., has no nutritional value), providing 7 kcal/gram. It contributes to weight gain just as any other energy source does.

Micronutrients are nutrients required in small quantities—typically micrograms to milligrams—or, in some cases, around a gram. Vitamins and minerals are micronutrients. **Vitamins** are organic molecules that are essential in small quantities for life because they cannot be synthesized by the body. The vitamins are divided into those which are water-soluble and fat-soluble; all are required in the diet. Vitamins often act as cofactors in enzymatic reactions. Because they are often recycled in reactions rather than broken down, they tend to be required in small quantities.

The required amounts of vitamins and minerals in the diet have been set by the Food and Nutrition Board of the National Academies of Sciences, Engineering, and Medicine based on observations of health effects related to deficiency, healthy status, and toxic effects. These levels are called Dietary Reference Intakes (DRI) and include an Estimated Average Requirement (EAR)—the amount meeting the needs of half the individuals in a group; Recommended Daily Allowance (RDA)—the amount estimated to meet the needs of virtually all healthy people; Adequate Intake (AI)—used when there is not enough data to determine an RDA; and Upper Limit (UL)—the limit above which toxic effects may occur.

Several of the B vitamins, namely **thiamine, riboflavin, niacin, pyridoxine, biotin**, and **pantothenic acid**, are involved in energy metabolism. Pyridoxine is also involved in amino acid metabolism. **Vitamin C** is most commonly known as an antioxidant but has other functions, including serving as a cofactor in collagen synthesis. The fat-soluble **vitamins A** and **D** function as hormones regulating the expression of a variety of genes and are also important in vision and bone formation respectively. **Beta (b)—carotene**—a precursor to vitamin A found in yellow and orange vegetables—is also a weak antioxidant. Beta-carotene is less toxic consumed in excess than fully formed vitamin A. **Vitamin E** is an antioxidant, and **vitamin K** is involved in blood clotting and bone formation. The sections below summarize the DRI, functions, effects, and sources of the vitamins.

 DRIs are for males between the ages of nineteen and thirty. DRIs vary with age and sex as well as pregnancy and lactation.

Vitamin C

DRI: RDA: 90 micrograms (μg); Tolerable Upper Intake Level (UL): 2,000 μg

Functions: antioxidant, cofactor for the synthesis of collagen, carnitine, and norepinephrine; drug, steroid, histamine, and tyrosine metabolism; fatty acid desaturation

Deficiency symptoms: scurvy, fatigue, anorexia, muscular weakness, infections

Toxicity symptoms: gastrointestinal (GI) distress, diarrhea

Food sources: fruits, vegetables

Thiamin (B-1)

DRI: RDA: 1.2 milligrams (mg)

Functions: cofactor for enzymes in carbohydrate metabolism/TCA cycle, BCAA metabolism, brain function

Deficiency symptoms: beriberi (dry): leg atrophy and peripheral neuropathy; beriberi (wet): cardiac hypertrophy and edema

Toxicity symptoms: At 100 × DRI: headache, convulsions, weakness, arrhythmia

Food sources: whole grains, yeast

Riboflavin (B-2)

DRI: RDA: 1.3 mg

Functions: cofactor for many enzymes involved in single and double electron transfer: important in carbohydrate, amino acid, and lipid metabolism (protection from oxidative stress)

Deficiency symptoms: cheilosis (lip lesions), glossitis (tongue inflammation), reduced numbers of blood cells: reticulocytopenia, leukopenia, thrombocytopenia

Toxicity symptoms: generally nontoxic

Food sources: meat and dairy products, leafy green vegetables

Niacin (B-3)

DRI: RDA: 16 mg; UL: 35 mg

Functions: required for the synthesis of nicotinamide adenine dinucleotide (hydride) [NAD(H)]; the central molecule in *H* transfer in energy metabolism

Deficiency symptoms: pellagra: lesions of skin including cheilosis, glossitis, and GI tract lesions; anemia, anxiety, depression, fatigue

Toxicity symptoms: flushing, itching, GI discomfort (nicotinamide is more toxic than nicotinic acid)

Food sources: meats, whole grains (when treated with alkali to release from niacytin)

Pyridoxine (B-6)

DRI: RDA: 1.3 mg; UL: 100 mg

Functions: central to amino acid metabolism, biosynthesis of neurotransmitters, central to the release of glucose from glycogen as a coenzyme of glycogen phosphorylase, involved in phospholipid synthesis, modulates steroid hormone receptors

Deficiency symptoms: weakness, peripheral neuropathy, cheilosis, glossitis, stomatitis, sleeplessness, impaired immunity

Toxicity symptoms: peripheral neuropathy, can interfere with L-dopa treatment in Parkinson's disease

Food sources: meats, whole grains, vegetables, and nuts

Biotin (B-7)

DRI: AI: 30 μg

Functions: carboxyl carrier involved in gluconeogenesis, supplies oxaloacetate to TCA cycle, synthesis of fatty acids, oxidation of odd-number chain fatty acids, leucine degradation, regulates glycolysis

Deficiency symptoms: rare except when regularly consuming raw egg whites which bind it: dermatitis, glossitis, depression, anorexia, nausea, hepatic steatosis, hypercholesterolemia

Toxicity symptoms: generally nontoxic

Food sources: yeast, milk, liver, egg yolks, some vegetables, innate intestinal microfloral synthesis

Pantothenic Acid (B-5)

DRI: AI: 5 mg

Functions: as part of coenzyme A and acyl carrier protein, integral to fatty acid, amino acid, and carbohydrate metabolism; involved in protein, choline, sulfonamide, and amino sugar acylation; and fatty acid and triglyceride synthesis

Deficiency symptoms: rare except in severe malnourishment: burning sensation in feet, GI problems, depression, fatigue, insomnia, vomiting, muscle weakness, increased insulin sensitivity

Toxicity symptoms: generally nontoxic

Food sources: ubiquitous: meat, mushrooms, avocado, broccoli, whole grains

Folate/Folic Acid

DRI: RDA: 400 μg; UL: 1,000 μg

Functions: single-carbon metabolism (transfer of methyl groups): important in metabolism of the amino acid methionine and metabolism of nucleotides, which are the building blocks of DNA

Deficiency symptoms: mild deficiency: increased cancer risk (likely involving reduced DNA methylation), elevated blood homocysteine, and neural tube defects in developing embryos; more severe deficiencies: megaloblastic anemia with weakness, depression, neuropathy, skin lesions, poor growth, malabsorption, diarrhea—all due to impaired DNA synthesis

Toxicity symptoms: generally nontoxic

Food sources: liver, green leafy vegetables, beans, eggs

Cobalamine (B-12)

DRI: RDA: 2.4 µg

Functions: degradation of propionate from degradation of odd-number chain fatty acids, degradation of leucine, methylation of homocysteine-producing methionine and recycling folate

Deficiency symptoms: elevated blood homocysteine, pernicious anemia (also called megaloblastic anemia; due to lack of folate recycling, leading to decreased DNA synthesis), peripheral neuropathy; vegetarians are at risk as well as the elderly and those with GI issues due to the complexity of the absorption process in the GI tract

Toxicity symptoms: generally nontoxic

Food sources: animal related foods: liver, meat, fish, milk, eggs, some fermented foods, mushrooms

Vitamin A

DRI: RDA: 900 µg; UL: 3,000 µg

Functions: important in vision, normal differentiation of epithelial cells, skin maintenance, reproduction, embryonic development, bone metabolism, hematopoiesis, immunity, beta-carotene is an antioxidant

Deficiency symptoms: ocular lesions, night blindness, keratinization of epithelial tissues, possible increased susceptibility to cancer

Toxicity symptoms: from prolonged large overdoses: dry lips, mucosa and skin, skin scaling and peeling, hair loss, fragile nails, headache, nausea, vomiting, bone abnormalities, liver disease; smaller overdoses may lead to birth defects; beta-carotene is less toxic than vitamin A

Food sources: retinol: meat, fish, eggs, milk, oils; beta-carotene: yellow vegetables like carrots, green vegetables, legumes, fruits, seeds

Vitamin D

DRI: RDA: 15 µg (600 IU); UL: 100 µg (4,000 IU)

Functions: regulator of calcium/phosphate homeostasis, bone metabolism, required for Ca absorption, regulates many genes as a steroid hormone, involved in cell differentiation, membrane fatty acid composition, muscular function, pancreatic insulin production, immunity, neural function

Deficiency symptoms: bone/systemic disease (rickets) in children; osteomalacia in adults

Toxicity symptoms: relatively nontoxic; at very high doses: hypercalcemia, calcinosis (deposition of calcium in tissues), anorexia, vomiting, headache, diarrhea

Food sources: exposure of skin to sunlight, vitamin D- fortified foods (e.g., milk), fatty fish, egg yolks, mushrooms

Vitamin E

DRI: RDA: 15 mg; UL: 1,000 mg

Functions: antioxidant, protects membrane lipids

Deficiency symptoms: anorexia, myopathies

Toxicity symptoms: relatively nontoxic, supplements may increase small risk for hemorrhagic stroke, at very high doses may interfere with other fat-soluble vitamins and cause headache, fatigue, nausea, GI distress

Food sources: vegetable oils, seeds, nuts, and avocados

Vitamin K

DRI: AI: 120 µg

Functions: involved in blood clotting and bone formation

Deficiency symptoms: rare except in unsupplemented newborns, patients treated with antibiotics, and patients with GI malabsorption problems: causes hemorrhage

Toxicity symptoms: relatively nontoxic: very high doses can cause oxidative stress leading to anemia, hyperbilirubinemia, and jaundice

Food sources: leafy green vegetables, microbial synthesis in the gut

Minerals have many important functions. Although they are micronutrients, they are divided into macrominerals: calcium (Ca), phosphorus (P), potassium (K), magnesium (Mg), sodium (Na), chloride (Cl), and sulfur (S) as well as microminerals: iron (Fe), zinc (Zn), copper (Cu), iodine (I), selenium (Se), manganese (Mn), and chromium (Cr). The macrominerals are required in greater quantities than the microminerals. Minerals help maintain the proper pH and fluid levels/pressure of the blood. Sodium, phosphorus, and chloride are particularly significant in those roles. Sodium and potassium are responsible for transmitting electrical signals across nerve and muscle membranes. Calcium and phosphorus mineralize the skeleton. The release of intracellular Ca is involved in muscle contraction and many regulated cellular processes. Phosphorus is a component of the phospholipid cell membranes, and many enzymes are regulated by phosphorylation. Magnesium is also a component of bone. It helps activate enzymes and is necessary for the proper functioning of many signal transduction proteins in membranes.

Many of the microminerals (also known as trace minerals) are components of metalloenzymes and metalloproteins. An excess of some minerals can interfere with the absorption of other minerals. As an example, excess zinc can cause a copper deficiency. The following lists summarizes the properties and requirements for minerals:

Ca (Calcium)

DRI: RDA: 1,000 mg; UL: 2,500 mg

Functions: bones and teeth, intracellular messenger (e.g., muscle contraction and insulin secretion), cofactor for enzymes (e.g., blood-clotting enzymes and the digestive enzyme trypsin)

Insufficiency effects: rickets, reduced bone mass, increased risk for osteoporosis, colon cancer, and kidney stones

Toxicity: unusual, high levels in diet can reduce absorption of iron, zinc, and magnesium

Food sources: dairy products, leafy green vegetables, calcium- fortified foods, soft bones of fish

P (Phosphorous)

DRI: RDA: 700 mg; UL: 4 g

Functions: bones and teeth, DNA and RNA, energy compounds: ATP and creatine phosphate, phospholipid membranes, regulation/activation of enzymes, phosphoproteins, pH balance

Insufficiency effects: unusual except with excessive use of aluminum hydroxide antacids, rickets/osteomalacia

Toxicity: unusual

Food sources: meat, dairy products, eggs

Mg (Magnesium)

DRI: RDA: 400 mg; UL: 350 mg from supplements in addition to food intake

Functions: bone, enzyme activation, complexed with ATP, affects membrane ion transport

Insufficiency effects: impaired regulation of bone metabolism/Ca homeostasis, decreased blood Ca and K, irritability, muscle spasms; diabetes mellitus a risk factor for Mg deficiency

Toxicity: unlikely except with kidney disease

Food sources: fruits, leafy green vegetables, whole grains, nuts, beans

Na (Sodium)

DRI: AI: 1.5 g; UL: 2.3 g

Functions: fluid/electrolyte balance, nerve conduction, muscle contraction, absorption of glucose, amino acids, pH balance

Insufficiency effects: fluid loss, fatigue, muscle cramps, headaches, dizziness, death

Toxicity: unusual as long as sufficient fluid intake levels; elevated levels may increase risk for hypertension in some individuals

Food sources: salt, soy sauce, sport drinks, processed foods

K (Potassium)

DRI: AI: 4.7 g

Functions: fluid/electrolyte balance, pH balance, nerve conduction, muscle contraction, activates some enzymes, required for protein synthesis and insulin secretion

Insufficiency effects: muscle weakness, anorexia, nausea, cardiac arrhythmia, glucose intolerance, renal impairment

Toxicity: renal impairment, hyperexcitability

Food sources: fruits, vegetables, meat, milk

Cl (Chloride)

DRI: AI: 2.3 g; UL: 3.6 g

Functions: pH balance, fluid/electrolyte balance, formation of gastric hydrochloric acid (HCl), the chloride shift allowing passage of HCO_3^- (derived from CO_2) from red blood cells into the blood plasma

Insufficiency effects: rare except with Na deficiency, can occur with heavy sweating: loss of appetite, fatigue, dehydration, muscle weakness, and in extreme cases loss of muscle control

Toxicity: rare: high fluid retention/blood pressure, pH imbalance

S (Sulfur)

Functions: component of the amino acids *methionine* and *cysteine*, antioxidant peptide *glutathione*, coenzyme-A involved in aerobic energy metabolism, lipoic acid, chondroitin sulfate, mucous, the anticoagulant *heparin*

Insufficiency effects: unusual, but vegans need to take care to eat sulfur-containing foods

Toxicity: methionine in excess is toxic

Food sources: most plentiful sources: eggs, meat, poultry, fish; legumes, nuts, seeds, onions, garlic, cruciferous vegetables

Fe (Iron)

DRI: RDA: 8 mg; UL: 45 mg

Function: hemoglobin: oxygen transport in blood; myoglobin: oxygen transport and storage in muscle; component of enzymes in aerobic metabolism and ATP production, antioxidant protection, and metabolism of some amino acids

Deficiency symptoms: anemia, fatigue, sore tongue

Toxicity symptoms: increased iron storage in tissues leading to tissue damage

Food sources: meat most bioavailable source; whole grains, nuts, seeds, dark leafy greens, beans

I (Iodine)

DRI: RD: 150 μg; UL: 1,100 μg

Function: thyroid hormone: regulates energy metabolism

Deficiency symptoms: reduced growth, impaired reproduction, dry rough skin, goiter

Toxicity symptoms: does not occur from food sources; excessive intake is toxic, resulting in GI symptoms, mouth and throat burning, metallic taste, fever, rash, seizures

Food sources: iodized salt, sea vegetables, seafood, milk, eggs, strawberries

Cr (Chromium)

DRI: AI: 35 μg

Function: improves insulin sensitivity

Deficiency symptoms: low levels may contribute to insulin insensitivity, high cholesterol

Toxicity symptoms: may cause oxidative stress, organ, and DNA damage

Food sources: shellfish, dates, pears, broccoli, whole grains, tomatoes, mushrooms, meat

Zn (Zinc)

DRI: RDA: 11 mg; UL: 40 mg

Function: component of enzymes involved in digestion, energy metabolism, DNA, RNA, and protein synthesis, collagen processing, important to immunity and reproductive function

Deficiency symptoms: growth retardation, reproductive problems, anorexia, poor wound healing, immune disorders, mental disorders

Toxicity symptoms: moderate: interferes with Cu absorption; extreme: interferes with CU and Fe absorption, nausea, vomiting, diarrhea

Food sources: shellfish, meat, beans, nuts, seeds, whole grains, dairy products

Cu (Copper)

DRI: RDA: 900 μg; UL: 10,000 μg

Function: iron oxidation/transport, antioxidant defense, elastin synthesis, dopamine and norepinephrine metabolism

Deficiency symptoms: anemia, leukopenia, neutropenia, neuropathies

Toxicity symptoms: extreme: vomiting, hypotension, coma, jaundice; moderate: can interfere with Zn absorption

Food sources: nuts, seeds, beans, mushrooms

Se (Selenium)

DRI: RDA: 55 µg; UL: 400 µg

Function: component of antioxidant enzyme glutathione peroxidase and a variety of selenoproteins, activation thyroid hormone

Deficiency symptoms: Keshan disease: necrosis of heart muscle

Toxicity symptoms: nausea, nail changes, hair loss, diarrhea, fatigue, irritability

Food sources: seafood, nuts (especially Brazil nuts), mushrooms, beans, seeds, broccoli, cabbage, spinach

Mn (Manganese)

DRI: AI: 2.3 mg; UL: 11 mg

Function: mucopolysaccharide synthesis involved in formation of cartilage and bone, mitochondrial antioxidant, urea synthesis, cholesterol synthesis, carbohydrate metabolism

Deficiency symptoms: poor wound healing, skeletal abnormalities

Toxicity symptoms: rare except in Mn miners

Food sources: leafy green vegetables, fruits, nuts, whole grains

PRACTICE QUESTIONS

1. Which of the following is the most energy-dense macronutrient?

A) carbohydrates

B) sugars

C) fats

D) protein

Answers:

A) Incorrect. Carbohydrates provide 4 kcal/gram; this is less than fat.

B) Incorrect. Sugars are a type of carbohydrate and provide 4 kcal/gram.

C) Correct. Fats provide 9 kcal/gram; this is more than carbohydrates or protein.

D) Incorrect. Protein, like carbohydrates, provides 4 kcal/gram.

2. Which group of vitamins participates in energy metabolism?

- **A)** fat-soluble vitamins
- **B)** antioxidant vitamins
- **C)** most of the B vitamins
- **D)** folate and B-12

Answers:

- A) Incorrect. The fat-soluble vitamins have no direct role in energy metabolism.
- B) Incorrect. Antioxidants neutralize free radicals which can be a side effect of energy metabolism, but they are not directly involved in energy metabolism.
- C) **Correct.** All of the B vitamins—except folate and B-12—are involved in energy metabolism.
- D) Incorrect. Folate and B-12 are involved in transferring single carbons and deficiencies in intake manifest mainly as megaloblastic anemia.

NUTRITION STRATEGIES

Carbohydrates and fats are the main fuels for exercise and physical activity. Fat predominates during low-intensity activity. Both carbohydrates and fats play a role in fueling moderate-intensity exercise, whereas carbohydrates dominate at high aerobic capacity. Endurance training increases fat oxidation capability, sparing glycogen. Weight training increases glycogen reserves and carbohydrate oxidation capacity.

The sources of carbohydrates during exercise are blood glucose, muscle and liver glycogen, glucose from gluconeogenesis in the liver, and carbohydrates consumed during exercise. Fat is available from intramuscular triglycerides as well as those stored in adipose tissue. Fatty acid release and transport from adipose tissue occurs quickly upon initiation of exercise and is generally more than sufficient to meet the needs of the muscle. Blood lipoproteins are also a source of fat.

Protein can also provide energy for exercise through the oxidation of amino acids, especially when carbohydrate and fat stores are low. Endurance exercise stimulates the oxidation of amino acids at higher rates as intensity increases. Protein is not used as much as a fuel in strength training. However, both types of exercise can damage muscle fibers, leading to an increase in the need for dietary protein for repair.

The ***Dietary Guidelines for Americans 2010***, published by the US Department of Agriculture (USDA) and the US Department of Health and Human Services, recommends a dietary intake of 45 – 65 percent carbohydrates, 10 – 35 percent protein, and 20 – 35 percent fat, with no more than 10 percent saturated fat.

The USDA ***Food Guide Pyramid***, published in 1992, provided a visual guide for accomplishing this goal while consuming **nutrient-rich** foods (foods that contain a variety of nutrients). Nutrient-rich foods include whole grains, vegetables, and fruits. These foods are rich in vitamins, minerals, and other beneficial phytonutrients and are good sources of dietary fiber. Lean meats, fish, and low-fat dairy products are also nutrient rich and contain protein, moderate fat, and vitamins and minerals.

Eating a variety of nutrient-rich foods helps ensure that all nutritional needs are met. The Food Guide Pyramid divides foods into five **food groups** that segment similar types of foods and make recommendations for the number of servings of each that a person should consume for optimal nutritional health. The five groups are grain, vegetable, fruit, protein, and dairy. The consumption of simple sugars as well as fats and oils should be minimized.

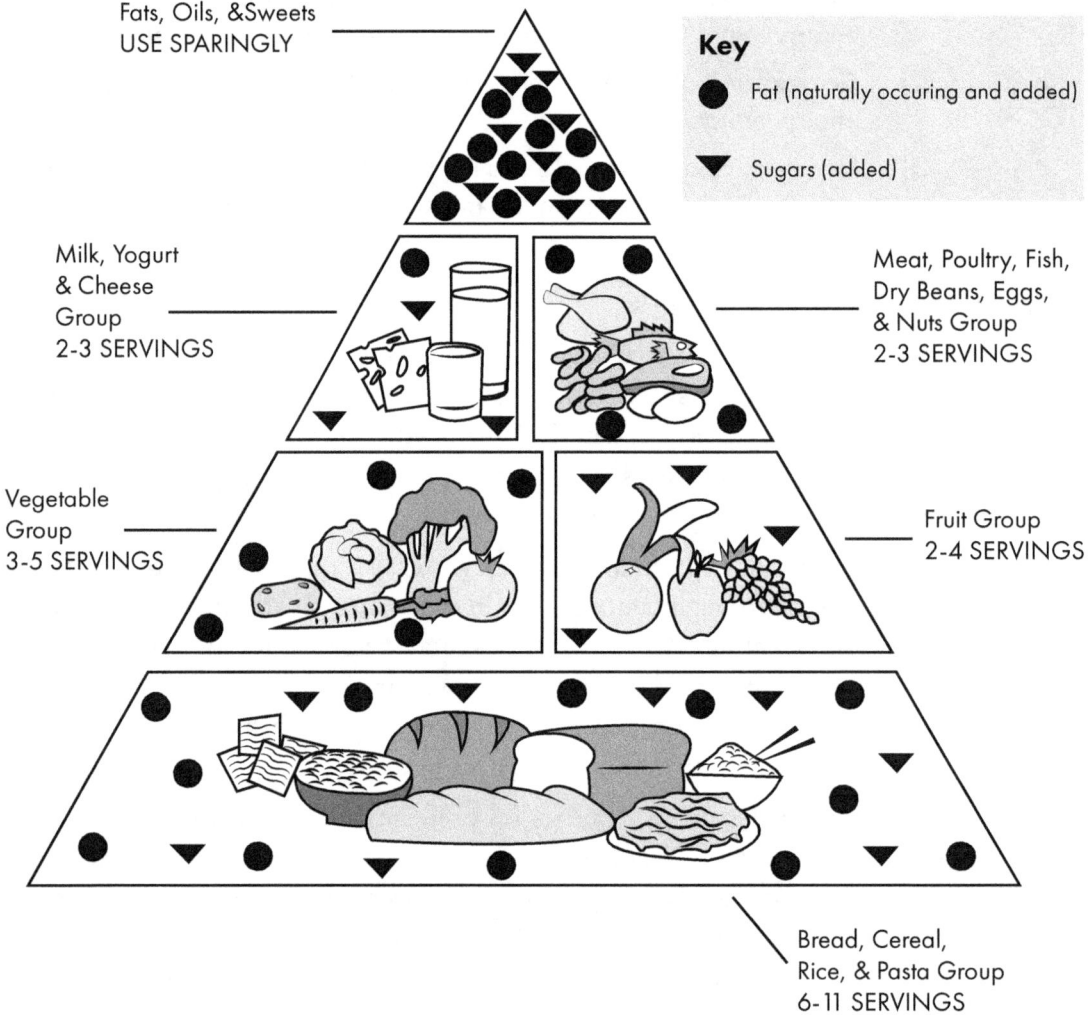

Figure 2.1. The Food Guide Pyramid

The serving sizes indicated by the Food Guide Pyramid are generally smaller than what the average American would consider to be a serving size. For instance a half cup of fruit or vegetables would constitute one serving. A cup of milk, 1.5 ounces of cheese, or 2 – 3 ounces of cooked lean meat or fish also equal one serving.

The Food Guide Pyramid was later replaced with MyPyramid, which was then replaced in 2011 with the MyPlate program. The MyPlate program uses a plate to illustrate the proper ratios of the five food groups: grains, vegetables, fruits, protein, and dairy in a healthy diet.

In contrast to the Food Pyramid Guide, the MyPlate program recommends a greater emphasis on fruits and vegetables, which are often more nutrient dense and rank lower in the **glycemic index** than grains. According to the MyPlate program, fruits and vegetables should occupy half of the plate. Clicking on the "All About" prompts next to the plate for each group leads the reader to selection tips for each food group and recommended daily servings for different sexes and age groups. There is also a calorie calculator based on age, sex, weight, height, and physical activity level that links to individualized recommendations for daily servings from the five food groups. This can be found at https://www.choosemyplate.gov/MyPlate-Daily-Checklist-input.

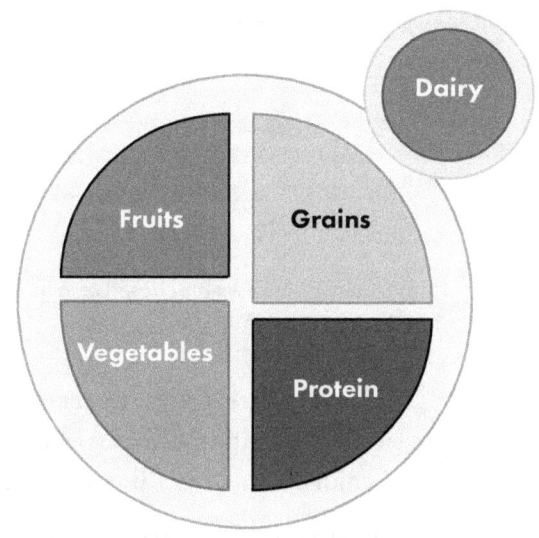

Figure 2.2. The MyPlate Program

> 🔍 The glycemic index is a measure of the rise in blood glucose caused by a standard amount of food—usually 50 grams. The blood glucose rise is plotted for two hours. The glycemic index is calculated as the area under the glucose curve (AUC) divided by the AUC of a standard food (white bread) times 100. Eating an excess of foods with a high glycemic index increases the risk for obesity and type 2 diabetes.

The MyPlate program recommends eating a variety of foods and limiting saturated fat, sodium, and added sugar. Oils should also be used sparingly. Lean sources of protein, including 8 ounces of cooked seafood per week (for nonvegetarians) are recommended. Low-fat or no-fat dairy products are recommended as well. The program encourages varying fruits and vegetables and choosing whole grains at least half of the time.

Meal timing can play a role in the health of a diet, especially when weight loss is desired. Eating several small meals throughout the day helps even out blood glucose and insulin levels and helps the individual avoid hunger. Eating one large meal can lead to overindulgence because of built-up hunger. Skipping breakfast is not a good way to lose weight as it may lead to snacking and overeating at later meals. Whether one eats several small meals throughout the day or three meals per day, it is important that attention is paid to portion sizes and the amount of calories consumed. The MyPlate program provides good guidance in this regard. Table 2.1 summarizes MyPlate recommendations for individuals who achieve less than thirty minutes of moderate exercise per day.

Table 2.1. MyPlate Daily Intake Recommendations for Low-Activity Individuals

Sex	Age	Vegetables (cups)	Fruits (cups)	Grains (oz.)	Protein (oz.)	Dairy (cups)	*Total Calories
Women	19 – 30	2.5	2	6	5.5	3	2,000
Women	31 – 50	2.5	2	6	5.5	3	2,000
Women	51+	2.5	1.5	6	5	3	1,800
Men	19 – 30	3	2	8	6.5	3	2,400
Men	31 – 50	3	2	8	6.5	3	2,400
Men	51+	3	2	7	6	3	2,200

*Total calories are estimates based on a height of five feet eight inches, a weight of 150 pounds (lb.), and a body mass index (BMI) of 23.

The MyPlate program recommends at least 150 minutes of moderate-intensity physical exercise per week, working up to that level gradually for those who are inactive. Total caloric intake is adjusted based on physical activity level.

Since oxygen is consumed in the utilization of fuel (carbohydrates, fat, and protein) for exercise, the volume of oxygen consumed (**VO2**) can be used to determine how many calories have been expended. Resting VO2 is about 3.5 milliliters (mL) of oxygen (O_2) per kilogram (kg) of body weight per minute. For every liter of oxygen consumed during exercise, about 5 kcal are burned. The American College of Sports Medicine (ACSM) publishes formulas for calculating VO2 for various activities, including walking, running, cycling, and stepping. These formulas are available at https://certification.acsm.org/metabolic-calcs.

Metabolic equivalents (METs) are another measure of exertion and can be related to caloric expenditure. A MET is the ratio of the working metabolic rate to the resting metabolic rate. One MET is equal to 1 kcal/kg/hour in caloric expenditure. One MET is also equal to an oxygen usage of VO2 of 3.5 mL/kg/minute. Both of these values are representative of energy expenditure when sitting quietly. It should be noted that MET values are averages determined experimentally and can vary based on the body composition and fitness of the individual. The table below gives MET values for some typical activities.

Table 2.2. MET Values for Common Activities

Activity	MET
sleeping	0.9
desk work	1.5
walking slowly	2.3
walking briskly (3 mph)	3.3
stationary bicycling (100 watts) light effort	5.5

Activity	MET
jogging	7.0
jumping rope	10.0

One of two formulas can be used to convert METs to caloric expenditure:

1. MET for given exercise × 3.5 mL oxygen/kg/minute × body weight (kg) × minutes exercised × 1 liter (L)/1000 mL × 5 kcal/L oxygen

   OR

2. MET for given exercise × 1 kcal/kg/hour × body weight (kg) × hours exercised

These two formulas give close—but not exactly the same—results.

When reproducing formulas from memory, it is important to remember that the units used will cancel out to give an answer in the desired units.

In formula 1, *mL* after 3.5 on top cancels with *mL* after *1,000* on the bottom; *kg* and *minutes* cancels with *kg* (body weight) and *minutes* (exercised) on top; and one *L* on top cancels with *L* (oxygen) on the bottom, leaving the answer with units of kcal.

Likewise in formula 2, *kg* and *hour* cancel with *kg* (body weight) and *hours* (exercised) on top, yielding an answer in kcal.

Athletes have additional nutritional needs over those of inactive individuals. Carbohydrate consumption is particularly important before, during, and after endurance events. The details of fueling such events will be covered in a later section.

Since *B*-complex vitamins are important in energy metabolism, athletes may have higher requirements than the standard Dietary Reference Intakes. However, athletes typically consume more calories to maintain their weight than inactive individuals, and if they eat a variety of foods—including plenty of vegetables, fruits, and whole grains—they should be able to meet their needs. Vitamin supplements may be appropriate in athletes with poor nutrition and also in individuals limiting their diet in an effort to lose weight.

Likewise, exercise may increase the need for the antioxidants b-carotene, vitamin C, and vitamin E as increased energy metabolism and mitochondrial activity can produce greater amounts of free radicals. As with the *B* vitamins, a diet rich in vegetables, fruits, whole grains, nuts, and seeds should be sufficient to meet this need. Supplementation may be considered for individuals with poor diets or who are trying to lose weight. There are, however, risks with excessive intakes of these vitamins, so supplementation should be minimal.

Athletes can have higher mineral requirements than the average person since many minerals are cofactors for energy metabolism and electrolytes—especially sodium and potassium—and can be lost through sweating. Sport drinks can be used to replenish fluids and electrolytes. Since some minerals interfere with the absorption of others and many are toxic in excess, obtaining minerals through a varied and balanced diet is generally the best way to meet mineral needs.

Athletes—especially endurance athletes—may have a higher requirement for iron. Aerobic exercise causes an increased loss of iron through the breakdown of hemoglobin in blood, an increased loss of iron in sweat and urine, and also increases the need for iron-containing myoglobin and respiratory enzymes. Meat is the most bioavailable source of iron. Female athletes who tend to eat less calories and less meat than men (in addition to experiencing menstrual losses) and vegetarian athletes are at risk for iron-deficiency anemia, also known as microcytic hypochromic anemia—smaller red blood cells lacking sufficient hemoglobin. A simple hematocrit test can detect iron-deficiency anemia. Since iron can be toxic in excess, iron supplementation should only be done under the supervision of a physician.

Finally, active individuals have a higher requirement for protein than sedentary individuals. Exercise increases the oxidation of amino acids for energy and can also damage muscle fibers, which need to be rebuilt. The protein *RDA* for inactive individuals is 0.8 g/kg body weight for nonvegetarians and 0.9 g/kg for vegans. For individuals who regularly participate in endurance exercises, these figures increase to 1.2 – 1.4 g/kg. For strength trainers, the recommendation is 1.6 – 1.7 g/kg body weight.

PRACTICE QUESTIONS

1. What are the names of the food groups?
   A) vegetables, fruits, grains, protein, and dairy
   B) vegetables, fruits, grains, protein, dairy, and oils
   C) vegetables, fruits, grains, meat, and dairy
   D) vegetables, fruits, grains, sugar, and dairy

   Answers:
   A) **Correct.** These are the five food groups designated by the Food Pyramid Guide and MyPlate program.
   B) Incorrect. Oils are not considered a food group and should be used sparingly.
   C) Incorrect. The more general term *protein* is used to refer to high-protein foods, examples of which are meat and seafood.
   D) Incorrect. Sugar is not considered a food group and should be consumed sparingly.

2. What is the energy expenditure for a 154 lb. man for one hour of jogging at 7 MET? (There is more than one correct answer.)
   A) 25 kcal
   B) 515 kcal
   C) 1132 kcal
   D) 490 kcal

Answers:

A) Incorrect. This is the product of MET × 3.5. There are more terms to the calculation.

B) **Correct.** The formula: 7 MET × 3.5 mL oxygen/kg/minute × 70 kg × 60 minutes × 1 L/1000 mL × 5 kcal/L = 515 kcal provides an accurate energy expenditure for the person described in the question.

C) Incorrect. Body weight must be converted from pounds to kilograms.

D) **Correct.** The formula: 7 MET × 1 kcal/kg/hour × 70 kg × 1 hour = 490 kcal provides an accurate energy expenditure for the person described in the question. (Note: this answer is close to answer choice B, which is also correct. So, approximately 500 kcal will be burned by a 154 lb. man who jogs for one hour at 7 MET.)

Hydration

Water comprises a large percentage of body weight, roughly 45 – 70 percent. In addition, lean muscle mass contains significantly more water than adipose tissue does. Water lubricates tissues and transports nutrients and other chemicals into, throughout, and out of the body. Water is the medium in which chemical reactions take place. Water volume maintains blood pressure, and the evaporation of water cools the body. With so many important functions, **hydration**—fluid intake sufficient to maintain optimal body water content—is critical to health and performance.

Normal body water loss is 1 – 2 liters per day, with about one tenth of that being lost through perspiration under inactive, cool, dry conditions. Exercise can increase the metabolic rate by up to 20 percent, dramatically increasing the need to cool the body through sweating. Along with water, electrolytes are also lost through sweating. **Electrolytes** are minerals that circulate in the blood as positively and negatively charged ions and include sodium, potassium, magnesium, calcium, chloride, and phosphate. The main electrolytes lost in sweat are sodium and potassium. These ions are responsible for the transmission of electrical signals across nerve and muscle cell membranes, and sodium is critical to maintaining blood volume. Dehydration—a decrease in total body water—can lead to GI distress, increased heart rate, greater muscle glycogen use, and most importantly, an inability to properly cool the body. The higher the temperature and humidity, the more sweating will occur, resulting in an increased need for water and electrolytes.

The ACSM recommends consuming 14 – 20 oz. (ounces) of fluid two hours before exercising to ensure good hydration at the start of exercise. However, more liquids may be required in hot environments. A drink or food containing carbohydrates will help supply blood glucose and maximize glycogen stores as well. Fruit juice or sport drinks are suitable for pre-exercise hydration. During exercise lasting more than one hour, fluids containing carbohydrates and electrolytes are recommended at 20 – 36 oz. per hour, preferably spread out at 15 – 20 minute intervals. Sport drinks are appropriate to meet this need. Fruit juice is too concentrated and delays gastric emptying, which slows down fluid absorption. Not only does hydration with sport drinks prevent overheating, it also improves performance and reduces glycogen use by supplying blood glucose.

Postexercise, food can replace lost electrolytes and water can be used for hydration. If food is not available, a sport drink containing electrolytes and carbohydrates is recommended.

Heat and humidity increase hydration needs but so can the cold, especially at high elevations. Cold increases the water vapor lost through respiration and may increase urinary losses. Heavy clothing may increase sweating and make cooling difficult as well.

PRACTICE QUESTIONS

1. What are the main electrolytes lost through sweating?
   - **A)** calcium and magnesium
   - **B)** chloride and phosphate
   - **C)** sodium and chloride
   - **D)** sodium and potassium

   Answers:
   - A) Incorrect. Calcium and magnesium are lost in only small amounts in sweat.
   - B) Incorrect. Chloride and phosphate are lost in only small amounts in sweat.
   - C) Incorrect. Sweat results in a significant loss of sodium but not in chloride.
   - **D) Correct.** While all of these ions can be lost in sweat, sodium and potassium are the electrolytes that experience the most significant losses.

2. Which type of fluid is recommended during lengthy exercise?
   - **A)** water
   - **B)** sport drinks containing electrolytes and carbohydrates
   - **C)** fruit juice
   - **D)** caffeinated beverages

   Answers:
   - A) Incorrect. While water can be used for short-term hydration, it can also dilute electrolytes during lengthy exercise. It is necessary to replace lost electrolytes.
   - **B) Correct.** Sport drinks replace both fluid and electrolytes and have the added advantage of supplying blood glucose for fuel.
   - C) Incorrect. While fruit juice does contain some electrolytes and carbohydrates, the sugars are too concentrated, resulting in slow gastric emptying and fluid absorption.
   - D) Incorrect. While a caffeinated beverage an hour prior to exercise might have benefits, caffeine is a diuretic and could decrease hydration during

exercise. For proper hydration during exercise, it is best to replace fluid and electrolytes and provide glucose for fuel.

Applications of Nutrition Concepts

Body Composition

The simplest indicator of a healthy versus an unhealthy weight is the **body mass index (BMI)**, which equals weight in kilograms divided by the height squared in meters. The BMI is a useful screening measure to determine if an individual is underweight or at a healthy weight versus whether the individual is overweight or obese, but it does not directly correlate with body fat. The table below gives the guidelines for interpreting BMI:

Table 2.3. Guidelines for Interpreting BMI

BMI	Weight Status
less than 18.5	underweight
18.5 – 24.9	healthy weight
25.0 – 29.9	overweight
30.0 and above	obese

While there is a correlation between BMI and the risk of diseases—such as diabetes and cardiovascular disease—BMI is not an accurate measure of a healthy weight for all individuals. For instance, people with heavier bones or with a large muscle mass from strength training may appear to be overweight according to BMI but actually be at a healthy weight.

Body composition is another way of assessing health. Body composition can be divided into fat mass (FM) and fat-free mass (FFM); FM is the weight of body fat, and FFM is the weight of everything else: muscle, soft tissues, skeleton. FM can be measured in laboratory settings through such techniques as densitometry (underwater weighing), and dual-energy X-ray absorptiometry.

Lean body mass (LBM) is composed of organs, tissues, bones, and muscle. It is similar to FFM but includes fatty tissues—such as the brain and spinal cord—and is equal to body weight (BW) minus body fat (BF). LBM is typically 40 – 90 percent of body weight, which would result in BF comprising about 10 – 60 percent of body weight.

High body fat—especially abdominal fat—is a risk factor for diabetes, cardiovascular and heart diseases, metabolic syndrome (dyslipidemia—high blood LDL cholesterol and triglycerides), insulin resistance, and high blood pressure. Risk factors also include some cancers and arthritis. Low body fat reduces the risk for these diseases, but taken to an extreme—as with anorexia nervosa—it can increase the risk for reproductive problems, osteoporosis, and a range of nutrient deficiencies. In general, a body fat range of 10 – 22 percent for men and 20 – 32 percent for women is considered healthy.

Measurements of body composition that can be done in a fitness setting are the BOD POD, bioelectric impedance, and skinfold measurements. The BOD POD uses air displacement similar to the way underwater weighing uses water displacement to compare weight to volume, but it is easier to use. Bioelectric impedance is based on the fact that fat contains less water than lean tissue and therefore is more resistant to the passage of an electrical current.

It is important that the measurements be done according to standard procedures and that the client is well hydrated and has not eaten for about three or four hours prior to the assessment. There are detailed procedures and formulas for measuring skinfold thickness with calipers and correlating the measurements to body fat percentage.

Other measurements that do not translate directly to body fat percentage but are indicators of the risk of disease are waist-to-hip ratio (WHR) and waist circumference. Since excess abdominal fat—otherwise known as an android pattern or apple shape—poses a risk for obesity-related diseases, these measurements correlate with disease risk. A WHR greater than 0.95 for men or 0.86 for women is considered unhealthy. Waist circumferences greater than 40 inches for men or 35 inches for women increase the risk of disease.

The most effective method to improve body composition is a combination of dietary change and increased exercise. Reducing calories through smaller portion sizes, healthier food choices, and less snacking decreases caloric intake. Aerobic exercise increases caloric expenditure. The combination of these behavioral changes can produce a net caloric deficit that leads to weight loss. Resistance training—although it does not expend many calories—can help build lean muscle mass, increasing resting metabolic rate (RMR) and possibly contributing to weight loss.

> Why is a combination of dietary change and exercise more effective/healthier for weight loss than diet alone? Think about the effect of exercise on lean body mass and cardiovascular health. Would a deficit of 3,500 kcal per week in diet alone cause excessive hunger/eating urges? Would it be sustainable?

Gradual weight loss of 1 – 2 lb. per week is preferable to dramatic weight loss as the behavioral adjustments that lead to gradual weight loss are more likely to be sustained as opposed to extreme diet and exercise changes. Also, lean body mass can be lost with rapid weight reduction, which can lead to a lower RMR. On average, it is necessary for an individual to expend and/or reduce intake by 3,500 kcal to lose one pound of body fat. Exercise should typically account for 2,000 kcal or more of the weekly deficit, with dietary change accounting for the rest.

Behavioral modification that stresses a lifelong commitment to healthy eating and exercise can be very successful in producing and maintaining weight loss. Elements of a behavior modification program can include education on healthy food choices—plenty of vegetables and fruits, whole grains, lean proteins, and low-fat dairy products—portion size control, identifying triggers for excessive/poor eating and eliminating them, nonfood rewards to celebrate successes, social support, and positive reinforcement.

PRACTICE QUESTIONS

1. How are the BOD POD and underwater weighing similar?
   - **A)** They can both be used in a fitness setting.
   - **B)** They both compare volume to weight to determine body composition.
   - **C)** They both can be directly correlated with BMI.
   - **D)** They both involve water displacement.

   Answers:
   - A) Incorrect. Underwater weighing is generally only available in a research setting.
   - **B) Correct.** Both measure volume by measuring the displacement of water or air and compare it to weight to determine the percentage of body fat.
   - C) Incorrect. BMI is a measurement of weight versus height and does not give complete information about body composition as does a measurement of weight versus volume.
   - D) Incorrect. The BOD POD involves air displacement.

2. What is/are some very simple measurements that do NOT determine body fat percentage but can indicate whether a client is at a healthy weight?
   - **A)** BMI, WHR, and waist circumference
   - **B)** skinfold measurements, BMI, WHR, and waist circumference
   - **C)** skinfold measurements
   - **D)** skinfold measurements and BOD POD

   Answers:
   - **A) Correct.** These are very simple measurements that can be made with a tape measure and scale, and although they are not directly relatable to body fat percentage, they do have a rough correlation to the risk of disease that certain body fat percentages can pose.
   - B) Incorrect. The procedures for performing and analyzing skinfold measurements are quite rigorous, and the data can be correlated with the percentage of an individual's body fat.
   - C) Incorrect. As with answer choice B, the data gathered through these measurements can be correlated with the percentage of an individual's body fat.
   - D) Incorrect. Both of these techniques are fairly complex; they also correlate with body fat percentage.

WEIGHT MANAGEMENT

The average woman needs an intake of 2,000 kcal per day to maintain weight while the average man needs an intake of 2,500 kcal to do the same. These, however, are only averages; the actual values will vary based on height, weight, age, and activity level. Individual maintenance levels can be calculated at https://www.choosemyplate.gov/MyPlate-Daily-Checklist-input. The Harris-Benedict equation may also be used to estimate caloric intakes for weight maintenance for both males and females:

For males: RMR = 66 + 13.8 × body weight (kg) + 5 × height (cm) − 6.8 × age

For females: RMR = 655 + 9.6 × body weight (kg) + 1.8 × height (cm) − 4.7 × age

Multipliers of RMR for various activity levels are 1.2 for bed rest, 1.3 for sedentary, 1.4 for active, and 1.5 for very active.

For individuals who are overweight and striving to lose weight, a dietary deficit of 250 – 800 kcal per day is recommended along with increased exercise. A total caloric deficit of at least 3,500 kcal is necessary for weight loss of one pound. Losing one pound/week can be accomplished with a dietary deficit of 250 kcal per day plus between four to six hours of aerobic weight bearing exercise per week, expending about 2,000 kcal. Daily intake of less than 1,200 kcal may not meet essential nutrient requirements.

Some individuals—for example body builders and some athletes—may wish to increase lean body mass and, as a result, their overall weight. In this case, a surplus of 400 – 500 kcal/day is recommended. This surplus will not exceed the body's capability to add muscle mass so that fat gain is minimized. Whether the goal is to lose weight or gain weight, a varied diet rich in nutrient-dense foods should be followed.

> **?** What strategies would you suggest for a client who wants to increase weight/muscle mass? Which foods would be good nutrient-rich snacks? What adjustments could be made to meals? Which types of exercise would be beneficial?

A number of factors can make losing weight difficult. The first law of thermodynamics states that energy can be neither created nor destroyed. A simple expression of this law is that calories in equals calories out. This relationship can be expressed as:

Caloric Intake = RMR + thermic effect of food + exercise expenditure + energy storage

In this formula, the thermic effect of food is the energy expended in the digestion, absorption, and processing of nutrients. When caloric intake exceeds the first three terms in the equation, the excess energy is stored as fat (and glycogen). When caloric intake is less than the first three terms, fat or other energy sources are burned. For individuals with "thrifty metabolism," or a low RMR, weight loss can be more challenging.

Sleep deprivation—even a thirty minute deficit per day—is associated with insulin resistance and obesity. Sleep is necessary to rejuvenate the brain and the body. When sleep is insufficient, levels of the hormones *cortisol* and *ghrelin* increase and cause hunger, while levels of *leptin*—which shuts down the appetite—decrease. As a result, sleep-deprived individuals tend to eat in greater quantity and choose high-calorie foods.

Endocrine abnormalities—like diabetes—can also make weight management difficult. The insulin resistance typical of type 2 diabetes means muscle is less responsive and less able to absorb glucose from the blood and use it to build glycogen stores. Insulin is often used to lower blood glucose in diabetics and can lead to the storage of that excess glucose as fat. Exercise can help burn blood glucose, which will lower the level of insulin necessary and help to prevent weight gain.

A number of drugs have side effects that increase insulin resistance, including birth control pills and some antidepressants and antipsychotics. These drugs may lead to weight gain. On the other hand, type 2 diabetics may take medications—such as metformin—which help improve insulin sensitivity. Metformin also appears to promote a small amount of weight loss.

It seems that there is always a new **fad diet** that promises easy weight loss. These diets tend to get a lot of press and become popular for a time. They typically prescribe removing whole categories of foods from your diet or extreme calorie reductions. There are serious problems with many of these. Starvation diets may cause quick changes in weight, but a lot of the weight that is lost is water—related to glycogen loss and the loss of lean body mass—because nutritional needs are not being met. Nutritional deficiencies caused by such diets can lead to illness. In addition, starvation diets are not sustainable; once they are ended, the weight is regained. This is true of many fad diets. Starvation diets may also lower RMR, making weight loss more difficult.

There are a variety of diets that recommend a lot of protein and very low levels of carbohydrates. Examples of these are the Atkins and Zone diets. The fact, however, is that glucose from carbohydrates is necessary to fuel the prolonged exercise necessary to achieve weight loss and build lean muscle mass. It is also necessary to completely burn fats and avoid the buildup of toxic keto acids in the blood. Excess protein consumption may also strain the kidneys (due to increased nitrogen excretion) and increase the risk for osteoporosis, kidney stones, and some cancers. Sustainable weight loss requires a lifelong commitment to calorie control with a balanced, nutrient-rich diet and regular exercise.

> **?** Individuals do sometimes lose weight with fad diets. Why? Think about the reduction in calories that comes from eliminating carbohydrates. How would you address the disadvantages/risks of fad diets with a client and counsel that individual regarding alternative ways to limit calories?

There are a variety of gimmicks advertised for short-term weight loss. Saunas, body wraps, and sweat suits may be used by athletes—such as wrestlers and jockeys—who need to get down to a particular weight to qualify for competition. These methods result in only water loss. They risk dehydration and are not appropriate for long-term weight loss. Vibrating belts and electric stimulators are advertised to burn fat in the specific body areas where they are applied. In reality, no significant energy expenditure takes place, and it is not possible to target specific body areas for weight loss as energy deficits will be met by fat loss throughout the body.

A variety of supplements are hyped as weight loss aids as well. Some of these include brindleberry (Garcinia cambogia), capsaicin, caffeine, ephedrine, *L*-carnitine, chromium picolinate, Ginkgo biloba, pectin, grapeseed extract, lecithin, and St John's wort. While there are theoretical reasons as to why one might expect many of these supplements to assist in weight loss, and some poorly controlled studies have indicated benefits, randomized placebo-controlled studies consistently find no effect on weight loss.

Some of these supplements can have undesirable side effects as well. For example, caffeine-ephedrine supplements have been linked with deaths. The only proven way to lose weight is through dietary caloric reduction and exercise.

While an increase in the level of exercise performed is a good recommendation for most people, there are some individuals who may become addicted to exercise and overdo it. Too much exercise can stress the body, leading to fatigue, depression, and frequent sickness. The body needs time to recover, especially after intense exercise. It is best to increase the exercise level gradually and always allow a couple of days for recovery after intense exercise.

PRACTICE QUESTIONS

1. Which of the following methods represents the most effective way to lose weight and keep it off?
    - **A)** reduce dietary intake by 400 kcal/day
    - **B)** do weight bearing aerobic exercise for one hour every day
    - **C)** reduce dietary intake by 1,000 kcal/day
    - **D)** reduce caloric intake by 300 kcal/day and do a one-hour aerobic workout or jog four to five times per week

    Answers:
    - A) Incorrect. This is an insufficient calorie reduction to lose one pound of fat per week. The addition of exercise would help to spur significant weight loss.
    - B) Incorrect. Many individuals would not be able to sustain this frequency of activity, and this may not create enough of a caloric deficit for significant weight loss.
    - C) Incorrect. This would be difficult to sustain and could cause nutrient deficiencies.
    - **D) Correct.** These are sustainable changes in behavior that would create a calorie deficit of around 4,000 kcal/week—enough to lose a little over one pound per week.

2. Which of the following is a sustainable way to lose weight and improve health?

- **A)** supplementation with Garcinia cambogia
- **B)** exercising in heavy or non-breathable clothing
- **C)** a high-protein, high-fat, very low-carbohydrate diet
- **D)** a moderately calorie-restricted, nutrient-rich, and varied diet coupled with regular exercise

Answers:

- A) Incorrect. Some poorly controlled studies have reported positive results. However, rigorous studies have found that Garcinia cambogia does not cause weight loss.
- B) Incorrect. This can lead to overheating, dehydration, and dangerous stress to the heart. Any weight loss experienced is also mostly water.
- C) Incorrect. This method does not provide adequate carbohydrates to fuel exercise and can strain the kidneys due to excess nitrogen excretion, resulting in buildup of toxic keto acids in the blood because of the incomplete metabolism of fat.
- D) **Correct.** This method uses moderate behavioral changes that are sustainable for a lifetime, which is the key to losing weight and keeping it off.

Eating Disorders

Despite the prevalence of obesity and a high number of individuals who are overweight, a very thin body image is something which is prized in modern society. In addition, athletes may feel pressure from both coaches and peers to maintain a slim physique. Women are especially prone to these pressures, though men may experience them too. Such oversensitivity to weight can lead to the clinical **eating disorders** anorexia nervosa and bulimia nervosa.

An extreme desire for thinness and fear of gaining weight characterize **anorexia nervosa**. Anorexic individuals abstain to such a degree from food that they do not maintain healthy levels of body fat and consume too little essential nutrients to meet these requirements. In women, the starvation of the body of nutrients and fat reserves leads to decreases in sex hormone production as well as amenorrhea—the ceasing of the menstrual cycle. This loss of sex hormones can also lead to osteoporosis, since estrogen stimulates bone mineralization. This condition puts female athletes at a greater risk for bone fractures. The syndrome is common enough in female athletes that the term *female athlete triad* has been coined for disordered eating, amenorrhea, and osteoporosis. Calcium, magnesium, and vitamin D supplements may be helpful in ameliorating bone loss caused by the female athlete triad.

The diagnostic criteria for anorexia nervosa as established by the American Psychiatric Association are:

+ the refusal to maintain a minimal normal body weight

- a strong fear of being overweight despite being at a normal weight
- an unreasonably poor body image
- amenorrhea

> 🔍 Some sports that emphasize leanness and increase the risk for the female athlete triad are dance, skating, diving, gymnastics, swimming, volleyball, running, cycling, and cross-country skiing.

Bulimia nervosa is also associated with an individual's obsession over his or her weight and body image, but it is characterized by an uncontrollable urge to binge followed by compensatory actions, such as purging, fasting, excessive exercise, and the use of laxatives, enemas, and diuretics to try to lose the calories consumed during the binge.

The diagnostic criteria for bulimia nervosa as established by the American Psychiatric Association are:
- binge eating at least twice a week for three months or more
- excessive actions to compensate for caloric intake, such as purging, using laxatives, and/or overexercising
- an unreasonably poor body image

Individuals who meet the diagnostic criteria for anorexia nervosa or bulimia nervosa should be referred to a health professional. In addition, subclinical eating disorders in which some of the criteria are not present—for instance, normal menses or binge eating of less than three months—are also cause for concern and may require professional help if the behaviors cannot be remedied.

PRACTICE QUESTIONS

1. Which of the following is NOT an aspect of anorexia?
   - **A)** a feeling of societal or sports-related pressure to maintain a very lean body
   - **B)** an insatiable desire for food
   - **C)** deficiencies of essential nutrients
   - **D)** extreme restriction of caloric intake

   Answers:
   - A) Incorrect. A feeling of pressure to maintain a lean body weight is a feature of anorexia.
   - **B) Correct.** Anorexia causes an aversion to eating, not an insatiable desire for food.
   - C) Incorrect. Inadequate dietary intake causes nutrient deficiencies.
   - D) Incorrect. Anorexic individuals drastically limit caloric intake.

2. Which disorder is defined by an insatiable desire to eat followed by extreme measures to compensate, such as purging or excessive exercise?

- **A)** anorexia nervosa
- **B)** obesity
- **C)** bulimia nervosa
- **D)** the female athlete triad

Answers:

- A) Incorrect. Anorexia nervosa is characterized by an unwillingness to eat enough.
- B) Incorrect. Obesity is extreme excess weight and does not necessarily entail any compensatory behavior.
- C) **Correct.** Bulimia nervosa involves binge eating with extreme compensatory behavior.
- D) Incorrect. The female athlete triad consists of anorexia nervosa, amenorrhea, and osteoporosis.

Maximizing Performance

The fuels used by runners change with the duration of the exercise. For sprinters, ATP and phosphocreatine are the first fuels used. For middle distance runners, anaerobic glycolysis fueled by muscle glycogen is the main source of energy. At a mile, blood glucose and liver glycogen become important, and fat from adipose tissue comprises a growing portion of energy. The graph below illustrates the mix of fuel sources used during

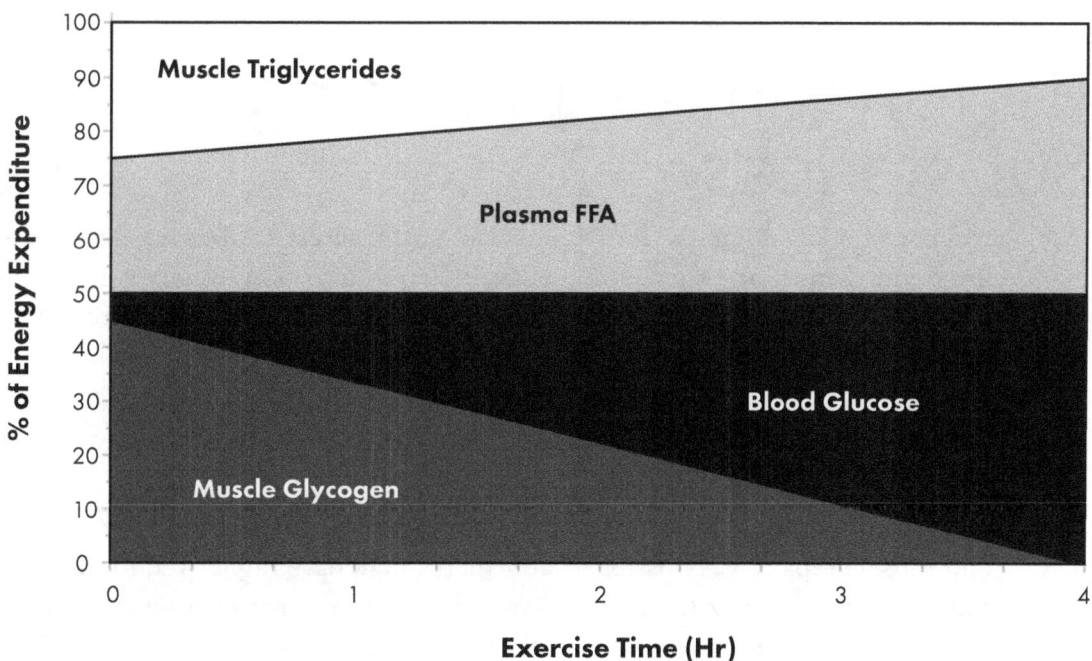

Figure 2.3. Fuel Use During Exercise at 65 – 75 percent VO2 Max

prolonged exercise at 65 – 75 percent VO2 max. As muscle glycogen is depleted, it is increasingly important that blood glucose be maintained for aerobic endurance.

A moderately sized pre-exercise meal is useful to maximize glycogen storage and provide blood glucose for fuel. This meal can be consumed one to six hours before the event. It should be high in carbohydrates, with some protein, and low in fat and fiber for ease of digestion. The consumption of carbohydrates during lengthy exercise can avoid depletion of blood glucose and glycogen stores and improve performance. Glucose, sucrose, and maltodextrin are superior to fructose in maintaining and replacing muscle glycogen. Four to eight ounces of a sport drink during every fifteen to twenty minutes of exercise helps maintain glycogen stores and blood glucose while also providing fluids and electrolytes. More may be required during exceptionally long events or at high temperatures.

Post-exercise-combined carbohydrate/protein meals are more effective at replenishing muscle glycogen than protein or carbohydrates alone, and protein also provides amino acids for muscle repair. Some fat is beneficial as well to replenish triglycerides.

The goal of strength training is to achieve muscle hypertrophy—the increase in muscle cross-sectional area that leads to increased muscle strength. Hypertrophy is the result of a combination of increased fluid/glycogen in the muscle and an increase in the size and number of the contractile proteins actin and myosin in the muscle fibers. This increase in muscle thickness occurs during the repair process following exercise. Adequate carbohydrates are necessary to fuel reps as well as replenish muscle glycogen post exercise, while protein is needed to provide the amino acids for rebuilding the muscle fibers. Recommendations for protein intake for strength trainers are 1.6 – 1.7 g/kg body weight/day. Protein intakes above those levels have not been shown to improve performance.

Performance-Enhancing Substances

Many athletes and active individuals take an interest in **dietary supplements** for improving health or performance. Protein and amino acid supplements may seem to make sense since muscle fibers are damaged by exercise and then repaired using amino acids to build protein. However, there is no evidence that protein intakes higher than the 1.2 – 1.4 g/kg body weight recommended for endurance athletes or the 1.6 – 1.7 g/kg body weight recommended for strength trainers will improve performance. These levels of protein intake are easily attained through diet.

Since vitamins and minerals are involved in energy metabolism, oxygen transport, and muscle repair, it is possible that athletes may have higher requirements of these than sedentary people. In practice, a varied diet with plenty of vegetables, fruits, whole grains, and adequate lean protein and calories can meet a person's vitamin and mineral needs. Supplements may be beneficial when diet is poor or restricted for weight loss purposes, but megadoses may be toxic and should never be taken.

Ergogenic aids are substances that are used to improve exercise or athletic performance by improving energy or strength. There are several **herbs**, including ginseng, yohimbe bark, and guarana (which contains caffeine), that are purported to increase energy. These herbs are **stimulants**, and although small quantities on occasion may be harmless, higher intakes can cause symptoms such as dizziness, a racing heart, and insomnia. Mexican sarsaparilla root may have anti-inflammatory effects, but there is no evidence for the claim that it is anabolic (i.e., promotes muscle growth).

Anabolic steroids are synthetic compounds that mimic the action of the male sex hormone testosterone. They can stimulate the growth of muscle, resulting in improved athletic performance. However, they are illegal in competition and have serious risks associated with them. Risks include mental challenges—such as irritability and paranoia—acne, swelling of the hands and feet, and undesirable sex-specific effects, such as shrinking testicles in men and increased facial hair in women. Long-term use can cause kidney, liver, and heart damage.

Diuretics are drugs that increase urine excretion. They are sometimes used by athletes to flush out anabolic steroids or other banned drugs in an effort to avoid detection. They may also be used by athletes who need to meet a maximum weight limit. Dehydration is a risk.

Beta blockers slow the heart and calm the symptoms of anxiety. Athletes sometimes use them to improve focus, steady the hands, and relieve competition anxiety. Since they slow the heart, they are not used by endurance or strength athletes but may be attractive to archers, shooters, or golfers who require steady hands and concentration. Like anabolic steroids, beta blockers are illegal in competition and carry serious risks, such as blood sugar problems, weakness, and heart failure.

Blood doping is another illegal method of improving performance. It is a practice that results in an artificial increase of the oxygen-carrying capacity of the blood in order to improve aerobic performance. A variety of methods can be used, including transfusions; erythropoietin (EPO), which stimulates red blood cell production; synthetic oxygen carriers; and cobalt chloride, which also stimulates red blood cell production. A variety of tests can detect the use of these techniques. Since EPO thickens the blood, it can lead to stroke and heart attack.

EPO is an example of a **peptide hormone**—a hormone composed of a short chain of amino acids that circulates in the blood and affects the activities of tissues and organs. Peptide hormones are banned in competition. Some examples are insulin; **human growth hormone (HGH)**, which is taken by body builders to increase lean body mass and decrease fat; human chorionic gonadotropin (HCG); and luteinizing hormone (LH), which increases testosterone levels in males and helps to restore testicular loss caused by anabolic steroid use. HGH can cause heart and nerve problems as well as glucose intolerance.

Some signs and symptoms of ergogenic aid abuse that the personal trainer should be on the lookout for are mood swings, depression, irritability, acne, male pattern baldness, enlarged male breasts, intramuscular abscesses, increased fatty acids in the blood, high blood pressure, heart problems, and—in women—a deepening of the voice and an increase in facial/body hair.

Creatine is a legal supplement that is used by athletes and fitness enthusiasts. Phosphocreatine (PCr) is plentiful in muscle and recycles ADP to produce the energy molecule ATP while simultaneously buffering hydrogen ions built up during muscle contraction. The formula below describes this process:

$PCr + ADP + H+ \longleftrightarrow ATP + creatine$

There is some evidence that creatine supplementation may improve performance in intense, short-duration events, such as sprinting and weight lifting. There is a limit as to how much creatine can be stored by muscles. Dietary sources of creatine are meat and fish. Thus, vegetarians may benefit more than those who consume meat. Short-term use of 20g/day up to five days appears to be effective and safe. The safety of long-term use is unknown, but there have been anecdotal reports of kidney damage and muscle cramps.

Carbohydrate loading—known as glycogen loading or muscle glycogen super-compensation—is a technique used by endurance athletes to maximize muscle glycogen stores. It involves eating a relatively low carbohydrate diet (50 percent of total energy) for three days, with an exercise regimen designed to deplete muscle glycogen. This is followed by three days with little exercise and a high carbohydrate diet (70 percent of energy) to fuel muscle glycogen repletion to the maximum possible level. The maximization of muscle glycogen can improve performance and endurance. Possible difficulties with this procedure are gastrointestinal distress with the dietary changes. Some athletes also report feeling heavy from the weight of the extra glycogen and associated water.

PRACTICE QUESTIONS

1. Which is NOT an example of a peptide hormone?
   A) human growth hormone
   B) testosterone
   C) human chorionic gonadotropin
   D) luteinizing hormone

Answers:

   A) Incorrect. Human growth hormone is a peptide hormone.
   B) Correct. Testosterone is a steroid hormone.
   C) Incorrect. Human chorionic gonadotropin is a peptide hormone.
   D) Incorrect. Luteinizing hormone is a peptide hormone.

2. Which ergogenic aid is illegal in competition?
   A) carbohydrate loading
   B) blood doping
   C) vitamin supplements
   D) creatine

   Answers:
   A) Incorrect. Carbohydrate loading is legal and simply involves a specific dietary regimen prior to competition.
   B) **Correct.** Blood doping is illegal as it gives an unnatural advantage and can also be dangerous.
   C) Incorrect. Vitamin supplements are just normal nutrients in supplement form and are legal.
   D) Incorrect. Creatine is a normal component of food and can be taken legally in supplement form.

THREE: ASSESSMENT

Basic Assessment Concepts

REASONS FOR ASSESSING CLIENTS

Creating an effective and individualized exercise program begins with conducting thorough assessments. An **assessment**, or test, is the process of determining the importance, size, or value of something through an evaluation process. A comprehensive fitness assessment is comprised of several measurements that help determine a client's past and present health, as well as his or her current fitness level. An assessment will also allow the personal trainer to help the individual set realistic and achievable goals. These goals can be used to improve adherence to the exercise program and encourage the positive lifestyle changes needed to reach each goal.

Fitness assessments also create a baseline of statistical information that allows progression to be accurately monitored. A **pretest** of abilities should be administered prior to beginning a training program to help the personal trainer determine the client's basic abilities. This will allow the exercise program to be accommodated to the individual's current training level and overall program objectives. Program progression or regression can be determined by using a midtest. A **midtest** is generally administered one or more times to assess the progress and effectiveness of a program. It also allows for proper modifications to be made to the exercise program, which will be needed in order to continue to maximize results. This includes allowing programs to be regressed or progressed according to client results.

Before beginning an assessment, the trainer should notify the client of what to expect the day of testing. Prior to the day of the assessment, the personal trainer should determine the preparedness of each individual to ensure that he or she knows exactly what to expect on the testing day. This information will increase preparation on the part of the client and eliminate the likelihood of cancellations. Pertinent information, such as proper pre-workout nutrition, hydration, and even what to wear will help prepare the individual for the assessment. A midtest should be scheduled after the initial assessment has been taken.

A **formative evaluation** is a periodic reevaluation that is based on the midtest. The formative evaluation allows the personal trainer to monitor progress and make any adjustments to the exercise program based on the individual's needs and concerns. This can also be used as a time to ensure that the training program remains interesting for the client and that he or she does not experience mental and physical staleness, which could lead to boredom and low compliance of the exercise program.

After the training program has been completed, the **post-test** can be administered to determine the overall effectiveness and success of the training program.

Validity and Reliability of Assessments

Assessment results can only be deemed effective if they measure what is supposed to be measured and if the measurement is repeatable. **Validity** refers to the degree to which a test or test item measures what it is supposed to. Validity is the most important characteristic of conducting successful testing.

There are several different types of validity that personal trainers can use to help determine the accuracy of their testing results. **Construct validity** refers to the overall validity, or the extent to which the test actually measures what it is designed to measure. Tests used to measure characteristics—such as movement skills, flexibility, and body fat—should be able to produce repeatable results. **Face validity** is based on a test *appearing* to measure what it is intended to measure. Face validity ensures that the individual will respond positively to the test due to the fact that the test appears to accurately measure what it is supposed to measure. **Content validity** is an assessment that ensures that the testing being conducted covers all the relevant component abilities in appropriate proportions. This may include body fat assessments and weight circumference measurements for individuals whose primary objective is to lose weight. In order to ensure content validity, the personal trainer should make sure all the proper components are represented during exercise testing. **Criterion-referenced validity** is the extent to which test scores are related to an outcome with some other measure or a test of the same ability.

Criterion-referenced validity is broken into three categories: concurrent, predictive, and discriminant. **Concurrent validity** is the extent to which test scores are related to those with other accepted tests that measure the same ability. **Predictive validity** is the extent to which the test scores correspond with future performance. Predicative validity is generally measured through comparison of a test score with some degree of the specific activity being evaluated. **Discriminant validity** is the ability of a test to distinguish between two different concepts and shows evidence of a low correlation between the results of the test and the results of a test of a different concept. An effective test demonstrates good discriminant validity when it eliminates an unnecessary waste in energy, resources, and time when administering tests that have a high correlation with each other.

Is a reliable test always valid? What would make a reliable test valid?

Finally, **reliability** is the measure of the degree of consistency or repeatability of a test. A reliable test should deliver the same score or result no matter when the test is administered. In order for a test to be valid, it must be reliable. Tests that have highly variable results have little to no purpose in determining if a test measures what it is supposed to measure.

PRACTICE QUESTIONS

1. What is criterion-referenced validity?
    - **A)** the extent to which the test score corresponds with future performance
    - **B)** the measure of the degree of consistency or repeatability of a test
    - **C)** the extent to which test scores are related to an outcome with some other test of the same ability
    - **D)** the degree to which a test measures what it is supposed to measure

    Answers:
    - A) Incorrect. The extent to which test scores correspond with future performance is predictive validity.
    - B) Incorrect. The measure of the degree of consistency or repeatability of a test is reliability.
    - C) **Correct.** Criterion referenced validity is the extent to which test scores are related to an outcome with another test of the same ability.
    - D) Incorrect. Validity is the degree to which a test measures what it is supposed to measure.

2. In order for a test to be reliable, which characteristics must the test display?
    - **A)** The test must be able to distinguish between two different concepts.
    - **B)** The test score must correspond with future performance.
    - **C)** The test must measure what it is designed to measure.
    - **D)** The test must deliver the same score or result.

    Answers:
    - A) Incorrect. The ability to distinguish between two different concepts is discriminant validity.
    - B) Incorrect. Test scores that must correspond with future performance demonstrate predictive validity.
    - C) Incorrect. The face validity of a test measures what the test has been designed to measure.
    - D) **Correct.** A test is said to be reliable if it delivers the same score or result.

Types of Assessments

Questionnaires and Interviews

In order to ensure each potential client has an individualized exercise program that is safe and effective, the personal trainer must be sure to collect as much information as possible in regards to their client's personal history, such as medical background, occupational history, and lifestyle history. Assessing an individual's general and medical history, as well as lifestyle, will provide the personal trainer with the information needed to begin designing an exercise program. The Physical Activity Readiness Questionnaire (PAR-Q) is widely used by personal trainers to determine the general readiness of an individual to begin an exercise program. This questionnaire is usually used for people who are between the ages of fifteen and sixty-nine.

The **Physical Activity Readiness Questionnaire (PAR-Q)** is a questionnaire that is used to help personal trainers determine whether individuals have any health, medical, or physical conditions that may prevent them from participating in an exercise program. The PAR-Q helps to identify individuals who may require further medical evaluation before beginning an exercise program. The primary objective of the PAR-Q is to help the personal trainer detect individuals who may be at a high risk for cardiovascular disease. Any individual who answers *yes* to one question or more should be referred to a physician for further medical screening before starting an exercise program. With this information, the personal trainer will be able to determine if an individual has any signs or symptoms of cardiovascular, metabolic, or pulmonary disease.

Obtaining the details of an individual's **medical history** will provide the personal trainer with information about known or suspected chronic diseases, such as high blood pressure, diabetes, or coronary heart disease. The medical history provides information about the client's past and present health status, as well as any past or recent injuries, surgeries, or chronic health conditions. Previous injuries or surgeries will serve as a predictor of future musculoskeletal injury. Past surgeries may have an impact on neural control of the muscles and joints affected by surgery. Pain, inflammation, and limited range of motion as a result of previous injuries or surgeries may also contribute to altered mechanics and muscle recruitment. Chronic pain, diseases, and conditions—such as arthritis, obesity, hypertension, and diabetes—can cause pain that may impact an exercise program. It is important for the personal trainer to know what conditions affect each individual to ensure a safe and effective exercise program. Medications may affect physiological factors, such as resting heart rate, exercise heart rate, and blood pressure. The personal trainer should be aware of each medication that the individual has been prescribed. The personal trainer should consult with the individual's physician to gain a better understanding of the physiological effects that each prescribed medication may have on the client's body. Gaining insight into family medical history will also help the personal trainer determine if the potential client may be at greater risk of chronic diseases, such as diabetes, obesity, and cardiovascular disease.

A collection of **general health history**—such as occupation and lifestyle—will provide the personal trainer with valuable information that will help the trainer create a safe and individualized exercise program. Gathering information about an individual's occupation can help determine repetitive movements performed at work, discover potential health and physical limitations, and recognize alterations in muscle function and postural abnormalities. Gathering knowledge about a person's general health will also provide information about the demographic, mental, and cultural background(s) of the potential client. All these factors should be taken into consideration when creating an exercise program to ensure the personal trainer is able to establish safe and effective exercise programs that are based on the objectives and needs of each individual.

Personal trainers can often overlook the importance of the daily general lifestyle activities and habits of their clients. The **lifestyle questionnaire** will allow the personal trainer to obtain information needed to determine if an individual should be referred to a medical professional prior to beginning an exercise program.

The lifestyle questionnaire includes questions about an individual's sleep habits, stress level, alcohol consumption, smoking habits, and recreational behaviors and activities. Insufficient sleep has been linked to health problems such as obesity, type 2 diabetes, cardiovascular disease, decreased immune function, unwanted weight gain, difficulty losing body fat, and impaired cognitive function. Chronic exposure to high stress levels can lead to problems such as muscular pain and postural distortion, high blood pressure, increased resting heart rate, and a weakened immune system. Research has also demonstrated that long-term exposure to high levels of stress can contribute to the development of several major diseases.

While alcohol may not have adverse effects when consumed in moderation, consuming larger amounts of alcohol has several negative effects on health. Some of the problems that are commonly associated with excessive alcohol consumption are high blood pressure, stroke, weakening of the immune system, liver damage, and an increased likelihood of developing certain cancers.

According to the Centers for Disease Control and Prevention (CDC), cigarette smoking is the leading preventable cause of death in the United States. Smoking increases the risk of developing heart disease, stroke, respiratory disease, and lung cancer. Smoking also adversely affects overall health by decreasing immune function.

Lifestyle questions also allow the personal trainer to gain an understanding of the activities that are performed outside of the workplace. Discovering which activities an individual participates in will allow the personal trainer to design an exercise program that focuses on the specific needs of each client.

STATIC POSTURAL ASSESSMENTS

Static posture, or how an individual holds his or her body while standing, will give the personal trainer an idea of the general baseline of an individual's movement foundation. A client's static posture will give the personal trainer an idea of how that client's body may be used during dynamic movements. A static postural assessment will provide information about joint misalignment, proper muscle length, possible muscular dysfunction, and overall poor posture. A static assessment is used to check the body for optimal alignment, symmetry, balanced muscle tone, and specific postural abnormalities. It provides the foundations from which the extremities will move and function. Using a static postural assessment can provide information about problem areas of the body that may need to be evaluated more in depth. It provides the personal trainer with the basis for developing the appropriate exercise strategy needed to target faulty movement patterns. Being able to recognize these postural abnormalities will ultimately affect exercise performance and body alignment and may interfere with the client's health and fitness goals.

While generally no equipment is needed for static postural assessments, the personal trainer must take the time to observe each kinetic chain checkpoint and know what to look for in order to make the proper determinations. Kinetic chain checkpoints allow the personal trainer to systematically view the body in an organized manner. This will allow for easy observation of the body. The kinetic chain checkpoint refers to the major joint regions of the body. The personal trainer will also view the body from three different angles in order to see gross deviations in posture. During the static postural assessment the following joint regions should be observed:

Anterior View:
+ foot/ankle: straight ahead and parallel, not flattened or externally rotated
+ knees: in line with toes, not abducted or adducted
+ lumbo/pelvic/hip complex (LPHC): pelvis level with anterior superior iliac spines
+ shoulders: level, not elevated or rounded
+ head: neutral position, not tilted or rotated

Lateral View:
+ foot/ankle: neutral position, leg vertical at right angle to sole of foot
+ knees: neutral position, not flexed or hyperextended
+ lumbo/pelvic/hip complex: neutral position, avoidance of lumbar extension or lumbar flexion
+ shoulders: normal kyphotic curve, not excessively rounded
+ head: neutral position, not falling forward

Posterior View:
+ foot/ankle: heels straight ahead and parallel, not overly pronated
+ knees: neutral position, not abducted or adducted
+ lumbo/pelvic/hip complex: pelvis level with both posterior iliac spines
+ shoulders/scapulae: level, not elevated or protracted
+ head: neutral position, not rotated or tilted

> **?** What are the three views used during movement assessments? Why are these views used?

Interpreting static postural assessment results will help personal trainers determine which muscles may be contributing to the posture that they are viewing. There are three deviations of posture that are generally observed during a static postural assessment. While observing static posture, common misalignments that may be seen are pronation distortion syndrome, lower crossed syndrome, and upper crossed syndrome. Pronation distortion syndrome is characterized by foot pronation, or flat feet, and internally rotated and adducted knees. Lower crossed syndrome is characterized by anterior pelvic tilt of the pelvis, which creates the appearance of an arched low back. Upper crossed syndrome is characterized by rounded shoulders and a forward head position.

PRACTICE QUESTIONS

1. When observing an individual during the static postural assessment, which position should be observed at the shoulder joint from the lateral view?

    A) level, not elevated or rounded

    B) neutral position, not flexed or extended

    C) normal kyphotic curve

    D) neutral position, not tilted or rotated

    Answers:

    A) Incorrect. The shoulders are observed as neither elevated nor rounded from the anterior view.

    B) Incorrect. The knees are observed as neither flexed nor extended from the lateral view.

    C) **Correct.** The shoulders should maintain a normal kyphotic curve and not be excessively rounded when viewed from the lateral angle.

    D) Incorrect. The head should be observed as neither tilted nor rotated while observing from the anterior view.

2. During the static postural assessment, which kinetic chain checkpoints are analyzed?

    A) the knees, shoulder, and head

    B) the feet and knees

    C) the foot/ankle, knees, lumbo/pelvic/hip complex, shoulders, and head

    D) the shoulder and head

    Answers:

    A) Incorrect. This view only examines three of the five kinetic chain checkpoints.

    B) Incorrect. This view only examines two of the five kinetic chain checkpoints.

    C) **Correct.** Each kinetic chain checkpoint should be viewed during the static postural assessment.

    D) Incorrect. This view only examines two of the five kinetic chain checkpoints.

Movement Assessments

Movement assessments are used to determine dynamic posture. After completing a static postural assessment, the personal trainer should begin to administer assessments that require the client to observe the kinetic chain in movement. Movement assessments should be focused around analyzing basic movement patterns, such as squatting movements, gait, and unilateral balance. These dynamic assessments will provide the personal trainer with reliable and valid measures of joint and muscle synergy. As the personal trainer has limited time to observe clients before beginning an exercise program, it is important that a systematic assessment protocol be administered. The overhead squat, single-leg squat, and gait assessment all provide detailed information about how an individual's body moves. After each assessment is performed, the personal trainer's findings should be recorded. This information will then help the personal trainer determine which exercises will be the most appropriate when creating an exercise program for each individual.

Overhead Squat Assessment

The purpose of the overhead squat assessment is to test neuromuscular efficiency, functional strength, and dynamic flexibility. The overhead squat assesses bilateral symmetry, mobility, and stability of the hips, knees, and ankles. It is also an indicator of the mobility of the shoulder and the extension of the thoracic spine. To complete the assessment, it is recommended to use a dowel rod or broomstick. This test may also be administered without a dowel rod by extending the arms above the head. In order to deliver a reliable and valid overhead squat test, the procedure and movement must be coached without overcueing to allow for proper testing.

Movement Procedure:
1. The individual should stand with feet shoulder-width apart with the toes pointed forward. The foot and ankle complex should be in a neutral position. Performing this assessment with shoes off will allow the personal trainer to have a better view of the foot and ankle complex during movement.
2. The individual should be instructed to raise arms overhead with elbows fully extended. The upper arm should bisect the torso.

Movement Execution:
1. The individual should be instructed to squat to a depth of comfort and return to the starting position.
2. The movement should be repeated for at least five repetitions. Be sure to observe the movement from all three positions (anterior, lateral, and posterior).

The feet, ankles, and knees should be viewed from the front (anterior) view. The feet should remain straight and in line with the foot. The lumbo/pelvic/hip complex, shoulder, and head and neck should be viewed. After completing the assessment, the personal trainer must be able to interpret the results. Compensations should be observed from all three angles.

Compensations from anterior view:
- feet: Do the feet flatten and/or turn out?
- knees:
  - Do the knees move toward the midline of the body (adduct and internally rotate)?
  - Do the knees move toward the outside of the midline (abduct and externally rotate)?

Compensations from lateral view:
- lumbo/pelvic/hip complex:
  - Does the lower back arch?
  - Is the lower back rounded?
  - Does the torso lean forward excessively?
- shoulder: Do the arms fall forward?

Compensations from posterior view:
- feet:
  - Do the feet flatten (excessive pronation)?
  - Do the heels rise off the floor?
- lumbo/pelvic/hip complex: Is there an asymmetrical weight shift in the hips?

Single-leg Squat Assessment

The purpose of the single-leg squat assessment is to evaluate single-leg functional strength, dynamic flexibility, balance, flexibility, core strength, and neuromuscular control. This test will allow the personal trainer to observe unilateral movement of the lower extremities.

Movement Procedure:
1. The individual should be instructed to stand straight ahead with hands on the hips. The head and neck should be neutral, with the eyes staring straight ahead.
2. The foot should be pointed straight ahead and the ankles, knees, and lumbo/pelvic/hip complex should remain in a neutral position.
3. The ankles, knees, lumbo/pelvic/hip complex, and shoulders should be viewed from the front. The knee should remain in line with the foot. The LPHC and shoulders should remain level and face straight ahead.

Movement Execution:
1. The individual should be instructed to squat to a comfortable level and return to the starting position.

2. At least five repetitions should be performed before switching sides. The personal trainer must observe the movement from three angles (anterior, lateral, posterior).

Movement Compensations: anterior view
- knee: Does the knee move toward the midline of the body (adduct and internally rotate)?
- lumbo/pelvic/hip complex:
    a. Does the hip of the raised leg elevate (hip hike)?
    b. Does the hip of the raised leg drop (hip drop)?
    c. Does the torso rotate inward?
    d. Does the torso rotate outward?

 Why is the overhead squat test beneficial for assessing movement patterns?

Gait Assessment

The purpose of the gait assessment is to determine dynamic posture. This test will allow the personal trainer to view each individual's manner of walking. It is important for the personal trainer to examine each kinetic chain checkpoint in order to determine movement compensations.

Movement Procedure: The individual should be instructed to walk on a treadmill at a comfortable pace at a zero degree incline.

Movement Views: From the anterior view, the feet and knees should be observed. The feet should remain straight ahead, with the knees remaining in line with the toes. From the lateral view, the low back, shoulders, and head should be observed. The low back should remain neutral. The shoulders and head should also maintain neutral alignment. From the posterior view, the feet and lumbo/pelvic/hip complex should be observed. The feet should remain straight, and the lumbo/pelvic/hip complex should remain level.

Compensations from the anterior view:
- feet: Do the feet flatten and/or turn out?
- knees: Do the knees move inward toward the midline of the body?

Compensations from the lateral view:
- lumbo/pelvic/hip complex: Does the low back arch?
- shoulders and head/neck:
    a. Do the shoulders round?
    b. Does the head travel forward?

Compensations from the posterior view:
- feet: Do the feet flatten and/or turn out?
- lumbo/pelvic/hip complex:

a. Does the pelvis excessively rotate?
b. Do the hips hike?

PRACTICE QUESTIONS

1. Which compensation is observed while performing the overhead squat at the lumbo/pelvic/hip complex when the individual is observed from the lateral view?

    A) an asymmetrical weight shift in the hips
    B) the low back rounding or arching
    C) the arms falling forward
    D) the knees adduct and internally rotate

    Answers:

    A) Incorrect. An asymmetrical weight shift in the hips would be seen from the posterior view.

    B) Correct. The lower back rounding or arching would be seen from the lateral view.

    C) Incorrect. The arms falling forward would be observed at the shoulder joint.

    D) Incorrect. The knees adducting and internally rotating would be observed at the knee joint.

2. What is the primary compensation seen while observing the knees from the anterior view during the single-leg squat assessment?

    A) the hips hiking
    B) excessive rotation of the pelvis
    C) the knees moving inward toward the midline of the body
    D) the knees traveling over the toes

    Answers:

    A) Incorrect. The hips hiking is a compensation seen at the lumbo/pelvic/hip complex.

    B) Incorrect. Excessive rotation of the pelvis is observed at the lumbo/pelvic/hip complex.

    C) Correct. The knees moving inward toward the midline of the body is the primary compensation seen at the knee checkpoint during the single-leg squat assessment.

    D) Incorrect. The knees traveling over the toes is not the primary compensation seen at the knee during the single-leg squat assessment.

ASSESSMENT 101

Core Stability and Balance

Balance Error Scoring System (BESS)

The purpose of the balance error scoring system is to assess static postural stability. This assessment is performed on two testing surfaces: the ground and the foam pad. The foam pad is used to challenge the task of balancing. The difficulty will vary depending on the individual's body weight. An increase in body weight will increase the likelihood of deformities around the foot, which can further challenge balance and stability. In order to properly administer this test, the personal trainer will need a stopwatch, a foam pad, a flat surface (or the ground), a BESS scorecard, the BESS testing protocol, and a spotter who will ensure that the individual does not fall during testing.

Movement Procedure:
1. The personal trainer should read testing protocol as it is written to ensure accuracy and test compliance.
2. The double leg stance is assumed by standing on a firm surface with the feet touching, hands on the hips, and eyes closed.
3. Each of the twenty-second trials is scored by counting deviations from the proper stance.
4. The test will consist of six twenty-second tests with three different stances and two surfaces.
5. This test will be performed with no shoes.

Movement Execution:
1. The following stances will be assessed on solid surface and then foam surface.
   a. double-leg stance
   b. single-leg stance (non-dominant leg)
   c. tandem stance (dominant leg behind front leg)
2. An error is credited to the individual when any of the following deviations occur:
   a. opening the eyes
   b. abduction or flexion of the hip beyond thirty degrees
   c. remaining out of the proper position beyond five seconds
   d. moving the hand off the iliac crests
   e. stumbling or falling
   f. lifting the forefoot or heel off of the testing surface
3. Subjects who are unable to maintain the testing posture for a minimum of five seconds are assigned the highest possible score of ten.
4. If the test subject commits multiple errors simultaneously, only one error should be recorded.

Star Excursion Balance Test

The purpose of this test is to assess dynamic balance, proprioception, and ankle stability. The personal trainer will need athletic tape to perform this assessment.

Movement Procedure:
1. The trainer should cut four strips of tape into lengths of six to eight feet.
2. Two pieces of tape will be used to form a *t*, and the other two pieces will be placed over the top piece to form an *x* so that a star shape is created. All lines should be separated from each other by a forty-five degree angle.

Movement Execution:
1. The subject should maintain a single-leg stance while reaching as far as possible with the opposite leg.
2. The subject should reach the opposite leg as far as possible in all eight directions.
3. The subject should reach in the following directions on each leg:

   1. anterior
   2. anteromedial
   3. medial
   4. posteromedial
   5. posterior
   6. posterolateral
   7. lateral
   8. anterolateral

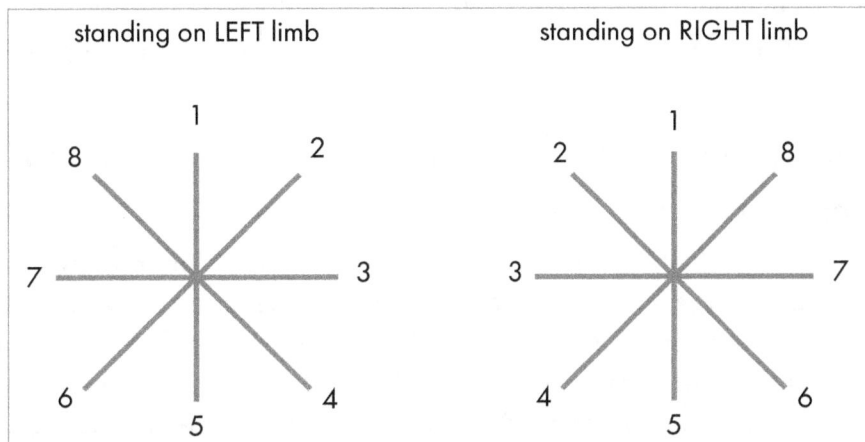

Figure 3.1. The Eight Directions That Should Be Reached While Standing on One Foot

PRACTICE QUESTIONS

1. What is the primary purpose of the Balance Error Scoring System test?
   - **A)** to assess single-leg strength
   - **B)** to assess static postural stability
   - **C)** to assess flexibility
   - **D)** to assess strength and neuromuscular efficiency

Answers:

A) Incorrect. Static single-leg strength can be assessed, but it is not the primary purpose of the BESS assessment.

B) **Correct.** The primary objective of the BESS test is to assess an individual's static postural stability.

C) Incorrect. The flexibility of the standing leg is not being assessed.

D) Incorrect. Assessing strength and neuromuscular efficiency is not the primary objective of the BESS test.

2. While standing on the left leg during the Balance Error Scoring System test, which direction should be reached by the test subject's second attempt?

A) lateral

B) posterolateral

C) anterior

D) anteromedial

Answers:

A) Incorrect. A lateral reach is performed on the seventh reach.

B) Incorrect. A posterolateral reach is performed on the sixth reach.

C) Incorrect. To initiate the test, an anterior reach is performed on the first reach.

D) **Correct.** An anteromedial reach is performed on the second reach attempt.

Muscular Strength, Endurance, and Power Assessments

Bench Press Assessment

The purpose of the bench press assessment is to determine training intensities of the bench press and the overall strength of an individual's upper body, or pressing musculature. As this assessment is considered advanced, it may not be suitable for every client. To perform this assessment, the personal trainer will need access to a bench, barbell, rack with safety pins, and weight plates (between two-and-a-half to forty-five pounds).

Movement Procedure:

1. The subject should lie face up on the bench with the head/neck, upper back, and butt on the bench. The feet should be placed firmly on the floor, with the hands shoulder-width apart.

2. The personal trainer should serve as the spotter at all times.

3. The individual should lower the bar under control to the midline of the chest and press up to return to starting position, fully extending the elbows.

Movement Execution:

1. The subject should warm up with a light weight (five to ten repetitions) without lifting to failure.

2. After a one minute rest, the subject should perform three to five repetitions with a moderately heavy weight.
3. After a two minute rest, the subject attempts one repetition with a heavier weight. If successful, the subject will rest three to five minutes, increasing the load by 5 to 10 percent for each of the following attempts.
4. Once the subject fails an attempt, a weight in an amount that falls between the last two successful lifts can be attempted.

Barbell Squat Assessment

The purpose of the barbell squat assessment is to determine bilateral maximal lower body strength. This test will determine training intensities for the squat. To perform this assessment, a squat rack with safety pins, a barbell, and weight plates (between two-and-a-half to forty-five pounds) will be needed.

Movement Procedure:
1. The subject should stand with feet shoulder-width apart (or slightly wider) and toes pointing straight ahead, with the knees in line with the toes.
2. The personal trainer should serve as the spotter at all times.
3. The individual should squat until the thighs are parallel to the floor and then return to the starting position.

Movement Execution:
1. The subject should warm up with a light weight (five to ten repetitions) without lifting to failure.
2. After a one minute rest, the subject should perform three to five repetitions with a moderately heavy weight.
3. After a two minute rest, the subject should attempt one repetition with a heavier weight. If successful, the subject will rest three to five minutes, increasing the load by 10 to 20 percent for each of the following attempts.
4. Once the subject fails an attempt, a weight in an amount that falls between the last two successful lifts can be attempted.

Push-Up Test

The push-up test is used to measure the stability of the muscular endurance of the upper body's ability to push muscles as well as upper body and lumbo/pelvic/hip complex stability. Since only the body is used to perform a push-up, no additional equipment is required.

Movement Procedure:
1. The individual should be instructed to start the assessment in the push-up position. The head, shoulders, hips, knees, and ankles should be in a straight line.
2. The individual's hands should be placed shoulder-width apart, and the elbows should be straight.

3. The personal trainer should place his or her closed fist under the chest of the subject.

Movement Execution:
1. The individual will proceed to lower the body to touch the closed fist and repeat for one minute or until exhaustion without movement compensations.
2. Only the total number of touches should be recorded.
3. If a full push-up position cannot be used, the individual may perform the test with the knees bent.

Movement View: The push-up is best viewed from the lateral angle. The cervical spine, shoulders, lumbo/pelvic/hip complex, and knees are the primary kinetic chain checkpoints.

Compensations from lateral view:
+ lumbo/pelvic/hip complex:
    a. Does the low back round?
    b. Does the low back sag?
+ shoulders:
    a. Do the shoulders elevate?
    b. Does the shoulder blade wing lift away from the ribcage?
+ head/neck: Does the head travel forward?

The Long Jump (Bilateral Broad Jump)

The purpose of the long jump assessment is to measure total body bilateral power. This test will measure the distance of the jump in the sagittal plane. It may also be performed in the frontal and transverse planes. The personal trainer should have access to a tape measure in order to properly administer this assessment.

Movement Procedure:
1. The personal trainer should place the measuring tape along a nonskid surface to create a start line with the athletic tape.
2. The individual should start with toes at the start line.
3. The individual should be allowed up to three attempts. The best measurement will be recorded.

Movement Execution:
1. The individual should jump out as far as possible, starting at the athletic tape.
2. After the jump, the personal trainer should record the relative distance of the edge of the starting line to the individual's heels.
3. If the individual falls backward, the body part nearest the starting line should be recorded.

Movement View: This assessment is best viewed in the front of the individual and slightly off to the side. This will allow the personal trainer to view the body during takeoff and landing.

Compensations:
- feet: Do the feet flatten and/or turn out?
- knees: Do the knees move inward or outward before the jump or after landing?
- lumbo/pelvic/hip complex: Does the lower back round before the jump or after landing?

Vertical Jump Assessment

The purpose of the vertical jump test is to measure total body bilateral power. In order to properly administer the vertical jump assessment, the personal trainer will need a Vertec. If a Vertec is not available, then the personal trainer should place tape on the wall. A yardstick or tape measure will also be needed.

Movement Procedure:
1. The personal trainer should measure the individual's standing reach when one arm is fully extended upward.
2. After the personal trainer marks the highest point on a wall, the trainer should then instruct the individual to jump and try to hit the marked point.

Movement Execution:
1. The jump will begin from a static start position with no drop step or side step.
2. The individual will jump as high as possible, using the arms to propel the body into the air. The body should travel straight up in an attempt to touch the highest point on the wall if a Vertec is not available.
3. There will be two jump attempts. A third attempt will be awarded if a new height is reached on the second attempt.

Movement View: This assessment is best viewed in the front of the individual and slightly off to the side. This will allow the personal trainer to view the individual's body during takeoff and landing.

The Reactive Strength Index Test

The purpose of this test is to assess an individual's ability to perform during plyometric activities by measuring reactive jump capacity, muscle-tendon stress, stretch-shortening cycle effort, and the ability to start, stop, and change direction. If available, the personal trainer should provide a jump mat for the assessment.

Movement Procedure: The individual should be instructed to perform continuous jumps.

Movement Execution:
1. The individual should perform three to five continuous jumps.
2. The personal trainer should use the jump mat to calculate the assessment results by using one of two methods:
    - jump height/ground contact time
    - jump height/time elapsed during takeoff
3. If no jump mat is available, assessment results should be determined using flight time/ground contact time.

Margaria-Kalamen Test

This purpose of the Margaria-Kalamen Test is to assess the lower body's power. To perform this test, the personal trainer will need a stopwatch, tape measure, and a flight containing twelve steps; each step should be seventeen-and-a-half centimeters in height.

Movement Procedure:
1. The personal trainer should mark a starting line six meters in front of the first step.
2. The third, sixth, and ninth steps should be clearly marked.
3. The athlete's weight should be converted to kilograms. (This can be done by dividing the individual's weight in pounds by 2.2.)

Movement Execution:
1. The individual starts at the tape that has been measured six meters before the first step.
2. On the *go* command, the individual will sprint to and up the flight of steps, taking three steps at a time. The individual should step on the third, sixth, and ninth steps.
3. The time will be recorded when the foot makes contact with the third step, and the time will be stopped when the foot makes contact with the ninth step. The personal trainer will record the time.
4. Three trials will be conducted; two to three minutes should be allowed between each trial.
5. After the completion of each trial, the following formula will be used to calculate the results of the test:

    P = Power (watts)
    M = Body Mass (kg)
    D = Vertical distance between steps three and nine
    T = Time (seconds)
    9.8 = Constant gravity
    $P = (M \times D) \times 9.8/T$

PRACTICE QUESTIONS

1. What is the purpose of the barbell squat assessment?
    - **A)** to determine lower body muscular endurance
    - **B)** to determine upper body strength
    - **C)** to determine maximal lower body strength
    - **D)** to determine single-leg strength

    Answers:
    - A) Incorrect. The barbell squat assessment is used to test maximal strength, not muscular endurance.
    - B) Incorrect. The barbell squat assessment is used to determine lower body strength, not upper body strength.
    - **C) Correct.** The barbell squat assessment is used to test an individual's maximal lower body strength.
    - D) Incorrect. The barbell squat assessment is used to determine bilateral strength, not unilateral strength.

2. Which assessment predicts an individual's ability to repeatedly absorb the stress of continuous jumping?
    - **A)** reactive strength index test
    - **B)** vertical jump test
    - **C)** Margaria-Kalamen test
    - **D)** long jump test

    Answers:
    - **A) Correct.** The reactive strength index test is used to determine an individual's plyometric capacity by measuring jump reactive ability.
    - B) Incorrect. The vertical jump test measures an individual's maximum vertical jump height.
    - C) Incorrect. The Margaria-Kalamen test measures lower body power.
    - D) Incorrect. The long jump test measures an individual's maximal horizontal jumping distance.

Speed, Agility, and Quickness Assessments

T-Test

The *t*-test determines an individual's overall agility while moving forward, laterally, and backward. The personal trainer will need a tape measure, stopwatch, and cones to perform this assessment.

Movement Procedure:
1. The personal trainer should set four cones (A, B, C, and D) in a *t* shape.
2. Three of the cones should be set five yards apart, and one cone should be placed ten yards from the middle cone.

Movement Execution:
1. On the command, the individual will sprint to cone B and touch the base of the cone using the right hand.
2. The individual will then turn left and shuffle sideways to cone C and touch the base of the cone using the left hand.
3. The individual will then proceed to shuffle sideways to the right toward cone D and touch the base of the cone with the right hand.
4. Finally, the individual will then shuffle back to cone B, touch the base of the cone with the left hand, and backpedal to cone A.
5. The test will be completed when the individual passes cone A.
6. The test will be performed three times, and the best time of the three trials will be taken.

Hexagon Test

The hexagon test determines an individual's ability to change direction and stabilize the body at high speeds. To perform this assessment, the personal trainer will need masking tape and a stopwatch. The test must be performed on a nonslip surface.

Movement Procedure:
1. Using masking tape, the personal trainer should create a hexagon on the ground (six sides, one hundred and twenty degrees), ensuring that each side measures twenty-four inches.
2. The individual should be instructed to stand in the middle of the hexagon, facing the same direction throughout the test.
3. One trial is allowed in order for the individual to get used to the pattern.

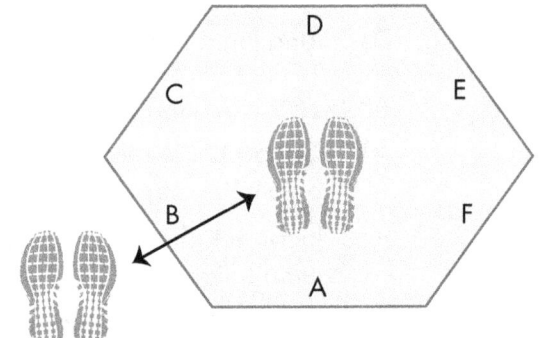

Figure 3.2. Pattern of the Hexagon Test (Footprints Demonstrate Landing Area Within Hexagon)

Movement Execution:
1. The personal trainer should give a *ready* command, at which point the individual should proceed to jump forward over the tape and then back into the hexagon.

2. The individual continues the pattern while making his or her way around the hexagon until all the sides have been jumped over.
3. This pattern should be continued for three nonstop revolutions of the hexagon.

Forty-Yard Dash

The forty-yard dash test measures an athlete's reaction capabilities and maximal speed. The personal trainer will need a tape measure, two cones, and a stopwatch to conduct this assessment.

Movement Procedure: The personal trainer should stand at the finish line.

Movement Execution:
1. The individual should sprint toward the forty-yard mark.
2. The personal trainer should begin timing with the individual's first movement and stop after the forty-yard mark has been touched.

Pro-Agility Test (5-10-5 Shuttle Test)

The pro-agility test measures lateral speed and agility. The personal trainer will need a stopwatch and three cones in order to perform this assessment.

Movement Procedure:
1. The personal trainer should place two cones at a distance of ten meters apart. The last cone should be placed at the midpoint.
2. The personal trainer should face the middle cone.

Movement Execution:
1. The individual should start by facing the personal trainer at the start/finish line (middle cone).
2. The timer begins on the individual's first movement toward the first cone.
3. The individual should start by turning to the left and sprinting for five yards, then turning to the right and sprinting for ten yards.
4. To end the test, the individual will turn back to the left and sprint the remaining five yards.

LEFT (Lower-Extremity Functional Test)

The purpose of this test is to assess an individual's ability to run in the sagittal and frontal plane. The personal trainer will need two cones and a stopwatch in order to properly perform this assessment.

Movement Procedure: Place two cones within ten yards of each other.

Movement Execution:
1. The individual will run to the first cone and then backpedal toward the starting cone.

2. The individual will change directions and perform a side shuffle to and from each cone.

3. The individual will then proceed to carioca to and from each cone and finally turn and run past the cone.

PRACTICE QUESTIONS

1. Which assessment would be most appropriate for athletes who want to improve their change-of-direction ability?

    A) the forty-yard dash

    B) the *t*-test

    C) the vertical jump test

    D) the hexagon test

    Answers:

    A) Incorrect. The forty-yard dash is used to measure straight-ahead speed.

    B) Incorrect. The *t*-test assesses an individual's ability to move forward, backward, and laterally but may not be the most accurate test for change-of-direction ability.

    C) Incorrect. The vertical jump test is used to assess an individual's maximal vertical jump height.

    D) **Correct.** The hexagon test is used to determine an individual's ability to change directions at a high speed.

2. What is the purpose of the 5-10-5 shuttle test?

    A) to assess lateral speed and agility

    B) to assess 180-degree direction-change ability, horizontal speed, and agility

    C) to assess the ability to run in the sagittal and frontal plane

    D) to assess an individual's maximal horizontal jumping distance

    Answers:

    A) Incorrect. The 5-10-5 test is used to assess lateral speed and agility.

    B) **Correct.** The 5-10-5 shuttle test is used to assess 180-degree-direction change ability, horizontal speed, and agility.

    C) Incorrect. The LEFT is used to assess an individual's ability to run in the sagittal and frontal plane.

    D) Incorrect. The long jump test is used to assess maximal horizontal jumping.

Flexibility Assessments

Overhead Squat

While the overhead squat is used as a movement assessment, it can also be used as an indicator of overall flexibility. The overhead squat requires flexibility in all the muscles that impact the joints of the kinetic chain checkpoints, such as the hip flexors, the abdominals, quadriceps, pectorals, adductors, hamstrings, latissimus dorsi, gastrocnemius, and soleus. Improving the flexibility of these muscles will allow clients to improve their overhead squat capabilities by increasing the range of motion in the joints.

Movement Procedure:
1. The individual should stand with feet shoulder-width apart and toes pointed forward. The foot and ankle complex should be in a neutral position.
2. The subject raises arms overhead, with elbows fully extended. The upper arm should bisect the torso.

Movement Execution:
1. The individual should be instructed to squat to a depth of comfort and return to the starting position.
2. The movement should be repeated for at least five repetitions. The trainer must observe the movement from all three positions (anterior, lateral, and posterior).

The feet, ankles, and knees should be viewed from the front (anterior) view. The feet should remain straight and in line with the foot. The lumbo/pelvic/hip complex, shoulder, and head and neck should be viewed. After completing the assessment, the personal trainer must be able to interpret the results. Compensations should be observed from all three angles.

Allowing the individual to perform this assessment with shoes off will allow the personal trainer to have a better view of the foot and ankle complex during movement.

Sit-and-Reach Test

This test is used to measure the flexibility of the lower back and hamstrings. In order to properly perform this assessment, the trainer will need a measuring stick, a twelve-inch high box (thirty centimeters), and tape.

Movement Procedure:
1. The individual may warm up for five to ten minutes prior to testing.
2. The individual's shoes should be removed prior to testing.
3. The individual should sit on the floor with legs fully extended and both feet placed against the box. The feet should remain in contact with the box for the duration of the test.

Movement Execution:
1. The individual places one hand on top of the other and slowly bends forward until he or she can no longer do so. Once this point is reached, the individual will hold this position for two seconds.
2. The personal trainer should mark the individual's end point.
3. The end point is measured at the individual's finger tips.
4. Three trials are performed, and the average of the three distances is used to determine the individual's score.

> The overhead squat is also used to assess flexibility. Even though it is generally used to assess dynamic posture, the overhead squat is also an excellent indicator of flexibility in the upper and lower body.

PRACTICE QUESTION

What does the sit-and-reach test assess?

- **A)** quadriceps flexibility
- **B)** shoulder flexibility
- **C)** lower back and hamstring flexibility
- **D)** hamstring strength

Answers:

- A) Incorrect. Quadriceps flexibility is not assessed during the sit-and-reach test.
- B) Incorrect. Shoulder flexibility is not assessed during the sit-and-reach test.
- **C) Correct.** The sit-and-reach test assesses lower back and hamstring flexibility.
- D) The sit-and-reach test is a flexibility assessment, not a strength assessment.

CARDIORESPIRATORY ASSESSMENTS

Three-Minute Step Test (YMCA Step Test)

The purpose of the three-minute step test is to provide a submaximal measure of cardiorespiratory fitness and assess how quickly the heart rate recovers from short bouts of exercise. In order to properly perform this assessment, the personal trainer will need a twelve-inch step, stopwatch, and a metronome.

Movement Procedure:
1. The personal trainer should demonstrate the alternating stepping cadence to the individual prior to testing to ensure movement competency.
2. The metronome should be set to ninety-six beats per minute.

Movement Execution:
1. The individual will begin stepping on and off the step to the beat of the metronome, following the *up, up, down, down,* cadence.

2. The test will continue for three minutes.
3. As soon as three minutes expire, the individual should stop immediately and the heart rate should be recorded.
4. A manual pulse reading is then performed, and the number of beats is counted for sixty seconds.

Rockport Walk Test

The Rockport walk test is used to estimate aerobic capacity (VO2 Max), and the trainer will need a treadmill or four-hundred-meter track and a stopwatch in order to properly perform this assessment.

Movement Procedure:
1. The personal trainer should inform the individual to walk, not jog.
2. The individual must walk as quickly as possible, trying to maintain the same pace for the entire mile.

Movement Execution:
1. At the *go* signal, the individual will begin walking as fast as possible until one mile is completed.
2. If using the radial pulse to determine the heart rate at the completion of the walk, the trainer will measure the heart rate for fifteen seconds and then multiply by four.

300-Yard Shuttle Test

The 300-yard shuttle test measures anaerobic capacity. The trainer will need two cones, a stopwatch, and masking tape in order to carry out this assessment.

Movement Procedure: The personal trainer should place two cones twenty-five yards apart on lines of a football field or lines created with masking tape.

Movement Execution:
1. The individual starts the test with his or her foot on the line. When instructed by the personal trainer, the individual will sprint toward the opposite cone.
2. The individual will touch his or her foot to the line, then turn and run back to the starting line.
3. This will be repeated six times without stopping.
4. After the initial test, the individual will rest for five minutes and repeat the assessment.

One-and-a-Half-Mile Run

The purpose of the 1.5-mile run is to measure an individual's aerobic power (cardiovascular endurance). In order to properly perform this assessment, the trainer will need a 400-meter track (or treadmill) and a stopwatch.

Movement Procedure: A proper warm-up should precede the 1.5-mile run, and a cool down should follow at the completion of the test.

Movement Execution:
1. The individual will complete 1.5 miles (six laps) as fast as possible.
2. The individual's heart rate and the time it takes for the person to finish the test will be determined at the completion of the assessment.

Twelve-Minute Run Test

This test measures aerobic fitness by determining the individual's ability to use oxygen pathways to produce energy while running. The trainer will need a track, stopwatch, and cones in order to carry out this assessment.

Movement Procedure:
1. The personal trainer should set cones at specific intervals that he or she determines are appropriate.
2. Each cone should be measured to ensure accuracy for total distance covered.
3. A ten-to-fifteen-minute warm-up should be completed before beginning the test.

Movement Execution: The individual will run or walk as much as possible in twelve minutes.

> **?** Which speed, agility, and quickness assessments would be the most beneficial for an individual who plays football?

PRACTICE QUESTIONS

1. When conducting the three-minute step test, the metronome should be set to how many beats per minute?

    A) 96
    B) 108
    C) 24
    D) 48

    Answers:

    A) Correct. The metronome should be set to ninety-six beats per minute.

    B) Incorrect. One hundred and eight beats per minute is not proper test procedure.

    C) Incorrect. There are twenty-four steps performed per minute, but the metronome is set to ninety-six beats per minute.

    D) Incorrect. Forty-eight beats per minute is not proper test procedure.

2. Which cardiorespiratory fitness assessment would most accurately measure anaerobic capacity?

- **A)** a 1.5-mile run
- **B)** the 300-yard shuttle test
- **C)** the Rockport walk test
- **D)** the twelve-minute run test

Answers:

- A) Incorrect. The 1.5-mile run measures aerobic power.
- **B) Correct.** The three-hundred yard shuttle test measures anaerobic capacity.
- C) Incorrect. The Rockport walk test is used to estimate aerobic capacity, or VO2 max.
- D) Incorrect. The twelve-minute run test is used to determine an individual's ability to use oxygen pathways for energy while running.

Physiological Assessments

Physiological assessments are used as indicators of a client's general fitness and overall cardiorespiratory health. Determining heart rate and blood pressure will help the personal trainer design and progress an individual's exercise program. This information will also ensure that the personal trainer creates a safe and effective program. When conducting each assessment, it is important for the individual to be relaxed, as emotions may alter resting heart rate and blood pressure measurements.

Resting Heart Rate

Determining an individual's resting heart rate can help the personal trainer get a general idea of a person's cardiorespiratory health and can also serve as an overall indicator of the client's fitness level. Calculating the resting heart rate will allow the personal trainer to create an individualized cardiorespiratory program. The resting heart rate can also be used to monitor the progression of an individual's exercise program. In order to determine the resting heart rate, the personal trainer must know how to find the correct pulse landmarks.

The two most commonly used pulse landmarks are the radial and carotid pulse. The **radial pulse** is the preferred method for determining resting heart rate; the **carotid pulse** should be taken with caution. In order to get an accurate reading, the personal trainer should teach individuals how to take their own resting heart rate since the resting heart rate is most precise when taken upon rising in the morning. It should be taken three days in a row to ensure validity.

Execution:

1. Radial pulse: Two fingers are lightly placed along the lateral aspect of the wrist, palpating along the base of the individual's thumb until the pulse is

felt. Once the pulse is felt, the beats should be counted for sixty seconds, after which the heart rate recorded.

2. Carotid pulse: The index and middle fingers should be lightly placed on the lateral aspect of the neck, just below the jaw. After the pulse has been found, it is counted for sixty seconds. The total number of beats counted within sixty seconds is the resting heart rate.

Using the rate of perceived exertion (RPE) method will allow clients to express how they feel while they are exercising. This method indicates how hard an individual is working, which will allow the personal trainer to estimate the level of difficulty of the activity being performed. The rating provides information on the individual's muscle fatigue, respiration rate, increases in heart rate, and overall fatigue.

Blood Pressure

Assessing blood pressure prior to beginning an exercise program will give the personal trainer a general idea of the client's overall health as well as notify the personal trainer if the client should be referred to a medical professional prior to beginning an exercise program. The first number (top number) is called *systolic*; this number represents the pressure in the arterial system after the heart contracts. The second number (bottom number) is called *diastolic*; this number represents the amount of pressure in the arterial system when the heart is resting and filling with blood.

According to the American Heart Association, an acceptable blood pressure is under 120/80. Blood pressure is measured with a sphygmomanometer or an electronic blood pressure monitor. If an electronic blood pressure monitor is not available, a sphygmomanometer should be used. To record the blood pressure, the personal trainer should take the following steps:

1. Ensure that the individual is seated comfortably.
2. Place the cuff directly above the elbow.
3. Place the stethoscope over the brachial artery while using minimal pressure.
4. Inflate the cuff twenty to thirty millimeters of mercury (20 – 30 mmHg) above the point at which the pulse can no longer be felt at the wrist.
5. Begin to release pressure at a rate of no more than 2 mm Hg per second, listening for a pulse.
6. In order to determine the systolic pressure, listen for the first sound of the pulse.
7. Determine the diastolic pressure by listening for the pulse as it fades away.
8. The test can be repeated on the opposite arm for validity.

PRACTICE QUESTIONS

1. What is the preferred pulse landmark for determining the resting heart rate?

    A) carotid

    B) femoral

    C) brachial

    D) radial

    Answers:

    A) Incorrect. The carotid artery is not the preferred landmark for determining resting heart rate.

    B) Incorrect. The femoral artery is not the preferred landmark for determining resting heart rate.

    C) Incorrect. The brachial artery is not the preferred landmark for determining resting heart rate.

    D) Correct. The radial pulse is the preferred landmark for determining resting heart rate due to the safety of its location and ease of finding it.

2. What does the systolic number represent?

    A) pressure in the arterial system after the heart contracts

    B) the point at which the pulse can no longer be felt

    C) the pulse fading away

    D) the sphygmomanometer

    Answers:

    A) Correct. The systolic number represents the pressure in the arterial system after the heart contracts.

    B) Incorrect. The point at which the pulse can no longer be felt occurs when the cuff is inflated 20 – 30 mmHg past the pulse point.

    C) Incorrect. The fading away of the pulse represents the diastolic pressure reading.

    D) Incorrect. The sphygmomanometer is the device used to determine blood pressure.

BODY COMPOSITION ASSESSMENTS

Body composition assessments are used to determine an individual's relative percentage of body weight that can be described as either fat mass or fat-free mass. Fat-free mass can be defined as muscle, bones, connective tissue, and teeth. Fat mass is described as essential fat (needed for normal body function) and nonessential fat (storage or adipose). Several methods are used to estimate body composition.

Personal trainers who do not have access to the specialized equipment that is usually found in exercise physiology laboratories frequently use **skinfold measurements** to assess body fat. These measurements are used to estimate the amount of fat found in subcutaneous regions of the body, which generally contain higher levels of the substance.

The skinfold measurement is the most common test to assess body fat due to the low cost, ease, and convenience of performing the test like this. There are several measurement sites that can be used, but the seven-site and three-site assessments are the most common. The validity of skinfold measurements can be affected by personal trainer experience, hydration, sex, and age. Marking anatomical landmarks should be done with proficiency to ensure accurate and consistent measurements.

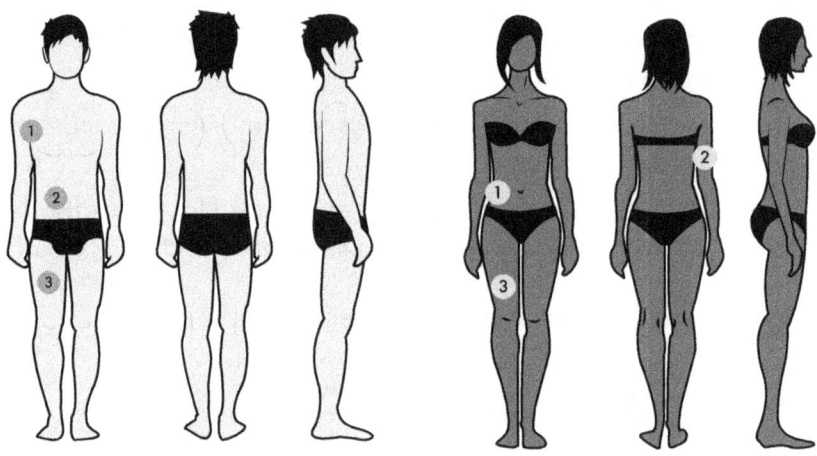

Figure 3.3. Three-Site Skinfolds Assessment in Men and Women

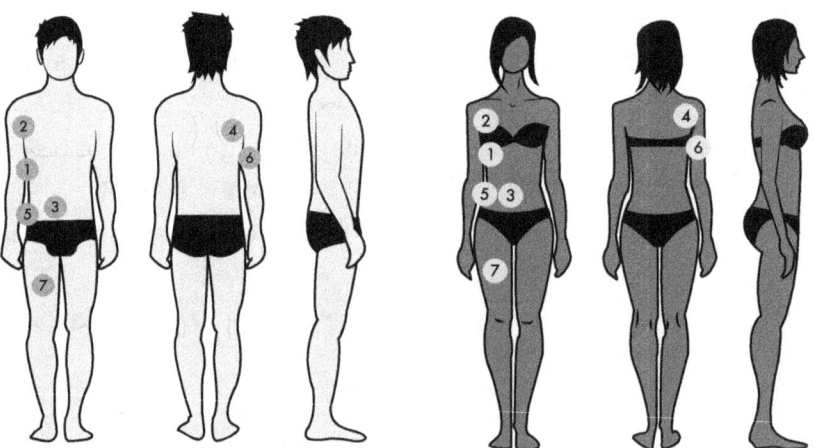

Figure 3.4. Seven-Site Skinfolds Assessment in Men and Women

The **air displacement plethysmography,** familiarly known as the BOD POD, is a whole-body densitometry device used to measure body composition. The BOD POD measures body mass by using a highly precise scale and volume while an individual sits inside. Once inside, body density can be measured. Once body density is determined, relative proportions of body fat and lean body mass are calculated. The BOD POD is highly recognized for its accuracy, speed, and safety.

Bioelectrical impedance analysis involves a low-level and safe electrical signal that is sent from metal electrodes that are in contact with the hands, feet, and abdomen. In handheld models, the electrical signal passes through the water that is present in the muscle tissue but meets resistance when fat is encountered. This form of testing is based on the premise that tissues that are high in water content will conduct an electrical current with less resistance than fat tissue that does not carry as much water.

The **near-infrared interactance (NIR)** method uses probes that are placed against an area of the body that emits an infrared light that passes through muscle and fat. The near-infrared light proceeds to use this information, along with activity level and age, to estimate body composition. The biceps are most often used.

Dual-energy x-ray absorptiometry (DEXA) uses two x-ray beams of different energy levels to measure bone mineral density. Once soft tissue absorption is measured, bone mineral density can be determined. The DEXA scan measures height, muscle mass, fat mass, and bone mass. The DEXA scan is widely known as the most accurate body composition assessment.

Circumference measurements measure the girth of body segments. These measurements are affected by muscle and fat. Circumference measurements can be used as an indicator of an individual's current health status and as a feedback source for clients who have body composition goals. In order for these measurements to be reliable, they must be consistent. For each location measured, the tape measure must be level and taut around the region which is being assessed. The following sites are generally measured:

+ Neck: Measurements are done across the Adam's apple or just above the collar bone.
+ Chest: Measurements are taken directly across the nipple line.
+ Waist: Measurements are taken at the narrowest point of the waist; if there is no narrowing of the waist, then measurements should be done directly around the navel.
+ Hips: Feet should be together and the widest portion of buttocks should be measured.
+ Thighs (upper leg): Measurements should be taken ten inches above the patella or the widest portion of the upper leg.
+ Calves: The largest portion of the lower leg, between the knee and the ankle, is the best place to take this measurement.
+ Biceps: With the arm fully extended and palms forward, the largest circumference of the bicep is measured.

The **waist-to-hip ratio** is used to assess the correlation of chronic disease and excess fat stored in the midsection. In relation to these two measurements, it has been shown that an increase in the waist-to-hip ratio reflects a rise in body fat. The waist-to-hip ratio is determined by dividing the measurement of the waist by the measurement of the hip. A ratio that is greater than 0.80 for women and greater than 0.95 for men may place these individuals at a greater risk for diseases, such as coronary heart disease or type 2 diabetes.

> ✏️ Practice how to identify anatomical landmarks in order to get accurate skinfold measurements. It will also be important to spend plenty of time becoming an expert with skinfold calipers.

Body mass index is used to determine what an individual's weight should be in proportion to height. Higher BMI measurements are related to an increased risk of disease, especially if the individual has a large waist circumference. BMI has been known to be an easy and inexpensive method to determine if weight is within a healthy range for an individual's height. BMI is calculated by dividing a person's weight in pounds by the square of height in inches and multiplying by 703. The reliability of BMI testing only takes weight into consideration but does not distinguish between fat mass and fat-free mass; therefore BMI is not the most accurate way to measure body composition but can still be used to determine if an individual has a high level of body fat.

PRACTICE QUESTIONS

1. Which method determines body fat by measuring body mass through the use of a highly precise scale while the individual sits inside the device?

    A) DEXA scan

    B) near-infrared interactance

    C) bioelectrical impedance

    D) air displacement plethysmography

    Answers:

    A) Incorrect. The DEXA scan uses two x-ray beams to measure bone density levels.

    B) Incorrect. Near-infrared interactance uses probes that emit infrared light that passes through muscle and fat.

    C) Incorrect. Bioelectrical impedance uses a low-level electrical signal to help estimate body fat percentage.

    D) Correct. Air displacement plethysmography uses a highly precise scale to help determine body fat percentage.

2. What method is most commonly used by personal trainers to determine body fat?

    A) skinfold measurements

    B) body mass index

    C) air displacement plethysmography

    D) circumference measurements (to determine girth)

Answers:

A) Correct. Skinfold measurements are the most commonly used form of body fat testing due to the ease, convenience, and low cost of performing this method of assessment.

B) Incorrect. Body mass index does not determine body fat; it only determines what an individual's weight should be in proportion to height.

C) Incorrect. Air displacement plethysmography is highly accurate, but it is not the most commonly used method.

D) Incorrect. Circumference measurements determine the girth of body segments but not the body fat percentage.

CALCULATING BODY COMPOSITION: THE FORMULAS

Body Mass Index:

Either one of the following formulas can be used to calculate body mass index:
- weight (kilograms) ÷ height (square meters)
- {weight (pounds) ÷ height (square inches)} × 703

Height is the measurement from head to foot of a standing individual; weight is the human body's relative mass.

Waist-to-Hip Ratio:
- waist circumference ÷ hip circumference

The waist to hip ratio is calculated by dividing the waist measurement by the hip measurement.

The waist measurement is determined by measuring the narrowest part of the client's waist. If the personal trainer cannot identify a narrowing of the client's waist, then the measurement should be taken directly around the navel.

The hip measurement is determined by measuring the widest portion of buttocks while the client is standing with feet together.

Fat Body Mass:
- total body weight × body fat percentage

Body fat percentage is the total amount of fat mass represented by a percentage of total body weight.

Lean Body Mass:
- total body weight - fat mass

Lean body mass consist of bones, ligaments, tendons, internal organs, and muscles.

For both fat body mass and lean body mass: The total body weight represents the human body's total mass. Fat mass consists of nonessential and essential adipose tissue, or fat. Essential adipose tissue is needed for proper body function while nonessential, or excess adipose tissue, is not needed to maintain necessary functions of the body.

Administering Assessments

ASSESSMENT PROCEDURES

In order to ensure that each assessment is reliable, the personal trainer should follow a strategically planned order. A comprehensive fitness assessment should always begin with gathering information about the potential client. After obtaining this subjective information, objective information can be collected. The following assessment sequence is recommended in order to prevent the client's performance from being affected during the subsequent test:

1. general and medical history
2. occupational, lifestyle, and medical information
3. physiological assessments (resting heart rate, blood pressure)
4. body composition testing (body fat measurements, circumference measurements)
5. static postural assessments
6. flexibility assessments (sit-and-reach test)
7. movement-based assessments (overhead squat, single-leg squat)
8. speed and power assessments
9. strength assessments
10. muscular endurance assessments
11. aerobic assessments

The order of fitness assessments should be based on prioritizing performance. Tests that rely on the ATP-PC energy system, for example, should be performed before tests that rely primarily on the glycolytic anaerobic system. Following this order will help the subject avoid fatigue without interfering with tests that rely on the quick-burst energy of the ATP-PC system.

PRACTICE QUESTION

Which of the following assessments would precede a flexibility assessment?

A) physiological assessments

B) aerobic assessments

C) muscular endurance assessments

D) strength assessments

Answers:

A) Correct. Physiological assessments should be performed in a resting state before a flexibility assessment takes place.

B) Incorrect. Aerobic assessments should be performed after a flexibility assessment.

C) Incorrect. Muscular endurance assessments should be performed after physiological assessments have been completed.

D) Incorrect. Strength assessments should be performed after physiological assessments have been completed.

RELATIVE AND ABSOLUTE CONTRAINDICATIONS

Exercise testing is the most effective way to begin an exercise program. It allows personal trainers to gather all pertinent information both for and about their potential client. Even though testing is necessary, there are still relative and absolute contraindications that may prevent the subject from completing exercise testing.

Relative contraindications are less threatening conditions that may pose a risk to the subject during testing. Examples of relative contraindications are severe high blood pressure, a history of heart illness, chronic infectious diseases (e.g., hepatitis, AIDS), uncontrollable metabolic diseases (e.g., diabetes), and neuromuscular and/or musculoskeletal disorders that are exacerbated by exercise. If a subject displays signs of any relative contraindications, the personal trainer must be sure that the benefits of testing outweigh the possible risks. The exercise test may also be modified to meet the needs of each individual.

On the other hand, a subject with **absolute contraindications** should NEVER proceed with exercise testing. Examples of absolute contraindications that would lead to the termination of a test are severe infections, uncontrolled symptomatic heart failure, unstable angina, and a recent history of myocardial infarction. The exercise test should be discontinued immediately if there are any signs of poor perfusion, such as dizziness, confusion, light-headedness, an onset of chest pain, failure of the heart rate to rise with an increase in workload, or if the subject requests to stop the exercise test.

The personal trainer should always deliver test results in a positive manner. The personal trainer should never aim to discourage or embarrass the individual. A negative delivery may impact the client-trainer relationship and discourage the individual from proceeding with the training program. The objective should be to improve the outlook and self-esteem of the individual rather than create a negative experience with exercise and the personal trainer.

PRACTICE QUESTION

Which of the following is an example of a relative contraindication?

- **A)** recent history of myocardial infarction
- **B)** unstable angina
- **C)** uncontrolled symptomatic heart failure
- **D)** severe high blood pressure

Answers:

- A) Incorrect. A recent history of myocardial infarction is an example of an absolute contraindication.
- B) Incorrect. Suffering from unstable angina is an example of an absolute contraindication in a client.
- C) Incorrect. When a patient exhibits uncontrolled symptomatic heart failure, it is an example of an absolute contraindication.
- D) **Correct.** Severe high blood pressure is a relative contraindication.

REASSESSMENT

In order to ensure that an exercise program is effective and to keep the client motivated, regular assessments of clients should be strategically scheduled. A reassessment will help the personal trainer determine the next plan of action. Reassessments are generally performed every four to six weeks. They should not be performed so often that adequate time has not passed to see noticeable changes. The reassessment should include identical test and measurements that were administered at the initial assessment. The measurements will give the personal trainer an individual basis for adjusting acute variables of the training program.

During the initial goal setting process, the personal trainer should encourage the individual to set physical, psychological, and mental goals. This will allow the individual to see continual success. It also allows the client to focus on accomplishing goals that aren't focused around altering body composition. Having goals that are focused on the mental and psychological benefits of exercise will help clients develop positive lifestyle habits that will make accomplishing physical goals more attainable.

After reassessing the individual, the personal trainer can make the proper modifications to the exercise program to help the individual stay on track or get back on track to accomplishing his or her goals. The reassessment period also serves as an excellent time to reevaluate the objectives of the exercise program to make sure that the original goals are still important to the client.

PRACTICE QUESTIONS

1. Which of the following is NOT a reason to reassess clients?

    A) to keep clients committed to the goals they have created

    B) to reevaluate goals

    C) to make sure the most appropriate exercises are being programmed to help the clients achieve their goals

    D) to introduce new assessments to see if the program is working

    Answers:

    A) Incorrect. Reassessing clients will help keep them committed to their goals.

    B) Incorrect. Reassessing client goals is a great time to reevaluate goals that were selected at the initial assessment.

    C) Incorrect. The reassessment period serves as an opportunity to modify the exercise program.

    D) Correct. When reassessing clients, it is important to keep the same test protocol.

2. Which types of goals does a personal trainer NOT address before beginning an exercise program?

    A) mental goals

    B) physical goals

    C) financial goals

    D) psychological goals

    Answers:

    A) Incorrect. Personal trainers will help their clients set mental goals. Mental goals may allow clients to overcome mental barriers that could interfere with accomplishing their overall goals.

    B) Incorrect. Personal trainers will help their clients set physical goals. Most clients will want to change their physical appearance when they begin working with a personal trainer.

    C) Correct. Personal trainers will not help their clients set financial goals as these are out of their scope of practice.

    D) Incorrect. Personal trainers will help their clients set psychological goals. Psychological goals may be determined in an effort to use exercise to combat common psychological problems, such as anxiety and stress.

REFERRALS

It is important for personal trainers to stay within their scope of practice when working with their clients. Personal trainers do NOT:

- diagnose disease or injury.
- prescribe medication or treatments.
- treat injury or disease.
- prescribe diets or nutrition advice outside of basic healthy eating information.
- administer diagnostic testing or procedures.
- provide psychological counseling.

Personal trainers DO:
- assess movement dysfunctions and muscular imbalances.
- use evidence-based protocols to enhance client exercise experience.
- administer pre-exercise assessments and screenings.
- design safe and effective exercise programs.
- provide basic information in regards to healthy eating.

If a client has several risk factors, or if the personal trainer believes the client's condition is out of his or her scope of practice, then the personal trainer should refer the client to a medical professional for further testing before proceeding with an exercise program. Risk factors that exceed the personal trainer's scope of practice include known cardiovascular, pulmonary, or metabolic diseases. If an individual exhibits one or more signs of these diseases, then the personal trainer should refer the client to a physician. The personal trainer must be sure to document pulse, blood pressure, pain, odd behavior, or abnormal respiration before, during, and after exercise testing.

Referring individuals to the proper medical professional will allow the personal trainer to help the individual get a clear and concise answer about possible medical problems. A referral to a medical professional will also show the client that the personal trainer cares about the client's health, and it will help build a strong professional relationship between the personal trainer and the client.

Once the personal trainer has determined that a medical clearance is needed, he or she should give the client a medical clearance form to be completed by the client's primary care physician. After the physician has determined if an unsupervised, supervised, or medically supervised exercise program is necessary, the personal trainer will adhere to the program recommendations of the physician until the individual is cleared to participate in normal activity. The personal trainer should be sure to retain a copy of the completed medical clearance form for records and verification of completion. The personal trainer should also maintain frequent communication between the client and physician to ensure that the goals of the client and the program recommendations of the physician are being met regularly.

The personal trainer should be sure to document any abnormal signs or symptoms during the assessments. This will allow the personal trainer to share the right information with the medical professional in case a referral is needed.

Assessments in Special Populations

When assessing special population groups, such as youth, senior, or prenatal clients, modifications and considerations have to be implemented to make sure a safe and effective exercise program can be designed. The personal trainer should know what to expect and which test will be the most effective for each population. The personal trainer should perform static and dynamic postural assessments as well as physiological assessments with each special population. Test selection should be based on safety and any special considerations.

The term *youth* generally describes individuals who are between childhood and adulthood. Children and adolescents between the ages of six and twenty are often considered youth clients.

When assessing children and adolescents, the personal trainer must be aware of the physiological differences between youth and adult clients in order to successfully and effectively determine fitness level. Considerations that the personal trainer must consider are:

- Youth have a higher oxygen demand than adults, which will increase the chance of fatigue and heat production.
- Youth have a decreased ability to perform longer duration, higher intensity tasks.
- Youth have less tolerance to environmental extremes, such as high heat and humidity.
- Youth are comparable to adults in their ability to perform endurance tasks.

> **?** What are the modifications that should be made for assessing the cardiorespiratory systems of youth clients?

The term *senior* is generally used to describe individuals who are sixty-five years of age or older.

When assessing the senior population, the personal trainer must be sure to consider the physiological and training considerations of people who are over the age of sixty-five. Normal changes that occur with aging include:

- a reduction in cardiac output
- reduced balance capabilities
- a decrease in coordination
- a decrease in muscle mass
- reduced VO2 max capacity

In order to effectively assess seniors, the personal trainer must select the test that would be most appropriate and beneficial for this population. Useful assessments for seniors would include:

- the overhead squat assessment
- the gait assessment
- the balance error scoring system
- the Rockport walk test or half-mile walk test

The term *prenatal* is used to describe a woman who is currently pregnant. Before assessing prenatal clients, the personal trainer should have an understanding of some of the absolute and relative contraindications for exercise this population may face.

Absolute contraindications include the following:
- multiple gestation (e.g., twins, triplets, etc.) that puts the client at a higher risk for premature labor
- pregnancy-induced hypertension
- premature labor during current pregnancy

Relative contraindications include the following:
- poorly controlled hypertension
- poorly controlled type 1 diabetes
- extreme levels of obesity
- history of high levels of a sedentary lifestyle

When assessing prenatal women, it is important that personal trainers be familiar with the physiological changes that women experience during pregnancy. Throughout pregnancy, women will experience a decrease in available oxygen for aerobic activity, an increase in metabolic demand to maintain proper energy balance, and an overall decrease in work capacity. The personal trainer should select tests that provide the information needed to create a safe exercise program. More importantly, tests that are safe to administer should be chosen. Safe assessments for prenatal women are:
- the Rockport walk test
- the overhead squat assessment
- the balance error scoring system

PRACTICE QUESTIONS

1. Considering the differences between youth and adult clients, which assessment would be the LEAST beneficial for testing most youth clients?

    A) one-repetition bench press test

    B) push-up test

    C) overhead squat assessment

    D) sit-and-reach test

    Answers:

    A) Correct. The one-repetition bench press test would be the least beneficial for testing most youth clients.

- B) Incorrect. The push-up up test would be a beneficial assessment for testing the muscular strength and muscular endurance of youth clients.
- C) Incorrect. The overhead squat would be a beneficial assessment for youth clients to help determine dynamic movement efficiency and dynamic flexibility.
- D) Incorrect. The sit-and-reach test would be beneficial to assess lower back and hamstring flexibility.

2. Which test would be the most appropriate for a prenatal client?
   - A) overhead squat assessment
   - B) one-repetition barbell squat
   - C) 300-yard shuttle
   - D) 1.5-mile run

Answers:
- A) **Correct.** The overhead squat would be the most appropriate exercise test for a prenatal client.
- B) Incorrect. The intensity of the one-repetition barbell squat test would not be appropriate for a prenatal client due to the high load and spinal loading of the barbell.
- C) Incorrect. The intensity of the 300-yard shuttle test would not be appropriate for a prenatal client.
- D) Incorrect. The 1.5-mile run test would not be the best option for a prenatal client; the Rockport walk test would be more appropriate due to its low intensity and shorter duration.

FOUR: EXERCISE TECHNIQUE

Fundamentals of Exercise Technique

Well-designed fitness programs should follow a progressive system that integrates all forms of exercise: cardiovascular, flexibility, core and balance training, plyometrics training, resistance or weight training and speed, agility, and quickness training.

Proper exercise technique is key to building muscle strength and endurance while minimizing injury. An athlete can risk injury just as much as a beginner can should they fail to follow proper form and breathing protocols. Focus should be on proper form and breathing techniques before adding a difficult weight load. The more controlled the exercise reps, the better quality the workout.

First, breathing is a key component to any good exercise technique, regardless of fitness level. Proper breathing helps control core activation, repetition tempo, and range of motion. In rested position, one should inhale through the nose which inflates the diaphragm and exhale through the mouth while exerting the muscle into power position. Then repeat the inhale to control the release back to resting position and so on, until all reps are complete in the set.

For example, the proper breathing technique for a chest press would be:

1. Exhale on **concentric** motion, or exertion point. Elbows push with power to straightened position contracting the pectoral muscles.

2. Inhale on the **eccentric** or lengthening motion. Bending the elbows back to rest position, with control, stretch the pectoral muscles.

Advanced lifters who are focused on heavy loads might adopt the **Valsalva breathing maneuver.** This breathing technique uses a forceful exhalation that is pushed through a tight airway causing decreased blood flow. Most feel this type of breathing during heavy lifting, particularly barbell deadlifts, squats, and chest press, supports the low back, reducing injury risk. However, this technique lowers one's heart rate and blood pressure, which can lead to dizziness and fainting.

 The term *isometric motion* refers to holding a certain muscle length.

Maintaining a neutrally aligned body position is another vital component in exercise technique. Good form and posturing will minimize injury risk and isolate the correct muscle groups when an exercise is performed. Personal trainers' primary goals should include giving feedback on form during sessions.

The following are the elements of a neutral standing body position:
+ head straight
+ chin back
+ legs at hip-width apart or slightly wider
+ shoulders relaxed and straight
+ palms facing the midline of the body (thumbs forward)
+ pelvis tucked in
+ navel pulled toward the spine (activates core)
+ knees soft
+ toes straight forward

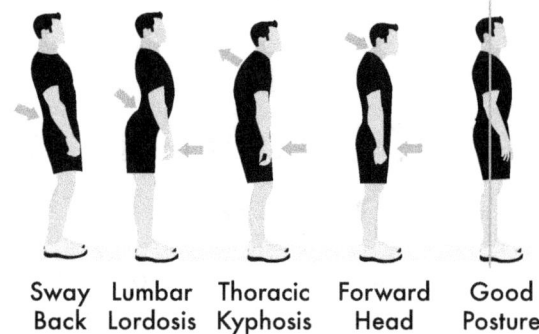

Figure 4.1. Posture

A client's potential postural **muscle imbalances** might have the following body position inefficiencies:
+ head and chin forward
+ palms facing **posteriorly**
+ shoulders jutting forward (thoracic kyphosis)
+ hips tilting upward (lumbar lordosis)
+ legs too wide or too narrow
+ **lateral** or **proximal** toe positioning

Proper body form in the **semi-supine** position should include:
+ laying on back
+ five points of contact
  ⋄ head
  ⋄ shoulders
  ⋄ glutes
  ⋄ right foot
  ⋄ left foot

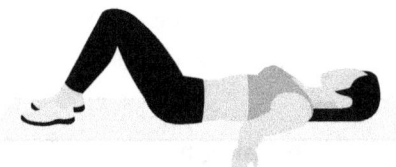

Figure 4.2. Semi-Supine Position

After a proper postural assessment, a trainer can design a routine that will help combat postural muscle imbalances. Proper posturing while the body is in motion will be discussed in greater detail for each exercise.

Along with proper body positioning, another way to isolate muscle groups with efficiency is using different types of **grips** while lifting barbells, dumbbells, and kettlebells, and while using weight machines. Grips will be defined in greater detail along with different exercises; familiarity with these terms will ensure proper audio cues for clients when visually demonstrating exercises.

> Use a long dowel or plastic PVC pipe to help your clients hold neutral body positioning. They should be able to maintain three points of contact—head, mid back, and buttocks—with the dowel. This will help them experience a strong neutrally aligned body position.

Bodybuilding can be very difficult on the body, because many lifters perform most exercises to their **sticking point**, where form is heavily compromised. Advanced clients may want to train to get past this sticking point; a proper program design focusing on form, **spotting**, and breathing can help with this.

When designing a program for a client, it is imperative to discuss goals to make sure the program aids in attaining those goals. Exercises can be classified into categories to help fitness professionals pick the right types of exercise for different fitness levels—either by muscle type recruitment or whether the **kinetic chain** is working from a fixed position. **Core exercises** recruit multiple large muscle groups (for example, the legs, back, or chest) and multiple joint motions at a time. Core exercises can be **structural**, posture-centered and load bearing, like a barbell deadlift or **power-based**, which are more reactive and explosive, like a medicine ball slam.

Assistance exercises typically activate smaller muscle groups (for example, arms, calves, and neck) and single joint motions. These types of exercises tend to be used for rehabilitative purposes because they focus on one muscle group and joint motion at a time.

The body's three systems—the nervous, muscular, and skeletal systems—need to work in synergy to complete the kinetic chain, making for the most effective and efficient workout. When the hands or feet are planted in a fixed position, like in a pull-up or squat, we consider these **closed kinetic chain** exercises; planting the limbs closes the chain of motion. Like core exercises, closed chain exercises engage both **Type I** (*postural muscles*) and **Type II** (*power muscles*) muscle groups for a more complex workout and more efficient caloric expenditure.

> If you had a client who was interested in burning more fat and all around body toning, which type of exercises would you prescribe?

Like assistance exercises, open kinetic chain exercises isolate one muscle group at a time. A machine leg extension or dumbbell biceps curl allows hand or foot movement, keeping the chain open.

PRACTICE QUESTIONS

1. Which muscles are considered Type I muscles?

    A) power muscles

    B) weak muscles

    C) postural muscles

    D) leg muscles

    Answers:

    A) Incorrect. Power muscles are considered Type II muscle groups. They are larger and tire easily.

    B) Incorrect. Weak muscles are not a type of muscle group.

    C) Correct. Postural muscles, or core muscles, are slow to fatigue, which are Type I muscles.

    D) Incorrect. Leg muscles fall into the Type II muscle group.

2. Exhale on the _____ of the exercise.

    A) hold point or isometric movement

    B) exertion point or concentric movement

    C) extension point or eccentric movement

    D) sticking point or failure

    Answers:

    A) Incorrect. One should still be inhaling at this point.

    B) Correct. Exhaling on exertion will help control and propel the user's force to complete the full range of motion.

    C) Incorrect. The user should inhale through the stretch of the exercise allowing for the breath and potential energy to be ready for the contraction of the muscle.

    D) Incorrect. This is not a part of muscle contraction.

Warm-Up and Cooldown Protocols

A warm-up prepares the body and mind for physical activity. Warm-ups should be based on the client's fitness assessment and should contain both full-body conditioning and targeted exercises. The primary goal of a warm-up should be to increase the range of motion before resistance training allowing for proper **neuromuscular efficiency**.

There are several benefits of warming up the body prior to exercise, including:

- Aiding in correcting muscle imbalances
- Increasing joint range of motion, while relieving joint stress
- Reducing muscle tension
- Improving response of muscle/joint connectors, or, the tendons
- Improving mind/muscle recruitment efficiency
- Improving overall body function.

Warm-Up Protocols

It is imperative to start a workout with a good warm-up and end with a cooldown. An effective warm-up should last at least 10 minutes at about 30 – 60 percent exertion, or low to moderate intensity, depending on a client's fitness level. Someone who is new to exercise or deconditioned may need to spend more time on a warm-up due to postural correction through stretching or poor cardiorespiratory endurance.

One should start with a general cardiovascular warm-up by using a treadmill or other cardio machine, jumping rope, or performing body weight exercises, like jumping jacks or high knees. This will help elevate body temperature and provide a general warm-up for all muscles of the body, which is necessary before any stretching begins.

After the body is warm, the client should be directed to briefly stretch the muscles they will be using in their workout. If a client has a muscle imbalance, like shortened hamstring muscles, be sure to give him special attention with **self-myofascial release** or **static stretching**, or both, to ensure proper form throughout the duration of his exercise session.

> To remember how to warm up a client use **RAMP** for her routine!
>
> **Raise** your body temp. Typically some sort of cardio training to warm up your body before any muscle lengthening or strengthening occurs.
>
> **Activate** key muscle groups and **Mobilize** joints and joint receptors (tendons).
>
> **Potentiate**, or increase, the power of the muscle groups or workout type one is performing, for example, reactive training for sports or power training for weight lifting.

End the warm-up with **dynamic stretching** to target the muscle groups the client will be focusing on during his workout session. These stretches should require more exertion (65 – 75 percent) than the general warm-up; as the client improves his cardio endurance, he can use these types of exercises in lieu of standard cardio machines. Performing several dynamic stretch exercises in a **circuit** can provide effective heart elevation and efficient muscle activation for a warm-up. Dynamic stretches may include butt kickers or prisoner squats for the lower limbs or arm circles and medicine ball chop/lifts for the upper limbs.

COOLDOWN PROTOCOLS

While it may be tempting to finish a tough workout and just call it a day, a cooldown will benefit the body because it:

- Promotes flexibility
- Removes waste products via the blood
- Alleviates potential for muscle soreness
- Avoids dizziness or fainting
- Provides a mental relief after exercise stress

Cooldown protocols should follow a similar pattern to the warm-up and should last about 10 minutes. Start with cardio at a low level that will aid in slowly reducing back to a resting level while still moving. Instead of dynamic stretching, one should go immediately into a few targeted static stretches and finish the cooldown session with self-myofascial release.

PRACTICE QUESTIONS

1. The general cardio warm-up should start with what?
    - **A)** dynamic stretching
    - **B)** agility ladders
    - **C)** cardiovascular training
    - **D)** PNF stretching

    Answers:
    - A) Incorrect. Warm-ups should start with general conditioning and end with dynamic stretches.
    - B) Incorrect. Agility training is too high of intensity.
    - **C) Correct.** This training can be modified for any fitness level and provides a general conditioning allowing the body temp to rise.
    - D) Incorrect. PNF stretching should not be done with cold muscles.

2. What are some physiological benefits of cooling down?
    - **A)** promotes flexibility
    - **B)** raises body temperature
    - **C)** builds lean muscle mass
    - **D)** mentally prepares a person for exercise

    Answers:
    - **A) Correct.** Stretching should be part of a cooldown routine, since the muscles have been worked and are still warm.
    - B) Incorrect. This is a benefit of warming up the body before exercising.

C) Incorrect. This is a benefit of resistance training.
D) Incorrect. This is another benefit of warm-ups.

Flexibility and Stretching Exercises

Flexibility in the fitness world is easily defined as the full range of motion in one's joints or the mobility of one's muscles for easy joint motion. While it is important to have pliable muscles that allow joints free and full range of motion, it is not necessary to be so flexible one can bend over and touch their nose to their knees. Flexibility is relative and specific to each person.

Stretching should have a multifaceted approach to help correct muscle imbalance and improve proper muscle and tendon elasticity and function.

Self-Myofascial Release

Self-myofascial release (SMR) or foam rolling is a good way to target any muscles that may be overactive or have apparent knots in the muscle fibers. SMR initiates **autogenic inhibition** within the muscle sensors called the Golgi tendon organs. These organs eventually release their tension once stimulated by the pressure the foam roller puts on them, causing them to relax and increase range of motion in the overactive fiber.

There are different densities of foam roller depending on the client's sensitivity to pressure, and other implements that can be used for self-myofascial release. Tennis balls, medicine balls, roller bars and textured rollers are a few other examples, but foam rollers are the most popular and accessible.

Special populations, like people with heart failure, bleeding disorders, organ failure, blood clots, contagious skin disorders, or open wounds should avoid SMR.

In general, these exercises should be performed by rolling over the tender spot for 30 – 60 seconds, depending on the clients' pain tolerance. It is best to do at least two sets of static stretches, so the muscles being relaxed can extend their range of motion in the second set.

Exercises

Place foam roller under the lower leg. Cross one leg over the other and push the body up so the hands and the foam roller are the only points of contact. Be sure the head and shoulders are aligned with the spine; palms are pressed firmly into the ground. Begin to slowly move the foam roller up and down the lower leg

Figure 4.3. SMR Gastrocnemius/Soleus (Calf)

by swaying the hips toward and away from the foam roller. Repeat this motion for 30 – 60 seconds. Release and switch legs.

> **?** If your client is rehabilitating from a strained calf and has trouble stretching on her own, how would you help her improve her muscle flexibility to ensure she does not create a muscle imbalance during her workout?

Wedge foam roller between the floor and the top of the hip. Activate the elbow closest to the floor and allow the hip to balance on the roller. Be sure the shoulders and hips are stacked; the top shoulder and hip should not lean over. Use the foot of the top leg as a guide to slowly move the body, from hip to knee over the roller. Repeat this motion for 30 – 60 seconds. Release and switch legs.

Figure 4.4. SMR Iliotibial (IT) Band

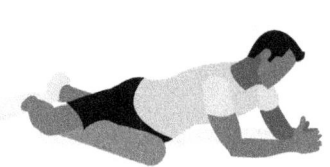

Figure 4.5. SMR Adductors (Inner Thigh)

Lying **prone** on the floor, place foam roller parallel to the body. With knees bent and wide apart, wedge roller under one leg so it is in contact with the inner thigh. Using the other knee, the forearms and elbows, lift the body off the ground and allow the roller to move from the groin to the knee. Repeat this motion for 30 – 60 seconds. Release and switch legs.

Sit on foam roller and cross one ankle to the opposite knee. Lean the body toward the bent leg. Balance the body on the foam roller so the straight leg and opposite palm are the only points of contact to the floor. Slowly guide the glute of the bent knee up and down the foam roller. Repeat this motion for 30 – 60 seconds. Release and switch legs.

Figure 4.6. SMR Piriformis

Figure 4.7. SMR Hamstring

Place foam roller under the upper leg. Cross one leg over the other and push the body up so the hands and the foam roller are the only points of contact. Be sure the head and shoulders are aligned with the spine; palms are pressed firmly into the ground. Slowly move the foam roller up and down the upper leg by swaying the hips toward and away from the foam roller. Repeat this motion for 30 – 60 seconds. Release and switch legs.

Wedge foam roller between the floor and under the armpit; extend arm overhead and bend top leg behind the body so foot is on the ground. Activate the bent leg's foot and the elbow closest to the floor and allow the side of the torso to balance on the roller. Roll the side up and down from armpit to hip. Repeat this motion for 30 – 60 seconds. Release and switch to the other side.

Figure 4.8. SMR Latissimus Dorsi (Large Back Muscles)

Begin in seated position. Place roller behind glutes and lean the small of the back against the roller. Lift glutes off the floor so the feet are the only point of contact to the floor and the back is balancing on the roller. This will cause the abdominals to activate; keep head, neck, and shoulders off the floor. Use the feet to help guide the roller up and down the spine from just below the shoulder blades, and continue rolling to the top of the shoulders. Repeat this motion for 30–60 seconds.

Figure 4.9. SMR Thoracic Spine (Mid Back)

PRACTICE QUESTIONS

1. Which populations should not use SMR in their warm-up protocols?
    - **A)** a person with vitiligo
    - **B)** a person whose body fat exceeds 30 percent
    - **C)** a person who is prone to blood clots
    - **D)** a person who has no flexibility

    Answers:
    - A) Incorrect. Vitiligo is a non-contagious skin condition.
    - B) Incorrect. Obesity is not a restricted special population for SMR.
    - C) **Correct.** Blood clots can move from the roller's pressure, causing an increased risk for them to travel to the heart, so SMR would not be recommended.
    - D) Incorrect. SMR would help a person who is inflexible release tension from strained muscle fibers.

2. What dictates the duration that a client should perform the SMR exercise?
    - **A)** the client's pain tolerance and sensitivity
    - **B)** the client's age
    - **C)** the client's fitness level
    - **D)** the client's flexibility

    Answers:
    - A) **Correct.** SMR can be uncomfortable, so the client should perform the exercise as long they can tolerate; between 30 – 60 seconds.
    - B) Incorrect. Age is not a factor.
    - C) Incorrect. Clients of any fitness level can use SMR.
    - D) Incorrect. Being flexible is not a factor.

STATIC STRETCHING EXERCISES

Like SMR, static stretching causes autogenic inhibition in the muscle spindles and Golgi tendon organs. To protect the muscles from injury, these sensors will relax and allow lengthening in the muscle fibers.

These stretches should be held at the muscle's point of *slight* discomfort for 30 seconds. It is best to do at least two sets of static stretches, so the muscles being relaxed can extend their range of motion in the second set.

Look Right and Left

Muscles Targeted: trapezius, scalene, and levator (neck muscles)

Stand in neutral body position; with relaxed shoulders, turn head to peak range of motion. Hold for 30 seconds. For greater stretch, lightly hold chin with finger. Change sides.

Neck Flexion and Extension

Muscles Targeted: trapezius, scalene, levator (neck muscles), and rhomboids (mid back)

Stand in neutral body position. With relaxed shoulders, bring chin to chest peak range of motion. Hold for 30 seconds. Then point chin upward and hold for 30 seconds.

Straight Arms Behind Back

Muscles Targeted: pectorals (chest), deltoids (shoulders), and biceps

Stand in neutral body position. With relaxed shoulders, lace fingers together and straighten elbows. Hold for 30 seconds. For intensified stretch in shoulders and chest, hinge body at hips, allowing arms to fall toward head. This progression will also stretch lower back and hamstrings.

Figure 4.10. Straight Arms Behind Back

Figure 4.11. Seated Lean Back

Seated Lean Back

Muscles Targeted: deltoids (shoulders), biceps, and forearms

Start in straight-leg seated position. Place palms on floor, fingers turned away from the body. Slide arms back and lean torso back until peak shoulder range of motion is met; do not let shoulders creep up to ears. Hold for 30 seconds.

Behind-Neck Stretch

Muscles Targeted: triceps (back of arm) and deltoids (shoulder)

Stand in neutral body position. With relaxed shoulders bring one arm overhead and use opposite hand to push elbow of the stretched arm so the palm is touching the nape. Keep shoulders relaxed. Hold for 30 seconds.

Figure 4.12. Behind-Neck Stretch

Figure 4.13. Cross Arms in Front of Chest

Cross Arms in Front of Chest

Muscles Targeted: deltoid (shoulders) and rhomboids (mid back)

In neutral standing stance, bring one straight arm across chest. Use the opposite arm to hold straight arm in place. Hold for 30 seconds. Change arms. For a more intense stretch, place chin on the shoulder of the arm stretched; this will activate and stretch the trapezius as well.

Arms Straight Above Head

Muscles Targeted: deltoids (shoulder), pectorals (chest), and forearms

In neutral standing stance, lace fingers and bring arms overhead so palms are facing the ceiling. Keeping the shoulders relaxed and pelvis pulled in, hold this position for 30 seconds.

Spinal Twist

Muscles Targeted: glutes, piriformis, biceps femoris, erector spinae, latissimus dorsi, pectorals, and shoulders

From a straight leg, seated position, cross one leg over the other. Use the opposite arm of the bent leg to hold a spinal twist; keep shoulders relaxed. Hold for 30 seconds. Switch sides. For an advanced stretch, lie in supine position with straightened arms on the floor; keep shoulders on floor. Bend one leg and pull it across the body to peak range of motion.

Figure 4.14. Spinal Twist

Semi-Leg Straddle

Muscles Targeted: hamstring, gastrocnemius, and glutes

From a straight leg, seated position, bend one leg so the foot touches the inner thigh of the opposite leg. Keeping back straight, pull the navel to the spine and reach for the toes of the straightened leg. Hold at peak range of motion for 30 seconds. (For a more advanced stretch, refer to Figure 4.19.)

Figure 4.15. Semi-Leg Straddle

EXERCISE TECHNIQUE 143

Forward Lunge

Muscles Targeted: hip flexors and glutes

Figure 4.16. Forward Lunge

From a tall kneeling position with both knees on the ground, bring one foot up to the ground so it is completely flat. Push the body into the lunged leg so the opposite hip begins to stretch. If heel begins to come off the ground while lunging, pull the foot further away from the body. Hold that position for 30 seconds. Switch sides.

Supine Knee Flex

Figure 4.17. Supine Knee Flex

Muscles Targeted: hip flexor and glutes

From supine position, draw one leg up to the chest while keeping the straight leg on the floor. Hold this position for 30 seconds. Switch legs. To modify this stretch, have the client begin in semi-supine position.

Side Bend

Muscles Targeted: obliques, latissimus dorsi, and deltoids

In a neutral stance with hips squared, reach one hand overhead while the other is on the hip for support. Hold at peak range of motion for 30 seconds; keep shoulders relaxed and hips square. Switch sides.

Side Quadriceps Stretch

Muscles Targeted: quadriceps and hip flexors

Figure 4.18. Side Quadriceps Stretch

Laying on side, keep hips and shoulders stacked; head propped up with bottom arm. With the top hand, grab the top foot and pull the pelvis forward while squeezing the glute. Hold this position for 30 seconds. Switch sides.

Sitting Toe Touch

Muscles Targeted: hamstrings, calves, and glutes

Seated with legs extended, shoulders relaxed and feet flexed, reach fingertips toward toes. Be sure the shoulders or back are not rounded. The goal should be to draw the navel toward the quadriceps. Hold at peak range of motion for 30 seconds.

Straddle Stretch

Muscles Targeted: inner thighs, hamstrings, and glutes

Figure 4.19. Straddle Stretch

Seated with legs extended and feet flexed, open legs until peak range of motion is reached. Then, place hands on floor and walk them out until that peak range of motion is met. Be sure the shoulders or back are not rounded and head is an extension of the spine. Hold for 30 seconds. For regression, see Figure 4.15. For progression, stand in a wide leg stance. Fold body, reaching for the ankles.

Butterfly

Muscles Targeted: inner thighs

Sitting tall, shoulders relaxed, and crown of head toward ceiling, bring souls of feet together. Grab the ankles and draw navel to floor so elbows touch the knees, pressing them to the floor. For an advanced stretch, use hands to pull ankles in to groin while folding torso over legs; keep the back straight. Hold for 30 seconds.

Figure 4.20. Butterfly

Wall Calf Stretch

Muscles Targeted: gastrocnemius (interior calf) and soleus (exterior calf)

Face a wall and place the palms on the wall. Keeping shoulders relaxed, step one leg toward the wall and bend the knee. The back leg should remain straight, toe pointed straight ahead and heel pressed down to the floor. Hold this stretch for 30 seconds. Switch legs. For a more advanced stretch, keep the feet together and lean toward the wall.

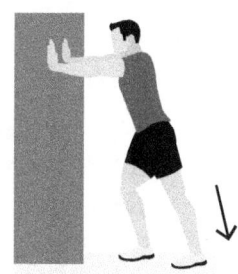

Figure 4.21. Wall Calf Stretch

PRACTICE QUESTIONS

1. At what point should one hold a static stretch?
   - **A)** as soon as feeling the stretch, before any discomfort
   - **B)** at the point of intense pain
   - **C)** at the point of slight discomfort
   - **D)** The stretcher should pulse the stretch, not hold it.

Answers:

A) Incorrect. The intention of static stretching is to challenge the fibers.

B) Incorrect. While it is important to seek a challenge, stretching should never be intensely painful; the individual risks pulling the muscle.

C) **Correct.** Slight discomfort alerts the stretcher that he is challenging his range of motion, but allows him to hold the stretch.

D) Incorrect. Stretchers should never bounce in a stretch; they could unintentionally pull a muscle.

2. What can be considered a regression for the static straddle stretch?
   - **A)** seated lean back
   - **B)** butterfly stretch
   - **C)** semi-straddle stretch
   - **D)** supine knee stretch

   Answers:

   - A) Incorrect. The seated lean back is a stretch for the shoulders, not the adductors.
   - B) Incorrect. The butterfly stretch is an adductor-only stretch; the straddle stretches the hamstrings and adductors.
   - C) **Correct.** The semi-straddle stretch allows one adductor and hamstring to be stretched at a time.
   - D) Incorrect. The supine knee stretch is a stretch for the hamstring and hip flexor.

DYNAMIC STRETCHING EXERCISES

Dynamic stretching exercises use force production and body momentum to activate a full range of motion and are ideal for warming up the body parts about to be used during a workout.

Arm Swings

Muscles Targeted: shoulders, upper and mid back, and chest

In neutral body position, lift straight arms with bladed fingers laterally. Swing arms in front of body so they crisscross in front of the body, allowing the momentum of the swings to be strong but controlled.

Lunge Walk

Muscles Targeted: glutes, hamstrings, hip flexors, and quadriceps

From a neutral stance, step one leg out, bending both knees at 90 degrees; front foot should be firmly on the floor. Using the heel of the front foot, lift the body up while driving the back leg forward to change lead legs. Torso should remain tall the entire time, do not lean forward.

Walking Knee Lift

Muscles Targeted: glutes, hamstrings, hip flexors, and quadriceps

From a neutral stance, step one leg out; bending both knees at 90 degrees, front foot should be firmly on the floor. Using the heel of the front foot, lift the body up while driving the knee of the back leg forward, changing lead legs. Torso should remain tall the entire time; do not lean forward.

Forward Lunge with Elbow Instep

Muscles Targeted: hip flexors and glutes, spine, and chest

From a tall kneeling position with both knees on ground, bring one foot forward so it is completely flat and lift the back knee off the ground. Lift the body with the opposite palm on the same plane as the front leg. Feel the opposite hip begin to stretch. Drive the elbow on the same side of the lunged leg into the instep, intensifying the glute stretch. Then, extend that arm overhead, and open the body toward the bent knee. If the heel begins to come off the ground while lunging, pull the foot further away from the body. Continue the elbow instep to the arm extension for a set amount of time or repetitions. Switch sides.

Figure 4.22. Forward Lunge with Elbow Instep

Heel-to-Toe Walk

Muscles Targeted: core, coordination, and balance

From a neutral stance, bring one heel in line with toe of the opposite foot, maintaining control and balance while stepping the back foot into the front position.

Walking Over and Under

Muscles Targeted: hip flexors, glutes, and core

From a neutral stance, drive one knee up and circle around with an exterior rotation, followed by the other; this knee should be interiorly rotating. Then, drop the initiating leg into a lateral lunge by sitting into one leg with heel of the bent leg taking the weight, while keeping the other leg straight. The torso should be straight; do not let the shoulders fall forward while in the lateral lunge position. Change lead legs and repeat the entire sequence.

Figure 4.23. Walking Over and Under

Inverted Hamstring

Muscles Targeted: core, hamstrings, quadriceps, glutes, and hip flexors

From a neutral stance, extend the arms laterally and hold torso tight. Press the weight of the body into one heel, keeping the knee of the standing leg soft; the other leg is extended slightly behind the body. Bend at the hip while

Figure 4.24. Inverted Hamstring

lifting the extended leg straight behind the body, ending in a flat bent-over stance. Maintaining a tight core and still pressing through the heel of the standing leg, hinge the body back up to standing. Switch legs and repeat.

Straight-Leg March

Muscles Targeted: hip flexors, core, and hamstrings

From a neutral stance, keeping the hips and shoulders square, lift a flexed foot to chest level, reaching the fingers of the opposite hand to toe. Lower with control. Do not allow the standing knee to bend or the torso to lean forward. This stretch can be performed either alternating the leg lift or completing a set of repetitions on one leg before going to the other.

Figure 4.25. Straight-Leg March

PRACTICE QUESTIONS

1. When would one use a dynamic stretch in the warm-up protocol?
    - **A)** as the first part of the warm-up protocol
    - **B)** before static stretching
    - **C)** only with advanced clients
    - **D)** as the last part of the warm-up protocol

    Answers:
    - A) Incorrect. A dynamic stretch is the last part of the warm-up.
    - B) Incorrect. Dynamic stretches come after static stretching.
    - C) Incorrect. A dynamic stretch is appropriate for all fitness levels.
    - **D) Correct.** A dynamic stretch is the last part of the warm-up. These stretches more intensely target the muscle groups used in the exercise routine than the general cardio warm-up does.

2. What type of dynamic stretch would be ideal for an upper body workout?
    - **A)** arm swings
    - **B)** lunge walk
    - **C)** inverted hamstring
    - **D)** walking over and under

    Answers:
    - **A) Correct.** Arm swings target the chest, back, shoulders, and arms.
    - B) Incorrect. Lunge walks are lower-body intensive.

C) Incorrect. The inverted hamstring stretch targets the lower body and core.

D) Incorrect. Walking over and under targets the lower body and primes the legs for lateral movement.

PNF Stretching Exercises (Proprioceptive Neuromuscular Facilitation)

PNF stretching exercises are an assisted stretching technique typically used in clinical or athletic environments. These stretches utilize a combination of static stretching and isometric contraction to increase range of motion and aid in muscle rehabilitation, while keeping the injury risk low. This technique is beneficial for increasing range of motion quickly. While some physical therapists may use different methods of stretching and contracting combinations, the common Hold-Relax PNF stretching protocol follows this sequence:

+ The stretcher takes the muscle to the end of its initial range of motion for 20 – 30 seconds.
+ The client contracts the muscle being stretched for 7 – 15 seconds, pushing with 20 percent effort against the person holding the tightened limb, allowing for the autogenic inhibition of the muscle to activate, decreasing its resistance to a new range of motion.
+ The stretcher begins passive (no contraction) or active (slight contraction) introduction to the muscle's new range of motion.
+ The client statically holds limb in new position for 20 – 30 seconds.
+ Repeat three times.

Hold one leg straight with one arm while pressing the client's foot into dorsiflexion with the hand. Use the wrist and forearm to bend the client's toes. Place the knee on the client's other leg to ensure that both hips are on the floor. After the position is established, hold it at the peak range of flexion for 30 seconds. Then, instruct the client to press the flexed foot against the pressure using 20 percent effort (be sure to counter the force) and continue this for 7 – 15 seconds. Instruct the client to relax as a new range of motion is established. Hold this static stretch for 20 – 30 seconds. Switch legs and repeat.

Figure 4.26. PNF Gastrocnemius (Calf) Stretch

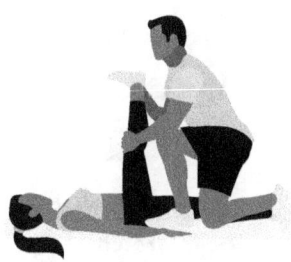

Figure 4.27. PNF Hamstring Stretch

Hold the client's leg straight with one hand on the knee or above. Hold the client's ankle with the other hand, and slowly guide the leg forward until the stretcher reaches her peak range of flexion. Hold for 30 seconds. Be sure both hips are on the floor. Then, instruct the client to press her flexed leg against the pressure using 20 percent of her effort (be sure to counter the force); continue this for 7 – 15 seconds. Instruct her to relax while a new range of motion is established. Hold this for 20 – 30 seconds. Switch legs and repeat.

Kneeling next to the client, place one hand on the small of her back while pulling her leg toward her glutes by the ankle. Be sure that her hips remain on the floor. Hold her leg at peak range of motion for 30 seconds. Then, instruct her to press her flexed leg against the pressure using 20 percent of her effort (be sure to counter the force); continue this for 7 – 15 seconds. Instruct her to relax while a new range of motion is established. Hold this for 20 – 30 seconds. Switch legs and repeat.

While kneeling next to the client, have the client bend his knee. Holding his leg up by the knee, guide the leg by the ankle toward his navel. Be sure his hips remain on the floor; anchor his body by placing a knee on his straight leg if necessary. Hold his leg at peak range of motion for 30 seconds. Then, instruct him to press his leg against the pressure using 20 percent of his effort. Be sure to counter the force, and continue this for 7 – 15 seconds. Instruct the client to relax while a new range of motion is established. Hold this for 20 – 30 seconds. Switch legs and repeat.

Figure 4.28. PNF Piriformis Stretch

Figure 4.29. PNF Biceps Femoris Stretch

Have the client lift his leg straight up from a supine position. Holding the leg behind the knee to keep it straight, grab his foot and guide the leg across the body to his peak range of motion. Hold for 30 seconds, ensuring his hips remain on the floor. Then, instruct him to press his flexed leg against the pressure using 20 percent of his effort. Be sure to counter the force, and continue this for 7 – 15 seconds. Instruct the client to relax while a new range of motion is established. Hold this for 20 – 30 seconds. Switch legs and repeat.

From a supine position, have the client point her foot. Anchor her leg by placing one hand above her knee. Press on the top of the foot. Hold for 30 seconds at peak range of motion, ensuring her hips remain on the floor or table. Then, instruct the client to press her pointed foot into dorsiflexion against the pressure using 20 percent of her effort. Be sure to counter the force, and continue this for 7 – 15 seconds. Instruct them to relax while a new range of motion is established. Hold this for 20 – 30 seconds. Switch legs and repeat.

From a tall seated position, have the client place his hands behind his head. Place hands on the client's elbows and put one knee into his back, leaning his body against it. Pull the client's elbows toward each other until reaching peak range of motion. Hold for 30 seconds. Then, instruct the client to pull his elbows in the opposite direction using 20 percent of his effort. Be sure to counter his force, and continue this for 7 – 15 seconds. Instruct him to relax while a new range of motion is established. Hold this for 20 – 30 seconds.

Figure 4.30. PNF Chest Stretch

From a supine position on a bench or bed, have the client lift her arm straight overhead. Hold the arm by the elbow and wrist, keeping it straight. Press the arm down and toward the body until peak range of motion is established. Make sure her shoulders stay square on the bed or bench. Then, instruct the client to press her arm against the pressure using 20 percent of her effort. Be sure to counter her force; continue this for 7 – 15 seconds. Instruct the client to relax while a new range of motion is established. Hold this for 20 – 30 seconds. Switch arms and repeat.

Resistance Training

Strength training, a type of exercise that recruits muscle growth through resistance, provides exponential health benefits to the body by increasing bone, tendon, and ligament strength, as well as improving metabolism and increasing cardiac health. Effective resistance programs should include a progressive system allowing for the body to build strength from a solid foundation, with proper form and core strength.

The first step, **stabilization**, focuses on building strength through core training, controlled instability, lighter loads and higher rep counts; focusing on decreasing body fat; and improving muscle endurance.

The next step, **strength**, focuses less on stability training and more on **prime mover** strength training through increased weight load and **synergistic** muscle group recruitment. One will put more emphasis on building lean body mass and joint strength by lifting heavier loads with more sets and less reps.

The final step, **power**, puts the emphasis on muscle speed and strength/force production. Instead of just lifting heavy loads with a few reps, the program should incorporate **supersets** of lighter, explosive exercises with a higher rep count. This will challenge the muscles to work speed and strength together.

Resistance training programs can be as varied as the health and fitness professional desires. With a plethora of body weight exercises, weight machines, free weights, kettlebells, and functional equipment (for example, sandbags, stability balls, suspension trainers, and resistance tubing/bands), one can create endless combinations to help clients in any tier of their progressive system.

PRACTICE QUESTIONS

1. In the power tier of resistance training, what should be the primary focus of an exercise regimen?

    A) fat loss

    B) force production

    C) proper form

    D) core strength

Answers:

A) Incorrect. This is a prime focus of stabilization training.

B) Correct. Increasing force production in prime movers is the focus of power training.

C) Incorrect. Feedback on proper form is more of a focus in stability training, even though form is always a factor in strength training.

D) Incorrect. Building core strength is mostly focused on in stabilization training.

2. What is a physiological benefit of resistance training?
   A) increased flexibility
   B) healthy skin
   C) increased metabolism
   D) longer stride

Answers:

A) Incorrect. This is a benefit of stretching.

B) Incorrect. This is a benefit of proper nutrition.

C) Correct. Building lean mass through resistance training allows for more caloric expenditure as muscles burn more calories than fat.

D) Incorrect. Speed, agility, and quickness training attribute to a longer stride.

Resistance Machines

Cam and pulley machines use a combination of the body's concentric and eccentric force, gravity, friction from the pulleys, and weight loaded to dictate the speed of the machines and range of motion. Iron weights are loaded on the machine either by moving a pin or loading a plate weight, to create resistance. Cam machines help lock the position of the body in place so one can isolate specific muscle groups, which is beneficial to improving form. Pulley machines allow the body to activate secondary muscle groups because the user must use more of their body to maintain proper form.

Air and hydraulic machines provide a fixed amount of resistance through a specific range of motion, so no matter how fast you move, the resistance stays the same. These machines provide a smoother range of motion for the user but don't typically offer a varied resistance level.

Suspension Training allows users to leverage their own body weight for resistance to focus on more core activation and balance training while targeting other muscle groups. While body weight limits strength production, suspension training offers a very efficient training technique for increasing neuromuscular efficiency, tendon strength, and flexibility.

Shoulder Press

Primary Muscles Targeted: **medial** and **anterior deltoids** (top and front shoulders)

Machine Set: Seat position should allow for full foot contact.

Body Position: Back and shoulders should be firmly pressed into the back support. Hands should have a loose **pronated, hook** grip.

Starting Position: Elbows bent to rib cage.

One Repetition: Using palms, press arms into straight position, exhale on exertion, and inhale controlling arms back to starting position.

Triceps Pushdown

Primary Muscle Targeted: triceps

Machine Set: Standing in front of the cable handle, move the pulley to a notch on the machine that allows the handle to hang at shoulder height. Use a rope, straight bar, or V-bar handle depending on availability.

Body Position: Stand in a neutral position, a bent arm's length from the machine. Draw the navel to the spine and keep knees soft to ensure core activation.

Starting Position: Hands should have a **neutral** grip (for rope or V-bar) or pronated grip (straight bar). Elbows should be pinned to rib cage.

One Repetition: Hinging only from the elbows, pull the handle down to the pelvis. Exhale on exertion. Inhale, controlling the arm movement back to starting.

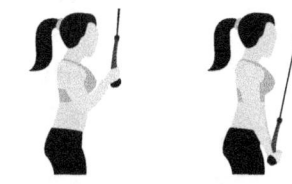

Figure 4.31. Triceps Pushdown

Pec Deck

Primary Muscle Targeted: pectorals (chest)

Machine Set: Seat position should allow for full foot contact.

Body Position: Back and shoulders should be firmly pressed into the back support. Hands have a pronated grip, with forearms pressed into pads.

Starting Position: Elbows are at 90 degrees; arms are open.

One Repetition: Pull arms to meet at centerline of the body. Exhale on exertion. Inhale, controlling arms back to starting position.

Vertical Chest Press

Primary Muscle Targeted: pectorals (chest)

Machine Set: Seat position should allow the full foot to rest on the foot pad. Position handles so they are slightly in front of the chest and shoulders.

Advanced users can position handles so they are in line with the chest and shoulders for greater range of motion.

Body Position: Back and shoulders should be firmly pressed into the back support. Hands should have a pronated grip.

Starting Position: Elbows are at 90 degrees. Hands are in line with the shoulders.

One Repetition: Press the palms into the handle and straighten the arms. Exhale on exertion. Inhale, controlling arms back to starting position.

Abdominal Crunch

Primary Muscles Targeted: transversus and rectus abdominis

Machine Set: Seat position should allow for knees to be bent at 90 degrees and for elbows to rest on the pads.

Body Position: The back, shoulders, and head should be pressed into the back support. Hands should have a neutral grip.

Starting Position: The body should be rested against the machine, with knees bent.

One Repetition: Using upper body, pull elbows toward knees; exhale on exertion. Inhale, controlling torso back to starting position.

Lateral Pulldown

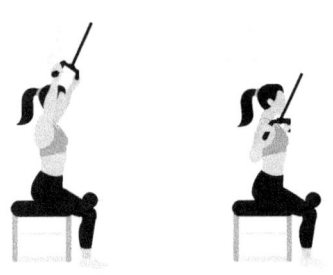

Figure 4.32. Lateral Pulldown

Primary Muscles Targeted: latissimus dorsi (large back muscles) and **posterior deltoids** (rear shoulder)

Machine Set: The seat position should allow the full foot to rest on the foot pad. Position the leg roll to keep the legs and buttocks wedged between it and the seat.

Body Position: The upper body should be tall, with the crown of head toward the ceiling. Grab the pulldown bar with a pronated grip.

Starting Position: Keep elbows extended, shoulders stretched overhead, and hands slightly wider than shoulder-width apart.

One Repetition: Pull bar down, bringing elbows toward the rib cage; exhale on exertion. Inhale, controlling arms back to starting position.

Seated Row

Primary Muscles Targeted: latissimus dorsi, rhomboids (mid back)

Machine Set: Seat position should allow for full foot on footrest. Set chest pad so the arms are fully extended in starting position.

Body Position: Upper body should be tall, crown of head toward the ceiling. Grab handles with a neutral grip. Some machines do have a supinated grip option. That will primarily target the rhomboids and posterior deltoids.

Starting Position: Arms extended forward, feeling a stretch through back.

One Repetition: Pull arms toward chest, bringing elbows past the rib cage; exhale on exertion. Inhale, controlling arms back to starting position.

Low Pulley Seated Row

Primary Muscles Targeted: erector spinae, core latissimus dorsi, rhomboids (mid back), and posterior deltoids

Machine Set: Sit on bench so knees are slightly bent and arms are fully extended in starting position.

Body Position: Upper body should be tall, with the crown of the head toward the ceiling. Grab handles with a neutral grip. There is no chest support on the pulley machine, forcing the core to activate and maintain straight posture.

Starting Position: Arms are extended forward; the user feels a stretch and activation through the entire back.

One Repetition: Pull arms toward the chest, bringing elbows past the rib cage; exhale on exertion. Inhale, controlling arms back to starting position. DO NOT hinge at the hips. The back should say straight; only the arms move.

Hip Sled (Leg Press)

Primary Muscles Targeted: glutes (buttocks), quadriceps (front of legs), hamstrings (back of legs)

Machine Set: Do not load the machine with weight until the foot plate is set. Typically, there is a handle that one rotates out, moving the plate rests. There is a position for shorter legs and one for longer legs. Use the position where knees are straight. Secure the safety handle and load the machine.

Body Position: Lower back, shoulders, and head should be pressed into backrest. Grab side handles to maintain body position while legs are moving.

Starting Position: Knees are extended and slightly soft. Heels are pressed into the foot plate and legs are hip-width apart. The user starts in power position.

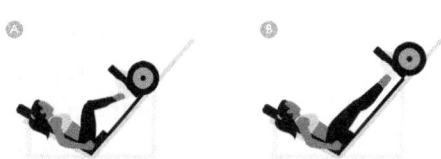

Figure 4.33. Hip Sled (Leg Press)

One Repetition: Use toes to slightly lift the plate to remove safety. Now legs are taking the weight. Inhale, controlling the foot plate. Keep weight in heels, allowing knees to bend. The hamstrings and glutes should be fully extended. Using the heels, press the legs back to starting position, exhale on exertion. DO NOT lock knees when moving legs back to starting position.

Seated Leg Extension

Primary Muscle Targeted: quadriceps

Machine Set: Position the backrest so the backs of the knees are aligned with the front of the seat. Position the foot roll so it rests where the top of the foot and ankle meet.

Body Position: Lower back is pressed against the backrest; hands are either resting on the legs or gripping the handles on the side of the machine. Make sure hips do not lift off the seat while working. If this happens, lower the weight.

Starting Position: Feet are flexed and firmly holding onto the foot roll.

One Repetition: Keeping feet flexed, fully extend the leg; exhale on exertion. Inhale while slowly lowering the legs back to starting position.

Seated Leg Curl

Primary Muscle Targeted: hamstrings

Machine Set: Position backrest so the leg roll rests right above the knees or immediately below them, depending on user comfort. Position the foot roll so it rests right above the foot, on the Achilles tendon, or right under the calf.

Body Position: The lower back is pressed against the backrest; hands are either resting on the leg roll or gripping the handles on the side of the machine. Make sure the hips do not lift off the seat while working. If this happens, lower the weight.

Starting Position: Feet are flexed, resting on the foot roll.

One Repetition: Keeping feet flexed, flex the legs, fully bending the knees; exhale on exertion. Inhale while slowly lifting the legs back to starting position.

Standing Calf Raise

Primary Muscle Targeted: gastrocnemius (calves)

Machine Set: Typically no settings are required.

Body Position: Nestle body between the footrest and shoulder pads; position the balls of the feet hip-width apart on the rest. Keep the body in a neutral standing position. Grab handles with a pronated grip.

Starting Position: Allow the heels to drop below the footrest, feeling a stretch in the calves.

One Repetition: Point toes; exhale on exertion. Inhale, slowly lowering heels back to starting position.

Seated Calf Raise

Primary Muscle Targeted: gastrocnemius

Machine Set: Typically no settings are required.

Body Position: Use the safety handle to lift the load up, while wedging the quadriceps under the leg pad.

Starting Position: The balls of the feet are resting on the foot pads. Allow the heels to drop below the foot pads, feeling a stretch in the calves.

One Repetition: Release safety, allowing calves to take the weight. Point toes, exhale on exertion. Inhale, slowly lowering heels back to starting position.

PRACTICE QUESTIONS

1. What kind of training allows users to leverage their body weight to target muscle groups while working the core?

    A) plyometrics
    B) balance
    C) suspension
    D) cardiovascular

    Answers:

    A) Incorrect. Plyometrics uses explosive movements to target muscle groups and core.
    B) Incorrect. Balance increases proprioception while building core strength.
    C) **Correct.** Suspension training allows the user to leverage his or her own body weight at different angles to target muscle groups while using the core as well.
    D) Incorrect. Load-bearing activities are not considered cardiovascular training.

2. Cam machines are considered what type of machine?

    A) hydraulic machine
    B) cardiovascular machine
    C) friction machine
    D) air machine

    Answers:

    A) Incorrect. Hydraulic machines use compressed air or water to create resistance.
    B) Incorrect. Cardio machines use incline or electronic resistance.
    C) **Correct.** Cam machines use weight, pulley friction, and gravity to create resistance.
    D) Incorrect. These machines use air only to create resistance.

FREE WEIGHT TRAINING

Like weight machines, free weights use gravity to force the body into concentric and eccentric motion to counteract and control the weight. Free weights typically are considered dumbbells of a specific weight and barbells where weight can be added. However, kettlebells, sandbags, and resistance tubes are becoming increasingly popular functional fitness tools because of their versatility and power maneuvers.

Exercises

Barbell Biceps Curl

Primary Muscle Targeted: biceps brachii

Starting Position: Maintaining a neutral body alignment, keep the elbows close to the body, the arms extended, and a supinated grip on the barbell. Do not lock the knees.

One Repetition: Curl the barbell to the shoulders; exhale on exertion. Inhale while extending arms, with control, back to starting position.

Hammer Curl

Primary Muscle Targeted: biceps brachii

Starting Position: Neutral body alignment, elbows close to body, neutral grip with dumbbells, arms extended at sides. Do not lock the knees.

One Repetition: Curl dumbbells to shoulders, keeping elbows at 90 degrees; exhale on exertion. Inhale while extending arms, with control, back to starting position.

Figure 4.34. Hammer Curl

Lateral Shoulder Raise

Primary Muscles Targeted: medial deltoids, trapezius (neck muscles)

Starting Position: Neutral body alignment, arms extended, holding dumbbells with neutral grip. Do not lock the knees.

One Repetition: Raise arms laterally to shoulder level, keeping the elbow soft; exhale on exertion. Inhale while extending arms, with control, back to starting position.

Lying Barbell Triceps Extension

Primary Muscle Targeted: triceps

Starting Position: Lie down on bench, so head, neck, and shoulders are supported. Feet are flat on the floor. Lower back should be pressed into bench. Start in power position. Arms are extended straight from chest, holding the barbell with a pronated grip. Barbell should be in line with forehead.

One Repetition: Hinging only from the elbows, inhale, lowering the barbell with control just above the head. Exhale on the lift back to starting position.

Flat Barbell Bench Press

Primary Muscles Targeted: pectorals and anterior deltoids

Starting Position: Lay down on bench so that head, neck, and shoulders are supported and feet are flat on the floor. The lower back should be pressed into the bench, and the forehead should be in line with the barbell while resting on the supporting rack. Grip the bar with a pronated grip while the bar is still on the rack; hands are a little wider than shoulder-width apart.

One Repetition: Push palms into barbell, releasing it from the rack, bringing the bar in line with the chest. In power position, inhale, lowering the bar with control until it is hovering just above the chest. Exhale on exertion, bringing the barbell back to starting position.

Dumbbell Bench Press

Primary Muscles Targeted: pectorals and anterior deltoids

Starting Position: Lay down on bench, so head, neck, and shoulders are supported and feet are flat on the floor. The lower back should be pressed into bench and elbows bent, holding the dumbbells with a pronated grip.

One Repetition: Push arms straight up from chest; exhale on exertion. Do not lock elbows, allowing the chest to stay contracted. Inhale, lowering the dumbbells, with control back to starting position. Holding the dumbbells with a neutral grip will protect injured or problematic shoulders. It also targets the triceps.

Wrist Curl

Primary Muscle Targeted: forearm

Starting Position: While seated on a bench, keep shoulders back and back straight. Using a supinated grip on the barbell, lean torso forward so the elbows are resting on the knees and the wrists are straight.

Figure 4.35. Wrist Curl

One Repetition: Hinging only at the wrists, curl palms toward shoulders, exhale on exertion. Inhale, slowly bringing the wrists back to starting position.

Wrist Extension

Primary Muscle Targeted: forearm

Starting Position: While seated on a bench, keep shoulders back and back straight. Using a pronated grip on the dumbbells, lean torso forward so elbows are resting on the knees and wrists are relaxed.

Figure 4.36. Wrist Extension

One Repetition: Hinging only at the wrists, curl tops of hands toward shoulders; exhale on exertion. Inhale, slowly bringing the wrists back to starting position.

Flat Dumbbell Fly

Primary Muscles Targeted: pectorals and medial deltoids

Starting Position: Lay down on the bench so that the head, neck, and shoulders are supported and feet are flat on the floor. The lower back should be pressed into the bench. Holding the dumbbells with a neutral grip, keep arms straight out from chest. Elbows stay slightly soft.

Figure 4.37. Flat Dumbbell Fly

One Repetition: Lower the arms to side with control feeling the pectorals stretch at the bottom of the extension, inhaling the whole time. Exhale while bringing the arms back to starting position, contracting the pectorals.

Incline Dumbbell Fly

Primary Muscles Targeted: pectorals and medial deltoids

Starting Position: Position the adjustable bench to a 30 – 45 degree incline. Lay down on the bench so that the head, neck, and shoulders are supported and the feet are flat on the floor. The lower back should be pressed into the bench. Holding the dumbbells with a neutral grip, keep the arms straight out from the chest. Elbows stay slightly soft.

One Repetition: Lower the arms to the side with control, feeling the pectorals stretch at the bottom of the extension. Inhale throughout the entire movement. Exhale while bringing the arms back to the starting position, contracting the pectorals.

Changing the incline of the bench targets the pectoralis major, which helps define the upper part of the chest. The pectoralis minor is located under the pectoralis major and is considered a stabilizer. It can be targeted by declining the bench.

Bent-Over Row

Primary Muscles Targeted: rhomboids, posterior deltoids, erector spinae

Starting Position: Stand in a neutral position, holding the barbell with a pronated, hook grip. Then, hinge at the hips, with knees slightly bent, bringing the torso as close to parallel as possible while maintaining a straight back and shoulders. Arms should be hanging straight down and the navel is drawn in, activating and supporting the core.

Figure 4.38. Bent-Over Row

 Holding the barbell with a supinated grip will target the latissimus dorsi and biceps.

One Repetition: Drive the elbows up, past the rib cage, squeezing the shoulder blades together and activating the core; exhale on exertion. Lower the arms with control back to starting position; inhale in extension.

One-Arm Dumbbell Row

Primary Muscles Targeted: latissimus dorsi (large back muscles) and posterior deltoid

Starting Position: Place one knee and one palm on a bench for support. Arm is extended, allowing the shoulder to release. Hold the dumbbell with a neutral grip.

Alternately, instead of bending, more experienced athletes may stagger the feet and hinge the torso over the front leg. They place one hand on the quadriceps for support or maintain core integrity with no support.

One Repetition: Drive the elbow up past the rib cage, squeezing the shoulder blade at the top of the move; exhale on exertion. Lower the arms with control back to starting position; inhale in extension. Do not allow the torso to rotate; the latissimus dorsi must do the work.

Back Loaded Squat

Primary Muscles Targeted: glutes, hamstrings, quadriceps and erector spinae

Starting Position: Load barbell at shoulder level using a squat rack. Stand in a neutral position in front of the rack, and back up until the barbell is resting on the upper back. Hold the barbell with a wide, pronated, hook grip. Legs should be wider than hip-width apart; toes face forward.

One Repetition: Once positioning is secure, the user will take the load onto the back and walk forward, clearing the rack. Inhale and slowly sit back as though sitting down onto a bench, sinking into the heels, eyes gazing forward, while maintaining a straight back. Do not allow the shoulders or torso to come forward onto quadriceps. Exhale while powering back up into a standing position, keeping the weight of the body in the heels. Do not lock the knees upon standing or push the pelvis forward.

Front Load Squat

Primary Muscles Targeted: glutes, hamstrings, quadriceps, and erector spinae

Starting Position: Load barbell at shoulder level using a squat rack. Stand in a neutral position in front of the rack. Walk toward the barbell and place

Figure 4.39. Front Load Squat

hands palms up, using the clean grip. Hands are shoulder-width apart, legs are hip-width apart, and toes face forward.

One Repetition: Once positioning is secure, the user will take the load onto the shoulders and walk backward, clearing the rack. Inhale and slowly sit back as though sitting down onto a bench, sinking into the heels, eyes gazing forward, while maintaining a straight back. Do not allow the shoulders or torso to come forward onto front of the legs. Exhale while powering back up into a standing position, keeping the weight of the body in the heels. Do not lock the knees upon standing or push the pelvis forward.

Forward Step Lunge

Primary Muscles Targeted: glutes, hamstrings, and quadriceps

Starting Position: Stand in a neutral position, holding dumbbells with a neutral grip at the sides.

One Repetition: Inhale and step one foot forward, allowing the heel to strike the ground. The whole foot should be on the ground; both knees are bent at 90 degrees. Using the heel of the front leg, exhale and push the body back up to standing, making sure to keep the torso tall. Change lead legs and repeat.

Step-Up

Primary Muscles Targeted: glutes, hamstrings, and quadriceps

Starting Position: Stand in a neutral position. Hold the barbell on the upper back with a wide, pronated grip, or hold dumbbells with a neutral grip at the sides. Step one foot up on a box, making sure that the full foot is on the box and that the knee is at a 90-degree angle.

One Repetition: Press the body up to standing on the box, making sure the weight of the body is in the heel of the foot on the box; exhale on exertion. Inhale while lowering the body back down to the floor with control, maintaining tall torso. Change lead legs and repeat.

Good Morning

Primary Muscles Targeted: glutes, hamstrings, latissimus dorsi, and erector spinae

Starting Position: Stand in a neutral position, holding barbell on the upper back with a wide, pronated grip. Legs should be slightly wider than hip-width apart; toes are facing forward.

One Repetition: Once positioning and load are secure, inhale and hinge at hips with control, until a stretch is felt in the hamstrings. Knees should maintain a slight bend. Keep body weight in heels

Figure 4.40. Good Morning

and the back strong and straight. Exhale, pulling the torso back up to starting position.

Deadlift

Primary Muscles Targeted: glutes, hamstrings, latissimus dorsi, and erector spinae

Starting Position: Stand behind the loaded barbell on the floor in a neutral position. Legs should be hip-width apart, toes facing forward and under the barbell. Sitting into the heels, bend the knees until the hands can grip the barbell with a pronated or alternating grip just outside of the knees. Eyes should gaze forward, ensuring a straight back and shoulders.

Figure 4.41. Deadlift

One Repetition: Once positioning and load are secure, push through the heels into standing; keep arms straight, still holding the barbell. Exhale on exertion. Inhale while lowering the weight back to the floor with control, returning to the starting position.

Stiff-Leg Deadlift

Muscles Targeted: glutes, hamstrings, latissimus dorsi, and erector spinae

Starting Position: Stand behind the loaded barbell on the floor in a neutral position. Legs should be hip-width apart; toes are facing forward and under the barbell. Sitting into the heels and maintaining soft knees, hinge the torso forward at hips so that the hands can grip the barbell with a pronated or alternating grip just outside of the knees. Do not bend the knees; the user should feel a stretch in the back of the legs. Eyes should gaze forward, ensuring a straight back and shoulders.

Figure 4.42. Stiff-Leg Deadlift

One Repetition: Once positioning and load are secure, push through the heels and hinge back into standing, keeping arms straight while still holding the barbell. Exhale on exertion. Inhale while lowering the weight back to the floor with control, returning to the starting position.

Romanian Deadlift

Muscles Targeted: erector spinae, latissimus dorsi, rhomboids, hamstrings, glutes, quadriceps, rectus and transversus abdominals, and internal and external obliques.

Starting Position: Set squat rack supports at the hip level and load the bar. Stand behind the bar in a neutral position; legs should be hip-width apart, toes

Figure 4.43. Romanian Deadlift

facing forward, and knees soft. Grab the loaded barbell with a pronated or alternating grip just outside of the knees, keeping arms straight. Clear the rack by stepping back.

One Repetition: Once positioning and load are secure, inhale and sit into the heels while hinging the torso forward at the hips with control. Lower just below the knees, feeling the stretch through the back of the legs. Push up through the heels and hinge back into the starting position. Exhale on exertion.

Seated Barbell Shoulder Press

Primary Muscles Targeted: anterior and medial deltoids

Starting Position: Seated on a bench, keep shoulders and back straight with feet firmly planted on the floor. Hold barbell just below the shoulders (resting on the chest), using a pronated grip. Draw the navel into the spine.

One Repetition: Exhale on exertion, pushing arms straight overhead; do not lock elbows. Inhale while lowering the barbell with control back to starting position.

Holding two dumbbells with a neutral grip is called a *military press*.

Upright Row

Primary Muscles Targeted: anterior and medial deltoids, trapezius (upper back)

Starting Position: With a neutral stance, keeping shoulders and back straight, feet firmly planted on the floor, and knees soft, hold barbell or dumbbells using a pronated grip. Arms are straight and the navel is drawn into the spine.

One Repetition: Exhale on exertion, pulling arms to chest or shoulder level; elbows wing out to the sides and wrists stay straight. Inhale while lowering the barbell with control back to starting position.

For regression, the dumbbell upright row allows the user a wider row, ensuring the wrists do not bend.

Push Press

Primary Muscles Targeted: anterior and medial deltoids, core, glutes, and calves

Starting Position: Load the barbell with a squat rack at chest level. With a neutral stance, keeping the shoulders and back straight, the feet firmly planted on floor, and knees soft, hold the heavy barbell just below the shoulders (resting on the chest), using a pronated grip. Draw the navel into the spine.

One Repetition: Inhale; sit into a shallow squat. Exhale, and explode into a standing position, using the momentum of the lower body to help propel the barbell into an overhead press. Inhale while lowering the barbell with control back to starting position. Repetitions are fast and explosive; this technique is only appropriate for an advanced user.

For regression, see the barbell shoulder press; for progression, see the push jerk (Figure 4.44).

Push Jerk

Primary Muscles Targeted: anterior and medial deltoids, core, glutes, quadriceps, and calves

Starting Position: Load the barbell with a squat rack at chest level. With a neutral stance, keep the shoulders and back straight, the feet firmly planted on floor, and knees soft. Rest the heavy barbell on the shoulders, using a pronated grip at shoulder-width. Draw the navel into the spine.

Figure 4.44. Push Jerk

One Repetition: Inhale; sit into a shallow squat keeping the weight in the toes. Exhale, and explode into a standing position, using the momentum of the lower body to help propel the barbell into an overhead press. Drop into a shallow squat and hold the extended arms briefly into a snatch grip. Inhale; power back into the toes. While controlling the barbell, drop back to the starting position. Repetitions are fast and explosive; this technique is only appropriate for an advanced user.

For regression, see the push press; for progression, see the power clean (Figure 4.45).

Power Clean

Primary Muscles Targeted: glutes, quadriceps, hamstrings, calves, latissimus dorsi, core, and trapezius

Starting Position: Inhale. Stand behind the loaded barbell on the floor in neutral position. The legs should be hip-width apart, with the toes facing forward and under the barbell. Sitting into the heels, bend the knees until the hands can grip the barbell with a pronated grip just outside of the knees. The eyes should gaze forward. The navel should be drawn into the spine, ensuring a straight back and shoulders.

Figure 4.45. Power Clean

One Repetition: Once positioning and load are secure, exhale and explode through the toes into standing position using the momentum of the lower body to help propel the barbell into an upright row. Allowing the hands to switch from a pronated grip to a clean grip, catch the barbell onto the shoulders, squatting under the barbell. Stand. Inhale and exhale pushing the barbell off the shoulders into a hanging pronated grip and back to starting position. Repetitions are explosive; this technique is only meant for an advanced user.

For regression, see upright row; for progression, see power snatch (Figure 4.46).

Power Snatch

Primary Muscles Targeted: glutes, quadriceps, hamstrings, calves, latissimus dorsi, core, trapezius, and deltoids

Figure 4.46. Power Snatch

Starting Position: Inhale. Stand behind loaded barbell on the floor in a neutral position. The legs should be hip-width apart, with toes facing forward and under the barbell. Sitting into the heels, bend the knees until the hands can grip the barbell with a pronated grip just outside of the knees. Eyes should gaze forward. The navel stays drawn into the spine, ensuring a straight back and shoulders.

> **?** During the stabilization level of strength training, one can add proprioceptive moments to many open kinetic chain exercises, such a single leg stand while the client does a bicep curl. Can you think of another way to increase a client's proprioception?

One Repetition: Once positioning and load are secure, exhale and explode through the toes into standing using the momentum of the lower body to help propel the arms straight into a snatch grip. Transition quickly from an upright row into a shoulder press, squatting under the barbell and moving into standing. Arms stick the overhead position briefly. Inhale and exhale dropping the barbell with control into a hanging pronated grip and back to starting position. Repetitions are explosive; this technique is only meant for an advanced user.

For regression, see power clean (figure 4.45). For progression, add a squat to the power snatch.

PRACTICE QUESTIONS

1. What is a progression of a Romanian deadlift?
   - **A)** push jerk
   - **B)** upright row
   - **C)** still-leg deadlift
   - **D)** inverted hamstring

Answers:

- A) Incorrect. While the push jerk is considered a more advanced move, it is not the direct progression.
- B) Incorrect. The upright row targets the shoulders and trapezius, not the lower body.
- **C) Correct.** The still-leg deadlift is the next progression, as the user would use the full range of motion allowing the barbell to go all the way to the floor, as opposed to stopping mid-shin.
- D) Incorrect. The inverted hamstring would be a rather dynamic stretch for the Romanian deadlift.

2. A push press would be a progression for:
    - **A)** triceps extension
    - **B)** biceps barbell curl
    - **C)** step up
    - **D)** barbell shoulder press

Answers:

- A) Incorrect. The primary mover for the triceps extension is the triceps; the exercise does not share a similar movement pattern with the push press.
- B) Incorrect. The primary mover for the biceps barbell curl is the biceps; the exercise does not share a similar movement pattern with the push press.
- C) Incorrect. The primary mover for the step up is the lower body; the exercise does not share a similar movement pattern with the push press.
- **D) Correct.** The barbell shoulder press is the same move as the push press, except it does not require a shallow squat to initiate a forced repetition. The primary movers are the shoulders, as in the push press.

SPOTTING

Supporting another person to ensure safety while he or she lifts a heavy weight is a practice called spotting. Only allow spotting if a user is not sacrificing form to lift the weight or if the spotter is needed to help support the weight. The spotter should not be lifting a substantial portion of the weight. The number of spotters needed for an exercise varies depending on the situation or weight. Structured exercises, like barbell squats and deadlifts, can use up to three spotters, while bench presses and free weight exercises are more appropriate for one spotter.

General body placement for a spotter should contain a wide **stagger stance** where one foot is in front of the other one; knees are soft to ensure a quick reaction in case the lifter goes into **failure**.

Spotting a Bench Press: The spotter should be at the head of the bench, behind the lifter. Use an alternating grip in between the lifter's grip. Unless the spotter needs to take the bulk of the weight because of failure, fingertips or open palms should be the only point of contact with the bar. Spotters are there only to support form or to implement **forced repetitions**.

 If the spotter is consistently taking on a substantial portion of the weight, the load is far beyond the lifter's capability, and therefore they should reduce the weight.

Spotting a Dumbbell Press: Spotting a dumbbell press, either seated or laying down, is similar to spotting a bench press. The key difference is the spotter's hand placement, since one is dealing with two dumbbells and not one barbell. Hands should hover just under the lifter's wrists, palms facing up to reduce the risk of weights falling on the lifter. If the spotter needs to aid the lifter, support the arms by holding the wrists; holding the elbows might force the lifter to overextend their elbows inward.

Spotting a Back Loaded Barbell Squat: This exercise can be spotted either with two spotters on either end of the barbell, one spotter behind the lifter, or a combination of the two. Ideally, there should be a person behind the lifter mimicking the squat move with their hands under the armpits to guide and maintain torso integrity, protecting the low back. The spotters on either end of the barbell should face the lifter with a wide stance, hands ready to grab the barbell should the lifter not be able to straighten his or her legs and rerack the bar.

PRACTICE QUESTIONS

1. When is it acceptable to use a spotter?
- **A)** The lifter has poor form and cannot lift the weight.
- **B)** The lifter is using proper form but needs support to complete reps.
- **C)** The lifter has poor form and can lift the weight.
- **D)** The lifter wants a spotter.

Answers:
- A) Incorrect. The lifter should only use a spotter if their form is correct and they should be doing most of the work.
- **B) Correct.** The lifter should be able to maintain core integrity and good form at all times.
- C) Incorrect. Like answer choice A, the lifter should always have correct form first and foremost.
- D) Incorrect. If a lifter doesn't feel secure with the weight lifted, they should not go up in weight.

2. What type of exercise uses a free weight?

A) hydraulic shoulder press

B) air propelled rowing machine

C) plyometric box jump

D) dumbbell bench press

Answers:

A) Incorrect. This is a compressed air or water resisted machine.

B) Incorrect. This is an air propelled machine.

C) Incorrect. This is a body weight exercise

D) **Correct.** Dumbbells are considered free weights.

Core Stability and Balance Training

The muscles that initiate trunk rotation, or waist rotation, are considered the core muscle group, which is the body's center of gravity and starting point for all movement. It controls posture, acceleration, and deceleration of movement and is an integral part of injury prevention. Weak core functionality can be the primary source of most muscle imbalances. A common misconception is that the abdominal muscles solely comprise the core. However, the core's anatomy contains abdominal and hip muscles (**lumbo-pelvic hip complex**) and the **thoracic** and **cervical** spine muscles.

 Proprioception is an individual's ability to sense where his or her body is in space.

Core training goes hand in hand with **balance training**, allowing clients to increase their proprioceptive ability, or sense of where their body is positioned in a space. Even if a person closes his eyes, he will know whether his foot is on the floor or lifted slightly off it. Core training uses controlled instability to build **proprioception** and balance. Standing on one leg or sitting on a stability ball while performing a simple exercise will increase core stabilization and postural strength. Having a client stand on one leg while closing her eyes is a good way to assess her proprioception.

Table 4.1. Types of Muscles

Intrinsic Core Stabilizers	Movement System
Transversus and Rectus Abdominis	Latissimus Dorsi
Internal and External Oblique	Erector Spinae
Lumbar Multifidus	Hip Flexors
Pelvic Floor Muscles	Hip Adductor Complex
Diaphragm	Hip Abductor Complex
Cervical Spine Complex	

Exercises

Plank

Muscles Targeted: movement and postural core systems

Starting Position: Lying **prone** (on the stomach), keep elbows at chest level, palms facing the floor and toes curled under the feet. The head should be an extension of the spine; the navel is drawn in to activate the core.

One Repetition: Inhale and lift the body up from the floor so the toes and forearms are the only points of contact. Hold this position while maintaining a straight spine; do not allow the shoulder blades, hips, or head to sink. Slowly exhale, maintaining a steady breathing pattern throughout the duration of the hold.

For regression, hold the plank from the knees instead of the toes.

Bird Dog

Muscles Targeted: movement and postural core systems

Figure 4.47. Bird Dog

Starting Position: Start in a **quadruped position**, on hands and knees. The hands are positioned directly under the shoulders, and the knees are directly under the hips. Keep the head as an extension of the spine; do not lock the elbows.

One Repetition: Inhale and lift the opposite leg and arm at the same time, testing balance. Exhale and slowly lower the leg and arm. Repeat on the opposite side.

For progression, on the exhalation, slowly draw the elbow and knee together. Inhale back to straight, then lower to starting position.

Bridge

Muscles Targeted: pelvic floor, glutes, and hip flexors

Starting Position: Start in semi-supine position.

One Repetition: Inhale. Exhale, draw the navel into the spine, press the heels into the floor, and lift the hips, squeezing the glutes. Hold briefly. Inhale, lowering the hips slowly back onto the floor.

For progression, extend one leg straight up.

Abdominal Crunch

Muscles Targeted: postural core systems

Starting Position: Start in semi-supine position with fingers laced behind the head to support the neck.

One Repetition: Inhale. Exhale, draw the navel into the spine, and lift the chest toward the knees, making sure the eyes gaze up and the chin stays off the chest. Do not pull on the head for momentum. Hold briefly. Inhale, lowering torso back to the floor with control.

Figure 4.48. Abdominal Crunch

For progression, complete the full sit-up.

Bent Knee Sit-Up

Muscles Targeted: movement and postural core systems

Starting Position: Start in semi-supine position with fingers laced behind the head to support the neck.

One Repetition: Inhale. Exhale, draw the navel into the spine, and lift the elbows to the knees, making sure that the eyes gaze up and the chin stays off of the chest. Do not pull on the head for momentum. Inhale, lowering the torso back onto the floor with control.

For progression, complete the full sit-up with straight legs.

Reverse Crunches

Muscles Targeted: movement and postural core systems

Starting Position: Start in a semi-supine position, with the arms extended at the sides with palms down. Lift bent legs off the ground, keeping the knees bent.

Figure 4.49. Reverse Crunches

One Repetition: Inhale. Exhale, draw the navel into the spine, and lift the hips off the ground, bringing the knees toward the chest. Try not to press the palms into the mat for help. Inhale, slowly lowering the hips back to the floor.

For progression, straighten the legs completely.

Ball Crunches

Muscles Targeted: postural core systems

Starting Position: Start seated on the ball. Walk the body down the ball so the lower back is on the ball. Lower the torso so that a stretch is felt along the abdominals. Lace the fingers behind the head to support the neck.

One Repetition: Inhale. Exhale, draw navel into the spine, and lift chest toward the ceiling until peak contraction, making sure eyes gaze up and chin stays off chest. **Torso should only come to straight. Do not sit all the way up on the ball; do not pull on the head for momentum.** Hold briefly. Inhale, lowering torso back to starting position with control.

For regression, see abdominal crunch (figure 4.48).

Cable Rotations

Muscles Targeted: obliques, erector spinae, and hip flexors

Starting Position: Set the pulley machine to the chest level. Lace the fingers around the handle and face perpendicular to the anchor point. Arms should be fully extended from the chest, while maintaining a neutrally aligned body; feet are wider than hip-distance apart. Walk away from the anchor point until the arms feel a slight tug.

One Repetition: Exhale, draw the navel into the spine, and pivot body away from the anchor point. Make sure the arms stay straight. Hold briefly. Inhale, slowly bringing the torso back to the starting point.

Figure 4.50. Cable Rotations

Soccer Throw

Muscles Targeted: movement and postural core systems and deltoids

Figure 4.51. Soccer Throw

Starting Position: Stand in a neutral position, keeping feet hip-width apart. Hold the medicine ball just overhead, with arms bent.

One Repetition: Inhale, reaching the arms back behind the head as far as possible. Exhale, activating the abdominal wall and stepping one leg forward, throwing the ball forcefully at a target. Be sure to utilize as much of the core musculature as possible when throwing the ball. Retrieve the ball and repeat, changing lead legs.

Rotation Chest Pass

Muscles Targeted: postural and movement core systems, pectorals, triceps, and deltoids

Starting Position: Stand in a neutral position with feet wider than hip-width apart. Turn perpendicular to the wall or a partner, holding the medicine ball at the navel.

One Repetition: Inhale, and pivot the body away from the target as if winding up for a pitch. Exhale; activate the core, and pivot back toward the target, forcefully throwing the ball from chest height toward the target. Be sure

Figure 4.52. Rotation Chest Pass

to utilize as much of the core musculature as possible when throwing the ball. Retrieve the ball and repeat, changing sides.

Medicine Ball Pullover Throw

Muscles Targeted: movement and postural core systems, deltoids, and triceps

Starting Position: Start seated on the ball. Walk the body down the ball so the lower back is on the ball. Lower the torso so a stretch is felt along the abdominals. Hold the medicine ball overhead, keeping arms bent.

One Repetition: Inhale. Exhale; draw the navel into the spine. Lifting the torso with power to a seated position, throw the ball overhead toward the target.

Ball crunches are a good option for regression; alternatively, omit the ball and do the exercise from the floor.

Figure 4.53. Medicine Ball Pullover Throw

Single-Leg Balance

Starting Position: Stand in a neutral position, keeping the crown of the head toward the ceiling.

One Repetition: Inhale. With soft knees, lift one leg off the floor. Shift the body weight into the heel of the standing leg. Exhale slowly while holding the position.

For progression, close the eyes.

Figure 4.54. Single-Leg Balance

Single-Leg Balance and Reach

Starting Position: Stand in a neutral position, keeping the crown of the head toward the ceiling. Inhale. With soft knees, lift one leg off the floor. Shift the body weight into the heel of the standing leg.

One Repetition: Inhale. Straighten the lifted leg in front of body on an exhale. Return to start on an inhale. Reach the lifted leg laterally, bring it back to the starting point, and then move it behind the body. Return to start. Switch legs and repeat the pattern.

For regression, see single-leg balance (figure 4.54).

Single-Leg Windmill

Starting Position: Stand in a neutral position, keeping crown of head toward ceiling; one leg is lifted posteriorly. Shift the body weight to the heel of the standing leg.

One Repetition: Inhale. Exhale, hinging the body with control, parallel to the floor. Reach one hand toward the floor and the other hand toward the ceiling; switch arm positions. Come back to standing, switch legs, and repeat.

For regression, see single-leg deadlift (Figure 4.57).

Figure 4.55. Single-Leg Windmill

> 🔍 A great way to work on balance is to focus the eyes on a point on a wall. Even with rotational moves, find a starting point and a finishing point to focus on!

Single-Leg Squat

Starting Position: Stand in a neutral position, keeping the crown of the head toward the ceiling, hands on the hips, and one leg lifted posteriorly. Shift the body weight to the heel of the standing leg.

One Repetition: Inhale. Exhale, and bend the knee of the standing leg with control, into a shallow squat. Inhale and straighten the leg. Switch sides and repeat.

Figure 4.56. Single-Leg Squat

For regression, see single-leg balance and reach.

Single-Leg Deadlift

Starting Position: Stand in a neutral position. Keep the crown of the head toward the ceiling; arms are extended at the sides, with one leg lifted posteriorly. Make sure back leg is straight. Shift the body weight to the heel of the standing leg.

Figure 4.57. Single-Leg Deadlift

One Repetition: Inhale. Exhale, hinging the body parallel to the floor with control. Reach the opposite arm of the standing leg toward the floor. Pushing through the heel, bring the torso back to standing, switch legs, and repeat.

For regression, see single-leg squat (Figure 4.56).

Lunge to Balance

Starting Position: Stand in a neutral position.

One Repetition: Inhale while stepping one leg out, bending both knees at 90 degrees. The front foot should be placed firmly on the floor. Using the heel of the front foot, exhale and push the body

Figure 4.58. Lunge to Balance

back up to standing, driving that knee up, holding the single-leg stance. Return to start, switch legs, and repeat.

For regression, see single-leg balance and reach.

Single-Leg Box Hop-Up

Starting Position: Stand in a neutral position in front of a short box. Keep the crown of head toward the ceiling and one leg lifted posteriorly. Shift the body weight to the heel of the standing leg.

Figure 4.59. Single-Leg Box Hop-Up

One Repetition: Inhale, while bending the standing leg into a shallow squat. Exhale, activate the core and the glute, and hop off the floor using the arms to help propel the body onto the box, stabilizing the body through the standing leg. Step back down to the floor. Switch legs and repeat.

For regression, step up to balance. Instead of hopping up onto the box, step up onto the box and lift the knee of the leg opposite the standing leg. Maintain the balance position with the knee raised for a few seconds and step back down to the floor. Switch legs and repeat.

Single-Leg Box Hop-Down

Starting Position: Stand in a neutral position on top of a short box. Keep the crown of the head toward the ceiling and one leg lifted posteriorly. Shift the body weight to the heel of the standing leg.

Figure 4.60. Single-Leg Box Hop-Down

One Repetition: Inhale while bending the standing leg into a shallow squat. Exhale, activate the core and the glute and hop off the box. Stabilize the body with the standing leg. Switch legs and repeat.

For regression, step up to balance. Instead of hopping up onto the box, step up onto the box and lift the knee of the leg opposite the standing leg. Maintain the balance position with the knee raised for a few seconds and step back down to the floor. Switch legs and repeat.

Multiplanar Single-Leg Hop

Starting Position: Stand in single-leg balance position. Inhale.

1. Exhale and hop forward, landing on the opposite foot. Stabilize the body on the single leg; inhale. Exhale and hop backward back to starting leg and stabilize the body on that leg; inhale.
2. Exhale and hop to the side on the opposite foot. Stabilize the body on a single leg; inhale. Exhale and hop back to the starting leg while stabilizing the body; inhale.

3. Hop and rotate the body, landing on the opposite foot. Stabilize the body. Hop back to the starting leg, and stabilize the body.

For regression, try lunges without the hop.

PRACTICE QUESTIONS

1. All these muscle groups comprise the core EXCEPT
    - **A)** the hip adductor complex.
    - **B)** the erector spinae.
    - **C)** the biceps brachii.
    - **D)** the internal obliques.

    Answers:

    A) Incorrect. The hip adductor complex is part of the core, as it supports trunk rotation and posture.

    B) Incorrect. The erector spinae is part of the core, as it supports trunk rotation and posture.

    C) Correct. The biceps brachii are the muscles located in the anterior side of the arms.

    D) Incorrect. The internal obliques are part of the core, supporting trunk rotation and posture.

2. Which of the following terms describes an individual's sense of his or her body position in space?
    - **A)** muscle imbalance
    - **B)** proprietary
    - **C)** core control
    - **D)** proprioception

    Answers:

    A) Incorrect. Muscle imbalance is inconsistency in a muscle's length around a joint.

    B) Incorrect. The term *proprietary* relates to the ownership of something.

    C) Incorrect. Core control relates to an individual's ability to control the muscles of the core during an exercise.

    D) Correct. Proprioception describes having a sense of the body and its relationship to the surrounding space; it also refers to the ability to balance.

Speed, Agility, and Quickness

These three components can also be considered reactive training. Adding this type of training to a client's workout regimen is beneficial for both the athlete and everyday person. Speed, agility, and quickness (SAQ) training preps the body and mind to react quickly to everyday scenarios, like playing with a child or walking a dog, as well as training for many different sports and is a great challenge to add to any fitness program. SAQ training can benefit the body by strengthening the connecting tissue of the muscles.

Speed refers to the body's ability to move in one direction as quickly as possible. **Agility** refers to bursts of movement starting, stopping, or changing the direction of the body. **Quickness** is the body's ability to react to a cue that propels the change.

These can be included as cardio training for advanced clients. It takes a great deal of strength, stability, and balance to perform these exercises properly; use caution when adding these exercises to a program to minimize injury risk.

SAQ Exercises

Fast Feet

Fast feet is ideal for a dynamic warm-up. The athlete must stay light on her toes and move from the wide to narrow stance as fast as possible; her arms are pumping, her knees are soft, and she is moving on the balls of the feet. Sets should only last about 30 seconds.

A-Skip

The A-skip is ideal for a dynamic warm-up. Drive one knee up and hop forward, repeating on the opposite leg. Repeat this movement as fast as possible.

Figure 4.61. A-Skip

Cone Drills: 5–10–5 Drill

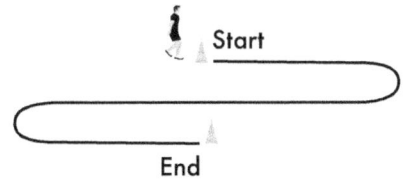

Figure 4.62. 5-10-5 Drill

These cone drills (5–10–5) promote speed, deceleration, and direction change. Two cones should be set 10 yards apart; a third cone is set at the 5-yard marker in between. The athlete starts at the middle cone, runs 5 yards in one direction, 10 yards in the other direction, then 5 yards back to the starting position .

Cone Drills: T-Drill

T-drills promote speed, acceleration, and deceleration; they also enhance rotational and lateral movement. **Shuffles** consist of small lateral hops, and

Exercise Technique 177

backpedaling refers to running backwards. A more complicated shuffle is the **carioca shuffle**, where the athlete crisscrosses their feet forward and back, while moving from side to side.

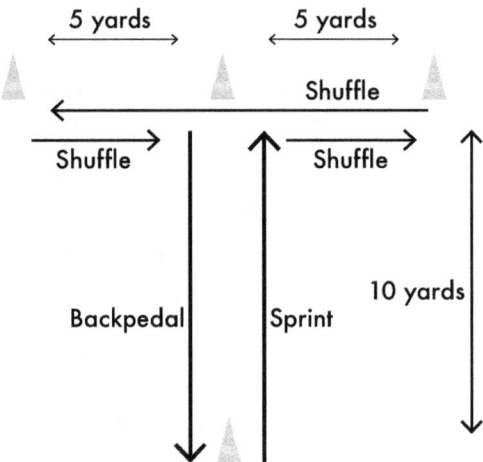

Figure 4.63. T-Drill

Cone Drills: Star Drill

Star drills promote speed, acceleration, deceleration, rotational, and lateral movement. Star drills can be varied by having the athlete change directions quickly from point to point, or he can sprint and backpedal from point to point.

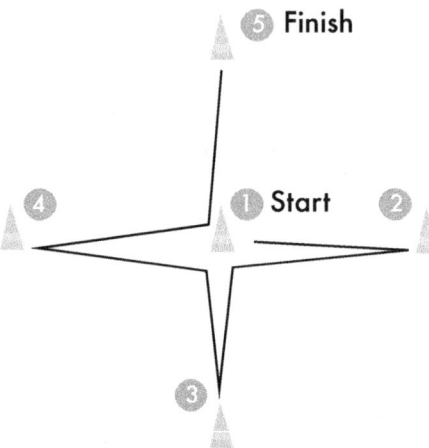

Figure 4.64. Star Drill

 Carioca shuffles are also known as grapevines. Carioca is pronounced *kare-ee-OH-ka*.

Cone Drills: Box Drill

Box drills promote speed, acceleration, and deceleration; they also enhance rotational and lateral movement. Cones should be set 5 yards apart. The athlete makes her way around the cones in a square (box) formation, varying her gait on each leg of the square.

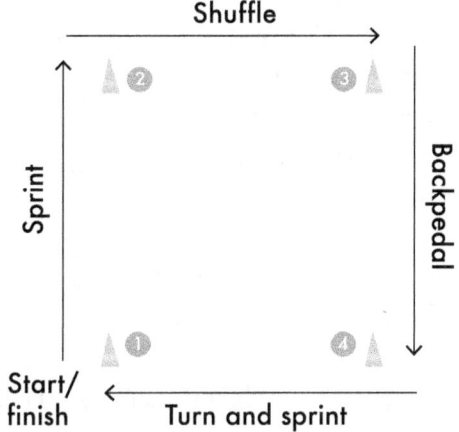

Figure 4.65. Box Drill

Cone Drills: Z-Drill

The Z-drill promotes speed, acceleration, and deceleration; it also enhances rotational and lateral movement. Athletes run in a Z formation around cones set up on a field or court. This drill is intended for the athlete to stay in forward sprint the entire time, cutting directions quickly.

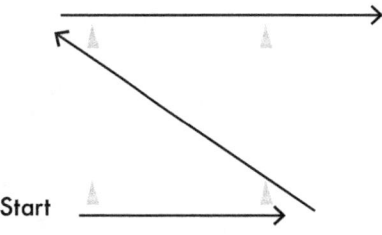

Figure 4.66. Z-Drill

Agility Ladder Drills: Ali Shuffle

The Ali shuffle is useful for lateral movement and footwork training. In this drill, the athlete starts in a staggered stance, using a hop to switch feet and move laterally through the pattern.

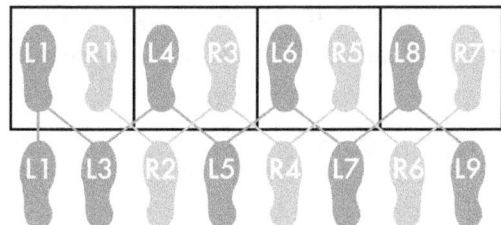

Figure 4.67. Ali Shuffle

Agility Ladder Drills: Ickey Shuffle

The Ickey shuffle is especially useful for deceleration and lateral movement training. The athlete must be light on her toes to change weight between feet quickly. Knees must stay high and arms pumping to help transfer body weight quickly.

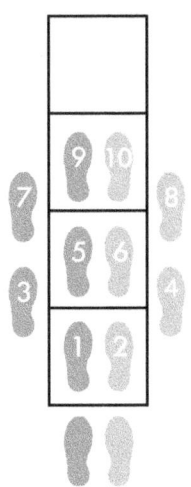

Figure 4.69. In and Out

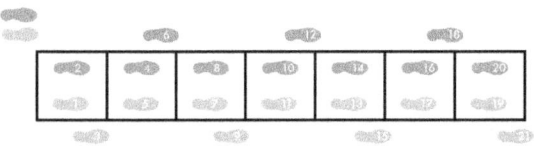

Figure 4.68. Ickey Shuffle

Agility Ladder Drills: In and Out

Agility ladder drills are useful for footwork and deceleration training. In the In and Out drill, the athlete must stay light on his toes, keeping the knees high while moving through the pattern hopping in and out of squares.

Speed and Overspeed Training

Resisted Sprinting

Resisted sprinting is a technique used to promote speed and start power by attaching a power band, sled, or speed parachute to the athlete. The athlete runs as fast as he can with the implement anchoring him. This training is for sprint training, so only push the athlete for short distances, about 20-yard intervals, with a rest between sets.

Assisted Sprinting

Assisted sprinting promotes speed and start power by attaching a bungee cord to the athlete. The athlete runs as fast as she can with the implement pulling her. The cord is affixed to a point or to a person faster than the athlete. This technique is used for sprint training, so only push the athlete for short distances, about 20 – 50 yard intervals, with a rest in between sets.

PRACTICE QUESTIONS

1. Cone drills focus on
   - **A)** speed training.
   - **B)** quickness training.
   - **C)** agility training.
   - **D)** resistance training.

Answers:

- A) Incorrect. Speed training is not the primary focus of cone drills. Resisted and assisted sprints focus on speed.
- **B) Correct.** Cone drills focus on reaction time and direction change.
- C) Incorrect. Agility training is not the primary focus of cone drills. Ladders drills focus on agility.
- D) Incorrect. Resistance training is not the primary focus of cone drills. Weight machines and free weights focus on resistance training.

2. Fast feet and A-skips are ideal for
   - **A)** speed, agility, and quickness warm-ups.
   - **B)** agility cooldown.
   - **C)** cardio endurance training.
   - **D)** static stretches.

Answers:

- **A) Correct.** Fast feet and A-skips are ideal dynamic warm-ups because they focus on increasing the range of motion for the lower body while adding quickness and footwork.
- B) Incorrect. Fast feet and A-skips are not ideal for cooldowns as they are high intensity.
- C) Incorrect. Fast feet and A-skips are to be done in shorter bursts. Endurance focuses on longer cardio bouts of training.
- D) Incorrect. Fast feet and A-skips do not represent static stretching protocols.

Plyometric Training

Also referred to as power training, plyometrics focuses on building the body's strength through maximum force production in the minimum amount of time. While SAQ training can also be considered part of the reactive training continuum, plyometrics training primarily focuses on explosive movement in a full range of motion; SAQ training keeps the exercises compact.

Plyometric training recruits multiple muscle groups and requires significant proprioceptive ability and core control. It is imperative the client be in the power level of training to perform these exercises appropriately to minimize risk of injury.

Exercises

Squat Jump

Starting Position: Stand in a neutral position with feet wider than hip-width apart; toes should be turned out slightly.

Movement: Inhale, and sink into squat position while bending the arms to the shoulders, activating the glutes and core. Shift the body weight to the heels. Exhale while pushing with power through the toes, jumping as high as possible. Use the arms to help propel the body upwards. Repeat as fast as possible.

Figure 4.70. Squat Jump

> **?** As a client gets stronger, it might be more difficult to find aerobic training that is challenging yet enjoyable to them. What kind of plyometric training or SAQ training exercises might be used in a circuit as a viable cardio option for an advanced client?

Double-Leg Box Jump

Starting Position: Stand in front of a box in neutral position with feet wider than hip-width apart; toes should be turned out slightly.

Movement: Inhale, sink into a squat position, and bend arms to shoulders, activating glutes and core; shift the body weight into heels. Exhale while pushing with power through the toes, jumping onto the box. Use the arms to help propel the body upwards. Step or hop down to starting position. Repeat as fast as possible.

Figure 4.71. Double-Leg Box Jump

Figure 4.72. Single-Leg Box Jump

Single-Leg Box Jump

Starting Position: Stand in front of a box in a single-leg balance position.

Movement: Inhale, and sink into the single-leg squat position. Bend arms to shoulders, activating the glutes and core; shift body weight into the heel. Exhale while pushing with power through the toes, jumping onto the box. Stabilize body. Use the arms to help propel the body upwards. Step or hop down. Repeat as fast as possible.

Lateral Box Jump

Starting Position: Stand to the side of a box in a neutral position with feet hip-width apart.

Movement: Inhale, and sink into a squat position. Bend arms to shoulders, activating the glutes and core; shift body weight into the heels. Exhale while pushing with power through the toes, jumping laterally to the box. Use the arms to help propel the body upwards. Step or hop down to the other side and repeat as fast as possible.

Figure 4.73. Lateral Box Jump

Alternate-Leg Push-Off

Starting Position: Stand with one foot on top of a box. Make sure the heel is on the box.

Movement: Inhale, reach the arms back, and slightly bend the back knee, activating the glutes and core; shift the body weight into the heels. Exhale while pushing with power through the leg on top of the box, straightening the leg and jumping as high as possible. Change lead legs while in midair. Use the arms to help propel the body upwards. Repeat as fast as possible, alternating legs.

Figure 4.74. Alternate-Leg Push-Off

Multiplanar Jumps

Starting Position: Stand in a neutral position with feet wider than hip-width apart; toes should be turned out slightly.

1. Inhale into a squat position. Exhale and jump forward, landing with soft knees; the glutes and core are activated. Inhale. Exhale and jump backward back to the starting position, landing with control; Inhale.

2. Inhale into a squat position. Exhale and jump laterally, landing with soft knees; the glutes and core are activated. Inhale. Exhale and jump laterally back to the starting position, landing with control. Inhale.

3. Inhale into a squat position. Exhale and jump rotating the body midair, landing with soft knees; the glutes and core are activated. Inhale. Exhale and jump back to the starting position, rotating the body midair and landing with control. Inhale.

Butt Kicks

Starting Position: Stand in a neutral position with feet hip-width apart.

Movement: Inhale, and sink into a squat position. Bring arms overhead, activating the glutes and core; shift weight into the heels. Exhale while pushing with power through the toes, jumping as high as possible; heels are kicking back into the glutes. Use the arms to help propel the body upwards. Repeat as fast as possible.

Figure 4.75. Butt Kicks

Tuck Jumps

Figure 4.76. Tuck Jumps

Starting Position: Stand in a neutral position with feet hip-width apart.

Movement: Inhale, and sink into squat position. Bring arms overhead, activating the glutes and core; shift body weight into the heels. Exhale while pushing with power through the toes, jumping as high as possible and tucking the knees into the chest. Use the arms to help propel the body upwards. Repeat as fast as possible.

Box Run Steps

Starting Position: Stand in a neutral position behind a low box or step.

Movement: Step lightly up and down, pumping the arms to aid in speed and intensity. Keep eyes on the box to reduce risk of injury. Repeat as fast as possible.

Ice Skaters

Starting Position: Stand in a neutral position with feet hip-width apart.

Movement: Leap from side to side as quickly as possible, maintaining soft knees to challenge balance and build lateral force production. Pump the opposite arm with the standing leg to increase intensity and coordination.

Figure 4.77. Ice Skaters

Single-Leg Tuck Jump

Starting Position: Stand in a neutral position with feet hip-width apart.

Movement: Inhale, and sink into a single-leg squat position. Bring the arms behind the body, activating the glutes and core; shift body weight into the heel. Exhale while pushing with power through the toes, jumping as high as possible;

tuck the knees into the chest. Use the arms to help propel the body upwards. Repeat as fast as possible.

Figure 4.78. Single-Leg Tuck Jump

Double-Leg Vertical Jump

Starting Position: Stand in a neutral position with feet wider than hip-width apart; toes are turned out slightly.

Movement: Inhale, and sink into squat position. Reach the arms behind the body, activating the glutes and core; shift body weight into the heels. Exhale while pushing with power through the toes, jumping as high as possible. Propel the upward motion by reaching the arms straight up overhead. Repeat as fast as possible.

Figure 4.79. Double-Leg Vertical Jump

Front Barrier Hop

Starting Position: Stand in a neutral position behind a barrier with feet hip-width apart.

Movement: Inhale, and sink into a squat position. Bring the arms behind the body, activating the glutes and core; shift body weight into heels. Exhale while pushing with power through the toes, jumping forward and as high as possible; tuck the knees into the chest to clear the barrier. Use the arms to help propel the body upwards.

Figure 4.80. Front Barrier Hop

4-Hurdle Drill

Starting Position: Stand in a neutral position in the center of the hurdles, feet-width apart.

Movement: Starting clockwise, jump forward, laterally, backward, and laterally again over all four hurdles, coming back to center after each jump. Do this as fast and accurately as possible. Repeat counterclockwise.

Power Skip

Starting Position: Stand in a neutral position, with feet hip-width apart and toes facing forward. Hands should be at sides.

EXERCISE TECHNIQUE

Figure 4.81. Power Skip

Movement: Drive one knee up while pushing with power through the toes of the opposite leg, propelling the body straight up or straight forward. Alternate this movement as fast as possible.

Backward Skip

Starting Position: Stand in a neutral position, with feet hip-width apart and toes facing forward. Hands should be at sides.

Movement: Drive one knee up while pushing with power through the toes of the opposite leg. Step back with the bent leg while in midair, propelling the body backward. Alternate this movement with the other leg as fast as possible.

Figure 4.82. Backward Skip

Figure 4.83. Single Arm Alternate-Leg Bound

Single Arm Alternate-Leg Bound

Starting Position: Stand in a neutral position, with feet hip-width apart and toes facing forward. Hands should be at sides.

Movement: Push off with power on one leg, allowing the other leg to extend as far forward as possible. Use the opposing arm to help propel the body forward. Alternate the legs as fast as possible.

Double Arm Alternate-Leg Bound

Starting Position: Stand in a neutral position, with feet hip-width apart and toes facing forward. Hands should be at sides.

Movement: Push off with power on one leg, allowing the other leg to extend forward as far as possible. Extend both arms to help propel the body forward. Alternate the legs as fast as possible.

Figure 4.84. Double Arm Alternate-Leg Bound

Depth Jump

Starting Position: Stand in a neutral position on top of a box; another box is positioned at a distance in front of the first box. Feet should be hip-width apart and toes are facing forward. Hands should be at sides.

Movement: Inhale, and sink into a squat position. Bend the arms to the shoulders, activating the glutes and core; shift body weight into the heels. Exhale while pushing with power through the toes, jumping off the box with control in a shallow squat position. Immediately jump onto second box, landing softly. Use the arms to help propel the body upwards. Repeat as fast as possible.

Figure 4.85. Depth Jump

Single-Leg Depth Jump

Starting Position: Stand in a neutral position on top of a box. Feet are hip-width apart and toes are facing forward. Hands should be at sides.

Figure 4.86. Single-Leg Depth Jump

Movement: Inhale; sink into a single-leg squat position, activating the glutes and core. Shift body weight into the heels. Exhale while pushing through the toes, hopping off the box. Land in a single-leg squat position and immediately perform a single-leg jump, landing softly. Use the arms to help propel the body upwards. Switch legs and repeat.

Depth Jump with Lateral Movement

Starting Position: Stand in a neutral position on top of a box. Feet are hip-width apart and toes are facing forward. Hands should be at sides.

Movement: Inhale; sink into a single-leg squat position, activating the glutes and core. Shift body weight into the heels. Exhale while pushing through the toes, hopping off the box. Land in a single-leg squat position; immediately cut to one side and sprint. Switch legs/sides and repeat.

Chest Pass

Starting Position: Stand in a neutral position with feet hip-width apart, toes facing forward, and knees bent. Hold a ball at the chest.

Movement: Inhale. Exhale and pass the ball from the chest with power while stepping forward. Hands clasp the ball at the palms, and the wrists rotate so that the fingers

Figure 4.87. Chest Pass

EXERCISE TECHNIQUE 187

complete the pass toward the chest, propelling the ball forward. Switch legs and repeat.

Two-Handed Overhead Throw

Starting Position: Stand in a neutral position with feet hip-width apart, facing the target. Hold a ball straight overhead.

One Repetition: Inhale, reaching arms back behind the head. Exhale, activate the abdominal wall, and throw the ball at the target. Be sure to utilize as much of the core musculature as possible when throwing and catching the ball. Repeat as quickly as possible.

Figure 4.88. Two-Handed Overhead Throw

Power Drop

Figure 4.89. Power Drop

Starting Position: Start in a semi-supine position. Hold a medicine ball at chest level.

Movement: Inhale. Exhale and throw the medicine ball from palms to fingers toward the ceiling as high as possible. Press the heels and lower back and shoulders into the floor to activate the core, aiding in force production. Catch and throw as fast as possible.

PRACTICE QUESTIONS

1. Which level in the training continuum should a client be in to implement plyometrics exercises in their routine?

A) Power

B) Strength

C) Stabilization

D) Core and Balance

<u>Answers:</u>

A) Correct. These exercises focus in prime mover force production.

B) Incorrect. These moves do not focus on building muscle or tendon strength.

C) Incorrect. These moves do not focus on building correct form or reducing body fat.

D) Incorrect. These are types of exercises not a training continuum.

2. What type of movement is plyometrics?

- **A)** balance
- **B)** sprinting
- **C)** jumping
- **D)** sliding

Answers:

- A) Incorrect. Balance is controlled instability.
- B) Incorrect. Sprinting is forward movement.
- **C) Correct.** Plyometrics promotes force production with explosive upward or forward movement.
- D) Incorrect. Sliding is a movement pattern utilized in advanced core training.

Aerobic or Cardiorespiratory Endurance Training

Aerobic or cardiorespiratory (cardio) training emphasizes inducing stress to the cardiorespiratory system, so almost any activity can be considered a form of aerobic training, but usually, any load-bearing activity is not considered aerobic-centered training.

Aerobic training will benefit any person, regardless of his or her fitness level. Aerobic training can decrease fatigue, anxiety, hypertension, obesity, and coronary artery disease, while increasing general body performance, immunity, glucose tolerance, and an overall sense of well-being.

> Some clients might ask about a "fat-burning zone" while doing cardiovascular training. Steer them clear of this line of thinking by explaining the **Law of Thermodynamics**: fat burning only occurs when more energy is being expended than consumed.

Typically, cardio equipment is used in training. Certain machines are available in almost any gym or fitness center.

Treadmills are the most common piece of cardio equipment. They allow a person to walk or run in place. The speed and incline on the machine can be increased, providing varied challenges for any fitness level.

There are several pre-designed programs available on a treadmill; the machine can change speeds and incline to automatically provide the user with a challenging workout.

When choosing a program, follow the prompts, which will ask for time and intensity level, ranging from 1 – 20.

When in doubt, or if the user only wants a quick 5-minute warmup, simply hit the Quickstart button, which will slowly start the machine. The user can then change the speed. To stop the machine quickly, there is an *Emergency Stop* button on the machine.

Make sure the user starts with their hands on the machine for safety, and once they feel the machine start, they can remove their hands. Holding a tall, neutral position while on the treadmill will ensure one is using their body as much as possible, thus putting stress on the heart, training for increased cardio efficiency, which is the goal.

The higher the incline, the harder it will be to keep hands off the machine, which is natural. When the user feels uncomfortable, they should place their hands on the handles or side bars to make sure they do not slip off the machine.

Some populations with knee issues or who cannot walk with proper posturing should be encouraged to try a stationary bicycle.

Stationary and recumbent (reclined seat) bicycles are another common piece of equipment in a gym or fitness center. Like treadmills, they also have the Quickstart button and a pre-designed set of programs.

Instead of incline, however, the stationary bike uses resistance to challenge the rider. The bicycle pedals have straps, which should be used to secure the feet while using the machine. On the upright bicycle, the seat should be about as high as the user's hip. It can be measured as the user stands next to the seat. Arms should be straight with soft elbows.

Seat positioning on the recumbent bicycle should allow the knees to be soft when they are at the lowest point of pedaling. The user should adjust the seat from a seated position.

Body positioning should be tall. Neither shoulders nor head should be bowed forward; rather they remain neutral as in exercises that require a seated position.

Elliptical trainers are increasingly popular cardio machines because both the arms and legs are in motion while the machine is used. They also have a lower impact on the joints, even though they facilitate a range of motion similar to running. Overweight populations tend to prefer these machines to treadmills.

They also have pre-designed programs and a Quickstart option. They use both resistance and incline to challenge the user.

To safely use this machine, the user should hold the stationary handles and then place the feet on the pedals. Push the balls of the feet on the pedals to start the

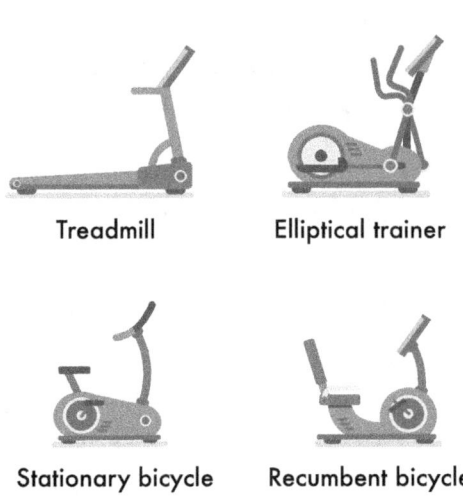

Figure 4.90. Cardiovascular Endurance Training Machines

machine in a forward motion. Once the user has chosen a program, he or she can take hold of the moveable handles.

The **stair climber or stair stepper** machines are considered more advanced and provide a great challenge for those at higher fitness levels. These machines are not recommended for users who lack high cardio endurance or who are in the stabilization level of training.

These machines also provide pre-designed programs and a Quickstart option, using speed and incline to challenge the user.

The stair stepper has pedals. Make sure the user always holds its handles for safety.

Only an advanced user can remove his or her hands from the stair climber. Body positioning should always be tall. The whole foot should stay on the pedal or step.

The **rowing machine** is becoming a popular item to have on the gym floor because it offers a full body and core challenge as well as a very tough cardio workout. It uses friction, air, or water for resistance. Air machines typically have a dial to increase or decrease the resistance.

Feet must be securely fastened to the pedals. Users should hold the handle with a supinated grip or a hooked grip.

Starting with the knees bent, the body tucked toward the handle, and the arms extended, row the body back by pushing the legs into extension and pulling the arms to flexion, leaning the torso back slightly to engage the core and upper back and shoulders. Control the body back to starting position.

Typically, the user does not pick a program for this machine. There is a display that shows caloric expenditure, distance in meters, and time. Use one of these as the goal when using the rowing machine.

The **arm bike** is probably the most obscure of cardio machines, but it does provide a targeted workout for those doing upper body exercises or those who cannot use their legs for cardio training.

Like other machines, arm bikes have pre-designed programs or a Quickstart option and use resistance to challenge the user.

Body positioning should be tall; shoulders and head should remain neutral as in exercises that require a seated position.

The most portable piece of cardio equipment is the **jump rope**, which is also believed to be the most efficient type of cardio training, requiring both coordination and body control.

To determine the length of a jump rope, anchor the folded rope under one foot. On advanced jumpers, the tops of the handles should reach just under the armpit, while on beginners, the handles should reach the tops of their shoulders.

Body position should be neutral, elbows slightly tucked into the body. The jumps should be on the toes and light, which is where body control is imperative. Even during a hesitation jump (two jumps between each rotation) the user's feet should have a minimal amount of sound when they contact the floor.

The most portable aerobic training equipment, of course, is the human body. **Walking** is a low impact form of cardio training that almost everyone can do. Keeping the body in a neutral stance with feet straight while propelling forward, striking the heel and rolling the foot to the toe, prevents the lower body from forming any muscle imbalances, while activating the core. The arms should swing naturally to aid in forward motion.

> **?** There's a big debate about the benefits of forefoot running versus heel strike running. Forefoot running will ensure a soft landing and forward propulsion, while heel strike running places strain on the joints and propels the body backward. What muscle and joint imbalances can come from heel strike running?

Jogging offers more of a challenge than walking by slightly increasing stride and pace. The jogger leans the body forward and pushes off with the toes. The legs should be under the body's center of gravity. The jogger lands softly on the midfoot or forefoot. The effort should be moderate intensity.

Running or **sprinting** is like jogging in body position except the pace is quicker, more explosive, and at a high intensity.

If the client is not landing softly on her feet, if her shoulders and head are hunched forward, or if her knees are drawing inward or toes are pointing outward, she should slow down or even regress to a lower impact form of cardio training.

Swimming is a viable option for populations suffering from joint injury or other problems that make walking or running difficult. Using water as resistance and all four limbs, clients benefit greatly from swimming as a low impact option. Those who cannot swim can use kickboards, allowing them to traverse the length of the pool by kicking their legs. They may even run in place at the shallow end of the pool.

PRACTICE QUESTIONS

1. All the following aerobic machines use the upper body EXCEPT
    - **A)** the recumbent bicycle.
    - **B)** the rowing machine.
    - **C)** the elliptical machine.
    - **D)** the arm bicycle.

    Answers:
    - **A) Correct.** The recumbent bicycle is a leg powered machine.
    - B) Incorrect. The rowing machine uses the upper and lower body.
    - C) Incorrect. The elliptical machine uses the upper and lower body.
    - D) Incorrect. The arm bicycle uses the upper body only.

2. What is the most challenging form of cardiorespiratory training?
   - **A)** walking at an incline
   - **B)** swimming with a kickboard
   - **C)** using an elliptical machine
   - **D)** jumping rope

Answers:

- A) Incorrect. While walking at an incline is challenging, it does not use the full body.
- B) Incorrect. Swimming with a kickboard is challenging, but it does not use the arms and is low impact.
- C) Incorrect. While an elliptical machine challenges both the upper and lower body, it is less intense than jumping rope.
- **D) Correct.** Jumping rope requires the user to recruit their full body and it is higher impact than the other choices.

FIVE: PROGRAM DESIGN AND IMPLEMENTATION

The following chapter discusses the importance of proper program design and some aspects to consider in implementing exercise programs. Additionally, it discusses some key terms and concepts associated with exercise program design, how to design a program, aerobic exercise programming, program periodization, and working with special populations. The concepts will give the trainer an understanding of how to properly create and implement well-rounded exercise programs for a wide variety of clientele.

Fundamentals of Exercise Program Design

First, it is important to know the components of exercise programs in order to properly design a program that meets the needs of the client. Components of an exercise program include a dynamic warm-up, the training stimulus, and proper cooldown. All these factors must be implemented into the program before it can be considered complete. This section discusses many of the key concepts and terminology found in a training program and gives examples of what a training program utilizing these concepts might look like.

THE DYNAMIC WARM-UP

A warm-up should always be performed before beginning an exercise routine because it effectively prepares the body for activity. With this in mind, it is important to consider what type of activity is going to be performed during the workout and make sure to design the warm-up based on this activity. For an individual preparing to do a back squat exercise, for example, an appropriate exercise to incorporate in the warm-up would be performing dynamic stretches that involve the quadriceps, hamstrings, glutes, and lower back muscles. The program design should always consider which muscles will be stimulated during the routine and prepare those muscle groups for the forces that will be placed on them during dynamic movements.

Traditional warm-ups used to utilize static stretching to prepare the body for exercise; however, static stretching does not adequately prepare the human movement system for the dynamic exercises found in nearly all fitness routines. **Static stretching** involves holding a muscle in a lengthened position for thirty seconds or more to elicit an elongation of the muscle being stretched. This type of stretching is helpful in improving the flexibility of the muscles but has also been shown to limit strength and power output for hours post-stretch. To prepare muscles for any dynamic activity, such as weightlifting, running, biking, swimming, tennis, baseball, football, ice hockey, or other sports-related activity, a dynamic warm-up should be incorporated into the workout. **Dynamic stretching** involves exercises that mimic the day's activity and short-duration stretches to prepare the muscles for the forces they will encounter during the workout. (See chapter 4 for more information on static and dynamic stretching.)

> Helpful Hint: There are several types of stretching: static stretching, dynamic stretching, ballistic stretching, and proprioceptive neuromuscular facilitation (PNF) stretching. Ballistic stretching is a high-speed version of dynamic stretching that can be potentially harmful to the joints. PNF stretching requires the assistance of a trainer and can be more effective than static stretching at increasing range of motion.

Prior to designing the dynamic warm-up, it is important to consider which joints will be used during the activity, what patterns and plane of motion the joints will be moving in, and which muscle groups will be involved in the activity. A well-rounded dynamic warm-up should include about five minutes of low-intensity aerobic exercise that uses a large percentage of the body's muscle mass, or at least the muscles that will be the focus of the workout. For example, starting a warm-up with five minutes of light jogging, cycling, stair climbing, etc. will help improve blood flow and muscle elasticity for exercise. Following this low-intensity aerobic exercise, the dynamic warm-up should include five or more **repetitions** of exercises that relate to the movements in the workout. A repetition is the performance of specific exercise through a single full range of motion. For example, an individual may perform a walking lunge in a dynamic warm-up to prepare the quadriceps, hamstrings, and glutes for weighted stationary lunges in a weightlifting routine. A variety of these dynamic stretches should be performed for fifteen minutes prior to the workout or activity.

> Testing Tip: Watch a sporting event and try to develop a dynamic warm-up for one of the players based on the movements in their sport. Practice with different types of sports and make sure to perform the warm-up yourself to feel its effectiveness.

THE TRAINING STIMULUS

When considering a training stimulus, the overall goal of the fitness program needs to be defined. A training stimulus refers to the type of exercises being applied in the program, and how they are implemented can have varying effects. This is why it is important to develop goals before the start of any training program. For example, if the goal is to increase muscle size, a program designed to focus on muscular hypertrophy is optimal for the client. However, if the goal is to develop speed and agility, exercises that develop muscular power may need to be incorporated as a training stimulus. Therefore, it is important for the trainer to know what type of training stimulus elicits the desired effect to reach the client's goals. Additionally, training **specificity** should also be taken into consideration. Specificity refers to developing a training program to achieve a specific goal determined by the trainer and client. Training specificity can be applied to both resistance training and cardiovascular training. For example, if a client's goal is to run a 5-kilometer race, the client's primary mode of cardiovascular training should be running or jogging.

It is important to understand the key terms involved in program design in order to develop a training protocol for the client to follow. Programs that follow a proper **progression** of intensity tend to yield the best results. Progression refers to an increase in program difficulty through increased frequency and intensity of exercise throughout the client's fitness program. Therefore, it is important for the trainer to assess the client's abilities and implement an appropriate number of **sets** and repetitions.

A set involves performing several repetitions of a specific exercise, ranging from one repetition to many repetitions, until fatigue is reached. When performing multiple sets of the same exercise, a **rest period** should be implemented between consecutive sets. A rest period is a set amount of recovery time between sets or exercises that allows the muscles to sufficiently replenish to properly perform the exercise again. For example, if the client performs ten repetitions of a bench press, a rest period of between thirty and ninety seconds is advisable.

Too little rest may prevent the client from completing the goal number of repetitions or may lead to improper form, while too much rest can reduce the beneficial response of the exercise. The rest period will vary based on the **load** involved during a specific exercise. The load is the amount of weight lifted with proper form, rather than simply a predetermined single repetition maximum for that exercise. As an example, an individual may do a barbell back squat for a single repetition maximum of 200 lbs., but that individual will be able to perform the same exercise for only ten repetitions at 75 percent or 150 lbs. The **volume** of training programs should also progress according to the client's fitness level and goals. Volume refers to the total number of sets, repetitions, and exercises, and varies according to the goal of the fitness program.

THE FITTE PRINCIPLE

Following the FITTE principle is very helpful in designing effective fitness programs. FITTE stands for *frequency* of exercise, *intensity* of exercise, *time or duration* of exercise, *type or mode* of exercise, and *enjoyment* of exercise. Utilizing this principle will help the trainer to plan the client's program to achieve appropriate fitness gains. Much of the FITTE principle will be determined by the fitness level of the client and the client's progress through the fitness program. These variables should start off moderately and progress to higher intensities as the program progresses.

Frequency in strength training programs will vary for each client. Beginners may be able to tolerate only two days of total body strength training per week focusing on the same muscle groups. Training the same muscle groups two days per week will provide adequate stimulus for musculoskeletal adaptations to occur. The frequency can eventually be progressed to three days per week of total body exercise, which should be performed on non-consecutive days to avoid overuse injuries. Individuals who have experience with strength training and are on a current strength training program will benefit most from training all major muscle groups three days a week. Exercise tolerance will vary per client; however, the body adapts to exercise and requires further overload via continuous training stimuli. Advanced exercisers may be able to tolerate a split resistance training routine that breaks up workouts into muscle groups. This type of program design takes a significant amount of dedication since the client would work out four or more times per week, focusing on different areas of the body. For example, the client might do an upper body workout on Monday and a lower body workout on Tuesday, take a day off from training on Wednesday, then do another upper body workout on Thursday and another lower body workout on Friday. These programs are often difficult to sustain long-term and are not recommended for everyone. If a client is already struggling to complete three resistance training days a week, it may not be advisable for that client to do a four-day split routine.

For cardiovascular training, frequency will also depend on the client's goals. Clients looking to perform in long-distance cardiovascular events will need to dedicate more time to cardiovascular exercise for improvement. When a client is beginning a cardiovascular exercise program, the trainer should insist the client dedicate at least two to three days a week of moderate-intensity cardiovascular exercise, such as jogging, swimming, cycling, dancing, or rowing, for at least thirty minutes per session. Other activities that elevate the heart rate for a sustained duration of at least thirty minutes can also be considered cardio. For example, if the client plays recreational sports such as racquetball, basketball, hockey, or soccer, these sports can make up a portion of the client's cardio for the week. If the training is for a specific event, the principle of specificity should be applied to improve the client's performance in the event.

Intensity of the workouts should follow a steady progression throughout the exercise program to ensure that the client's musculoskeletal system is prepared for the forces it will face. Additionally, a well-designed program will help ensure that the principle of **overload** is achieved with each workout. Overload refers to gradually increasing the difficulty of each successive workout by manipulating the training variables. The principle of overload will help ensure that the muscles receive stress that is significant enough to induce a beneficial adaptation to exercise. Prior to adjusting the intensity of the workout, however, the trainer should consider whether the client has reached a high level of proficiency with the current exercises. This is important because a rapid progression of exercise difficulty could lead to a plateau in progress or potential injury. Overuse injuries are common in individuals who attempt to increase the difficulty of their exercise routines too quickly. There are a number of ways to adjust the intensity of the workout, including increasing the weight, decreasing the stability (e.g., standing on an unstable surface while performing a squat), changing the center of gravity (e.g., performing an overhead squat rather than a traditional back squat), and increasing the rate at which the exercise is performed (e.g., power-developing exercises such as plyometrics or Olympic lifting). Modifying these training variables can make the workout significantly more difficult but modifications should be made only when the client has gradually progressed through easier exercises.

Progression of intensity in resistance training is critical for achieving the goals of the client. Lower-intensity workouts focusing on developing muscular endurance should be the starting point. Lighter loads and higher repetition ranges are best for new clients. As an example, the client may start with one set of each exercise at 65 to 75 percent of the client's one-repetition maximum (1RM) for ten to fifteen repetitions, then progress to multiple sets in the same load range. This will help develop the client's muscular endurance and improve neuromuscular adaptations to exercise. After six or more weeks, the trainer should increase the intensity of the workouts by increasing the load. Repetitions will decrease to a minimum of eight to twelve; however, the load is increased to between approximately 65 and 80 percent of the client's 1RM. This intensity will help the client develop muscle size, also known as muscular hypertrophy. The next progression in resistance training intensity focuses on developing muscular strength. This is achieved by again increasing the weight to between 85 and 100 percent of 1RM and decreasing the repetition range to between one and eight repetitions. The key concept to remember with resistance training progression is that the intensity increases as the weight increases.

The intensity of cardiovascular workouts can also be adjusted to gradually progress the client's program. This can be achieved by monitoring the heart rate during cardiovascular exercises such as running, swimming, stair-climbing, dance classes, cycling, rowing, and other activities. If the client is having difficulty tracking heart rate, the trainer can teach the client how to utilize a rate of perceived exertion to judge how challenging the cardiovascular workout is. The rate of perceived exertion uses a scale of one to ten to judge the exercise difficulty, with one being almost no exercise and ten referring to complete exhaustion. Beginners should try to accomplish at least two cardiovascular workouts a week for at least thirty minutes per session. This is a very general guideline and may need to be adjusted according to the client's abilities. Some individuals may not be able to tolerate a full thirty minutes depending on their activity level prior to engaging in an exercise routine.

Similar to resistance training, cardiovascular training should be progressively increased by increasing the time, rate, or distance of exercise. However, with clients who are just beginning to do cardiovascular exercise, a good rule of thumb is to try and continue a conversation with a partner throughout the workout. This provides a good starting point for how difficult the workout should be. If the client is unable to continue the conversation and is continually gasping for breath, the workout may be too challenging.

Time or *duration* of a workout routine should also be considered when designing a program for a client. The client will need to develop a tolerance for longer workouts by building up muscular and cardiovascular endurance. For resistance training programs, the earlier phases may emphasize dynamic warm-up and technique practice prior to loading, and stretching and cooldown following loading. As the client progresses, more time can be dedicated to weightlifting and the duration of the workouts can increase. The duration of the workout is often determined by how much time the client can dedicate to fitness. Early programs, however, should include around eight exercises that work all the primary musculature of the body. Progression and allotted time will often limit the duration of the workout. Likewise, cardiovascular training will start with short durations and gradually increase as the client's tolerance for the exercise increases. If clients were previously sedentary, the trainer may need to start off the program utilizing short intervals of light jogging interspersed with walking. Some clients may have to start by walking only for the desired duration of the exercise routine, with variables such as pace and incline being manipulated to adjust difficulty. This is common for clients who develop joint pain from the impact of running. The duration of cardiovascular sessions should be approximately thirty minutes but may vary by client.

Type or *mode* of exercise can be determined by the client's and trainer's goals prior to beginning the program. This concept goes hand in hand with the principle of training specificity discussed earlier in the chapter. When selecting the type of exercise, the trainer should take into account the client's recreational activities, sports, fitness goals, time available for an exercise program, and any limitations that may prevent certain modes of training. The exercises selected for training programs should specifically help clients accomplish their goals. For example, if the client's goal is to improve the ability to play tennis, the trainer should incorporate exercises that focus on lateral movements and agility, core strength and power, shoulder and rotator cuff stability, and reaction time. Incorporating these drills into a client's program will help the client develop the ability to change direction quickly, hit the ball harder and more easily, prevent shoulder overuse injuries, and improve the ability to react to tough shots from an opponent. This concept should be considered in cardiovascular training too, depending on whether the client is exercising for general fitness and weight loss or training for a sporting event. Clients exercising for general fitness need not worry about the mode of cardiovascular exercise. However, if the client is a competitive swimmer, for example, more benefits will be gained from a cardio routine based on swimming than on cycling or running.

Finally, *enjoyment* of exercise is important when designing an exercise program because it promotes client compliance. Program compliance can be challenging when the client is not a fitness enthusiast. This is why it's important to find exercises the client likes and design the program accordingly. For example, some clients thrive on a regular routine and prefer a linear, predictable program, while others like a program that is constantly changing. The trainer should try to use this information in program design to prevent the program from becoming stale.

Exercise Regression and Progression

Often a trainer will find that a client is unable to complete an exercise with proper technique. It is important for the trainer to understand both the proper progression and the proper **regression** of an exercise. Regression refers to a decrease in exercise difficulty to accommodate individuals who cannot perform an exercise due to either physical limitations or inexperience. A trainer must understand that not everyone is capable of performing the same exercises, and this has become more of a concern with the increasingly sedentary lifestyle and the deleterious effect it has on the human body. Individuals suffer from the adverse effects of poor posture, excessive weight, previous injuries, and other conditions that prevent them from performing some exercises properly. It is important to assess the client's capabilities and design an exercise plan with an appropriate level of difficulty.

Additionally, the human body goes through motor learning phases that can help determine exercise progression. These stages include the *cognitive*, *associative*, and *autonomous* learning stages. The cognitive learning stage is associated with faltering while performing a skill and may look awkward. For example, someone learning to ride a bicycle for the first time is often shaky and may fall to the side. When teaching an exercise technique, this stage of learning may indicate that the exercise is too difficult and requires regression or modification. The associative stage is defined by more precise movement patterns but still maintains a level of difficulty that prevents unhindered movement. The individual learning to ride a bicycle no longer falls, but there is visible instability signified by the handlebars shaking. This stage of learning shows an appropriate level of difficulty for a client. The client is able to perform the exercise with proper technique, but with subtle yet obvious difficulty. Finally, the autonomous phase of learning indicates that the client has mastered the technique and requires further progression of the exercise. This can be compared to an individual who has been riding a bike for years and can do so with little thought. The movement is now automatic for the bike rider.

 Helpful Hint: Create your own chart of exercise regressions and progressions and use it for reference with future clients and training tests.

Progression should always be implemented into a program with the client's goals in mind. If the client is preparing for an athletic event involving increased power or agility, then the trainer should design the program to reach that goal by progressing the exercises from basic to advanced. For example, power exercises, such as a jump squat, should be implemented at the start of the program and advanced exercises, such as single-leg box jumps, should be implemented at the end of the program. It is important not to advance the client too quickly because rapid progression can lead to poor technique and possibly injury.

Table 5.1. Regression and Progression*

Movement	Regression #1	Regression #2	Standard	Progression #1	Progression #2
Squat	Wall Sit	Dumbbell Squat	Back Squat	Front Squat	Overhead Squat
Hinge	Hip Bridge	Cable Romanian Dead Lift (RDL)	RDL	Single-Leg RDL	Kettlebell Swings
Lunge	Split Squat	Assisted Reverse Lunge (TRX)	Walking Lunge	Multi-Directional Lunge	Split-Squat Jumps
Push (bodyweight)	Wall Push-up	Stability Ball Push-up	Push-up	Archer Push-up	Plyometric Push-up
Push (external load)	Machine Chest Press	Barbell Bench Press	Dumbbell Bench Press	Single-Arm Dumbbell Press	Split-Stance Single-Arm Cable Press
Horizontal Pull	Seated Row	Dumbbell Row	Bent-Over Row	Split-Stance Cable Row	Split-Stance Cable Row w/ Rotation
Vertical Pull	Lat Pulldown	Assisted Chin-up	Chin-up	Pull-up	Weighted Pull-Up
Press	Machine Shoulder Press	Kneeling Shoulder Press	Shoulder Press	Single-Arm Shoulder Press	Push Press

*Foundation of Fitness Program, National Strength and Conditioning Association, 2015 (modified for clarity)

Detraining

The human movement system goes through both short- and long-term changes as a person progresses through a training program. With effective program design and implementation, neuromuscular changes can occur in as little as two weeks, while true gains in muscular strength will occur over six to eight weeks. However, it is important for the trainer to understand how quickly the effects of **detraining** occur when stopping a fitness program. Detraining refers to the body's deleterious reaction to stopping a training program, which can become evident in as little as two weeks. In this short time frame, detrimental effects occur in both cardiovascular fitness and muscular fitness. Improvements in cardiovascular fitness from aerobic training programs—such as improved cardiac output, maximal oxygen uptake, and mitochondrial function in skeletal muscle—decline rapidly after stopping aerobic exercise. Furthermore, continuing aerobic activity following a long hiatus does not return the individual to the peak level of cardiovascular fitness; this can take months of training at lower intensities and gradual progression. It is more beneficial to the client to lower the intensity of the cardiovascular workout and continue to train at lower intensities than it is to stop aerobic training completely.

Muscular fitness, however, declines more gradually following cessation of a weight-training program. Though there is a limited effect on the strength of the muscle, the muscular cross-sectional area is reduced gradually over time. In individuals who have previously been training, the effects on muscular fitness after discontinuing strength training are less significant, since the body retains some of the strength gains achieved through resistance training following weight-training cessation. A decline in strength after weeks of detraining can be attributed to the loss of muscle cross-sectional area. With the effects of detraining in mind, the training program should be regressed by utilizing lighter loads or easier modifications following a period with no resistance training.

Training Protocols

Many different exercise program designs can effectively elicit the positive effects of general adaptation syndrome. However, creating an exercise program should always take into consideration the goal of the client and proper progression. A single-set protocol, which focuses on performing one set of each exercise, may be beneficial for those just starting a strength-training program, because they often do not have the muscular endurance to make it through multiple sets of an exercise using the same muscle groups. It gives their body time to adapt gradually to the exercises without causing excessive fatigue and the delayed onset muscle soreness that accompanies weight training.

 Check Your Understanding: List and describe the aspects of the FITTE principle.

Eventually the client can be progressed to **multiple-set** programs for strength training, which focus on performing two or more consecutive sets of each exercise in one session. For example, the program may include three sets of ten repetitions of the deadlift exercise. The sets would be performed consecutively with a rest period between each set until all three sets are complete. These sets would be completed before moving on to the next exercise in the program.

As the client progresses, the program complexity can be progressed as well. An example of this would be the **super set**, which involves performing a first exercise for one full set, immediately followed by working the antagonist or opposite muscle groups for one full set. An example of this would be performing the bench press exercise for one set of eight repetitions then immediately performing one set of eight bent-over rows. The bench press trains the pectoral muscles of the chest, triceps, and anterior deltoids while the bent-over row trains the trapezius, rhomboids, and latissimus dorsi of the back, biceps, and posterior deltoids. This type of program design can be performed at most repetition ranges; however, it is more easily accomplished with heavier loads since it allows the client to transition between exercises more easily. The client is allotted more time for rest periods with heavier loads and does not have to rush, minimizing the chance of poor technique.

Another advanced program design is the **pyramid set,** which involves selecting an exercise and performing consecutive sets at increasing loads, followed by sets of decreasing loads. Using the lat pull-down exercise, the client would perform the first set using a light load and ten repetitions at 75 percent of 1RM followed by a heavier load and fewer repetitions (eight repetitions at 80 percent of 1RM) followed by an even heavier load and even fewer repetitions (six repetitions at 85 percent of 1RM). Once a predetermined peak weight or repetition range is reached, the client then goes down to the original light-load and high-repetition range. In this example, the trainer would instruct the client to go back down from six repetitions and 85 percent of 1RM to eight repetitions and 80 percent of 1RM, and so forth. The client is working with multiple repetition ranges and weight categories within a single workout, which requires both muscular endurance and muscular strength.

Another beneficial and often time-saving program design is called **circuit training**. In circuit training each exercise in the program is performed for one set until all exercises are complete, and then the same cycle of exercises is repeated in the same order for additional sets. This style of training is beneficial for clients who tend to get bored waiting around for the next set because it keeps them in continuous motion. Short rest periods can be incorporated between exercises with a longer rest period occurring at the end of the circuit. When selecting exercises for a circuit training session, the trainer should consider which muscle groups are primarily being used and try to utilize different muscle groups with each exercise. This approach will help to avoid absolute fatigue, minimizing rest periods, and will provide a well-rounded workout that prevents muscular imbalances.

Designing a circuit that minimizes rest by selecting various muscle groups is called **vertical loading,** which is often done by starting at the top of the kinetic chain and working down to the bottom. In contrast, **horizontal loading** refers to performing consecutive exercises for the same muscle groups with intermittent rest periods. Because of the reduced rest periods involved in circuit training, the client's fitness level should be considered before beginning this type of program. The intensity of circuit training can be modified for beginners by changing the training variables to suit the client.

Manipulation of Training Variables

When deciding how to adjust the fitness program, the trainer must analyze which energy systems are being utilized in the client's activity. The training program should improve the client's ability to perform using the energy system most commonly used in that activity. For instance, if the individual plays a sport that involves short sprints (such as football), the client will benefit most by following a periodized program that develops muscular power. The trainer needs to consider how to adjust the training variables to mimic the energy requirements of the sport.

PRACTICE QUESTIONS

1. Regression refers to

    A) the gradual increase in exercise intensity over the course of a periodized training program.

    B) reducing the intensity of an exercise due to physical limitation or poor technique.

    C) performing an exercise for one full range of motion.

    D) the downward movement phase during the repetition of an exercise.

    Answers:

    A) Incorrect. The gradual increase in intensity throughout an exercise program refers to *progression*.

    B) Correct. Regression is the reduction or modification of an exercise due to physical limitation or poor technique.

    C) Incorrect. Performing an exercise through one full range of motion is a *repetition*.

    D) Incorrect. The downward movement phase during the repetition of an exercise is the *eccentric phase*.

2. Which of the following is the definition of *volume* as it refers to a training program?

    A) the amount of weight lifted for a single repetition

    B) the act of performing a specific number of repetitions through their full range of motion

    C) the principle that involves gradually increasing the difficulty to elicit muscular adaptation over the course of the periodization

    D) the total number of sets multiplied by the number of repetitions of a particular exercise

    Answers:

    A) Incorrect. The weight lifted for a single repetition is the *load*.

    B) Incorrect. Performing a specific number of repetitions through their full range refers to a *set*.

    C) Incorrect. The principle of gradually increasing difficulty to elicit muscular adaptation through the course of the periodization is the *overload principle*.

    D) Correct. Volume is the number of sets multiplied by the number of repetitions of an exercise.

PERIODIZATION

An important concept that all trainers should be familiar with is periodization of training programs. **Periodization** refers to the planned breakdown of the overall training program aimed at achieving a specific fitness goal and peak performance. It is essentially the blueprint of a client's program and how it will be implemented. The trainer's job is to design each phase of the program, the timelines to follow, when to adjust training variables and when the client should transition to the next phase. The goal of periodization is to elicit **general adaptation syndrome,** or physiological adaptations to exercise through proper periodization and use of the overload principle. The body is placed under excess stress and evolves to compensate and becomes stronger.

There are several different cycles, periods, and phases in the blueprint of the client's training program. *Macrocycle* typically refers to the overall program, which includes the **in-season** and **off-season** for athletes or a full program for general clients. In-season is the period in which athletes are actively practicing for and competing in their sport or event, and off-season is the period in which they are not involved in active practice or competition. *Mesocycles* typically involve a large portion of the program in which the load and volume are gradually progressed over a period of six to twelve weeks (dependent upon the timing of athletic competitions). Finally, *microcycles* are typically shorter cycles within a mesocycle, dedicated to a specific load and volume range that are aimed at a particular adaptation. Microcycles can be described as *phases* of training aimed at specific adaptations, such as *endurance phase, hypertrophy phase, strength phase,* and *power phase*. Each phase provides the trainer with the goal of the microcycle and what load and volume should look like.

The periods of an exercise program are important because they help determine how the client is progressing. The **preparatory period** refers to the start of a training program typically associated with lower intensities of exercise with the goal of improving muscular endurance, muscular hypertrophy, and the basic strength of a client. Exercises involved in this period may not follow the exact specificity of the client's sport or event and will be of lower difficulty. This period helps the client learn exercise technique and build a base of training for the next phase.

Transition periods occur after the preparatory phase and at the end of the periodization. The first transition period shifts the program toward more event-specific movements that improve peak strength and power prior to competition. This period should be planned to occur just prior to the start of the athlete's season, tryouts, or competition.

Following the first transition period is the **competitive period**, which occurs during the athlete's event or season and is defined by the absolute peak of performance with significant focus on power movements and sport-specific training or maintenance of fitness through moderate-intensity, higher-volume workouts. For instance, a client may have a short competitive period, such as with a track and field shot putter. Since the athlete's season is relatively short, the trainer should design the competitive period for peak performance when the athlete can focus on more specific movements, like power exercises at low volume and high loads. Additionally, the athlete will place more emphasis on throwing technique.

Athletes with longer seasons may require a focus on performance maintenance throughout the season. In this scenario, the trainer should design and implement a program that cycles back through the phases to have the athlete peak leading up to the most important competitive events, such as the first in-season match, toughest opponent, and playoffs.

Following the competitive period is typically a period of active rest, which is sometimes referred to as the *second transition period*. During this time, the athlete will take a break from the usual lifting cycles, skills and drills, and competition to actively recover through recreational activities that may not be related to their sport. The athlete should remain active during this time period; however, resistance training may be eliminated for about two weeks. This period allows athletes to recover from minor injuries and recuperate from the stress placed on the body during peak conditioning and competition.

> Testing Tip: Write down and/or voice record the terms in bold or italics and define each one to help your understanding. You can even create flashcards with the term on one side and definition on the other to speed up the process of learning new definitions.

The main goal of periodization is to have the client reach peak athletic performance exactly when needed. This is achieved through proper program design and implementation. There are two main types of periodization: linear periodization and undulating periodization. **Linear periodization** refers to a steady progression toward higher intensities: a standard endurance/hypertrophy phase, then a strength phase, then a peak strength/power phase. This method is highly beneficial to athletes preparing for competition because it allows the body to undergo general adaptation syndrome steadily and without risk of overtraining. Linear periodization generally allows for easy-to-follow resistance guidelines and simple transitions to the next phase for clients. **Undulating periodization** refers to a program that varies the intensity of the workouts within the microcycle, but that gradually increases the overall program intensity over the macrocycle. For instance, the first workout of the week may focus on loads and volumes aimed at increasing muscular hypertrophy, the second workout may be designed for improved strength, and the last for muscular endurance.

Periodization is an important way to optimize training programs for improved performance. The trainer should have significant knowledge of the principles of periodization and how to apply them. When evaluating a sport for program design, the trainer should consider the following: energy systems used in the sport, length of off-season, length of in-season, length of competitive period, and goal of program. Each of these factors will help the trainer to decide how to break down the training components from macrocycle to microcycle.

Table 5.2. Linear Periodization – Ice Hockey

Sept.	Oct.	Nov.	Dec.	Jan.	Feb.	Mar.	Apr.	May	Jun.	July	Aug.
In-Season								Off-Season			
Hypertrophy	Hypertrophy/Strength	Strength	Strength/Power		Power			Active Rest (2 weeks)	Endurance	Hypertrophy/Strength	Strength/Power
Preparatory Period				First Transition Period		Competitive Period		Second Transition Period	Preparatory Period and First Transition (Off-season)		Competitive Period (Tryouts)
Mesocycle 1									Mesocycle 2		
Macrocycle											

Training programs will vary greatly among sports and sometimes even by the position within each sport. For example, goaltenders in most sports require lateral movement speed and reaction time rather than straight forward movement speed. Therefore, the goaltender's periodization may include more emphasis on lateral movement plyometrics, agility, and reaction time drills in the first transition period and competitive period. Early stages in the periodization for the goaltender, however, will be similar to those for the other players. For example, the endurance, hypertrophy, and strength phases will involve higher volumes and lower loads with more basic resistance training exercises that progressively become more intense through the preparatory period. As the season progresses and the exercises get more specific, the trainer can incorporate exercises specifically for the position the athlete plays. This will occur during the first transition period through the competitive period.

Sports seasons vary greatly in duration and competitive periods. It is the trainer's responsibility to research and evaluate the sport prior to designing the athlete's exercise program. This will ensure the athlete is reaching peak performance at the start of competition. Athletes with long seasons may undergo multiple mesocycles during the course of the season. For example, professional baseball players have a season of 162 games from spring through fall, so planning a successful periodization around a baseball season is challenging. The trainer must be able to implement the principles of overload and specificity, and manipulate training variables throughout the exercise program. Since baseball has such a long in-season, the program may include four two-week microcycles: muscular hypertrophy, basic strength training, strength and power, and sports-specific power. The program will cycle back through these phases while program intensity will follow a steady progression of high volume, low load and low volume, high load. The off-season for the baseball player would begin back in the muscular endurance phase with very light loads and very high volume. It is not optimal to cycle muscular endurance during the season because it contributes to excessive fatigue that can hinder the athlete's performance.

Clients with shorter athletic seasons or fewer competitive events, such as triathletes, Ironman athletes, and marathoners, will have a somewhat different periodization; furthermore, the goal will be to peak for a single event rather than a full competitive season. In this example, the athlete can stretch out the mesocycles, implementing four-week microcycles of each phase. As with all programs, there should be a gradual progression of intensity to elicit the effect of general adaptation syndrome. The preparatory and first transition periods will be elongated compared to those of a baseball player, simply because unlike professional baseball players, triathletes and marathoners do not have three or four competitions per week during the season. The competitive period for these athletes is shorter and culminates in the event itself, emphasizing heavy loads with minimal repetition involving power-based movements such as plyometrics.

PRACTICE QUESTIONS

1. Undulating periodization is characterized by microcycles that follow
    - **A)** varying loads and volumes throughout a microcycle with increasing intensity over the course of the macrocycle.
    - **B)** one load and volume through an entire mesocycle.
    - **C)** a steady progression of load and volume through a mesocycle and gradual progression of intensity throughout the macrocycle.
    - **D)** no particular pattern in progressions of loading.

    Answers:
    - **A) Correct.** The load and volume of an undulating program vary within a microcycle and progress steadily over the course of the periodization.
    - B) Incorrect. This pattern describes no particular progression or periodization.
    - C) Incorrect. This pattern describes a *linear periodization* rather than undulating.
    - D) Incorrect. There is no periodization that follows this pattern.

2. What is the most common order of periods throughout a program periodization?
    - **A)** first transition period, preparatory period, competitive period, second transition period
    - **B)** competitive period, first transition period, second transition period, preparatory period
    - **C)** macrocycle, second transition period, competitive period, preparatory period
    - **D)** preparatory period, first transition period, competitive period, second transition period

    Answers:
    - A) Incorrect. The sequence is out of order.
    - B) Incorrect. The sequence is out of order.
    - C) Incorrect. A macrocycle contains all of the periods.
    - **D) Correct.** This is the most common order of periods.

Designing an Exercise Program

CONDUCTING A NEEDS ANALYSIS

Conducting a needs analysis will help the trainer discern how to plan the exercise program, which should be designed according to the overall goal of the client. Some of the most common goals a trainer will encounter are exercise for weight management, athletic performance, fitness improvement, or general health benefits. The needs analysis should always be performed prior to starting the client's fitness program, so the trainer can properly adjust the components of the program. Starting a fitness program without first conducting a goal-setting or needs analysis will leave the trainer and client with no starting point and nothing to give either person a sense of accomplishment. An effective method for developing goals is to utilize the **SMART** goal acronym.

SMART goals are *specific, measurable, action-oriented, realistic,* and *time-stamped* goals that can be developed in the needs analysis with the client. Developing fitness goals using this model will help both the client and the trainer stay focused on what they can achieve together. Ideally, the client and trainer will record this goal and plan around it, making sure to keep track of progress along the way.

> **?** Check Your Understanding: Create a SMART goal for yourself and make sure it reflects all letters of the acronym: specific, measurable, action-oriented, realistic, and time-stamped.

Specific implies that the goal is detailed and tells exactly what the client hopes to accomplish. As an example, a specific goal would be "I want to lose ten pounds," rather than "I want to lose weight." *Measureable* implies that there is a specific number or amount to reach; for example, the client may want to be able to deadlift 250 pounds. The goal is a measurable number that can be recorded. A goal of "I want to be stronger" is good; however, it is not specific and measureable. *Action-oriented* goals require the client to put forth a significant effort in order for the goal to be accomplished. The goal is achievable, but only through hard work from the client and influence from the trainer. *Realistic* implies that the goal is not outside of the realm of possibility for the client. For example, a realistic goal may be that the client wants to lose ten pounds in ten weeks. Based on healthy and sustainable weight loss methods, about one pound per week is the ideal amount of weight to lose. However, if the client's goal is to lose thirty pounds in three weeks, the client needs to be aware that this goal is unrealistic within that time frame. *Time-stamped* goals have set start and end dates. The client should make a point to select a final date for achieving the goal. This gives the trainer an idea of how to properly design and implement the training program and how to set up the periodization for the client's goals.

Program Design for Weight Management

Exercise for weight management is one of the most common goals in fitness and will certainly come up in a trainer's career. An effective weight management program will include a combination of consistent cardiovascular exercise, a variety of resistance training, and proper nutrition. This chapter will discuss the methods for selecting training variables to achieve the client's weight management goals.

Weight management program design uses a steady progression of training variables aimed at improving muscular and aerobic fitness. The program should start with two days of resistance training and three days of aerobic training per week. This can eventually progress to three days of resistance training days and up to five days of aerobic training per week as the client becomes more comfortable with the training program. A set schedule of when to exercise can help the client comply with the program. As the client builds tolerance to exercising five or more days per week, the trainer can gradually increase the intensity of the program by manipulating other training variables.

Those focused on weight loss should begin a resistance training program by building muscular endurance. Muscular endurance is a standard starting point for most resistance training programs that is characterized by lighter loads and higher repetition counts. This phase results in a lower-intensity workout and less stress placed on the body. Because untrained individuals typically lack muscular endurance and exercise technique, starting with heavier loads could result in possible injury or early fatigue. Though traditional linear weightlifting—multiple sets combined with rest periods—is effective, circuit training may keep the client more engaged in the program. It is up to the trainer and client to decide which method the client finds more enjoyable.

Following muscular endurance, the program should progress to a muscular hypertrophy phase. Muscular hypertrophy benefits a weight-loss program because increases in muscle mass help to increase the client's resting metabolism. Therefore, any increases to muscle mass will influence further changes in body composition. The strength gains resulting from the increase to the muscle cross-sectional area will also allow the client to progress into higher-intensity strength workouts.

Power-based exercises are beneficial in that they are very high intensity; however, they are not always necessary in a weight-loss program. Exercises that help increase power, such as plyometrics and Olympic lifting, may also not be advisable for individuals who have excess weight due to the increased stress these exercises place on the joints. Some plyometric exercises that involve rapid deceleration of body weight impact as more than three or four times the client's body weight and may cause significant injury. Resistance training programs that involve all the major muscle groups and a variety of modes, including body weight, free weights, machine weights, cable resistance, resistance bands, and more, will provide the most benefit while preventing the program from becoming stale.

For weight loss, cardiovascular exercise is very important; however, the mode is not significant. Since the goal of the fitness program is to improve body composition, any form of cardiovascular exercise will benefit the client. With this in mind, the client can decide how to incorporate cardio and select the most enjoyable method. Trainers will need this information to properly design the gradual progression required to improve fitness.

Cardiovascular training for weight loss should also follow a steady progression. Moderate-intensity aerobic exercise should be performed three days a week, for thirty minutes per session. The trainer should instruct the client to progress in small increments (less than ten percent every couple of weeks) to avoid overuse injuries from advancing too quickly. Individuals who are less fit may need to start with intervals of cardiovascular exercise.

It is also important for the trainer to inform the client of appropriate weight-loss goals and healthy, sustainable weight-loss methods. Any well-rounded fitness program incorporates basic nutrition information that will assist the client with achieving those goals. A key concept to remember with a weight management program is that it is healthier to gradually increase or decrease weight rather than gain or lose it rapidly. Gradual weight changes typically involve about one to two pounds per week. Clients should be made aware of this early in the program to set a realistic expectation of how much time it will take to reach their goals.

Program Design for General Health Benefits

Designing a fitness program for general health benefits is similar to program design for weight management. The key concepts still include a gradual progression of frequency, intensity, and duration of exercise that also keeps the client engaged in the program. Also, the program should implement a combination of both cardiovascular and resistance training for optimal results. It can also be beneficial to find out the client's daily activities, recreational activities, and other interests in designing a fitness program for that client. The trainer can use this information to create the exercise program and loosely base the exercises on the client's interests and daily activities.

For general health benefits, it will be most effective to keep the program simple and follow the basic guidelines of the FITTE principle, the overload principle, and exercise progression. Beginner clients will spend a longer period of time developing muscular endurance, hypertrophy, and basic strength. The program design may not require highly technical power movements, and the trainer should consider the physical condition of the client when adding high-impact or high-intensity exercises like power movements.

A variety of training protocols, such as exercise circuits, multiple sets, pyramid sets, and supersets, can be used to keep the client engaged in the program. This should help to increase program compliance. The program should start with two sessions of muscular-endurance-based resistance training and three aerobic endurance workouts a week. A gradual progression will eventually include a potential third resistance training session and more frequent cardiovascular workouts after six weeks of training has been completed. Various periodizations can also be implemented at this point to promote program compliance. The two different periodizations (linear vs. undulating) are discussed in detail earlier in the chapter.

Cardiovascular training for general health benefits should also follow a gradual progression of intensity. Since the client is not training aerobically for improved performance, it does not matter what mode of exercise the client uses. The trainer can then base the aerobic endurance training on the client's interests in a particular cardiovascular activity. In keeping with the "E" in the FITTE principle, allowing the client to select an enjoyable form of aerobic fitness will help with program compliance. If the client enjoys a particular recreational activity, it may be more beneficial to plan the cardio training around the mechanical requirements of that activity. For example, if the client plays golf recreationally, then a fast-paced walk with varying inclines on the treadmill could be implemented in the fitness program.

Program Design for Athletic Performance

Designing an exercise program for athletes requires a particular focus on specificity. The trainer should analyze the sport or athletic event the client participates in and perform a fitness assessment based on the energy requirements of that activity. When designing the program, the goal should be to have the athlete reach peak performance at competition time. Key concepts such as the in-season, off-season, and different periods of training are discussed later in the section on periodization.

More competitive athletes will benefit from incorporating a linear periodization that progressively increases in intensity, weight, and power while simultaneously decreasing in volume. Loads at the beginning of the program will focus on muscular endurance development followed by muscular hypertrophy, eventually transitioning into strength and power development. Additionally, the mode of training will differ from that of a general fitness program because of the need for exercise specificity.

In general, sports are performed in multiple planes of motion. However, some sports place most of their emphasis on specific movements and the program design should model this performance. For example, many racquet sports involve lateral movements and lunging positions. The trainer must take this into consideration when selecting resistance training exercises, making sure to emphasize training in these planes of motion for improved performance and injury prevention.

In terms of cardiovascular exercise for athletic performance, the trainer should consider the energy system used to perform the activity. Many sports that seem to benefit from long-distance cardiovascular activity may actually be hindered by it. Long-distance cardiovascular exercise encourages the slow-twitch muscle fibers in the body to become dominant. Although these muscles are great at keeping the athlete moving for long durations, such as in a 5-kilometer race, they do little to improve the athlete's anaerobic capacity to sprint for short distances. This is better accomplished by performing anaerobic sprints, agility- and power-developing drills that work the same energy systems the body uses for sports such as tennis, basketball, baseball, football, soccer, and hockey. These sports require peak power development from fast-twitch muscle fibers. The trainer's analysis of the athletic event should reveal which energy system to focus on in the athlete's fitness program.

CONTINUE

Program Design for Fitness Improvements

The design of the exercise program for fitness improvements will depend on the client's goal and what the client would like to achieve. The client and trainer should set a fitness goal that reflects the components of SMART goals to help design the exercise program. Goals for fitness improvement could involve a variety of components. The client could be looking to improve muscular strength, improve muscular endurance, reduce body fat, build muscle, improve aerobic endurance, or improve something more specific, such as a particular lift.

If the goal is vague, the trainer should have the client narrow down the goal and follow the SMART protocol. Different goals will require different program designs, based on what the client would like to achieve. Then principles such as specificity, overload, and steady progression can be applied to reach the goal.

For example, the client may be interested in improving his 1RM bench press. This goal requires improvements to muscular strength in the pectoral, tricep, and anterior deltoid muscles. Prior to beginning the program periodization, the trainer should first assess the client's current 1RM bench press in order to set a goal that is realistic. Exercise selection should be specific and include exercises that relate to the bench press movement, gradually progressing from developing muscular endurance to hypertrophy and finally to strength and power movements. Although the goal of the program is to improve the strength of the primary muscle groups for bench press, exercise selection should not be limited to only these muscle groups but should also include exercises for the muscular antagonists of the pectorals, triceps, and anterior deltoids.

Proper programming also helps to reduce the chance of developing muscular imbalances due to unilateral program designs. One effective way to achieve this balance in a program aimed at improving single repetition maximum exercises is a four-day split routine. This routine dedicates alternating days to different muscle groups and their muscular synergists. The program would dedicate the first day to "push" muscles, such as the triceps, chest, and shoulders, a second day to "pull" muscles, such as biceps, scapular retractors, posterior deltoids, and back muscles, a third day to all major muscle groups in the legs (i.e., quadriceps, hamstrings, calves, glutes, and hip flexors), and a final day to core musculature.

Similarly, if a client's overall goal is to run a half-marathon, then the trainer must use this goal to design a periodized program aimed at increasing aerobic fitness to prepare for the event. Again, the client's current level of fitness should be assessed based on the mode of the event. The client's periodization should focus on developing aerobic endurance and the primary mode of exercise should be jogging and running, since this is the mode of exercise during the marathon event. The client and trainer should set the SMART goal together, and the trainer can design and implement the program to achieve the goal.

 Powerlifters focus on improving their one repetition maximum (1RM) on three specific lifts: bench press, back squat, and deadlift, none of which involve

> muscular power. The 1RM is a measure of muscular *strength*. Olympic lifters perform either the barbell snatch or barbell clean and jerk, which requires muscular *power*.

A program design for a half-marathon runner will benefit the client most by including more aerobic training. However, resistance training should be incorporated too because it helps improve maximal oxygen uptake (VO2 max), as well as lactic acid threshold and neuromotor control. All these components are essential to a runner's fitness profile. The improved VO2 max will help with cardiovascular efficiency, improved lactic acid threshold will help reduce the buildup of lactic acid in the bloodstream, and improved neuromotor control will help with running technique and efficiency. Aerobic endurance training should be performed up to five days a week and progressed as tolerated by the client at 10 percent or less every two weeks. Resistance training should involve all the major muscle groups of the body to promote muscular balance. The resistance training goal should be to increase intensity gradually in an attempt to peak just before the event, with exercises focused on muscular strength/power.

Manipulating Training Variables for Specific Outcomes

The trainer should know exactly how to manipulate training variables in a client's program for desired outcomes. This is especially important for a well-developed training periodization. Important variables to keep in mind are the number of sets, repetitions, rest periods, and load used for a specific muscular adaptation to exercise. Table 5.3 lists the factors associated with resistance training and how they influence the muscles.

Table 5.3. Resistance Training Factors

	Sets	Repetitions	Rest Period	Load
Muscular Endurance	1 – 3	15+	30 seconds or less	60 – 70% 1RM
Muscular Hypertrophy	3 – 5	8 – 12	60 – 90 seconds	65 – 80% 1RM
Muscular Strength	3 – 5	1 – 8	3 minutes	80 – 100% 1RM
Muscular Power	1 – 3	3 – 6	2 – 3 minutes	0 – 60% 1RM

PRACTICE QUESTIONS

1. Choose the best answer that explains why the following is NOT a SMART goal:

   The client is starting her program in early April and would like to lose weight in the three months prior to her vacation at the end of June.

   A) The goal is not measurable.

   B) The goal is not action-oriented.

   C) The goal is not specific.

   D) The goal is not time-stamped.

Answers:

A) Incorrect. The goal is measurable because the trainer is able to weigh the client on a scale.

B) Incorrect. The goal is action-oriented because it requires the client to actively participate in the fitness program to achieve the goal.

C) **Correct.** The goal is not specific. The client neglected to decide how much weight to lose prior to her vacation.

D) Incorrect. The goal is time-stamped because the client wants to complete it prior to the vacation start date.

2. When designing an exercise program for clients focused on weight management, which training method may NOT be advisable for beginners due to excessive forces placed on the joints?

   A) training for muscular power using plyometrics
   B) training for muscular hypertrophy using resistance cable weights
   C) training for muscular endurance using free weights
   D) training for aerobic endurance using the recumbent bicycle

Answers:

A) **Correct.** Due to excessive forces placed on the joints by plyometric exercises, beginner programs may not require muscular power exercises.

B) Incorrect. Training for muscular hypertrophy is beneficial to clients looking to lose weight because it helps to change their body composition by increasing muscle mass and increasing resting metabolism.

C) Incorrect. Training for muscular endurance helps build a foundation to prevent muscular fatigue and promote neuromotor control.

D) Incorrect. Training for aerobic endurance is beneficial for clients focusing on weight management because it helps improve body composition by utilizing the body's adipose tissue as a fuel source.

Choosing Exercises

It is important that trainers base exercise selection around the data collected from the client's needs analysis, medical background, and fitness assessment. The selection of appropriate exercises will vary significantly from client to client, even when many clients will have the same goals in mind. This is due in part to many factors, including the client's health status, the time frame to reach the goals, recreational activities or sports the clients are involved in, and muscular imbalances that may need to be addressed in training. The following section will go into detail on these concepts and provide examples for many situations.

Goal setting can often assist the trainer in deciding how to fine-tune the exercise program. Additionally, collecting the client's medical history and performing a fitness assessment can help to identify areas of caution for the trainer. Prior to the start of any fitness program, the trainer must ensure the client is cleared for exercise by a physician, if this is indicated by the client's medical history and a Physical Activity Readiness Questionnaire (PAR-Q). If the client is deemed healthy, the client and trainer can sit down to discuss exactly what they would like to accomplish in their time together. During this session, the trainer should discuss the importance of setting a goal that reflects the SMART goals system. Goals that are vague can lead to poor program compliance, and progress can often be difficult to track.

Exercise selection becomes easier to determine after the client's goal is set. For instance, the client may decide he wants to reduce his weight by 5 percent in two months. If the client is 190 pounds, he must lose 9.5 pounds in eight weeks. The goal meets all of the necessary aspects of the SMART system, and the client is medically cleared for exercise. Additionally, the client's fitness assessment did not uncover any areas of significant weakness and the client has an overall fair score. With this knowledge the trainer can create the exercise program aimed at improving body composition.

The program should include a variety of resistance training exercises targeting all the major muscle groups for the client to perform for two to three sessions per week. The start of the program should be high volume and low intensity, focusing on improving muscular endurance and basic exercise techniques. Gradual progression in load should be applied every two weeks while staying between 65 and 75 percent of the client's 1RM. Cardiovascular training should follow the same pattern of progressing intensity; however, since the client is exercising for general health benefits and weight management, the mode is not important. Frequency of aerobic exercise should start with at least two to three sessions per week and increase as the client's tolerance increases. Also, the trainer should discuss with the client the importance of nutritional habits that will increase the client's chance of successfully achieving the goal. Although it is not within the trainer's scope of practice to develop a meal plan for the client, a trainer may provide research-based recommendations on dietary guidelines for weight loss.

Often the client's medical history or health status will create difficulties in designing a fitness plan. The trainer must be aware of past injuries, surgeries, and current health concerns, such as elevated blood pressure, smoking, and heart conditions, which may be affected by exercise. It is common for trainers to work with clients that have some sort of health concern due to more sedentary lifestyles, and increasing numbers of overweight and obese individuals. The trainer should create a program to help address these concerns without going beyond the scope of practice. Exercises selected should accommodate the individual and his or her health concern. For example, if the person had recent knee surgery and struggles to sit in chairs, the trainer can address this concern and help the individual strengthen the leg and core muscles associated with this activity. Regressions of the squat exercise can be beneficial in this situation as long as the client can tolerate the force on the affected knee joint.

Appropriate regressions can be found for nearly every exercise and the trainer must be creative in selecting exercises for muscular balance and variety. Other medical concerns uncovered during the medical history, such as increased blood pressure or heart conditions, may require the trainer to monitor the client throughout the cardiovascular workout to make sure the client knows what intensity is ideal for them. Aerobic training will help in weight management and improve the client's cardiovascular endurance and function. To avoid a medical event, the individual's cardiovascular and strength training routines may need to start at a lower intensity than that for healthy clients. Lower-intensity exercises will not elevate the heart rate and blood pressure as much. This should be taken into consideration when designing the exercise program.

When the trainer comes across areas that need improvement during the fitness assessment, this information should be recorded and addressed through the program design. During the assessment process, the trainer should attempt to test all of the major fitness components, including body composition, flexibility, cardiovascular fitness, muscular strength, and muscular endurance. The results of the client's fitness assessment can be compared to national normative values to evaluate which areas need improvement and which areas require maintenance only. For example, the client may be in great shape and meet the healthy criteria for body composition, cardiovascular fitness, muscular strength, and muscular endurance; however, the client's flexibility may be well below normal values for their age and gender. The trainer can then design a fitness program that emphasizes improving flexibility while maintaining a standard periodization for peak fitness in all other categories. This may include dedicating more time at the end of the fitness routine to static stretching or possibly initiating a proprioceptive neuromuscular facilitation (PNF) program for improved flexibility. It is up to the trainer to decide whether to include additional testing for the client.

Some advanced clients may benefit from sport-specific assessments of power, agility, anaerobic endurance, or even a functional movement screen. Periodic retesting will also help in exercise selection and program design. Retesting should occur after approximately six to twelve weeks, depending on the length of the program, to see if the client is making progress. This will allow the trainer to fine-tune the exercise program and select exercises for areas needing further improvement.

Exercise Selection to Promote Muscular Balance

Exercise selection should always promote muscular balance of the movement system. Muscular imbalances are often caused by overuse related to the client's occupation, while postural deviations may be related to daily sedentary habits and unilateral training programs. Training muscles that are already shortened or tight because of poor posture can further emphasize the muscular imbalance and potentially cause injuries. For example, office workers who sit for forty or more hours a week tend to have forward-rounding shoulders from being crouched over their desks, and tight hip flexors from being in a seated position. This muscular imbalance should be assessed through a visual examination of posture and addressed by strengthening the scapular retractors of the upper back, stretching the muscles of the chest and anterior deltoids, and stretching the hip flexors sufficiently post workout.

When developing the client's fitness program, the trainer should make sure to include exercises that work all the major muscle groups of the body, without exception. This is true even in situations where the client's goal is to increase her 1RM bench press load. Exercises that work the muscular antagonists of bench press movement, such as bent-over rows, should be implemented to decrease risk of muscular imbalances in the shoulders. Muscular balance is also based on the planes of motion in which the exercises are performed. Human movement occurs in distinct planes of motion: the sagittal plane, frontal plane, and transverse plane. Since many muscles work in multiple planes of motion, it is very important that the trainer incorporate a wide variety of exercises for each muscle group. For instance, the client's program may include the dumbbell bench row exercise to address the trapezius, latissimus dorsi, and bicep muscles in the sagittal plane of motion; however, the same muscles function during a pull-down exercise in the frontal plane of motion. Performing both these exercises will help promote muscular balance of the trapezius, latissimus dorsi, and bicep muscles.

 Testing Tip: Create a list of exercises that primarily work the muscle groups opposite to those listed below to promote muscular balance:
- bench press (chest, triceps, anterior deltoids)
- lat pulldown (latissimus dorsi, biceps, lower trapezius)
- stiff-leg deadlift (hamstrings, gluteus maximus, lower back)
- machine hip adduction (inner thigh or hip adductors)

Exercise Selection for Sports Specificity

Choosing exercises to improve sports performance requires analysis of the sport itself, in conjunction with the overall fitness assessment. The trainer should consider the movement patterns and associated muscle groups of the sport when selecting exercises for an athlete's program. Additionally, the fitness assessment should test the energy systems being used during the sport and incorporate exercises to improve the identified energy system.

The training program should always follow the principle of *specificity* when it comes to improving sports performance. Many common sports, such as baseball, softball, basketball, football, tennis, hockey, and lacrosse, are multiplanar, requiring most of the major muscle groups of the body. Also, differences in the position played in the sport can provide vital information for the trainer's program design. Development of leg and core power is essential for all of the sports mentioned; however, the position the athlete plays may change the energy systems utilized during performance. For instance, goalkeepers in sports such as soccer generally do not run as much as the other players and are active for less of the match. They are standing and waiting for large portions of the match, compared with the center, who is running or moving for longer durations and distances. Because of differences in the energy system used by each player, it would benefit the goalie more to work on short bursts, jumping, and agility drills that involve lateral movement, whereas the center would benefit more from utilizing the length of the whole field for anaerobic cardiovascular endurance. Additionally, further research into the position will show the trainer that even in soccer, the players are not running the entire match. This should eliminate the addition of long-distance aerobic endurance bouts in the training programs. The trainer should incorporate sprint intervals that mimic the length of running bouts during the match, interspersed with brief rest periods.

Utilizing the planes of motion, muscle groups, and energy systems can save the trainer a lot of time when attempting to identify which exercises are best for the athlete. However, some sports may be more challenging for a trainer to identify which exercise is best for a particular muscle group.

It might seem that the bench press is the best upper body exercise for football players since they are constantly pushing off one another with their arms. This is a common misconception, since the bulk of force required is generated by the leg and core musculature and transmitted to the upper body. Football players will benefit more from performing the push-press exercise that forces the athlete to generate force with the legs, stabilize with the core, and transmit the force to the arms and shoulders to press the weight overhead. The bench press eliminates the use of both the legs and core, focusing on the strength of the triceps, chest, and anterior deltoids. This does not necessarily mean the athlete should not perform the bench press but simply that the bench press should not be utilized as a measure of the athlete's fitness for the sport.

> **Did You Know?** Athlete Training Combine events for professional athletes test various aspects of fitness related to their sport, such as muscular power, sprint speed, VO2 max, strength and endurance. Ice hockey players test leg power by performing the standing broad jump, an exercise requiring the athlete to jump straight forward as far as possible from a dead stop. Some hockey players can jump over 10 feet.

Aerobic and anaerobic endurance athletes, such as sprinters, cross-country runners, swimmers, and cyclists, also benefit greatly from resistance-training programs. The mode of cardiovascular exercise they perform should be identical to their event, but these athletes benefit as much as the previously mentioned athletes in power and agility sports.

One major benefit that aerobic and anaerobic endurance athletes achieve through resistance training programs is improved biomechanical efficiency. As fatigue sets in, the body tends to compensate during movement and lose efficiency, contributing to further fatigue. Anaerobic athletes receive the added bonus of increasing their speed by developing muscular power.

Programs will vary based on the distance of the athlete's event. For example, a sprinter may incorporate overspeed training, such as sled drag sprints, parachute sprints, and downhill and uphill sprints for increased foot contact speed. Long-distance runners such as cross-country runners may choose not to incorporate these drills and may focus more on resistance training and plyometrics for the neuromotor benefits and final push of the run. The trainer's examination of the athletic event will help determine which specific exercises will be most beneficial. For example, sprinters and long-distance track runners will benefit most from strength training exercises such as lunges, and power exercises such as broad jumps and bounding. These exercises develop athletes' leg power and the ability to explosively propel themselves forward. Athletes such as hurdlers and swimmers may benefit more from plyometrics that incorporate upward movement akin to jumping over hurdles or pushing off the wall of the pool while turning.

PRACTICE QUESTIONS

1. Which exercise will benefit a football lineman MOST during the course of the game?

    A) bench press

    B) seated lateral pull-down

    C) standing military press

    D) push press

    Answers:

    A) Incorrect. The bench press does not involve the core or leg muscles that are necessary for a football lineman's position.

    B) Incorrect. The seated lateral pull-down also eliminates use of the legs and is not specific to the position.

    C) Incorrect. Although the standing military press may benefit the player, since it includes the core and leg muscles, it is not the MOST beneficial exercise on the list because it does not develop power.

    D) Correct. The push-press forces athletes to generate power using their legs, stabilize with their core, and transmit force from the legs through the arms in a pushing motion. These are all specific to the common movements associated with a football lineman.

2. What should the trainer make sure to do first, prior to starting a training program with a new client with medical concerns indicated on their medical history paperwork?

    A) set SMART goals

    B) make sure the client has been cleared by a physician for exercise

    C) perform a fitness assessment

    D) test the client's flexibility

    Answers:

    A) Incorrect. Setting SMART goals should be done prior to program design, but the client has medical concerns that need to be addressed.

    B) Correct. If the client has a medical concern that may be affected by exercise, the client should see a physician to make sure she is healthy enough to begin an exercise program.

    C) Incorrect. The fitness assessment may exacerbate a medical concern such as heart arrhythmias, high blood pressure, etc.

D) Incorrect. Flexibility tests are typically included in the fitness assessment and can create problems for clients with existing medical conditions.

Exercise Order

The key concepts of exercise order are: always start with a dynamic warm-up prior to a workout, and try to perform exercises from highest intensity to lowest intensity. Following these concepts will help to reduce the risk of injury and early fatigue. The following section discusses the ideas behind the order of exercises as they pertain to the type of workout, muscle groups of focus, and the client specifically.

The dynamic warm-up should always be performed prior to the fitness program. Exercises in the dynamic warm-up should follow movement patterns similar to those listed in the day's workout. Performing similar, low-intensity versions of the same exercises helps to prepare the muscles that will be involved, making them more elastic and initiating muscular activation. Additionally, the increased blood flow to the muscles supplies the oxygen needed for increased activity levels. As an example, if the program design involves performing lunges and Romanian deadlifts for strength, the dynamic warm-up may include a lunge and trunk twist for five repetitions per leg to warm up the quads, glutes, and hamstrings, and a straight-leg kick to stretch out the hamstrings and warm up the hip flexors.

The warm-up itself should involve ten minutes of stretches and dynamic movement patterns that involve most major muscle groups, and five minutes of light, progressive aerobic exercise to increase blood flow to the muscles. The warm-up may also include performing self-myofascial release techniques involving a foam roller or various tools. This technique focuses on compressing the connective tissue surrounding the muscles to release adhesions that may cause movement compensation or limit flexibility, without the deleterious effects associated with static stretching.

Following the dynamic warm-up, the exercise should start with high-intensity, large-muscle-group exercises. There are several reasons for starting the workout with higher intensity exercises: Following the warm-up, the body has not depleted much of its energy sources, which means that fatigue has not yet set in and technique will not be compromised. When muscles become fatigued, they begin to recruit their synergists for repeated movements in compensation, causing technique to break down. Therefore, exercises that involve a lot of technique, such as Olympic lifting, plyometrics, and agility training, should be implemented early in the workout.

Resistance training should follow high-intensity exercise. Resistance training is higher intensity than aerobic activity but lower intensity than power- and agility-based movements. Therefore, the resistance-training phase of the program should be completed between the highest- and lowest-intensity exercises. There are certain types of training methods that will incorporate combinations of power- and strength-based movements; however, they should be reserved for experienced exercisers.

Finally, cardiovascular training can be saved for the end of the workout. The lower- to moderate-intensity cardiovascular portion of the training session is typically less technique oriented and form will not suffer as much from the fatigue of the resistance-training portion of the workout. Additionally, the energy system being utilized by the body differs once the client has reached the three-minute mark. Unlike the phosphagen system used in the first six seconds of high-intensity exercises or anaerobic glycolysis utilized in the first three minutes, aerobic exercise is based around the body's ability to convert oxygen to ATP using the body's adipose stores. This lower-intensity activity is easier to sustain for longer durations and should be saved for the end of the workout just prior to flexibility training.

Flexibility training should be completed at the end of the workout. Methods should be determined by the trainer to meet the needs of the client. If the trainer assesses that the client has poor flexibility during the initial fitness assessment, time should be taken to address the areas of concern. Common flexibility issues due to sedentary lifestyles or careers tend to evolve from long periods of sitting. The shoulders tend to slouch or round forward, the hips are in a constant state of flexion, and the hamstrings are shortened. The sitting position contributes to issues throughout the kinetic chain and can often be corrected through stretching and strengthening. Goniometry may be performed to assess various areas of tightness among the muscles. Practiced trainers can often determine the areas of concern via a visual examination in conjunction with goniometric measurements.

Flexibility training can involve a number of methods, such as static stretching, assisted stretching, and PNF stretching, to improve the range of motion in the client. PNF should be performed only by trainers who are well trained in the methods, because knowledge of biomechanics is necessary for proper form. Flexibility and stretching should be performed at the end of the program because the muscles become more elastic once they are warmed up through exercise, and the client can achieve greater ranges of motion. The elasticity also makes it safer for the client and prevents overstretching, which can lead to prolonged weakness and sometimes injury.

The **exercise order** will occasionally vary based on the client. Clients with health concerns that cause rapid fatigue may benefit more from performing cardiovascular exercise first, allowing for a longer warm-up period prior to resistance training. Some individuals may not be healthy enough for certain dynamic stretching movements and just pedaling on the recumbent bike will elicit a stretch for their legs. The trainer should take this into consideration while designing the exercise program.

In general, the warm-up should include movements similar to the exercises that are planned in the workout, and the workout should start with higher-intensity, large muscle groups. The client's strength and conditioning status should also be taken into consideration while designing an exercise program. Clientele who are exercising for general health benefits and have been training previously may be able to tolerate a circuit that incorporates a combination of higher- and moderate-intensity exercises alternating throughout the program. This method can often keep the client interested and more compliant. In this case, the workout should still start with a dynamic warm-up, followed by higher-intensity exercises at the start of the circuit and lower-intensity exercises toward the end of the circuit. For example, after warming up, the client may start with box jumps, overhead squats, and ice skaters. Two plyometric exercises are separated by a resistance training exercise; however, they are all high intensity and use large muscle groups so they are placed at the start of the workout. Such clients should save the cardiovascular exercise for afterwards or for a separate day, and save static stretching for the end of each workout.

The order of exercises for those with specific training goals will follow a similar pattern as described above: dynamic and specific warm-up, high-intensity resistance training using large muscle groups, lower-intensity resistance training using smaller muscle groups, cardiovascular training (following the specificity of the client's goals), and finally, flexibility training.

PRACTICE QUESTION

A workout should always start with

- **A)** high-intensity exercises.
- **B)** flexibility training.
- **C)** small-muscle-group resistance training.
- **D)** a dynamic warm-up.

Answers:

- A) Incorrect. This is dangerous because the muscles are not prepared for exercise yet.
- B) Incorrect. Flexibility training involving static stretching and PNF stretching should be saved for last.
- C) Incorrect. This is dangerous since the muscles are not prepared for exercise yet.
- **D) Correct.** A dynamic warm-up that addresses the muscles that will be utilized during the workout should be done first.

Training Frequency and Rest Periods

Exercise frequency and rest periods will depend on a number of factors: the client's availability, training goals, and fitness level. Novice exercisers will likely have a significantly different recovery time than those who have previously trained. The trainer should take this into consideration while developing the exercise program.

Clientele beginning a new exercise program will often require longer and more frequent rest periods during workouts. The **work-to-rest ratio** is simply defined as how long the client is exercising compared with how long they are waiting in recovery. When the client is starting an exercise program, a work-to-rest ratio of 1:1 should allow adequate recovery for most healthy individuals. The trainer should observe the client through the training program and adjust this rest period accordingly. For example, clients who are significantly more sedentary, current or ex-smokers, or clients struggling with weight may require this ratio to be adjusted to allow for more rest between sets or exercises. The trainer should also inform the client of the amount of recovery between certain exercises at the various loads and volumes for the optimal results. Differences occur during resistance training and cardiovascular training in terms of rest periods and recovery methods.

Resistance training **rest periods** will depend primarily on the load and volume being utilized in the workout. Resistance training for muscular endurance using high repetition ranges and low loads should allow for only thirty seconds of recovery. Muscular hypertrophy rest periods can range from thirty to ninety seconds, while muscular strength and power exercises require a longer rest period of around three minutes. The rest periods will depend on the load the client lifted and should generally lengthen with increasing loads.

Certain training methods can change the rest period. For example, using circuit training, supersets, or pyramid sets can decrease rest periods; however, the trainer should wait until the client has progressed enough to tolerate the lack of recovery. Rest periods in circuit training should be brief (ten to fifteen seconds) between exercises and longer (ninety seconds) at the end of the circuit. For supersets, the rest period between exercises will depend on the load and volume. If the load is lighter, the rest period may be only long enough to perform the opposing exercise. This can make the workout more challenging for novice clients.

For cardiovascular exercise, rest periods will be determined by the goals of the client and type of cardiovascular training method being used. Clients who are participating in specific events should use the same method as their training event in preparation. If the client is training for a marathon, it makes sense for that individual to utilize running as their primary type of cardiovascular activity. Clients exercising for general health benefits or fitness gains may not require a specific form of cardio and will benefit most from a variety of sources. Those starting new cardiovascular activities should always begin with low to moderate intensity and may even incorporate rest periods into the workout. For instance, when a client is starting a running program, it is unlikely that the client will be able to perform thirty minutes of continuous running or jogging. The trainer should consider the difficulty for the new runner and have the runner start by performing walking and jogging intervals at a work-to-rest ratio of 1:1, or even 1:2 if the runner is struggling. Starting with a duration that the client is able to complete will also provide encouragement and keep the client more compliant. Clients who are more advanced exercisers may be able to tolerate higher-intensity workouts. As these clients progress, the trainer can advance them to work-to-rest ratios that minimize the rest period and increase the work period. Additionally, these clients will benefit from working with varying degrees of intensity during their cardiovascular workouts.

Assigning Training Frequency Based on Training Goals

Training frequency will depend on the client's current fitness level and goals set with the trainer prior to starting a fitness program. General health guidelines indicate that resistance training should be performed at least two to three times a week, whereas cardiovascular training should be performed at least three to five days a week. With novice clientele, resistance training should be performed on two non-consecutive days per week to allow for adequate recovery between workouts. New exercisers should also start with fewer cardiovascular training days and gradually progress. The trainer and client should discuss a specific schedule that includes both cardiovascular and resistance training workouts and the client should add it to his or her calendar. The act of writing down the workout in their schedules may help keep clients accountable for the daily exercise schedule and improve their commitment to the program.

Goals can help determine how to progress frequency in a client's training program. For improvements to fitness gains, such as an increase in weight lifted, the trainer may consider implementing a four-day split lifting routine for intermediate and advanced clients. This allows clients to focus on specific muscle groups on separate days and promote muscular hypertrophy and strength.

Clients seeking improvements on long-distance running, biking, or swimming times may require fewer resistance training days to allow for additional cardiovascular training. The trainer should consider utilizing a two- or three-day, full-body resistance training program in addition to cardiovascular training five days a week. The addition of resistance training to the client's workout routine will help to increase maximum oxygen uptake and lactate threshold, and improve body mechanics and movement efficiency, improving the client's cardiovascular performance.

Frequency can play a major role in overtraining and overuse injuries. It is important for the trainer to understand the consequences of training too often and inform clients of the risks of overuse associated with resistance and cardiovascular training. Clients who consistently perform resistance training on the same muscle groups on consecutive days are at higher risk of developing overuse injuries. For instance, if clients insist on improving their bench press and ask to incorporate the exercise more frequently, the trainer should explain that constant training of the same muscles could lead to overuse injuries. Constantly loading the chest and shoulders can cause inflammation of the bursae and tendons and wear down the cartilage. This scenario is similar in cardiovascular training. However, cardiovascular overtraining is caused by a combination of duration, distance, and frequency. It is a common issue with those training for long-distance running events to try and progress too rapidly. The runner decides to attempt another mile and places too much stress on the body, causing overuse injuries and, as a result, must rest for several weeks, impeding progress. The trainer must understand the importance of training frequency and proper progression.

Monitoring Exercise Intensity

There are numerous ways to monitor exercise intensity, including heart rate, perceived exertion, VO2 max, and metabolic equivalents (METs). Exercise intensity helps the trainer determine if the client is achieving the workout goal for the day. Using the simpler methods, such as determining a target heart rate zone or rate of perceived exertion, can help the trainer save time and maximize the efficiency of the workout.

Target heart rate zone can be determined by calculating the client's estimated maximum heart rate using the **Karvonen formula**, whereas the **rate of perceived exertion (RPE)** is simply described on a scale of how hard the client feels they are working. Though RPE is not quite as accurate as determining target heart rate zone, it saves the time of stopping the client to check his pulse and determine if he is at 65 percent of his maximum heart rate.

VO2 max is more complicated to determine and accuracy requires expensive laboratory equipment. There are formulas to calculate maximal oxygen uptake, but they still require more time than utilizing the target heart rate zone or RPE scales.

Metabolic equivalents **METs** are a measurement of the body's caloric energy consumption during exercise compared to its consumption at rest. Resting in a seated position, the body has a MET level of 1 kilocalorie per kilogram of bodyweight per hour. While exercising, an individual's MET level is a multiple of this number depending on the intensity of exercise. Moderate intensity is typically equated to between 3 and 6 METs, and high intensity is equated to over 6 METs. Occasionally, cardiovascular equipment will automatically calculate an approximate MET level based on the speed and incline used for the workout. For the client's sake, it is simpler to ask the client to utilize either RPE or the talk test to determine intensity. Table 5.4 depicts an RPE chart based on a 1 – 10 scale.

Table 5.4. RPE Chart (Rate of Percieved Exertion)

10	**Max Effort Activity**	Feels almost impossible to keep going. Completely out of breath, unable to talk.
9	**Very Hard Activity**	Very difficult to maintain exercise intensity. Can barely breathe and speak a single word.
7-8	**Vigorous Activity**	On the verge of becoming uncomfortable. Short of breath, can speak a sentence.
4-6	**Moderate Activity**	Feels like you can exercise for hours. Breathing heavily, can hold short conversation.
2-3	**Light Activity**	Feels like you can maintain for hours. Easy to breathe and carry a conversation.
1	**Very Light Activity**	Anything other than sleeping, watching TV, riding in a car, etc.

CONTINUE

PRACTICE QUESTIONS

1. When performing consecutive sets of an exercise, resistance training rest periods depend primarily upon the

    A) load and volume.

    B) strength of the client.

    C) power of the client.

    D) There is no rest period in resistance training.

    Answers:

    A) Correct. The load and volume of an exercise will primarily determine the rest period in between consecutive sets of that exercise.

    B) Incorrect. The strength of the client will help to determine the weight rather than the rest period.

    C) Incorrect. The power of the client determines the velocity at which an exercise is performed.

    D) Incorrect. The rest period allows for adequate recovery of muscle energy systems to perform the exercise at the same load properly.

2. Clients looking to improve strength gains will benefit most from

    A) two days of resistance training and three days of cardiovascular training a week.

    B) increasing resistance training to four days a week when using an upper body/lower body split program.

    C) simply performing the same bodyweight workout two to three days a week.

    D) training the same muscle groups on consecutive days, multiple times a week.

    Answers:

    A) Incorrect. Though this is beneficial for general health benefits, clients looking to increase strength will benefit more from increasing the resistance training frequency to more than two days a week.

    B) Correct. A four-day split routine will provide adequate stimulation for improved strength.

    C) Incorrect. Performing the same bodyweight workout two to three days a week will eventually become too easy and not provoke an overload effect.

    D) Incorrect. Training the same muscle groups on consecutive days, multiple times a week may cause overtraining and potential injury.

TRAINING LOAD AND REPETITION

Performing an exercise assessment can often help the trainer identify what loads the client should be utilizing for the assigned repetition range. It can also be helpful in assigning cardiovascular training capacities per workout. Once it has been determined that the client is healthy and ready for exercise, the assessment process may include a 1RM test for larger muscle groups. Additionally, the trainer can determine the client's target heart rate zone for exercise using the client's resting heart rate and a simple formula. This will ensure the training program is incorporating the principles of overload and progression for optimal training results.

Assigning a training load can be achieved through repetition maximum testing. The **1RM test** is an accurate tool for developing training loads with athletic clients or clients who are currently participating in a training program. The 1RM test involves the client performing a single repetition of an exercise, typically, the bench press and back squat or leg press. The client must perform a single repetition with good technique through the full range of motion. If the client is able to perform more than a single repetition, she must wait for full recovery and perform the exercise again at a slightly higher load. This weight can then be used to determine a multiple repetition maximum to elicit different training goals.

For instance, training for muscular endurance typically requires about 60 percent of 1RM. Therefore, if the client's 1RM bench press is 200 pounds, his 15RM bench press should be approximately 120 pounds. If the same client is in a hypertrophy phase, that is about 75 percent of 1RM, or 150 pounds. If the client was looking to determine the load for muscular strength gains, he would want between 80 and 95 percent of 1RM, or 160 to 190 pounds. These numbers are approximate only and will vary by client. However, this method of determining repetition ranges based on the 1RM test can be very effective.

Since the 1RM test relies heavily on technique and full range of motion, it is not necessarily the best method for clients who are new to exercise. With beginner clients, it is more beneficial to have them perform a multiple repetition maximum test and then estimate a 1RM. For this type of test, a lighter load is selected for the exercise and the client is asked to perform repetitions to fatigue. The lighter weight should allow the client to perform the exercise with better technique and less risk of injury. Once the number of repetitions is determined based on the weight, the trainer can then calculate the estimated 1RM.

The same calculation can also be used to determine other resistance training ranges, for instance, if the client performs an eight repetition maximum test at 160 pounds. Knowing that eight repetitions is approximately 80 percent of the client's maximum, a 1RM can be estimated by plugging in higher numbers and multiplying by 0.8 until 160 is achieved. In this case, multiplying 200 by 0.8 gives the client's 8RM weight of 160 pounds.

Assigning a **target heart rate** for new clients requires the trainer to first determine the client's maximal heart rate in beats per minute (bpm). There are several methods to determine a client's maximal heart rate: estimation based on age, the Karvonen formula, and exercising stress test protocols.

Stress testing protocols typically involve complicated and expensive equipment that is not found in fitness centers and therefore is less practical. Estimating maximum heart rate based on age can help the trainer to quickly determine exercise target heart rate zones. In this formula, the trainer simply subtracts the client's age from 220 to determine the estimated maximal heart rate. The trainer can then multiply the resulting number by the percentage of maximal heart rate they want the client to achieve during their cardiovascular workout. For instance, if the client is twenty years old, the estimated maximal heart rate would be 220 − 20 or 200 beats per minute. The trainer can then take percentages of 200 beats per minute to determine the client's estimated target heart rate zone. If the client is trying to perform steady-state aerobic endurance training, she would want to keep her heart rate somewhere between 50 and 85 percent of the maximum, or between 100 and 170 bpm.

A more accurate measure of target heart rate zone can be determined using the **Karvonen formula**, a more complicated formula that utilizes the client's estimated maximal heart rate described above, his target heart rate training zone, and his resting heart rate. Prior to exercise, the trainer should first determine the client's resting heart rate and calculate the client's estimated maximal heart rate. As an example, a client of age thirty with a resting heart rate of 68 bpm who wants to perform cardiovascular exercise at 65 percent of maximum heart rate would have a Karvonen formula that looks like this:

> Target Heart Rate = Resting Heart Rate + (0.65 × [Estimated Maximal Heart Rate − Resting Heart Rate])
>
> Target Heart Rate = 68 + (0.65 × [190 − 68]) = 147 bpm

If the client wants to perform aerobic exercise of at least 65 percent of their maximum heart rate, he would need to be exercising at 147 beats per minute based on his resting heart rate and age.

The Karvonen formula provides the client a more accurate representation of how hard he should be training in terms of his cardiovascular exercise. If the same client were looking to improve his lactate threshold via anaerobic endurance training, the trainer would simply change the 0.65 to 0.90 and keep the rest of the numbers the same. Determining the client's training goals can allow the trainer to calculate the client's target heart rate zone for cardiovascular activity. However, the fitness level of the client should be considered prior to assigning the training heart rate zone. Additionally, the trainer should gradually progress the training program toward the client's goal. If the goal is to complete a marathon or long-distance cycling challenge, the program may not necessitate performing above certain percentages of the client's maximal heart rate.

Volume

Volume is a function of the number of sets, repetitions, and exercises in a workout. Manipulating this variable can contribute to differences in muscular fitness and is typically accompanied by a variance in load. Unless the client is on a current fitness plan and switching to a new one, periodization starts with high volumes and very low loads to promote muscular endurance.

Volumes of fifteen or more repetitions develop the muscles' ability to sustain very light loads over longer durations. Depending on the strength and conditioning level of the client, the trainer should implement between one and three sets per exercise for beginners and at least three sets for advance clients. Additionally, the rest periods for this volume should be as short as thirty seconds for optimal results.

In linear periodization, the next logical volume to progress to focuses on increased muscular hypertrophy using light to moderate loads with slightly lower volumes. The repetition range for this category is eight to twelve repetitions with a slightly heavier load than that of the muscular endurance category. The goal of this phase is to increase the size of the muscle. Muscular hypertrophy requires rest periods of approximately sixty to ninety seconds, and the client should perform three sets per exercise. The closer the repetition range and load come to 1RM, the more emphasis is placed on building muscular strength. Training volumes for muscular strength are anywhere between one and eight repetitions. The heavier the weight, the more stress that is placed on the muscles, tendons, and central nervous system; therefore, training for muscular strength should be done after clients have developed significant conditioning to heavier weights.

Along with an increase in load associated with lower training volumes is an increase in the length of the rest period to three to five minutes. The number of sets associated with muscular strength training will again vary per the client's fitness level. The optimal number of strength sets is at least three; however, beginners may perform only one to three sets per workout as they progress. The object of muscular strength training is to increase the maximal amount of weight the client is able to lift, which can be assessed via the 1RM test.

Finally, muscular power development involves the velocity at which the exercise is performed and shares similar volumes and rest periods with strength-based movements. Three or more sets of up to six repetitions is optimal for gains in power, but the exercise should be performed at a faster rate to influence muscular power. Since the goal of the exercise is maximal force production in a given time period, control of the exercises requires a lighter load than with muscular strength training. For example, the client's back squat 1RM weight may be 200 pounds but the jump squat weight will top out at 60 pounds and six repetitions. Power exercises are typically the highest intensity and should be implemented in a progressive manner as well.

PRACTICE QUESTIONS

1. What volume and load are associated with the development of muscular hypertrophy?

    A) very light loads with very high volumes

    B) very heavy loads with very light volumes

    C) moderate volumes and loads

    D) very light volumes with light loads performed at a high velocity

Answers:

- A) Incorrect. This load and volume range is associated with muscular endurance development.
- B) Incorrect. This load and volume is associated with muscular strength gains.
- **C) Correct.** Muscular hypertrophy involves performing moderate volumes of moderate loads.
- D) Incorrect. Since velocity is the goal, these volumes and loads are for power development.

2. In general, as training volume goes down, training load
   - **A)** goes up.
   - **B)** goes down.
   - **C)** stays the same.
   - **D)** goes down for athletes only.

Answers:

- **A) Correct.** As training volume goes down, the load lifted should increase.
- B) Incorrect. This is the opposite of what should happen.
- C) Incorrect. Without increasing the load, decreasing the volume may cause a loss of overload, leading to lack of progression.
- D) Incorrect. All clients will benefit from increasing the load while decreasing the volume.

PROGRESSION

The goal of exercise progression is to accomplish the principles of training overload and specificity by manipulating the training variables in a program. Progression refers to a gradual increase in the intensity of a training program by manipulating training variables incrementally. Progression can be applied to the principles of overload and specificity to make sure the training stimulus is challenging enough to elicit the body's natural adaptation to the stress. Overload requires the trainer to adjust one variable of the program, such as frequency, intensity, time or mode, in order to make consecutive workouts more difficult. Consistent overloading during consecutive workouts will ensure the client is adequately stressed with each workout and will avoid the risk of reaching a training plateau. The term *plateau* in training refers to a point in the client's training program where no further progress is being achieved. Reaching a plateau means the client is seeing no strength gains, weight loss, or fitness improvements even though they are continuing to exercise. Plateaus are dangerous for the client's compliance because they discourage the individual. Clients who do not see tangible results often place blame on themselves or the trainer and the likelihood of giving up is higher. Manipulation of training variables to elicit the overload effect will help prevent training plateaus, so it is important that the trainer follow this principle.

> **?** Athletes who are in competition will go into a short maintenance period of resistance training where they are not making exercise gains. How does this differ from a training plateau?

In order to ensure progressive overload is being achieved, the trainer should know when and how to adjust training variables in a program. Adjusting a client's training variables will depend mostly on how the client adapts to the exercises. The trainer should be aware of the stages of learning described earlier in the chapter and use these to adjust the program accordingly. If the client is obviously in the autonomous phase of learning an exercise technique, it is certainly in her best interest to increase the difficulty of the exercise. In contrast, clients in the cognitive phase of learning an exercise should remain at or below that exercise difficulty until they have mastered the technique. Increases to the training load should not exceed 10 percent and should be applied when the client has been able to complete the current workout without compensation more than once. This will ensure that overload is achieved without the risk of overtraining and potential injury.

Once a client has mastered an exercise technique, the trainer can increase the intensity of the exercise. For example, the trainer may notice the client is executing a bent over barbell row with little to no compensation and is in the autonomous phase of learning. One logical progression to elicit the overload effect would be to increase the weight on the bar, making the exercise more intense. Another method would be to progress the client to using dumbbells rather than a bar. With the dumbbells, each hand would have to stabilize a portion of the weight without help from the other, which may be enough of a challenge for the client to benefit from overload. When adjusting the difficulty of resistance training programs, it is safest to modify only one variable from workout to workout. This means that if the trainer is planning to increase the weight used for the exercises, the trainer should avoid also increasing the number of exercises in the workout. Adjusting a single variable is enough to provoke the overload response, obviating additional adjustments.

Cardiovascular program design should also follow a steady progression. Adjustments to cardiovascular mode, intensity, duration, and frequency should not exceed 10 percent per workout because there is a higher risk of overtraining beyond that point. Therefore, the client and trainer will need to track the distances, time, and intensity utilized in the cardiovascular workouts. For example, clients training for distance running events at steady paces can increase the distance by multiplying their previous distance by 0.1 and adding that amount to their previous total distance, making sure not to exceed the new distance during the next run. The trainer should ask the client to be aware of how his body responds to the adjustment and avoid increasing the distance, duration, or frequency if he is still experiencing significant muscular soreness following a workout. The delayed-onset muscle soreness is a sign that the overload principle was accomplished and no further increase is required until the body has adapted.

Assigning Progression Based on Training Goal

The needs analysis performed at the beginning of a training program will help the trainer determine how to progress toward the client's training goal. In general, a safe progression of strength training programs follows the order of muscular endurance training, muscular hypertrophy training, muscular strength training, and then muscular power training. However, the goal can change exercise selection, weight selection, duration of cycles and periods, and frequency of workouts. Because of the time frame of their competitions, clients seeking sports performance improvement will have a different progression than clients seeking general health benefits. The trainer should still observe how the client is reacting to the exercises and increase the difficulty based solely on the rate at which the client masters the exercise techniques.

Major differences in training progression toward the client's goal will rely on the specificity of exercise. Clientele seeking improvements to sports or recreational activities will follow a progression from non-specific exercises for improved muscular endurance to very specific exercises to improve performance. As an example, client programs that are designed for fitness improvements with athletic performance will be similar at the start of the programs, but the program designs will vary toward the end because of specificity of the goals. Clients seeking fitness improvements may want to perform exercise variations to boost their record lifts and specific fitness achievements, whereas clients seeking athletic performance improvements should progress to exercises that mimic key movements in their specific sports. More specifically, the fitness improvement client may have a goal to increase back squat weight over the course of the program. This is a double-leg, multi-joint exercise using many large muscle groups. The client will benefit from keeping this exercise in the training program, for the sake of specificity, and will also possibly benefit by incorporating different varieties of the same exercise. For example, having the client perform a sumo squat will help to develop strength in the adductors of the inner thigh and may be beneficial for improving the standard back squat. The program will gradually overload the client by steadily increasing the weight lifted, while making little change to the mode of the exercise.

In contrast, the client looking to improve sports performance may also start with the back squat as a primary multi-joint exercise. However, if this client plays a sport involving running or balancing on a single leg, it is in the client's best interest to progress toward specificity. Their program design will branch out to involve more single-leg, multi-joint exercises, such as lunges and single-leg squats, toward the end of the program. The goal of the fitness program helps determine how to progress the exercise mode, intensity, time, and frequency.

PRACTICE QUESTIONS

1. What is a training plateau?

   A) when the client has reached peak performance

   B) when the trainer has the client performing the same workout on several consecutive training days

   C) when the client is not seeing fitness improvements even though the client is still training

   D) when the trainer progresses the client's program to reach a desired goal

   Answers:

   A) Incorrect. This is not the definition of a training plateau.

   B) Incorrect. A training plateau does not refer to the described training design.

   C) **Correct.** A training plateau occurs when the client is not seeing any benefits from the exercise program due to lack of overload.

   D) Incorrect. This describes the principle of progression.

2. When should a training program be progressed?

   A) every workout

   B) when the client has reached the cognitive phase of learning the exercises

   C) when the client is still having significant delayed-onset muscle soreness

   D) when the client has completed the workout without compensation in technique more than once

   Answers:

   A) Incorrect. The client may still be learning how to master the techniques of the exercises in the program and could overtrain by progressing further.

   B) Incorrect. The cognitive phase shows that the client is still struggling to complete the task and requires further practice to eliminate compensatory movements.

   C) Incorrect. If the client is still having significant delayed-onset muscle soreness, the client is still achieving overload and should not progress yet.

   D) **Correct.** The client has mastered or nearly mastered the training technique and is ready to increase the difficulty of the workout through the manipulation of training variables.

Aerobic Endurance Training

Aerobic endurance training is an important part of a well-rounded fitness program. Program design and implementation should include not only resistance training but also some form of cardiovascular training. A key determinant of how to implement an aerobic endurance training program is the client's goal.

Cardiovascular activity has many variations that each elicit a different adaptation in the body. Steady-state heart rate training is generally what people think about when trainers refer to cardio. There are other methods of cardiovascular training, however, such as interval and zone training, that can be incorporated into a client's program for exercise variety. The client's goal will help to determine which type of aerobic endurance training is best for the client's progress. For example, clients who are training to perform in a 10-kilometer race will benefit more from steady-state, long-distance running than from interval training.

Steady state refers to running at the same pace or maintaining the same heart rate throughout the duration of the cardiovascular workout. This form of cardio helps to develop the capacity of the cardiovascular system to sustain long durations of aerobic exercise through increased cardiac output and mitochondrial function at the muscles. Additionally, steady-state aerobic exercise utilizes the body's excess adipose tissue as a fuel source rather than depleting the muscles' glycogen stores that are utilized during resistance training and interval training. Another reason steady-state cardio benefits long-distance competitors is that it develops the slow-twitch, type I muscle fibers that are the key to improving aerobic metabolism for sustained activities. Since steady-state aerobic training is at a lower intensity over a longer duration than interval training, the stress on the client is lower.

The downside to this type of aerobic training is that it can negatively affect the performance of strength and power athletes, such as those in football, baseball, lacrosse, ice hockey, tennis, and many other sports. Therefore, the trainer should implement steady-state aerobic endurance training in programs for long-distance athletes and clients exercising for general health benefits.

> Did You Know? There are ultra-triathalon competitions that span three days: day 1 involves a run of over 50 miles, day 2 involves a bike ride of over 300 miles, and day 3 involves a swim of over 6 miles.

Interval training uses a different energy system from steady-state training and tends to be performed at greater than 90 percent of the client's maximum heart rate. The work-to-rest ratio associated with interval training is best determined by the client's physical condition or goals. Programs for athletes should utilize the duration of the work-to-rest ratio associated with their sport.

Interval training develops the type II muscle fibers of the body that are associated with high-intensity sports performance and the anaerobic glycolytic energy system. This type of endurance training has several advantages over steady state: it takes much less time to complete a workout, burns more calories in a shorter period of time, and keeps the workout interesting. The high-intensity workout stimulates the body to produce hormones associated with weight loss and muscular hypertrophy and promotes caloric expenditure through excess post-exercise oxygen consumption for hours following the workout.

The downside to interval training is that the higher intensity workout puts more stress on the joints and muscles. This means that clientele may have to progress to the level where their body can tolerate the training. Intervals do not necessarily need to be high intensity to be effective. Utilizing an interval style of training can also help prepare individuals seeking to improve in longer-distance running or swimming. The client can take periodic breaks to recover the necessary energy to continue for a thirty-minute running session, for example. Breaking long-distance events into manageable intervals can be beneficial for clients new to training.

Finally, a **zone training program** can be built around simple measurable intensities, using the **rate of perceived exertion (RPE)** or the client's ability to hold a conversation while exercising. This type of training method is typically broken down into several zones that use ventilatory threshold levels associated with increasing intensities of exercise. The progression of exercise still involves an increase of 10 percent or less to avoid overtraining, and clients stay in the first zone until they are able to accumulate a half hour of sustained cardiovascular exercise. If using RPE to measure the intensity, the client should be around four out of ten while exercising in this zone, and should be able to hold a conversation while exercising.

The second zone marks the breach of the first ventilatory threshold that signifies an increase in respiration rate associated with higher-intensity exercise. The client's RPE should increase to five or six and the start of the phase may incorporate intervals to build up the client's aerobic fitness levels. At this stage, the client will have difficulty holding a conversation as the respiration rate increases and intensity climbs. Additionally, lactic acid levels will begin to increase, but the increased breathing will help to buffer the blood, allowing the person to continue exercising.

Finally, the third zone is indicated by a second ventilatory threshold and an additional increase in the respiration rate. This zone is characterized by high-intensity anaerobic activity, the inability to hold a conversation, and reaching lactate threshold. At this stage, the interval lengths will drop significantly as lactic acid levels in the blood continue to rise at a rate the body cannot buffer. Rest periods are required for the body to be able to continue at the same pace.

Zone training is advantageous in that gradual progression toward higher intensities will increase fitness levels, burn calories more efficiently, promote compliance through exercise variability, and improve lactate thresholds. One disadvantage to this style of training is that different clients will respond to increases in exercise intensities differently. Their ratings of perceived exertion on a scale of 1 – 10 are subjective and will vary based on each client's tolerance to increasing exercise intensities, similar to differences in pain thresholds among medical patients. Another drawback is that higher intensity zones are more stressful on the body mechanically, and the uncomfortable feeling of breaching the lactate threshold may turn some clients off to this type of training.

Table 5.5. Effects of Acute and Chronic Cardiovascular Training

		Effort	Effect
Improve Fitness	Maximize Performance	Maximum 90 – 100%	Benefit: helps fit athletes develop speed
		Hard 80 – 90%	Benefit: increases maximum performance capacity for shorter sessions
		Moderate 70 – 80%	Benefit: improves aerobic fitness
	Lose Weight	Light 60 – 70%	Benefit: improved basic endurance and fat burning
		Very light 50 – 60%	Benefit: helps with recovery

Both aerobic and anaerobic cardiovascular training produce short- and long-term effects in an exercise program. The acute effects associated with aerobic endurance training include increased cardiac output, increased blood flow to the musculoskeletal system, blood pressure regulation (including a post-exercise decrease in blood pressure for up to 15 hours), increased respiration, decreased stress, and increased myocardial blood flow. Chronic effects of aerobic training include improved stroke volume, improved oxygen uptake, or VO2 max, decreased resting heart rate, decreased blood pressure, reduced body fat, improved capillary density, and the development of slow-twitch muscle fibers.

Anaerobic cardiovascular training has similar acute responses such as an increase in heart rate, respiration, blood flow, cardiac output, and oxygen uptake. Another response is the acute systolic increase in blood pressure specific to physical activity. Chronic adaptations to anaerobic training involve improvements to lactate threshold, fast-twitch muscle fiber development, reduced body fat percentage, muscular strength and power development, and sprint performance. Applying these principles to an exercise program design can help the trainer identify which protocols to follow based on the client's goals. Clients seeking general health benefits may have success with both modes of cardiovascular training, whereas clients seeking improved performance should rely more on the method that is specific to their athletic event.

PRACTICE QUESTIONS

1. Steady-state cardiovascular activity is
    - **A)** more intense than anaerobic endurance training.
    - **B)** short-duration aerobic training of less than five minutes.
    - **C)** good for power athletes like sprinters, football players, and Olympic lifters.
    - **D)** appropriate for cross-country runners.

Answers:

- A) Incorrect. It is less intense than anaerobic endurance training.
- B) Incorrect. It is typically longer duration, and beginner programs should start at twenty to thirty minutes.
- C) Incorrect. Steady state is not specific and can cause increased influence of the wrong type of muscle fibers for power athletes.
- **D) Correct.** Steady-state activity is an appropriate form of cardiovascular activity for long-distance runners such as cross-country runners.

2. Performing cardiovascular exercise at near-maximal efforts (over 90 percent of maximum heart rate) will help to improve
    - **A)** development of type I muscle fibers.
    - **B)** recovery rate from a tough workout.
    - **C)** lactate threshold and movement speed.
    - **D)** decreased resting heart rate.

Answers:

- A) Incorrect. It helps to develop type II muscle fibers.
- B) Incorrect. It is already a tough workout and will cause further soreness.
- **C) Correct.** This intensity level is good for improving lactate threshold and movement speed.
- D) Incorrect. Steady state, long-distance cardiovascular activity helps to lower resting heart rate.

Special Populations

Often the trainer will encounter clientele who fall into the category of **special populations**. Special populations refers to senior adults, children and adolescents, pregnant women, and clientele who have limitations due to health concerns. It is important for the trainer to know how to train these special populations and what is within the scope of practice. This section will discuss how to handle various situations in exercise program design and implementation for special populations.

Exercise for Seniors, Children and Adolescents, and Pregnant Women

It is a common misconception that seniors, children, and pregnant women should not exercise or take part in resistance training. However, the benefits of exercise for these special populations far outweigh the concerns. Seniors who regularly partake in resistance training programs can help to maintain bone mineral density, improve their balance, and maintain a healthy posture. Additionally, seniors who perform cardiovascular exercise on a regular basis keep their respiratory and circulatory systems healthy, preventing numerous health-related risks associated with sedentary lifestyles. A common myth associated with resistance training for children is that it may stunt their growth or damage the growth plates in their bones. But resistance training in children and adolescents can help to develop healthy bones and has no effect on their overall growth. Women who are pregnant also benefit greatly from both strength training and cardiovascular activity. Continuing training during pregnancy helps to reduce the risk of many potentially harmful conditions associated with pregnancy, such as gestational diabetes and hypertension.

It is in the trainer's best interest to learn the appropriate methods for training these special populations, since caution should be exercised when designing exercise programs for them. Resistance training for **seniors** should emphasize working the major muscle groups associated with activities of daily living. For example, the step-up exercise is helpful in improving balance when climbing stairs. Seniors often struggle with balance, and adjusting the box height for the step-up exercise is a simple modification for progression and regression. Strength training two times a week at lower to moderate intensities, ranging from 40 to 70 percent of 1RM, is ideal. The exercises should include working the larger muscle groups of the body for one to two sets of ten or fewer exercises per session, at low load and higher volumes (approximately fifteen repetitions).

Cardiovascular training for seniors should include up to five sessions per week at thirty to sixty minutes of low- to moderate-intensity aerobic exercise up to five sessions per week. The trainer should recommend using heart rate monitoring or perceived exertion to track the intensity of the client's cardiovascular activity. If the client is struggling to complete a full thirty minutes, the training session can be broken up into smaller increments throughout the day until the client's conditioning has improved. Finally, the trainer should consider the possibility of arthritic joints among seniors and try to avoid exercise methods that cause excessive stress, such as plyometrics, running, and many types of calisthenics.

> **Did You Know?** Human bones develop quickly at a young age and eventually stop producing more bone tissue as a person ages. That is why it is important to start weight-bearing exercise at a young age.

For youth populations, the key concepts a trainer must consider are proper supervision, load, and safe progressions. **Children and adolescents** should always have adult or professional supervision while performing new exercise programs. The fine motor skills that develop with age are not always present in youths, which can cause improper technique during resistance training exercises. Additionally, children and adolescents should not be progressed too quickly or given inappropriately heavy weights. Exercise for children and adolescents should equate to around sixty minutes per day throughout the week and can be a combination of resistance training, sports, and aerobic training. Resistance training two to three days a week is beneficial to children as long as the trainer is focusing more on developing form and technique and less on increasing the weight lifted. The intensity of the child's activities should be moderate to high, or enough to make the child break a sweat and cause heavy breathing. Resistance training protocols should focus on lighter loads and higher volumes, emphasizing form over everything else.

Trainers should make sure that children and adolescents take frequent water breaks to ensure proper hydration, since it promotes thermoregulation and prevents potential overheating. In addition, children and adolescents benefit most from participating in a wide variety of physical activities in order to prevent potential overuse injuries from repeated sessions of the same movements. Overuse is evident, for example, in youthful baseball pitchers requiring surgery from repeated high-intensity stress to the elbow from throwing.

Pregnant women who are cleared for exercise benefit significantly from continuing their resistance and cardiovascular training programs. During pregnancy, the trainer and client will need to monitor the intensity of the activity throughout training sessions. Resistance training for pregnant women is recommended two to three times per week. Proper breathing technique should be emphasized, longer rest periods are advisable, and intensity should be kept moderate. The trainer should incorporate large muscle group exercises at repetition ranges of ten to fifteen and in one to three sets. Time between sets can be increased to ensure resistance training intensity is kept at a safe level.

> **?** Check Your Understanding: Compare the rest periods in resistance training for general populations and for women who are pregnant.

Cardiovascular recommendations for pregnant women should include at least thirty minutes per session on most days of the week. Aerobic activity modes should be low risk, non-contact, and moderate intensity to avoid risk of fetal injury. For instance, pregnant women can continue cycling as long as it is stationary, but contact sports are prohibited, and they should be able to hold a conversation through their cardiovascular exercise to keep the intensity at moderate levels. Pregnant women should perform abdominal exercises while seated slightly upright rather than flat on their backs. The trainer should make every effort to ensure pregnant clients pay attention to the signals their bodies are giving them during their workouts, and discontinuing exercise if need be.

Training Individuals with Stable Chronic Conditions

Numerous other chronic conditions that are cause for concern must be considered in designing and implementing exercise programs. Conditions that can have potentially dangerous outcomes include stable coronary artery disease and other cardiovascular diseases, diabetes mellitus, obesity, metabolic syndrome, hypertension, arthritis, chronic back pain, osteoporosis, chronic obstructive pulmonary disease (COPD), and chronic pain.

> Testing Tip: Figure out what kind of learner you are: visual, auditory, kinesthetic, or a combination, and make that your primary learning tool. Visual learners tend to excel through reading information thoroughly, auditory learners through hearing the

> information, and kinesthetic learners through performing actions associated with the information.

Prior to the start of any fitness program for clients with these diseases, the trainer must require that these individuals seek medical attention and exercise clearance before continuing. Additionally, the trainer may require the clients to ask their physicians about any other limitations that should be implemented in the exercise program. For people with many of these conditions, progression may be substantially lower than with the average person, and frequency, intensity, time, and mode may vary by client. In particular, **cardiovascular diseases** may require the trainer to start exercise far below standard recommendations.

For clients with **diabetes**, monitoring blood sugar levels before and after exercise may be indicated, and the trainer should make sure to monitor the patient for signs and symptoms of rapid changes in blood sugar. If the client experiences sudden slurring or changes in speech, dizziness, lightheadedness, and excessive fatigue, the trainer should discontinue exercise and keep juice on hand to counteract the effects.

Obese clients may require exercise modification to minimize joint stress or difficulty performing certain exercises. Additionally, the trainer should avoid high-contact exercises that involve jumping, since this will place added stress on the joints. Obesity can also increase the client's risk of overheating and may trigger difficulty breathing.

Clients with **hypertension** under control by medication will benefit from any exercise, from walking to high-intensity workouts. The trainer should educate clients with high blood pressure on increasing their activity levels through simple methods and following the recommended weekly guidelines for exercise. Hypertension can increase the client's risk for heart attacks or stroke, and should be monitored by the trainer in a new training program.

Arthritis can cause a decrease in range of motion, joint pain, instability, and muscular atrophy at the joints it affects. For clients with arthritis, the goal of resistance training should be to develop stability through strengthening the muscles that support the joint. Resistance training at moderate loads with high volume can help to improve muscular strength and tone and provide joint stability. The trainer should implement cardiovascular training that minimizes joint impact to reduce further degradation of the joints, and instruct the client to static stretch post-exercise to maintain joint flexibility of the arthritic joints.

Clients who suffer from **chronic back pain** will benefit most from improved flexibility and core strength through isometric exercises such as planks. Often low back pain is influenced by muscular imbalances of the lower body due to sedentary lifestyle or careers. The trainer should emphasize performing abdominal bracing exercises and the plank regularly and should implement flexibility training for the hamstrings and hip flexor muscles. Exercises involving excessive flexion and extension of the spine should be limited or avoided completely unless instructed by a physician as part of a rehabilitation program.

Osteoporosis often affects seniors, especially women, and causes a deficit in bone mineral density. Clients with this chronic condition benefit most from load-bearing activities like resistance training. Exercise recommendations for these clients should include two to three days of eight to ten exercises that work the major muscle groups of the body. The earlier the client begins load-bearing exercises, the better the chances of preventing osteoporosis. People with osteoporosis will still benefit from weight training.

Chronic obstructive pulmonary disease (COPD) makes cardiovascular exercise and breathing very challenging. Trainers should consider the client's difficulty in breathing when designing the exercise program and should start the client with a shorter goal for the cardiovascular workout. Frequency should still start around three days a week; however, cardiovascular sessions may last for only fifteen minutes or less, depending on how serious the client's condition is.

Chronic pain sufferers may require the trainer to adapt the program on a day-to-day basis, making changes to the program during the session. The trainer should start the session by asking how the client is feeling and try to assess which exercises may not be indicated for the day. Frequent implementation of flexibility training may benefit these individuals and they will often feel better after the workout regardless of how much pain they had before.

PRACTICE QUESTIONS

1. What exercise precaution should be taken when training a pregnant woman?
    - **A)** Training frequency should be reduced.
    - **B)** Resistance training should be eliminated.
    - **C)** Rest periods should be increased.
    - **D)** Abdominal exercises should be eliminated.

    Answers:
    - **A)** Incorrect. Training frequency can remain the same during pregnancy as long as the mother is healthy and cleared for exercise.
    - **B)** Incorrect. Resistance training is still beneficial for expectant mothers.
    - **C)** **Correct.** Rest periods between sets should be increased to prevent overheating or excessive intensity.
    - **D)** Incorrect. Modifications should be made for abdominal exercises, but they should not be completely eliminated from the exercise program.

2. Clients with chronic obstructive pulmonary disease (COPD) have difficulty breathing and may require that their cardiovascular training
    - **A)** start at fifteen minutes per session, three days per week.
    - **B)** start at thirty minutes per session, three to five days per week.
    - **C)** start at thirty to sixty minutes per session, five days per week.

D) not start at all since COPD clients should not participate in cardiovascular exercise due to their difficulty in breathing.

Answers:

A) Correct. A shorter duration may be necessary to build up cardiovascular capacity before advancing to longer sessions.

B) Incorrect. Though these are the general guidelines for individuals starting a cardiovascular exercise routine, it will likely be too advanced for someone with COPD.

C) Incorrect. This recommendation is for intermediate to advanced exercisers with no current medical concerns.

D) Incorrect. COPD patients benefit greatly from cardiovascular training and should not completely eliminate it.

SIX: CLIENT RELATIONS AND COACHING

Building Professional Relationships

The primary goal of building a fitness business, or any business, is to create and keep customers. To be a successful trainer, it's important to extend the highest quality of personalized customer service to clients.

Clients must feel as though they are receiving great workouts, that their workouts are tailored to their goals, and that they trust the professional trainer they are paying to help them reach those goals.

This section breaks down the key components in creating a strong system for building client relationships while being an effective coach.

The first step in building a sustainable relationship is building a strong **rapport** with the client, a relationship based on similarity and agreement. This connection between trainer and client could be considered as important as the expertly designed training program. Trust is the product of rapport. If clients do not feel like the personal trainer can relate to them or **empathize** with (understand) their experiences, they will not feel the environment allows them to be vulnerable with the trainer. Open dialogue between client and trainer is key to a well-planned program, in combination with motivational elements and goals to ensure adherence.

Communication techniques are essential in building rapport. Because verbal communication is only a small part of how we express ourselves, fitness professionals must be aware of other aspects of communication in working with clients. **Verbal communication,** or what we say, comprises only about 7 – 10 percent of how we express ourselves. Surprisingly, the rest of our communication is **non-verbal,** such as tone of voice and body language. Therefore, health and fitness professionals must be consistent, not only in what they say, but also in how they say it and how they look while saying it. It's important that trainers come across as genuine.

Table 6.1. Body Language

Positive Body Language	Negative Body Language
Direct eye contact (interest in the other person)	Downcast, shifting eyes (uncomfortable, lying)
Relaxed brows (comfortable)	Lowering of chin (doubting, angry)
Leaning forward (interested)	Yawning (not interested, bored)
Eyes open slightly larger (welcoming)	Fidgeting in chair (uncomfortable, anxious)
Nodding, slowly or quickly (actively listening)	Tapping foot or fingers (anxious, uncomfortable)
Tall posture (confidence)	Hunched shoulders (tired, not interested)
Firm handshake (sincere and welcoming)	Tightly clenched or wringing hands (anxious, angry)
Open arms/palms/jacket (interested, attentive, welcoming)	Arms crossed/body turned slightly away (not interested, uncomfortable, defensive)

Non-verbal communication consists of **body language,** a broad category that includes postures, gestures, facial expressions, eye movements, and tone of voice. Some types of body language convey a negative expression, while others convey a positive expression (see Table 6.1). Body language can either help or hinder a trainer's efforts to build rapport with a client.

Tone of voice conveys the real emotion someone is feeling, regardless of what the person is saying. If the trainer tells the client he or she is doing a good job in a monotone voice, the trainer may not sound very genuine. However, praising the client in an energetic voice will sound more positive and believable to the client.

Non-verbal communication is contagious; people tend to gravitate toward positive energy and avoid negative energy, so creating a positive presence using non-verbal communication is essential to building rapport with a client.

When meeting with a client, whether for the first time or the tenth, the trainer should exude confidence, enthusiasm, and professionalism, allowing the client to feel both at ease and confident that the trainer is the right one for the fitness journey.

When a trainer exudes *confidence*, he or she is communicating the ability to do the job well and keep clients safe. This confidence gives the client a sense of trust in the fitness professional, and in response the client will work harder and communicate more easily with the trainer. The trainer then has more ability to tailor an integrated fitness plan targeted to the client's goals. For example, non-verbal cues of confidence include definitive and sure statements and strong eye contact with the client. Trainers who display hesitation in their voices or cross their arms may convey a lack of confidence or lack of interest.

By exuding *enthusiasm*, the trainer communicates interest in helping the client meet his or her goals. Enthusiasm is contagious. Greeting a client with a big smile, high energy, and a high five will put the client in a positive, high-energy mood to get the most out of the training session. If the trainer is sitting or seems distracted and greets the client with a monotone voice, the client will mirror that behavior. By being positive and happy to see the client, the trainer will seem approachable and ready to answer the client's questions or concerns. Genuine enthusiasm speaks volumes in rapport-building and client retention.

By exuding *professionalism*, the trainer communicates a high degree of competence and a commitment to giving their clients the best service possible. Small details separate the professional from the pack. A professional and driven personal trainer maintains the highest standards in the following areas:

- wears proper, tasteful athletic attire (no jeans or business pants, or short, revealing, or otherwise inappropriate clothing).
- maintains proper hygiene, is always well-groomed, and avoids wearing strong colognes and perfumes.
- appears approachable, and is never slouched over a piece of equipment, avoiding eye contact, or hiding behind a trainer's desk.
- focuses on their client; cell phones should be put away during a session, and the trainer should provide feedback while clients are exercising or asking questions.
- maintains strong eye contact and speaks in a professional manner, clearly and deliberately, and refrains from using profanity.

The practice of **active listening** allows verbal and non-verbal communication to mingle while working with a client. When the client is speaking, the trainer should maintain eye contact and an open body position, indicating a genuine willingness to listen. Once the client has finished speaking, the trainer should then repeat key elements of the client's statement to show that he or she has heard the client. For example:

> Trainer: How was your day? Did you do anything special at work today?
>
> Client: I set up for a co-worker's birthday party, so my back feels a little stiff, but all in all, it was a good day; my co-worker was so surprised!
>
> Trainer: How nice of you to go the extra mile for your co-worker! But, it sounds like your back might need a little more attention in our warm-up today. Let's make sure we use the foam roller as part of your warm-up. I'll also skip the stability ball crunches today and instead focus on some balance with the core. Does that sound like a good plan?
>
> Client: Yes, sounds great.
>
> Trainer: Be sure to let me know if any of the routine is too much for your back.
>
> Client: Will do, thanks!

In this situation, active listening allowed the trainer to connect with the client on a personal level and also get some key information about the client's back. This kind of listening is a win-win for the trainer, allowing the trainer to connect personally with the client, and by repeating the client's key messages, the trainer also demonstrates an understanding of the client's needs. This instills a sense of trust in the client's mind and helps to build rapport between client and trainer.

Building a professional relationship is a simple but continual process. Using positive body language and an energetic voice in speaking clearly and professionally indicates the trainer is knowledgeable, enthusiastic, and professional. By using open and attentive body language and actively listening during any encounter with the client, the trainer will continue to build rapport in the relationship. Rapport creates trust, and trust builds a lasting relationship, ensuring the trainer can help clients reach their goals and improve their quality of life. The trainer should stay focused on being genuine, being passionate, and being professional.

One can practice active listening while cultivating open and positive body language:
1. Do not cross the legs or arms.
2. Maintain active eye contact (smile with the eyes), but do not stare.
3. Nod slowly while the client speaks.
4. Relax the shoulders but do not slouch.
5. Lean toward the client, but not too closely.

PRACTICE QUESTIONS

1. Body language encompasses all the following, EXCEPT:
  A) hand gestures.
  B) words.
  C) facial expressions.
  D) eye movement.

Answers:
  A) Incorrect. Hand gestures are body language.
  B) Correct. Words are verbal communication.
  C) Incorrect. Facial expressions are body language.
  D) Incorrect. Eye movement is body language.

2. Professionalism includes the following characteristics, EXCEPT:
  A) using profanity while speaking with their client.
  B) wearing proper and tasteful athletic attire.
  C) focusing only on the client.

D) staying approachable by using open body language.

Answers:

A) **Correct.** A trainer should refrain from the use of profanity while speaking with a client.

B) Incorrect. Trainers should always look the part; avoid jeans or clothing that is revealing or too tight.

C) Incorrect. A trainer should always be attentive to the client, especially in a session. Avoid talking on cell phones or texting.

D) Incorrect. Personal trainers should always be approachable and available to answer any questions.

Effective Coaching Communication

Effective and balanced communication *during* a training session is a fine art when working with a client. When a trainer is able to motivate, correct form, and deliver *tough love*, yet also stay sensitive to prevent a client from overdoing it, a lasting relationship between client and trainer is forged.

Knowing how the client best interprets information is the foundation of effective coaching communication. Each person is unique; each of us comprehends information differently, so a strong personal trainer must be able to deliver instructions in a variety of ways to ensure the client knows how to properly perform an exercise. A client may be an **auditory** or verbal learner, a **visual** or sight learner, or a **kinesthetic** or physical learner—or a combination. An effective trainer should use specific movements or words to help each type of learner fully understand what is being said. This technique is called **cueing.**

An auditory learner needs to *hear* effective descriptors to make sure he or she understands and can follow the trainer correctly. This type of learner typically waits until the trainer completely describes the exercise, from form to execution, before getting into position. Try to think of the client as being blind and needing everything described, from body position to correct execution of a single rep, to vocal feedback after the client has performed the exercise. Therefore, it is important for the trainer to use specific cueing strategies to keep the client informed and motivated. An auditory learner tends to stay motivated if the trainer counts down the reps, rather than up, so he or she knows how to adjust the intensity to finish the last few reps. A trainer must describe form corrections specifically, rather than saying, "do this" or "follow my lead." The auditory cues in Table 6.2 are helpful guides to get the auditory learner moving.

CONTINUE

Table 6.2 Auditory Cues

Alignment Cues	**Exercise Cues**
Toes forward and feet shoulder-width apart.	Squats: "Sit back as if to sit in a chair; keep the torso tall."
Pelvis tucked in.	Squats/lunges/balance: "Keep the weight of the body in the heels or in the heels of the standing/moving leg; keep the torso tall."
Draw belly button in toward the spine.	Breathing technique: "Inhale to control the release; exhale on exertion."
Big chest.	Rep technique: "Control to resting and power through the contraction."
Shoulders relaxed and back.	Upper body moves: "Do not 'break' wrists, keep them strong; do not lock the elbows, keep them soft."
Head straight, eyes forward.	Postural correction: "Keep the knees soft to continue core activation; keep the torso tall, shoulders back, pelvis in."

A visual learner needs to *see* the exercise performed while the demonstration is paired with specific cues. This tends to be the most common style of learning in the fitness industry. It is important that the trainer be able to perform the exercise precisely and efficiently while describing it. A visual learner tends to start mimicking the trainer after one or two repetitions. It is helpful to think of this type of learner as someone who cannot understand an explanation in English and needs to see physical gestures instead. For instance, if the trainer is trying to tell the client to activate the core, the trainer may need to place both fists at his or her own stomach to indicate that the abs need to be contracted.

Visual learners need the movements and cues to be concise and specific. The trainer cannot use complex movements or try to teach the whole exercise all at once. It is more efficient to break down a complex exercise and teach one move at a time. To demonstrate a squat to overhead shoulder press, the trainer should cue and describe the squat first, then cue and describe the shoulder press, and finally put them both together. When demonstrating an exercise for a visual learner, the trainer should be sure to indicate which area of the body the exercise is activating. This will help the client visualize where he or she will feel the exercise. While demonstrating a squat, for example, it would be helpful for the trainer to indicate that the glutes and hamstrings are the primary movers.

When correcting a client's form, it would be more effective to mimic the client's movements, and then show how to transition to the correct form while describing the correction. For example, during a bicep curl, the client's elbows might float away from his or her body. Help correct the client's form by mirroring the incorrect form and indicating that it can be corrected by pulling both elbows in toward the ribcage.

> **?** When cueing an exercise, there are numerous aspects to consider: body positioning, breathing, exercise execution, primary movers. Which order would result in the most efficient exercise demonstration for a client?

Kinesthetic learners need to *feel* the specific cues. As with visual learners, they need the trainer to demonstrate the exercise a few times before doing the movement, and the cueing must indicate where the client will feel the exercise, or which muscle groups will be worked. A key difference with kinesthetic learners is that they usually respond best when the trainer indicates the relevant muscle group on the client's body. With the client's permission, of course, a one- or two-finger touch on the client's mid back will indicate the need to activate the shoulders, and a touch on the client's hips during a cable rotation will indicate that he or she must keep the hips steady and rotate only through the torso. The more a trainer can indicate where a kinesthetic learner will feel an exercise, the more the client will successfully understand how to perform it properly. Essentially, kinesthetic learners need a combination of visual, touch, and verbal cues.

A client's **kinesthetic awareness**—the ability to coordinate muscle groups to function cohesively while maintaining spatial awareness—may give the trainer some indication of fitness level and help the trainer understand how quickly the client might progress through the three levels of the training continuum, as discussed in chapter 4. The following three stages of learning can be good guidelines to understand where a client can start training.

In the *cognitive stage* of learning the client typically has difficulty with exercises because the movements seem foreign. This indicates that the trainer should spend a prolonged period in the stabilization level of training. In this stage the trainer can focus on exercises that will allow the client to gain basic muscle memory with lighter weights and simple movement patterns. Basic squats, abdominal crunches, or bicep curls benefit a client in the cognitive stage of learning, since these teach the fundamentals of exercise technique.

In the *associative stage* of learning the client shows a kinesthetic connection to exercise. He or she understands the fundamentals of exercise technique (e.g., the proper neutral stance, proper form for basic exercises, and the proper use of cardio equipment). The client should be able to transition from the stabilization level of training to the strength level faster than a novice, using complex exercises and heavier weight.

In the *autonomous stage* of learning a client demonstrates a clear under-

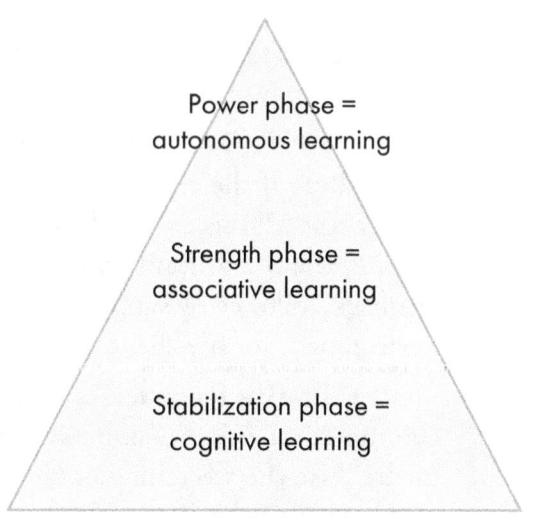

Figure 6.1. The Training/Learning Continuum

standing of exercise technique and needs challenging moves to help progress in both strength and force production, so he or she will be ready to focus on personal goals in the power level of training.

These stages of learning are progressive, so a client should build on an initial skill to reach each phase that corresponds with the training continuum.

During a session, a client will continue to learn through **feedback** that will help him or her improve motor function through muscle memory while reducing the risk of injury. A gifted trainer will be able to utilize different types of feedback to provide useful information while keeping the client positively motivated to improve and optimizing each training session.

Feedback can be either internal or external.

Internal feedback involves the client using personal kinesthetic awareness to correct motor function. As a client gets more "in tune" with his or her body, internal feedback will play a more integral role in the client's improvement. However, internal feedback can also be guided by the trainer by utilizing various forms of external feedback.

External feedback comes from outside resources, primarily through the trainer's exercise performance evaluation and improvement. **Descriptive feedback** is ideal to use while a client is performing exercises because the trainer can be specific and technical when providing feedback meant to improve form and technique. This feedback should be frequent and technical; it does not necessarily have to be positive, but it should never sound negative or the client will lose confidence in his or her ability to improve. For example, when a client is performing a squat, the trainer might observe that the client's knees buckle inward.

The trainer could critique the client's form by saying, *"While squatting, be sure to focus on pulling those knees apart to prevent them from drawing inward. Just think about putting more weight on the outer foot to keep those knees straight."*

Supportive feedback is a great way to end the descriptive feedback because it positively reinforces the corrections made. After the client finishes doing the squats with the corrected form, the fitness professional can provide supportive feedback: *"Pulling the knees out really made those squats look strong! That correction will ensure that you continue to build a balanced lower body. Did you feel the difference?"*

Asking if the client felt the difference will help improve the client's kinesthetic awareness. All this external feedback helps clients hone their internal feedback skills, helping them maintain good form even when the trainer is not there. Descriptive feedback, followed by supportive feedback, helps create a positive and nurturing learning environment for the client.

Evaluative feedback is an effective tool that a fitness professional can use to summarize the client's improvements during the session and suggest future improvements. Use the stretching or cooldown phase to connect with a client, and after the cooldown, dedicate the last five minutes to give the client evaluative feedback. The trainer should maintain focus on the client when giving any feedback, but especially evaluative feedback. The trainer should make warm eye contact with the client and begin with **targeted praise**, emphasizing an aspect or two of the workout where the client really showed great improvement. Keeping that warm eye contact, mention an aspect of the workout the client struggled with, reiterate some of the descriptive and supportive feedback mentioned during the session, and assign things the client can do outside the sessions to improve. Finally, ask the client if there are any questions or concerns, and actively listen to the client, continuing to build rapport with each session.

 External feedback can also be referred to as Knowledge of Results.

If a client shows negativity concerning their performance, showing **empathy** or understanding for their concerns will help connect with the client. Empathy shows clients that their imperfections are simply human qualities. And when the client knows he or she has the support of the trainer, that will provide further motivation.

Be sure the client has a welcoming environment to stay motivated and comfortable while in a session. Some clients may feel self-conscious when working out, so be sure to maintain some privacy for these clients. This might prove challenging in a busy gym, but it helps to keep the motivational comments or feedback at a level where only the client can hear them. If there is an unoccupied group fitness room or a less-utilized area of the gym, using these areas may help keep the client comfortable, depending on the exercises planned.

 Learn how to READ clients to build strong relationships.
Rapport and trust are established as the foundation of the relationship.
Empathy helps the trainer know why the client is motivated to start.
Assessments measure the client's fitness level to set the right goals.
Develop an effective program that reflects the client's goals.

Keep in mind the client's taste in music and what type of learner he or he is. If a client is an auditory learner, keeping the music at a lower level will help in hearing vocal cues. Regardless of genre, be sure to play "clean" versions of music. Profanity can be distracting during a session, and it can make some clients very uncomfortable.

? Body language is one way that trainers and clients can communicate non-verbally, both positively and negatively. If the client shifts focus away from the trainer or crosses his or her arms during a trainer's demonstration, are these positive indicators? How would you as a trainer interpret this body language? How would you address it?

The smallest of details can make or break a session. Building a professional relationship with the client will help make all these details easier to plan and keep the client coming back week after week.

CLIENT RELATIONS AND COACHING 253

PRACTICE QUESTIONS

1. A kinesthetic learner

A) interprets information through watching the trainer do one or two reps while explaining.

B) interprets information through listening to the trainer explain the movement.

C) interprets information through a combination of watching the trainer while they explain where the client should feel the exercise.

D) interprets the information through thinking through an explanation of the exercise.

Answers:

A) Incorrect. This is a description of a visual learner.

B) Incorrect. This is a description of an auditory learner.

C) **Correct.** This is a description of a kinesthetic learner.

D) Incorrect. This does not describe visual, auditory, or kinesthetic learning.

2. The power phase of training coincides with the _____ stage of learning.

A) cognitive

B) supportive

C) autonomous

D) associative

Answers:

A) Incorrect. This stage of learning coincides with the stabilization training phase.

B) Incorrect. This is a form of feedback, not learning.

C) **Correct.** At this stage of learning, the movement is almost second nature to the client.

D) Incorrect. This stage of learning coincides with the Strength Training Phase.

Motivation

Trainers must be realistic about the current fitness climate in America. According to the Centers for Disease Control, only about 45 percent of adults in the United States get the minimum recommended levels of physical activity. With most of the workforce sitting in front of a computer eight hours a day, five days a week, inactivity is the new normal, and so is obesity (Figure 6.2).

While everyone should get some physical activity in each day, for a majority of the population, the need for exercise is imperative. Fitness is trending: corporations are building onsite fitness centers as company perks, activity trackers are being bought at astronomical rates, and gym memberships are up. However, individual adherence to a fitness regimen after six months drops 50 percent. Now, more than ever, the role of the personal trainer is vital in helping the population get back on track. Keeping clients motivated is the key to making exercise the new norm, so that clients can improve their health and quality of life.

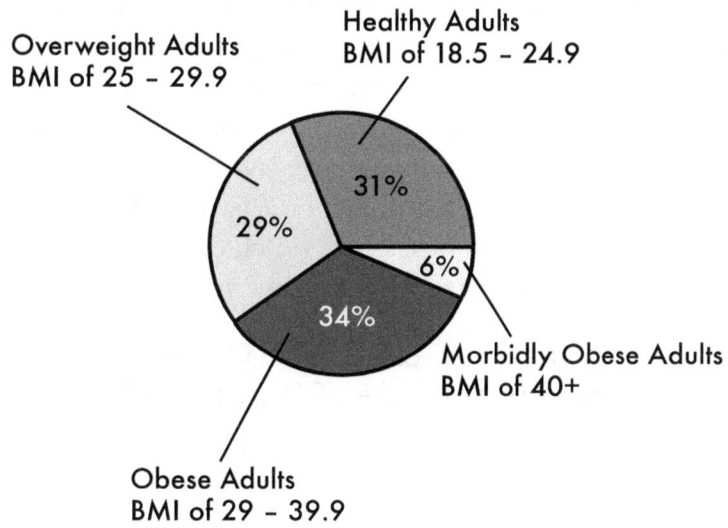

Figure 6.2. Obesity in America

Motivation, the reason why someone does something, is the spark that draws a new participant into initial communication with a personal trainer. Each person has a reason for wanting the help of a trainer to improve their health. These motivators can be classified as **intrinsic** or **extrinsic** factors. If a client hires a personal trainer solely because of his or her desire for self-improvement, that client is intrinsically motivated. Usually, an intrinsically motivated client will adhere to an exercise program because he or she already enjoys the benefits of exercise but wants a few sessions to learn how to use a different type of equipment or spice up an existing routine. On the other hand, extrinsically motivated clients are motivated by outside factors. These clients might want to lose weight for a high school reunion or wedding, or they might want to get healthier because they have young grandchildren or because a doctor has said they need to exercise to lower their risk for Type II diabetes. Regardless of their reasons, clients who are extrinsically motivated will need help, both in finding an intrinsic motivation and in adhering to an exercise regimen. These clients will need convincing reasons to change their behaviors and to work through the initial weeks of discomfort and exhaustion that will inevitably tempt them to stop. Mentally, extrinsically motivated people are not wholly committed to introducing new behaviors to their existing lifestyle; some may feel backed into a corner.

Breaking down the barriers to exercise adherence will require persistence for both the client and the trainer, because people who are not used to making fit and healthy choices equate them with discomfort. Potential roadblocks on the path to success fall into three categories: personal attributes, environmental factors, and physical activity factors.

Exercise adherence–voluntarily committing to an exercise program, or not—can be determined by environmental factors, such as accessibility, time, weather, and social support. These factors can be addressed when discussing short-term goals to aid in changing behaviors. Accessibility refers to the ease of accessing an exercise facility; the more convenient the location, the more likely a participant will stick with the program. Lack of time is one of the most commonly cited factors; participants say they do not have enough time to fit a workout into their busy schedules. Usually, when someone enjoys a regimen, he or she will find the time to fit it into her schedule; this is key to helping a time barrier become a thing of the past. Bad weather can cause a participant to miss scheduled sessions or classes, which can spiral into several days of missing scheduled sessions, interfering with the new rhythm.

 Adults should engage in at least two-and-a half hours of moderate physical activity each week, according to the US Department of Health and Human Services.

Lack of social support from family and friends is arguably the strongest deterrent to fully committing to a new lifestyle. Support from a spouse will allow the client to get to his or her sessions without worrying about family needs. Support from friends helps in making good decisions and provides support in difficult times.

When a participant decides to take the plunge into a new lifestyle, adherence is more likely if the client feels he or she can keep up with the fitness regimen. This is known as the physical-activity factor. Many people drop out if they don't enjoy the exercise or think it's too intense, so properly assessing a client's fitness level is key to creating the right progressive program. Also, if the client is injured, a long period of rest or the fear of reinjury may prevent him or her from returning. The trainer should stay in contact to plan a recovery strategy and ensure the client is motivated to return.

Personal attributes refer to physical or other personal aspects, such as age, gender, income, body composition, fitness level, lack of knowledge, **self-efficacy**, and **locus of control**. These can be the most difficult factors to overcome in changing behaviors. Increasing age can be a factor because those who are older may fear injuring themselves or have life-long habits to combat. Men tend to have more adherence than women because they tend to see results faster. This fact can be especially difficult for women who are externally motivated.

Those at lower income levels have a harder time starting and adhering to exercise programs because of the cost. Participants who are overweight or less physically fit can find exercise programs uncomfortable or hard to keep up with, causing them to feel discouraged. For new exercisers, lack of knowledge can be overwhelming; fear of the unknown can inhibit someone before he or she even starts.

Those with an **external locus of control** believe their lives are not in their control; their personal attributes, environmental factors, and physical-activity factors control their lives, and they do not have a well-developed self-efficacy. For example, if a client does not believe he has the power to change his life and meet his goals, he will have a hard time continuing with a program if he doesn't see results right away, or he may even sabotage his own success without knowing it.

Figure 6.3. Locus of Control

Those with an **internal locus of control** believe they are the masters of their fate; only they can determine life changes. This kind of person believes that with hard work, he or she can change anything. A person who embodies an internal locus of control is usually internally motivated, believes in his or her own willpower and strength, and has a well-developed self-efficacy.

Never underestimate the power of a good strategy in improving someone's self-efficacy. A positive and knowledgeable trainer can determine whether someone is driven by an internal or an external locus of control because of what motivates him or her to come for training in the first place. This is a key factor in strategizing the client's roadmap to successful behavior change, which in turn leads to an exponential growth in self-efficacy that will determine whether he or she will stick with the lifestyle change.

Understanding what factors might affect motivation and exercise adherence can help the fitness professional begin to mold and change unhealthy behaviors. It is also vital that the trainer understand behavior change theories, because those will help the trainer determine what factors can

Figure 6.4. Social-Ecological Model of Behavior Change

CLIENT RELATIONS AND COACHING 257

truly cultivate self-efficacy, regardless of what may mentally or physically block a client's success.

The **socio- or social-ecological** behavior change model (Figure 6.5) focuses on understanding and appreciating the relationship between an individual and his or her environment. This model believes that successful behavior change does start with the individual, but can be successful only if all levels of his or her society are supportive.

+ Individual: Shelly decides to walk every day for thirty minutes.
+ Interpersonal: Shelly's husband agrees to be home at a certain time, so Shelly can go for her walk while he is home with their two children.
+ Organizational: Shelly's neighborhood association uses funds to put a walking trail in the well-lit community park.
+ Community: The neighborhood association partners with the local watch to patrol the park, ensuring its safety after dark.
+ Public Policy: Funds were also appropriated to add large sidewalks and pedestrian crossings to make walking to the park easy and safe from Shelly's house.

Social cognitive theory states that when people observe someone performing a behavior and the consequences of that behavior, they remember the sequence of events and use this information to guide successive behaviors. For example, Mary watched her sister's progress after she joined a gym and employed the help of a personal trainer. After seeing her sister's energy skyrocket and her self-confidence soar, Mary is ready to give it a try herself. She joins the same gym as her sister and uses the same trainer, hoping for the same results.

Theory of planned behavior states that *attitude* (personal feelings) towards behavior, *subjective norms* (social network), and *perceived behavioral control* (self-efficacy), together shape an individual's *behavioral intentions* (readiness to perform behavior) and *behaviors* (response to the given situation).

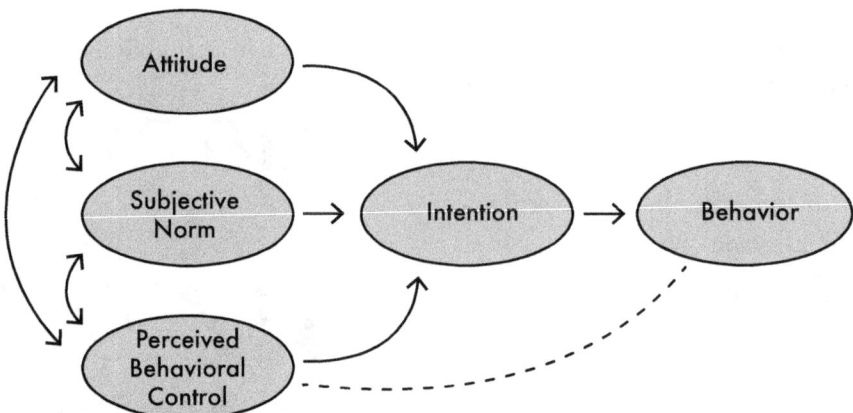

Figure 6.5. Theory of Planned Behavior

This theory, like the others, demonstrates that a combination of factors—environmental, personal, and social—will have a direct impact on whether a person is ready to make a change in his or her behavior. Knowing how important these factors are in a person's life will allow for the trainer to build empathy for that client's process.

The **readiness-to-change** theory differs from the other behavior change models because it indicates distinct stages of change and focuses on a person's intrinsic growth. This can be a useful tool for a fitness professional to track a client's self-efficacy cultivation and locus of control shift to facilitate behavior change. Using this theory, a personal trainer can come up with an effective strategy to plan and keep the client motivated, cultivating his or her behavior change to adhere to an exercise program. Table 6.3 translates the readiness-to-change theory into a strategy to facilitate exercise adherence, while building professional fitness relationships and client self-efficacy.

An individual at the first step in the Readiness-to-change theory, *precontemplation*, sees no problem at this point; in fact, she is resistant to change. She does not believe she can change anything about herself, so she denies there is a problem. Her family members, friends, or doctors see the problem; she does not. She initiates a change only because there are external motivators forcing her to, but once the pressure is gone, she stops trying to initiate change. Low self-efficacy and external locus of control dominate people in the precontemplation phase; they believe their situation is hopeless and would rather ignore it.

When this individual reaches the *contemplation* phase of change, she finally acknowledges she has a problem and wants to get out of it. Even though she realizes she needs to do something, she, like other contemplators, still has low self-efficacy, and has no idea how to begin breaking down the barriers that inhibit a solution.

When this individual decides to initiate a plan to solve her problem within a month or so, she is in the *preparation* phase. Going public with her problem is an important step, but she is still fearful that she may not be ready; her self-efficacy is low, but her motivation is internal, unlike in the precontemplation phase.

In the *action* phase of change, she has taken definitive steps to change her behavior. She has made a plan, is facing her fears, and is focused on creating long-term solutions to her problem. This is the phase that requires the most energy, focus, and time; these changes are apparent to those closest to her. Her self-efficacy has grown substantially and her locus of control is beginning to shift more from external to internal.

The *maintenance* phase will test this individual the most. Her goals have been reached, and now it is imperative that she have a plan set against relapses or setbacks. Her self-efficacy has reached its highest and greatest potential, but her internal motivation must endure years of trials.

The *termination* phase is the ultimate goal; the problem no longer tempts this individual. She is free of the struggles and believes her life is her own and she can achieve whatever she wants. Some believe, however, that problems will keep individuals in the maintenance phase for the rest of their lives.

Table 6.3 Readiness-to-Change Model

Stage of Change	Goal	Connections	Self-Efficacy Level	Locus of Control
Precontemplation – *The client is in denial about needing help; be open and approachable.*	Make the client's inactivity an issue of concern	+ Provide information to the client on the benefits of exercise. + Offer to answer questions.	Low	External
Contemplation – *Plant the seeds of a relationship. The client is not ready for action but is looking for support.*	Get the client interested in any type of activity	+ Provide opportunities to ask questions. + Ask client to make a pros/cons list of being active. + Give free exercise tips.	Low	External
Preparation – *Client is ready to initiate connection to ask questions and identify concerns.*	Get the client interested in a regular activity	+ Provide opportunities to ask any questions. + Offer assessment. + Have the client complete *I-statements*, defining the importance of exercise to him or her.	Low	Shifting
Action – *The client is ready to start working with a trainer to help pinpoint and facilitate goals.*	Maintain regular activity	+ Help the client set goals. + Create plan/schedule for regular sessions/classes. + Reinforce the client's actions with positive communication. + Have the client write a contract to himself or herself.	Medium	Internal

Stage	Goal	Strategies		
Maintenance – *The client may continue sessions systematically or periodically to stay on course.*	Prevent relapse	+ Reinforce the client's actions thus far with positive communication. + Provide feedback and solutions for potential barriers. + Educate the client on the probability of relapses or setbacks. + Set new goals and write new contract. + Educate the client on ways to keep fitness challenging. + Provide continued support.	High	Internal
Termination – *The client has reached all his or her goals and is ready to enjoy a healthy lifestyle independently.*	Maintain activity on his or her own	+ Provide continued support. + Identify signs of burnout or overtraining. + Help create a reward system for continued success.	High	Internal

During the action and maintenance phases of change, the client will need strategies to stay on track and motivated and prevent relapses or setbacks. The trainer should create a plan for the client that includes several specific strategies and detailed actions.

Self-monitoring holds the client accountable to a plan of action and helps denote problem areas. Specific actions include the following: Keep a diet journal. Do not simply record the food eaten, also record mood, time, and who else was there. Try to be as accurate as possible in terms of amount of food; add calories. Track activity or caloric expenditure. Note which exercise is done and how often. Incorporate weekly weigh-ins or circumference measurements, correlating caloric intake and expenditure to manage goal success and where to improve.

Environmental management, or *stimulus control*, minimizes opportunities to trigger unwanted behavior and promotes wanted behavior. Specific actions include the following: Put away foods immediately to promote portion control. Do not keep indulgent foods in plain sight. Keep gym bag or running shoes next to the door, or lay exercise clothes on the bed before leaving for work to ensure exercise stays on the schedule.

Alternative behaviors help in learning how to manage stressors with a new, healthier behavior. Specific actions include the following: Instead of reacting to anger or sadness with comfort foods, take a walk. Use rewards to positively reinforce a wanted behavior. Enjoy a spa day or buy a new fitness outfit after completing a specific goal.

Negative reinforcement is when a negative stimulus triggers a positive behavior. For instance, clients may observe that they feel sick after eating junk food and then working out, which could inspire them to improve their diet on exercise days, and improve their nutrition overall.

Social support is important for accountability and for emotional or physical support in reaching health and fitness goals. Specific actions include the following: Ask a friend to participate in the rewards or negative reinforcement tools, to build in accountability for both positive and negative actions. Enlist a friend or family member to be a workout buddy. Enlist the support of friends during social outings, to avoid feeling self-conscious about food and drink choices. Create or participate in a social media group for swapping healthy recipes.

Cognitive coping methods help prevent demoralizing oneself and help manage emotions during a relapse or after failing to reach goals. Specific actions include the following: Set reasonable and attainable goals to inhibit unsuccessful results. Practice positive self-talk to increase self-efficacy. Use positive imagery and self-soothing to manage negative emotions. Use cognitive reframing, which is the practice of identifying unwanted thoughts and finding positive alternatives for disputing them.

Time management is a tool to ensure one makes time for new priorities. Specific actions include the following: Schedule exercise like it's a daily appointment that can't be rescheduled. Hire a personal trainer or participate in scheduled enjoyable fitness classes. Prepare meals and snacks in advance by setting aside a day of the week to cook and package food. Plan a weekly menu and shopping list to reduce the need for a fast food meal.

Table 6.4. ABC Model of Behavior

	What It Is	**Example**
Antecedents	Event that triggers behavior	Mark sets his alarm 30 minutes earlier than normal.
Behavior	Behavior resulting from trigger	Mark can calmly make and eat his breakfast at home and prepare his lunch before leaving for work.
Consequence	Desirable or undesirable result from the preceding behavior	Mark's ability to wake up a little earlier allowed him to eat healthier throughout the day, which gave him energy to exercise on his way home.

Relapse prevention and recovery plans can identify triggers that could result in returning to unwanted activities. Specific actions include the following: Use the ABC model of behavior to identify triggers (Table 6.4). Create a contingency plan for social outings (e.g., limit alcoholic beverages so judgment is not impaired, have one portion of a trigger food after eating healthy options, etc.). If a relapse occurs, be sure to use positive self-talk to acknowledge successes. Do NOT focus on fault. Find an inspiring or motivational quote/picture and keep it available for quick reference to reframe an unhealthy mindset. Call a trusted friend or family member when feeling negative or vulnerable.

PRACTICE QUESTIONS

1. What are the six phases in the readiness-to-change model?
    - **A)** specific, challenging, attainable, measurable, proximal, inspirational
    - **B)** environmental management, alternative behaviors, reward, social support, cognitive coping, relapse prevention
    - **C)** precontemplation, contemplation, preparation, action, maintenance, termination
    - **D)** individual, introvert, interpersonal, organizational, community, public policy

    Answers:
    - A) Incorrect. These are six steps in effective goal-setting, according to the National Association of Sports Medicine (NASM).
    - B) Incorrect. These are six tools or techniques in behavior change.
    - **C) Correct.** These are the six phases of the readiness-to-change model.
    - D) Incorrect. Five of these words are the five tiers of the social-ecological behavior model. The sixth word, introvert, is a personality type.

2. Time management is a _____ _____ tool.
    - **A)** goal-setting
    - **B)** relationship-building
    - **C)** behavioral-change
    - **D)** self-efficacy

    Answers:
    - A) Incorrect. Time management is not a tool for setting goals.
    - B) Incorrect. Time management is not a tool for building relationships.
    - **C) Correct.** Time management is a tool for changing behaviors.
    - D) Incorrect. Time management is not a tool to build self-efficacy.

Setting Goals and Managing Expectations

When a client gets ready to start a new fitness program with a personal trainer, it is important that they communicate on how the trainer can best help the client. Setting goals is the best way to outline a plan to utilize sessions effectively and efficiently.

During the assessment and initial meetings, it is important that the trainer help the client verbalize his or her real motivations for using the trainer's services. A client will typically say the motivation is to "get in shape," "look better," or "feel better." These general statements aren't helping anyone, however, especially the client. Getting to the root of the motivation will help the client internalize the motivation, visualize the result, and manage expectations on how quickly the goal can be reached.

A trainer can be a vital tool in helping the client plan this fitness journey. Be pragmatic about how long and challenging the journey can be, and keep the client motivated by using a five-step planning strategy to help the client believe that he or she can achieve this goal.

Step 1: Establish the Client's Specific Goal

Helping a client get beyond the typical "I want to lose weight" response forces specific thinking to identify what he or she truly wants. Sometimes a client will not really know why he or she is there until the trainer takes the time to keep asking "why," and once will not be enough.

To help the client open up his or her mind, try asking **open-ended** *vision* questions requiring more than a single-word answer. Vision questions do not necessarily have anything to do with health or weight loss. These questions will open up the client's thought process to be specific in identifying what he or she wants. This process also allows for a more connected relationship with the trainer. These questions might be considered out-of-the-box thinking, but explain to the client that you are using an exercise that helps in goal setting.

Figure 6.6. Believe to Achieve!

Examples of vision questions:
+ Who are your role models?
+ What would you do if you won the lottery?
+ What kinds of experiences do you find so enjoyable that you forget about everything around you?

After the client has answered these questions, ask why he or she is enlisting the help of a trainer. If the client gives a superficial or general answer, ask why and keep asking why until the specific goal is revealed. For example:

> *Trainer: Why have you decided to hire a trainer?*
>
> *Maggie: Because I want to lose weight.*
>
> *Trainer: Why do you want to lose weight?*
>
> *Maggie: Because I want to look better.*
>
> *Trainer: Why do you want to look better?*
>
> *Maggie: So I can feel better about myself now that I am dating again.*
>
> *Trainer: I see. You want to feel more confident about yourself when you are out on dates.*
>
> *Maggie: Yes, I want to feel better about myself again.*

Continuing to ask Maggie *why* will help the trainer find the intrinsic motivator, which will motivate Maggie more than a superficial general goal would. This will also allow Maggie to feel more invested in her goal, because she vocalized her true desire to someone else.

 National Academy of Sports Medicine (NASM) also uses the acronym SCAMPI to describe goal-setting strategies:

S: Specific

C: Challenging

A: Approachable

M: Measurable

P: Proximal

I: Inspirational

STEP 2: SET SMART GOALS

After the client has visualized what he or she wants out of the sessions with the trainer, a plan can be formulated to get there. When setting goals, it is best to be **SMART** about them.

Specific goals, as shown in Step 1, will help transform the client's extrinsic motivation into intrinsic motivation, therefore making him or her invested in the goal and ready to work for success. Knowing the true goal is half the battle.

Measurable goals allow both trainer and client to measure progress and help the client build self-efficacy. Measuring steady progress will minimize the tendency to see success as all-or-none, so if there is a minor setback, the client realizes that success is just as likely as it was before.

Attainable goals create a stronger sense of confidence and motivation and allow for progress to the super-objective. If a client has a goal to lose twenty pounds in twelve months, breaking that goal down to one-and-a-half pounds a month will allow for the trainer to help cultivate a healthy lifestyle while keeping the client motivated each month.

Relevant goals keep the client motivated because the goal reflects what he or she wants to accomplish. If a client wants to be able to do five pull-ups by the end of the year, planning a marathon training program will not keep him or her coming to the sessions.

Time-bound goals keep the client motivated because the goals have a specific deadline.

STEP 3: BUILD SELF-EFFICACY

When someone takes on a challenge, such as improving their health or losing weight, they must believe they can achieve it. While specific goal setting is an integral part of this process, so is managing a client's inherent fear, uncertainty, and doubt.

Building self-efficacy is the foundation for success in fitness. Table 6.3 shows that the stages of change coincide with growth in self-efficacy. The trainer must nurture this growth by giving clients behavior-changing tools.

Giving a client modest goals to achieve progressive success builds confidence, erasing fear of the unknown and doubt that they can change themselves.

> **?** Many women in the United States are unhappy with their bodies, yet studies have shown that very few American women naturally have a body type that the American media has deemed the standard. This makes a personal trainer's job difficult. How can a trainer promote the balance between body acceptance and body change?

Specified visualization is a proven cognitive tool many athletes use to motivate themselves to achieve their goals and banish doubt. Ask the client to imagine a specific successful result to their goal. For example, a female client wants to lose 10 percent of her weight by her wedding and honeymoon. Ask her to visualize herself in her wedding dress posing for a picture with her new husband. Including vivid details, such as how the dress feels, what music is playing, etc., will allow her to draw on that "memory" every time she thinks her goal is too challenging to accomplish.

Scheduling negativity is a tool that can be used to battle negative thoughts that nurture self-doubt and a low self-efficacy. Ask a client to designate a "negative space" in his home, such as a chair in the corner of the living room, where he can sit for a specified time to allow for negative and fearful thinking. Once that time is up, he is no longer allowed to dwell on those thoughts; it's time to move on and get back on track. The allowable negative time should be no longer than thirty minutes and it must be a consistent time every day. This allows a specific time and place for negative feelings, but also keeps the client from letting them take over the whole day.

Step 4: Maintain Motivation

Successful people do not give up, no matter how hard they must work or how many times they make mistakes. This is persistence. To stay motivated in fitness, a client must understand that the key to success is to get back up, no matter how many times he or she falls. As with all things in fitness, a personal trainer should have techniques to help facilitate persistence.

Rewarding success is one technique to keep a client motivated. Trainers should invest in small rewards to facilitate positive reinforcement. If a client achieves an exercise goal, such as running a mile on the treadmill without stopping or doing a HIIT workout for the first time, rewarding the client with a token of achievement, no matter how small, will go a long way in motivating the client. It also helps strengthen the relationship between the trainer and the client.

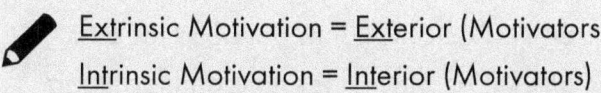
Extrinsic Motivation = Exterior (Motivators)
Intrinsic Motivation = Interior (Motivators)

Incentives help keep a client focused. If a client signs up for eight sessions, throw in a free reassessment to monitor his or her goals. This will help solidify the commitment to reaching a milestone and increase the motivation to stay focused, knowing there will be an opportunity to measure progress.

The trainer can do only so much to motivate a client. Encourage him or her to find a support network, whether that's a fitness class, family, or friends. A support network is a tool to ensure he or she achieves more and feels happier while doing it. Creating a *Network of Excellence* provides support, not only in times of need, but also in times of joy.

While it's important for a trainer to be positive, it's just as important to be pragmatic. Preparing a client for a setback or two will help manage those expectations. The best weapon in times of setbacks is to have a strategy in place. Each client is different and each setback has a different response, so knowing the client's specific triggers will be key to devising the best way to get him or her back on track.

Step 5: Measure Progress

Measurable goals allow the trainer to learn whether she is helping the client get closer to his long-term goals, or if the goals need to be adjusted.

Fitness assessments, session notes, body circumference measurements, and body composition measurements are all effective tools to measure a client's success. Encourage the client to self-monitor the sessions too, and ask him to rate his daily progress from zero to ten. If he wears a self-monitoring device, such a Fitbit® or UP® band, ask to see the information. Encourage him to monitor food intake in a journal and get some exercise outside the training sessions.

Together, the client and trainer can study the data and see where there are shortcomings and successes. Perhaps the client has been indulging too much on the weekends, or maybe he is not finding enjoyable cardiovascular exercise to do on days he is not with the trainer. Or perhaps he is not feeling challenged in the sessions. Whatever the case may be, it is up to the trainer and client to communicate effectively to find a solution that will keep the client motivated and working toward his goals.

PRACTICE QUESTIONS

1. When it comes to goal-setting strategies, what does the *S* in SMART stand for?
    - **A)** start
    - **B)** strong
    - **C)** specific
    - **D)** silly

    Answers:

    A) Incorrect. The *S* in the SMART acronym does not stand for *start*.

    B) Incorrect. The *S* in the SMART acronym does not stand for *strong*.

    C) **Correct.** The *S* in the SMART acronym stands for *specific*.

    D) Incorrect. The *S* in the SMART acronym does not stand for *silly*.

2. Scheduling negativity is a tool that helps combat
    - **A)** self-doubt.
    - **B)** positivity.
    - **C)** goal-setting.
    - **D)** exercise goals.

    Answers:

    A) **Correct.** Scheduling negativity is a tool that facilitates belief in oneself and combats self-doubt.

    B) Incorrect. Positivity is the opposite of the scheduling negativity tool.

    C) Incorrect. Goal-setting is a tool to help a person keep focused on his or her goals.

    D) Incorrect. Exercise goals help a person keep focused on his or her goals.

Client Privacy

Personal trainers obtain sensitive information from their clients in the first meeting. Each client provides medical and personal information in a PAR-Q, as well as information on body composition, emergency contacts, and payment. The personal trainer knows a lot about each client, and the client's privacy must be respected. Regardless if the trainer is a gym employee or an independent contractor, the trainer should have a plan in place that will provide protection from potential legal and liability issues. It is the job of the personal trainer to protect clients against theft and injury and prevent any need for litigation.

Have an agreement in place that outlines confidentiality policies. If working as an independent contractor in a gym, the trainer should have his or her own paperwork in place to assure the client that all the information provided is confidential, unless otherwise notified.

If working as a gym employee, the trainer must make sure there is a confidentiality clause in the agreement that protects both the trainer and the client.

All clients should complete and sign the following:
- medical disclosure form (outlining any preexisting conditions prior to exercise) and/or a medical consent form (usually provided by the client's physician)
- liability form
- PAR-Q (physical activity readiness questionnaire)
- a contract outlining the business relationship between the trainer and client. This contract gives the trainer the client's legal and medical consent to begin a training regimen.

Be sure all contracts, PAR-Qs, assessment forms, payment information, medical disclosures, and liability forms are under lock and key to ensure privacy and prevent theft and the fraudulent use of the information.

Electronic files have their own risk of breach by hackers and other cyberattacks. Be sure all computers and electronic devices are password protected and that anti-virus and malware protection software is installed. If working for a gym, be sure the client information is protected with passwords and administrative restrictions; only trainers and managers should see clients' information.

Unless the trainer obtains permission from clients, pictures or client reviews should not be posted on social media sites.

Keeping a client safe and motivated during a session should be a top priority, and offering knowledge about and insight to help a client achieve their goals creates a deeper relationship. However, a fitness professional must accept the reality that accidents and miscommunications can happen regardless of intention. To ensure all the bases are covered, the trainer should:
- Make sure the fitness space is clean and organized. Do not use faulty equipment and make sure to fully explain the proper execution of each exercise.
- Stay within the personal trainer's **scope of practice**, or field of specialty. If a client complains of a pain, do not diagnose anything; refer them to a doctor. Unless certified to do so, a trainer should not give specific dietary advice or diagnose allergies. Instead, refer the client to a registered dietitian or certified nutritionist.

+ Obtain personal trainer insurance, even if employed by a fitness center or gym. Contrary to popular belief, personal trainers are not fully covered under the insurance of a gym or fitness center. Personal trainers' liability insurance protects against defamation or wrongful invasion of privacy. Miscellaneous personal trainer insurance covers bodily injury claims based on delivering or failing to deliver services. There are several companies that offer a combination of both.

The **Health Insurance Portability and Accountability Act (HIPAA)** is a federal law to simplify obtaining and keeping health insurance, protect the privacy and security of healthcare information, and aid the healthcare industry in streamlining and minimizing administrative costs.

HIPAA applies to trainers because fitness centers and gyms collect medical disclosure and body composition information on their clients. Although fitness professionals are not held to the same scrutiny as doctors, they must keep all client information confidential. Clients trust that a personal trainer will not reveal their private information to anyone. Depending on the state, some businesses may be considered supportive to the medical profession, and while most personal trainers and gyms are not considered business associates, some states may think otherwise. Visit the National Commission of State Legislatures website for information: www.ncsl.org/issues-research/telecom/security-breach-notification-laws.aspx.

The **Family Educational Rights and Privacy Act (FERPA)** is a federal law that protects the privacy of student education records. The law applies to all schools that receive funds under an applicable program of the US Department of Education.

FERPA gives parents specific rights with respect to their children's education records. These rights transfer to the student when he or she reaches the age of eighteen or attends a post-secondary institution.

Schools must have written permission from the parent or student (over the age of eighteen) in order to release any information from a student's education record.

PRACTICE QUESTIONS

1. Even if a personal trainer is employed at a gym, he or she should invest in

    A) his or her own fitness equipment.

    B) liability insurance.

    C) a computer.

    D) business cards.

    Answers:

    A) Incorrect. Unless the trainer is working as a mobile fitness trainer, gyms should have plenty of equipment.

    B) **Correct.** Gyms do not have personal liability coverage for personal trainers.

- C) Incorrect. While it is important to have a computer, if employed at a gym, a trainer can manage without one.
- D) Incorrect. While these are always good to have handy, trainers at gyms tend to get plenty of leads without business cards; some gyms may also provide business cards for their trainers.

2. Clients should complete the following forms, EXCEPT:
   - **A)** PAR-Q
   - **B)** medical disclosure
   - **C)** demographic form
   - **D)** client contract

   Answers:
   - A) Incorrect. Clients should complete the PAR-Q.
   - B) Incorrect. The medical disclosure is one form that clients should be sure to complete.
   - **C) Correct.** The demographic form is not required for clients.
   - D) Incorrect. The client must complete the contract.

SEVEN: SAFETY AND RISK MANAGEMENT

Professional Liability

Responsibilities, Limitations, and Legal Implications for Emergencies

Certified personal trainers have several responsibilities in emergency situations, and must act quickly and within their scope of practice to ensure client safety. It is common practice for employers in the fitness industry to require trainers to be certified in cardiopulmonary resuscitation (CPR), automated external defibrillator (AED), and first aid to work at their facilities. Trainers who have these certifications must work strictly within the limitations of the certifications during emergency procedures. Attempting to perform these emergency procedures without proper certification can open up the trainer to potential lawsuits. For instance, if an employee without a current CPR certification performs CPR on a victim and breaks her ribcage in the process, this employee could potentially be sued by the victim. However, it may be within the responsibility of non-certified employees to alert emergency personnel and stay with the victim to keep her comfortable. An individual with the proper certification can then take on the responsibility of performing emergency procedures.

For other emergencies such as fire, flooding, or environmental emergencies, the fitness professional should abide by the state or federal regulations. It is up to the employees of a facility to help guide guests and customers to safety during an emergency. Additionally, fire escape plans and evacuation routes should be visibly posted throughout the facility to aid in the transportation to safer locations. Documentation on emergency action plans should also be accessible to all employees for review and should be updated when there are changes to the emergency plan. Lack of adequate safety procedures in these situations could result in a lawsuit.

Exercise Testing Protocols for Non-Licensed Professionals

The protocols for exercise testing can vary greatly for licensed and non-licensed professionals. Fitness professionals working in settings such as cardiovascular rehabilitation or stress-testing environments are often required to hold certifications indicating their competency in the field; however, the clinical setting does not give fitness professionals the same responsibilities that physicians have. In most rehabilitative or clinical testing laboratories, only exercise physiologists conduct testing procedures, and they do so under the supervision of a physician in case medical emergencies occur during the stress tests. The level of physician supervision in these environments will vary by facility, and a fitness professional must be aware that his participation has legal implications. Responsibility for medical procedures or intervention should typically be designated to the licensed professional responsible for overseeing the clinical testing protocol. The fitness professional in a situation such as this should receive clear and precise guidelines regarding his responsibility for the patients, and will receive adequate legal and liability coverage for his duties.

Licensed professionals should shoulder the responsibility of adequately preparing an exercise testing team of non-licensed professionals. In a situation requiring the presence of a physician, staff members are often trained to assess risk in patients, which can minimize the risk of an emergency. Additionally, the supervising physician is responsible for outlining all of the testing procedures and emergency protocols, triaging patients, and overseeing the test results. The physician must communicate all parameters of the procedures to the group of non-licensed professionals who typically oversee the actual exercise test.

Licensed physicians practice under strict laws and regulations, but for non-licensed professionals, the regulations are less strict and more loosely defined. Additionally, the regulations for non-licensed professionals can vary from state to state. Prior to agreeing to the terms of service, the fitness professional should receive guidance from the employer or physician on the limitations and regulations he is required to follow in the exercise testing setting. Any concerns about the duties should be discussed with the employer and supervising physician.

Personal Trainer Liability Insurance

When it comes to building a personal training business, purchasing adequate liability insurance coverage is an absolute necessity and it should be acquired before the trainer begins operating her business. Personal trainer insurance provides liability coverage for the various services that the fitness professional provides to clients, including her training methods, health screening procedures, fitness equipment, exercise testing protocols, and other risks. The fitness professional should discuss the insurance coverage and any limitations with the insurance company to ensure she has adequate coverage that fits the needs of her business.

> There are various ways to personalize insurance plans to meet the needs of a company or organization. Some training facilities provide insurance for personal trainers with employment. Be sure to ask the employer whether liability insurance is the responsibility of the trainer or the employer. Trainers must NOT begin work without this type of insurance coverage.

Personal trainer insurance helps to protect trainers against litigation they may face as a result of their work. In addition to the personal trainer insurance, other risk management methods are available to help prevent potential litigation. First, clientele must sign the necessary forms prior to joining a fitness center or starting a fitness program. Paperwork such as liability waivers, informed consent to exercise, and the assumed or inherent risks of starting a fitness program, all mitigate the risks to the trainer. These signed forms helps to reduce the possibility that a lawsuit will arise, simply because of the general risks inherent in exercising.

In addition to obtaining personal trainer insurance and using the necessary forms as part of standard operating procedures, fitness professionals should ensure client safety by following industry standards for items such as safe program implementation, proper emergency procedures, upkeep of exercise equipment, and proper credentialing for all trainers. Overly aggressive training programs can pose risks of injury that can open up avenues for lawsuits. These risks can be minimized with properly designed programs that are tailored to each client.

Most employers post signage on emergency procedures and practice those procedures throughout the year. Exercise equipment should be inspected regularly for wear and tear, and any damage should be reported and the equipment removed immediately from the fitness area. Finally, trainer certifications help to ensure a level of expertise in the field as long as the trainers practice within their scope. Additional certifications for safety, such as CPR, AED, and first aid, should also be mandatory to minimize risk in a fitness center. These issues are discussed in more depth in *Risk Management*, later in this chapter.

NEGLIGENCE IN TRAINING ENVIRONMENTS

Negligence is a common reason for lawsuits, and this is also true in fitness and training. Negligence can occur in the areas of fitness program design, fitness assessment, medical background, supervision of exercise techniques, cleanliness of facilities, equipment usage, and more. Therefore, it is essential for the fitness professional to follow appropriate risk-management strategies to prevent unnecessary lawsuits. To ensure the safety of new clientele, all clients must be thoroughly and carefully screened for their readiness for exercise. Each client also must complete a medical history form. The fitness assessment process should follow strict guidelines, and trainers should take precautions with clients to prevent injury during the assessment procedures. Clients should not be left unsupervised during training sessions. In addition, large group-training sessions that involve a lot of technique should have multiple trainers involved in supervision.

> **?** Consider your own experiences. When have you witnessed possible negligence in a facility or noted areas for improvement? Write down or think about some solutions that might solve this potential problem area. Be specific!

Fitness facilities should be thoroughly and regularly cleaned to reduce the risk of spreading infectious disease or bacteria. Equipment maintenance should be performed at regular intervals throughout the year to avoid potential injuries. Additionally, the cleaning and equipment-maintenance procedures should be well documented to provide corroboration of facility maintenance. Taking preventive steps to reduce the risk of negligence is essential in fitness.

PRACTICE QUESTIONS

1. Before beginning work with clients, what should the certified personal trainer acquire to help in emergency situations?

    A) personal liability insurance

    B) negligence insurance

    C) CPR, AED, and first aid certification

    D) a personal trainer certification

    Answers:

    A) Incorrect. Although it's a good idea to have personal liability insurance for legal protection, it will not help trainers in emergency situations.

    B) Incorrect. Negligence insurance should be included in adequate personal trainer liability insurance.

    C) **Correct.** CPR, AED, and first aid certifications qualify the trainer to be a first responder in emergency situations; these certifications should be obtained prior to the trainer beginning work with clients.

    D) Incorrect. Although a personal trainer certification helps to improve expertise in fitness, the certification does not include emergency responder training.

2. Negligence in training environments includes areas such as:

    A) the client acting inappropriately.

    B) an environmental emergency.

    C) the client performing appropriately designed workouts with the trainer present.

    D) equipment cleanliness.

    Answers:

    A) Incorrect. Clients acting inappropriately is not negligence on the part of the trainer; however, the trainer should attempt to limit this behavior.

    B) Incorrect. Environmental emergencies are not due to negligence.

- **C)** Incorrect. The client performing appropriately designed workouts with the trainer present reduces the risk of negligence.
- **D) Correct.** Equipment that is not cleaned regularly can lead to the spread of infectious diseases, resulting in a negligence lawsuit.

Risk Management

Safety Policies and Procedures

Implementing and documenting safety policies and procedures can help to eliminate the risks associated with emergency situations. Staff members of a facility should be oriented to safety policies and procedures immediately following their hiring to ensure the facility minimizes its risk. Documentation should be printed and kept in a place where it is easily accessible by all employees for review, and emergency drills procedures should be regularly practiced to ensure proficiency in executing emergency drills.

Additionally, signage should be posted to indicate where safety and emergency devices, such as first aid kits, fire extinguishers, fire exit plans, automated external defibrillators, etc. are located in the facility. Access to these emergency devices and emergency procedures should not be blocked by objects, and the emergency devices must be regularly maintained to ensure proper function. Any discrepancies found in emergency action plans and procedures could be grounds for a lawsuit against a facility for negligence and failure to prepare for emergency situations. Maintaining safety policies and procedures significantly helps in eliminating risks associated with emergencies.

The safety policies and procedures should also include injury prevention strategies. Certified personal trainers can help promote injury prevention by properly documenting programs. The documentation can include written examples of proper progression through an exercise program that would reduce the risk of overuse or overreaching injuries. In addition, to further manage risk, it may be advisable to assign supervisory roles, including training program oversight, to spot potential risks like rapid progression. Individuals running a one-person operation should consider reviewing their own programs for potential hazards prior to implementation. If the fitness professional is unsure of the program's safety, she must immediately review the appropriate literature on program design. It is up to each fitness professional to ensure his or her program is created safely, in order to reduce the risk of injuries related to poor program design.

Safety Precautions in the Training Facility

Risk management techniques also apply to the training facility. Operating a safe fitness center involves proper floorplan layout, cleaning schedules, and training surfaces. All equipment, including free weight areas with benches and Olympic lifting stands, should be properly spaced so that the moving parts will not collide with other objects or block walking paths or emergency exits. The area must be large enough to accommodate the person lifting the weights and up to three spotters for safety. Any equipment that could tip over or move must be bolted into the floor or walls for safety.

Equipment and floors should be cleaned regularly to prevent the spread of bacteria or infectious disease, and the cleaning procedures should be documented and initialed by employees. Accurate documentation shows the efforts being made to prevent the spread of infectious disease and eliminates the risk of follow-up visits by health authorities. A clean facility also helps with client retention. Finally, flooring should provide adequate traction for clients performing various types of exercises. Floors that get slick when wet can increase the risk of slip-and-fall injuries. Therefore, a rubber mat is better suited to fitness centers than hardwood, linoleum, or other smooth surfaces.

Different types of flooring may be needed for different types of exercise, however. For instance, hardwood flooring is preferred for fitness studios that hold dance-based aerobics since the hardwood allows for some sliding and prevents potential ligament damage from twisting. The type of exercise should be considered thoroughly before installing flooring.

SAFE TRAINING PRACTICES

Risk can also be managed through safe training environments, monitored exercise levels, and proper equipment setup. It is up to the fitness staff to care for and monitor the integrity of the equipment. Damaged equipment should be removed from the fitness floor, if possible, or signage should be placed to indicate the equipment is out of order.

Both the fitness staff and the facility members are responsible for keeping weight training areas free from clutter. The staff should take responsibility for putting away equipment they use and should also encourage members to return equipment to its proper place. Equipment that blocks walking paths could cause injury and result in legal action.

For outdoor training programs, environmental factors must be carefully considered. Rain, snow, ice, and extreme temperatures, either hot or cold, can negatively impact athletic performance, and under these conditions, it may be wise to keep the training session inside. Heat-related injuries resulting from inadequate hydration are common and should not be taken lightly. The outdoor area should also be inspected for any objects that could potentially harm clients during exercises.

> **?** How might a class schedule indicate the intensity of a group fitness class, other than saying low intensity, moderate intensity, or high intensity?

Monitoring the intensity of exercise is another method of risk management for the certified fitness professional. The trainer can help prevent dangerous situations by tracking the intensity of exercise based on the client's fitness level. Fitness assessments can help to measure the intensity at which a client should be working and therefore can help to lower the risk. The personal trainer can then use assessment results to program the client's workouts to achieve a desired intensity.

Compared with personal training sessions, fitness classes can present complications in monitoring the intensity and managing risk. A description of each class and its intensity level should be indicated on the fitness class schedules provided by the facility. Exercise classes should include modifications to exercises and clients should be encouraged to exercise at their own pace to avoid overtraining or injury.

Equipment Setup and Maintenance

The proper setup of equipment can help minimize risk. To prevent injury, trainers should encourage clients to utilize the equipment the way it was designed, without modifications or shortcuts, and should ensure proper safety mechanisms are applied. For barbells of all sizes, clips are required to hold the weight, regardless of the amount of weight on the bar. Safety rails on squat racks should be required for all clients, regardless of fitness status. The training staff should always be encouraging and accessible in case clients have questions and staff should be able to show clients how to properly set up each piece of equipment.

Regular maintenance should be performed on equipment and catalogued for appropriate risk management. For example, free weights such as barbells may require regular tightening of bolts, selectorized machine weights may require lubrication to allow proper movement of the weight plates, and cardiovascular equipment may require recalibration at regular intervals. The fitness professional or facility is responsible for some regular, routine maintenance to ensure that equipment lasts for a long time, and trainers should be familiar with what the equipment requires. Equipment upkeep instructions are often included with the equipment purchase.

If malfunctioning equipment requires a professional equipment mechanic to come out for service, this equipment should be marked with an *Out of Order* sign to prevent further damage to the equipment and injury to clientele. New equipment often comes with a service plan or warranty that will cover electrical or mechanical issues that arise within a certain time frame after purchase. Fitness professionals should become familiar with the service plan to make sure they are aware of what the warranty covers. Some key points to look for in a service agreement include: what is covered and not covered by the agreement, length of the warranty, what is involved in the service process, limits of liability of the product, and any guarantees of the product's integrity. Knowing these components of the service plan can help minimize costly risks associated with the purchase of exercise equipment. Additionally, trainers should become familiar with the service company's response time for equipment repairs. This is a smart way to ensure client satisfaction with a fitness center.

Components of an Emergency Action Plan

The key components of an emergency action plan are outlined by the United States Department of Labor. Below is a brief summary of the key components of an emergency action plan, according to the Occupational Health and Safety Administration (OSHA):

+ a method of signaling and alerting during emergencies, such as a fire alarm

- a procedure outlining emergency actions such as evacuations and emergency escape
- assigned tasks for employees that will ensure conditions do not become more dangerous for emergency responders
- a method, such as a head count, to ensure all employees have evacuated safely
- a direct resource for first responders to an emergency, such as fire departments and emergency rescue crews
- a list of employees and designated emergency duties in case of an emergency or evacuation protocol

The details of an emergency action plan will vary by the type of facility and working environment. The components outlined above will be adequate for many fitness centers; however, a fitness center with a child daycare may provide further details regarding emergency protocols for the abduction of children, for example. Emergency procedures should be documented in hard copy and should be easily accessible to all employees. The fitness professional in charge should make sure to explain the staff's responsibilities in emergency and evacuation plans during initial training, and should reinforce these methods through regular emergency drills. The guidelines of the US Department of Labor are the minimum regulations; each bullet point should be outlined in further detail by the employer regarding what specific measures the facility will take during emergencies. Having a well-designed emergency action plan is essential to the overall safety and risk management of a fitness center.

PRACTICE QUESTIONS

1. What is a good example of safe training practices?
    - **A)** performing outdoor workouts regardless of weather conditions
    - **B)** considering environmental factors prior to engaging in outdoor workouts
    - **C)** using a parking lot for a workout
    - **D)** relying on fitness center clientele to pick up equipment after usage

   Answers:
    - A) Incorrect. Weather conditions directly impact client safety because they can lead to slip-and-fall injuries.
    - B) **Correct.** When engaging in outdoor workouts, the fitness professional should consider environmental factors, such as heat, cold, rain, snow, ice, fallen leaves, etc.
    - C) Incorrect. Prior to engaging in the workout, the fitness professional needs to determine all potentially hazardous conditions, such as gravel, traffic, fallen leaves, and other environmental factors.

D) Incorrect. Though fitness professionals should encourage all clients to clean up their equipment following a workout, to ensure safety, the trainer should be responsible for this task.

2. What should the fitness professional do with malfunctioning equipment?
   A) place signage indicating the equipment is *Out of Order*, or remove the equipment from the fitness center floor
   B) inform clientele upon their arrival to the facility that the equipment is not working properly
   C) inform clientele about the equipment if the trainer sees a client using the equipment
   D) disassemble the piece of equipment

Answers:
A) **Correct.** Signage should be placed in a visible location on the equipment, indicating that the equipment is malfunctioning and should not be used.
B) Incorrect. Clients may not realize which piece of equipment the trainer is talking about and could injure themselves if they mistakenly use it.
C) Incorrect. Clients may be injured by broken equipment, so signage indicating the equipment is out of order should always be placed on the equipment immediately, before a client might inadvertently use it.
D) Incorrect. Certain pieces of equipment may have warranties and may require a technician's support. The fitness professional should not disassemble equipment.

Medical Clearance

Medical Clearance for Exercise

Ensuring clients are medically cleared for exercise is a high priority for the fitness professional, since this clearance can reduce the risk of a cardiovascular event during exercise and potentially prevent lawsuits resulting from negligence or liability. Identifying possible risks in new clientele can be done in various ways. The trainer should require all clients to fill out a medical history and PAR-Q. This way, the trainer will be aware of any health conditions of the client that may be exacerbated by exercise.

A number of fitness organizations have developed lists of risk factors to help trainers determine the risk stratification of new clientele. A list can be applied to a client's medical history to identify whether the client requires a physician's clearance prior to starting a new fitness program. The risk factors include:

+ age (the age risk varies by gender)
+ family history of cardiovascular diseases
+ smoking

- sedentary lifestyle
- obesity and/or diabetes or pre-diabetes
- high blood pressure
- high blood glucose

All clientele should be subject to risk stratification to lessen the complications that may arise from starting an exercise program. This precaution will help reduce the potential of medical emergencies. Based on clients' various health risk factors, they can be categorized as low risk, intermediate risk, or high risk. Low-risk individuals will have less than two of these factors present; intermediate-risk may have two factors, but they must be under a physician's care or asymptomatic; and high-risk clients will have evident and documented cardiovascular risk factors. Trainers should explain to clients in the high-risk category that a medical clearance from their physicians is required prior to participating in an exercise program.

These forms can also help the fitness professional determine the amount of supervision the client may require during exercise. In general, the higher the risk, the more supervision will be required. High-risk clients with known cardiovascular diseases may require a medically administered stress test to see if they are ready for physical activity or an individualized fitness program. After these clients receive a physician's clearance to work with a knowledgeable fitness professional, they may ease into a new exercise program. It is critically important that the fitness professional have the appropriate expertise for these clients' special needs.

A medical clearance form should provide space for the physician to detail the client's contraindications for exercise. The form should also indicate what precautions the fitness professional should take during exercise sessions. The client may have no cardiovascular contraindications to exercise, but other conditions, such as severe joint pain, may prevent him or her from performing certain types of exercise. These types of comments help to improve communication between the physician and the fitness professional and help prevent injuries. For certain conditions, the client may find it easier to ask that the physician speak directly with the fitness professional and provide advice on any contraindications for exercise. This level of commitment shows the client that the trainer prioritizes the client's health in planning an exercise program. Speaking with the physician does not replace the trainer's need for written medical clearance, however, and signed client paperwork should always be required for legal purposes.

> Print out examples of the four documents listed above and practice the initial client meeting with a friend. Practice can help reduce nervousness and help ensure that the actual client meeting runs more smoothly.

In addition to completing a medical history and PAR-Q form, the client must complete and sign the appropriate informed consent and liability waiver forms. On these forms the fitness professional outlines for the client exactly what is entailed in fitness testing procedures. These forms provide liability protection because the client must sign them and thereby affirm that he or she was fully informed about the testing procedures before participating in them.

To review, prior to beginning an exercise program the client must fill out and sign the following:

1. medical history (and obtain medical clearance if necessary)
2. PAR-Q (Physical Activity Readiness Questionnaire)
3. informed consent for exercise and fitness testing
4. liability waiver to begin the exercise program

This is an example of an informed consent for exercise:

Exercise Consent Form

I, the undersigned, hereby expressly and affirmatively state that I wish to participate in _____. I realize that my participation in this activity involves risk of injury, including but not limited to (list) _____ and even the possibility of death. I also recognize that there are many other risks of injury, including serious disabling injuries, which may arise due to my participation in this activity and that it is not possible to specifically list each and every individual injury risk. However, knowing the material risks and appreciating, knowing, and reasonably anticipating that other injuries and even death are a possibility, I hereby expressly assume all of the delineated risks of injury, all other possible risks of injury, and even death which could occur by reason of my participation.

I have had an opportunity to ask questions. Any questions which I have asked have been answered to my complete satisfaction. I subjectively understand the risk of my participation in this activity, and knowing and appreciating these risks I voluntarily choose to participate, assuming all risks of injury or even death due to my participation.

_____   _____
Witness   Participant

_____
Date

Figure 7.1. Exercise Consent Form

Additional forms are available to help trainers stratify risk and strategize for a more personalized exercise program.

REPUTABLE RESOURCES

Newly certified personal trainers will require additional education to ensure their methods meet industry guidelines. National research organizations such as the

American Heart Association offer guidelines on cardiovascular health. Certifying fitness organizations such as the National Academy of Sports Medicine (NASM), the American Council on Exercise (ACE), and the American College of Sports Medicine (ACSM), which develop their guidelines through peer-reviewed research are also credible resources for information on fitness. It's important that fitness professionals obtain certification through one of these organizations, not only to bolster their knowledge but also to provide evidence of expertise if clients research the trainer's background and qualifications. Fitness professionals can also direct clients seeking information to these reputable organizations. (See chapter 8 for more information.)

PRACTICE QUESTIONS

1. The medical history form is utilized to
    - **A)** protect trainers from liability if the client is injured.
    - **B)** assess potential medical concerns that may require a physician's clearance before the client can start an exercise program.
    - **C)** determine whether the client is interested in beginning an exercise program.
    - **D)** determine the intensity at which a client may begin an exercise program.

    Answers:
    - A) Incorrect. Liability cannot be prevented entirely by paperwork, and the medical history form is not an exception.
    - B) **Correct.** The medical history form helps the trainer decide whether the client requires a physician's clearance in order to begin exercising.
    - C) Incorrect. The client's interest in exercising cannot be determined by the medical history form.
    - D) Incorrect. Determining workout intensity is not the purpose of the medical history form.

2. A client who smokes, is diagnosed as obese, and has a documented family history of heart attacks would be at what level of risk?
    - **A)** no risk
    - **B)** low risk
    - **C)** intermediate risk
    - **D)** high risk

    Answers:
    - A) Incorrect. This individual has three cardiovascular risk factors.
    - B) Incorrect. A low-risk assessment is not correct, given the multiple cardiovascular risk factors.
    - C) Incorrect. An intermediate-risk assessment is too low for this client.

> **D) Correct.** This individual would be considered high risk and would require a physician's clearance to begin an exercise program.

Overtraining and Abnormal Responses to Exercise

Overtraining

Overtraining is the body's response to too much physical stress in too short a time. Overtraining means that the human body has not had adequate rest to develop the necessary adaptations to exercise prior to the next round of training.

Overtraining affects the human body both physically and psychologically. Fitness professionals should understand and be able to recognize the signs and symptoms or overtraining in order to prevent musculoskeletal injuries. They should also learn the proper treatment and recovery methods. Following is a list of the signs and symptoms of overtraining:

- sluggishness or generalized fatigue
- poor sleep
- loss of confidence
- increased anger or anxiety
- decrease in physical performance
- chronic muscle soreness or joint pain
- increase in resting heart rate
- change in blood pressure
- change in mood
- change in appetite
- depression
- excessive thirst

Though this list is not exhaustive, these signs are evidence that a client may be trying to fit too much into his workouts with inadequate rest and recovery. Not all clients will succumb to the same signs and symptoms, and it is up to the trainer to keep accurate training records to prevent the onset of this syndrome.

The fitness professional should approach overtraining cautiously and require that the client rest for up to twenty-four hours before overloading the same muscle groups. The athlete can still perform exercise to maintain fitness but should reduce the intensity of workouts. Psychologically, the overtrained client may require a scheduled break from training, a change of exercise methods or, in severe cases, a complete cessation of exercise.

The fitness professional must determine whether the client is experiencing overtraining and musculoskeletal injury, or rather acute muscle soreness and delayed onset muscle soreness (DOMS). Some muscular soreness and fatigue is a normal response to resistance training when the muscles are being properly overloaded. The onset of DOMS can occur between twenty-four and forty-eight hours post-workout and last up to several days, depending on the client and his or her training status. DOMS is different from overtraining in that the soreness will eventually subside without any chronic effect on the musculoskeletal system. Joint pain and soreness that does not go away could be a sign of overtraining, and should be taken seriously by both the client and fitness professional. Acute muscle soreness and DOMS are common in the muscles and tendons around the joints, but excessive joint pain refers to pain in the joint itself. Training programs should not cause this type of pain. If it occurs, the trainer should take precautions in future exercise programming to avoid overtraining.

 DOMS is actually caused by micro-tears in the fibers of the muscles and can even occur in well-trained athletes.

Other abnormal responses to exercise must be determined during training sessions. An in-depth understanding of exercise physiology can help the fitness professional make smarter decisions during emergency situations. Excessive breathlessness that does not subside following a cessation of exercise or after minimal effort is one warning sign. Other warning signs include dizziness, abnormal heart rate, or any signs of heart attack or stroke, which are listed in Tables 7.1 and 7.2.

Table 7.1. Warning Signs of a Heart Attack

Heart Attack Warning Signs

Men	Women
Chest pain/discomfort	Chest pressure
Rapid or irregular heartbeat	Unusual fatigue for several days
Feeling dizzy, faint of light-headed	Anxiety and sleep disturbances
Breaking out in a cold sweat	Back, neck, arm, and jaw pain
Stomach discomfort or indigestions	Nausea, feeling sick to stomach
Shortness of breath	Shortness of breath

If you have any of these signs, don't wait. Call 911

*froedtert.com/heart

Table 7.2. Warning Signs of a Stroke

Remember the key elements: FAST

F - Face	Ask the person to smile. Does one side of the face droop?
A - Arm	Ask the person to raise both arms. Does one arm drift down?
S - Speech	Ask the person to repeat a phrase. Is speech slurred or strange?
T - Time	If you see any of these signs call 9-1-1 right away

The FAST acronym describes the signs of a stroke and can save lives if the steps are quickly followed.

PRACTICE QUESTIONS

1. The difference between the symptoms of DOMS and the symptoms of overtraining is

    A) how sore the muscle is.

    B) which muscles are sore.

    C) nothing—DOMS is actually a symptom of overtraining.

    D) whether the soreness is acute or chronic.

    Answers:

    A)   Incorrect. Level of soreness is not a proper differentiation between DOMS and overtraining symptoms; both can elicit the same degree of soreness.

    B)   Incorrect. Overtraining and DOMS can occur in the same muscles.

    C)   Incorrect. DOMS is a normal physiological response to overloading the muscles, whereas overtraining is an abnormal response due to inadequate rest.

    D)   Correct. DOMS typically involves acute soreness, whereas overtraining involves chronic soreness.

2. The typical treatment for minor overtraining symptoms is to

    A) work the muscles at a lighter load.

    B) work the muscles at a lighter volume.

    C) temporarily stop exercising and get adequate rest.

    D) do cardiovascular exercise instead of resistance training.

    Answers:

    A)   Incorrect. Working the muscles, even at a lighter load, can continue to cause overtraining symptoms.

    B)   Incorrect. Symptoms of overtraining can still be caused by working the muscles at a lighter volume.

    C)   Correct. Temporary cessation of exercise and resting before restarting exercise helps the client overcome overtraining symptoms.

    D)   Incorrect. Cardiovascular exercise can still result in overtraining symptoms.

CONTINUE

Injuries and Medical Emergencies

Initial Management and First-Aid Techniques

It is in the best interest of fitness professionals to have proper protocols in place to quickly respond to medical emergencies and injuries. As previously discussed, fitness professionals must approach medical emergencies with caution and only within the scope of practice in which they are trained. For example, it may be appropriate for the fitness professional to supply a bandage or gauze pad so the individual can clean small open wounds. It is not within the scope of the trainer's practice, however, to attempt to stitch a wound closed.

Although treating injuries is not within the trainer's scope, trainers should be able to recognize the symptoms of various injuries and medical emergencies so they can respond appropriately to open wounds, musculoskeletal injuries, cardiovascular and pulmonary events, and metabolic disorders. Some possible situations are addressed below, along with the appropriate responses from a fitness professional with basic life support (BLS) and first-aid training.

Open wounds: The trainer should wash an open wound with clean water and apply a sterile dressing such as gauze or bandages. Apply pressure until bleeding stops, then reapply a fresh sterile dressing to the wound. The injured individual should be taken to the emergency room if bleeding persists, the wound is deep, or if the edges of the opening are wide. Injuries to limbs should be elevated above heart level.

Musculoskeletal injuries: Different types of injury require different first-aid procedures. For contusions, sprains, and strains, it is common practice to follow the RICE protocol (**R**est, **I**ce, **C**ompression, and **E**levation of the injury) within the first day to the first week of the injury to reduce symptoms. Rest the injured body part to prevent further injury; apply ice for up to thirty minutes per hour in ten-minute increments to reduce swelling, pain, and inflammation; apply a compressive wrap of gauze or bandage to the site of injury to reduce swelling; and, finally, elevate the injured site to further reduce swelling and enhance the drainage of excess internal fluid collection. If the client's pain, swelling, or other symptoms persist for longer than a few days, or if movement of the injury site produces grating, popping, or crackling sounds or unusual sensations under the skin, the client should seek immediate medical attention. If the trainer suspects a bone fracture has occurred, he or she should apply ice to the site and transport the injured person to an emergency department for medical treatment immediately. Similarly, with dislocated joints, the trainer should immediately apply ice and ensure the client is transported to the emergency department for medical attention.

 Bone fractures can be classified as simple, compound, open, closed, or comminuted.

Cardiovascular and pulmonary events: Cardiovascular events such as heart attack and stroke are often life threatening and must be considered emergencies. Trainers must immediately call 911. While awaiting emergency help, each employee responder should follow established emergency guidelines. Clients who fall unconscious due to suspected cardiovascular events may require CPR. Fitness professionals should follow the guidelines issued by the governing bodies on CPR. Severe cardiopulmonary events are discussed in detail below.

Chest pain can have many different causes and should be approached with extra caution. *Heart attacks* are often accompanied by chest pain with pressure, radiation of pain down the neck, arms, shoulders, and face, profuse sweating, feeling lightheaded, and shortness of breath. Any chest pain accompanied by these symptoms should elicit immediate medical attention. Additional medical emergencies involving chest pain include aortic dissection, pulmonary embolism, and unstable angina.

Tachycardia, an increased heart rate, can be a normal physiological response to exercise; however, tachycardia that occurs with inappropriate intensities of exercise could be cause for alarm. The heart rate increases with increasing intensities of exercise and should decrease with rest or reduced exercise intensity. Sustained elevated heart rate following cessation of exercise should be considered a potential cardiovascular event and emergency action may be required.

Bradycardia, a decrease in heart rate below normal levels, can be just as serious. Exercise should initiate an increased heart rate, but a low heart rate means that oxygen-rich blood is not being pumped to the tissues. This could result in sudden fainting. The causes of a low heart rate vary, but one potential cause could be damage to heart tissue, which prevents the proper conduction of electrical activity in the heart.

Hypertension, or elevated blood pressure, can lead to more serious conditions such as heart attacks and strokes. Clients with known hypertension should have their blood pressure checked prior to and following an exercise session. Over time, consistent exercise can help to reduce hypertension. Signs of hypertension often do not manifest until more severe conditions are apparent; therefore, it is important to check the blood pressure of incoming clients or refer them to their physicians for testing.

Hypotension, abnormally low blood pressure, can result from a rapid change in body position or from potential heart disease. The symptoms of low blood pressure include fainting, lightheadedness, dizziness, cold sweats, nausea, or blurry vision.

Hyperventilation, an increase in breathing rate, that occurs at rest could be a sign of a cardiac or pulmonary emergency. Breathing rate naturally increases with an increase in exercise intensity but should subside soon after cessation of exercise. Serious conditions that could present hyperventilation include heart attacks, excessive bleeding, panic attacks, chronic obstructive pulmonary disorders, and pulmonary emboli. If hyperventilation persists or other symptoms of cardiovascular events present themselves, call 911 immediately.

> Study prefixes and suffixes to remember medical terminology. For instance, the prefix *hypo–* means *below*, whereas *hyper–* means *above*. Studying lists or flashcards of prefixes and suffixes can make remembering medical terminology fast and easy with consistent practice.

Metabolic conditions such as **hypoglycemia**, or low blood sugar levels, can cause clients to experience *syncope*, or fainting. Patients who experience hypoglycemia are often diabetic and require rapidly available sugar to counteract the effects. Symptoms that could indicate dangerously low blood sugar include slurred speech, dizziness, confusion, sweating, loss of coordination, fatigue, irritability, tachycardia, blurred vision, and even loss of consciousness. If symptoms present prior to loss of consciousness, the fitness professional should administer readily available sources of glucose, such as hard candies or fruit juices. The client should sit down to avoid injury from falling and must be supervised while another individual obtains the glucose.

The opposite effect in diabetics is referred to as **hyperglycemia**, or high blood sugar, and can result in severe side effects if left unchecked. Typical symptoms include increased frequency of urination, increased thirst, high blood sugar levels in glucose testing, and increased sugar levels in urine testing. Severe cases can lead to diabetic comas and are typically preluded by ketoacidosis symptoms such as fruity-smelling breath, cottonmouth, vomiting, or shortness of breath. If a client is presenting these symptoms, call 911.

Other metabolic conditions include hyperthermia and hypothermia. **Hyperthermia,** an abnormally increased body temperature, is more common than hypothermia in exercise settings. The potential for hyperthermia is elevated in extremely hot and humid climates that do not allow the body's thermoregulation mechanisms, such as sweating, to work properly. The sweat will not evaporate and cooling does not occur. The symptoms of hyperthermia include mood changes, lack of sweat, rapid pulse, flushed skin, fainting, and loss of consciousness. The client should lie down and cold compresses should be applied to the major arteries and to the groin and armpits. Fluids should be encouraged if the client can drink, and the client should be removed from the heat and sun immediately.

Hypothermia, a decrease in body temperature below normal levels, is more of a concern in very cold climates. Clients involved in outdoor winter sports are more susceptible to hypothermia; however, hypothermia can also be caused by cold rain and temperatures above freezing. Signs and symptoms include confusion, drowsiness, loss of coordination, and even frostbite of the extremities, and any exposed skin. Clients experiencing these symptoms should be removed from the cold, stripped of wet clothing, covered with dry clothing and blankets, and given a warm beverage free of alcohol or caffeine.

Obtaining Basic Life Support (BLS) and First-Aid Training

As previously discussed, certified fitness professionals must also receive training in CPR, AED, and basic first aid. Basic Life Support (BLS) classes provide training in CPR and in AED. Many training organizations will include basic first-aid training, which should be a priority for fitness professionals, who may encounter bleeding, broken bones, and other common incidents. The BLS certification will prepare the fitness professional to provide emergency first response.

Several organizations provide these certification courses, including the American Heart Association, the Occupational Safety and Health Administration (OSHA), and the American Red Cross. Certification courses can typically be completed in one or two days through in-classroom training or in a blended course that combines online work followed by in-classroom testing protocols. Required training may vary for individual employers or states. Courses are offered nationwide, and the certifications typically need to be renewed every two years.

Client Health History and Emergency Contacts

It is important to closely control access to clients' confidential information. A paper copy of each signed document should be stored in a locked cabinet that is easily accessible in case of emergency. Client information can also be scanned and stored in an electronic file for even quicker access. Whether stored physically or electronically, all confidential client information must be protected. Electronic information must be password-protected to prevent violation of privacy.

 Why might it be wise to keep medical history forms easily accessible?

PRACTICE QUESTIONS

1. Over time, hypertension can lead to
    - **A)** overuse injuries.
    - **B)** musculoskeletal injuries.
    - **C)** delayed onset muscle soreness.
    - **D)** heart attacks and strokes.

    Answers:
    - A) Incorrect. Hypertension leads to cardiovascular events and is not typically related to overuse injuries.
    - B) Incorrect. Musculoskeletal injuries are typically related to overtraining or physical trauma.
    - C) Incorrect. Delayed onset muscle soreness, or DOMS, is the natural physiological result of overloading the muscle and is a normal occurrence.

- **D) Correct.** Hypertension can lead to heart attacks and strokes.

2. Through what organizations can a fitness specialist obtain CPR, AED, and first-aid training?
    - **A)** the American College of Sports Medicine (ACSM)
    - **B)** a local hospital
    - **C)** the same organization that provides personal trainers' insurance
    - **D)** the American Heart Association (AHA), OSHA, or the Red Cross

Answers:

- A) Incorrect. The ACSM provides personal training certifications; however, it does not provide CPR, AED, or first-aid certifications.
- B) Incorrect. Though courses may be held at local hospitals, the leading organizations that provide this training are the American Heart Association, OSHA, and the Red Cross.
- C) Incorrect. Personal trainer insurance organizations do not provide CPR, AED, or first-aid training.
- **D) Correct.** The AHA, OSHA, and the Red Cross are reliable organizations for obtaining certifications in CPR, AED, and first aid.

EIGHT: PROFESSIONAL DEVELOPMENT AND RESPONSIBILITY

Personal trainers, like all certified professionals in the **allied healthcare continuum**, must adhere to certain standards to maintain the industry's credibility. This section outlines the general framework of responsibilities and parameters for a certified personal trainer.

Scope of Practice

Certified personal trainers are included in what the American Council on Exercise calls the *allied healthcare continuum*, a network of licensed, certified, or registered professionals who provide invaluable healthcare resources to the general population. The healthcare continuum includes doctors, nurses, dieticians, nutritionists, physical therapists, psychologists, and massage therapists, who all work to keep people healthy every day. This network depends on the integrity of all members to give participants the best care possible.

Each credentialed professional must work within legal parameters, or a **scope of practice**, which allows the patient or participant to get the most informed and well-researched information available. A physician typically is at the top of the healthcare *chain of command* and is assisted by nurses. General physicians typically refer patients to specialists if the treatment needs are beyond the physicians' expertise. For example, an orthopedic surgeon might prescribe the patient to receive rehabilitative treatment from a physical therapist, who might then refer the patient to a personal trainer for continued strength training. A physician or specialist might refer the patient to a registered dietician or nutritionist to aid in pre- or post-surgery diet corrections.

A certified fitness professional's scope of practice is focused on exercise program design, fitness assessments, exercise technique, body composition measurement, fitness goal setting, exercise adherence, and motivation. As with the other professionals in the allied healthcare continuum, the personal trainer must positively enforce the trainers' scope of practice. This ensures the integrity and necessity of the fitness professional as a valued part of the healthcare alliance.

> **?** A client comes into his training session complaining of a numbing pain in the left side of his lower back. After the warm-up portion of his session, he continues to hold his back and mentions frequent trips to the bathroom and painful urination. What would be the proper way for a personal trainer to handle this situation?

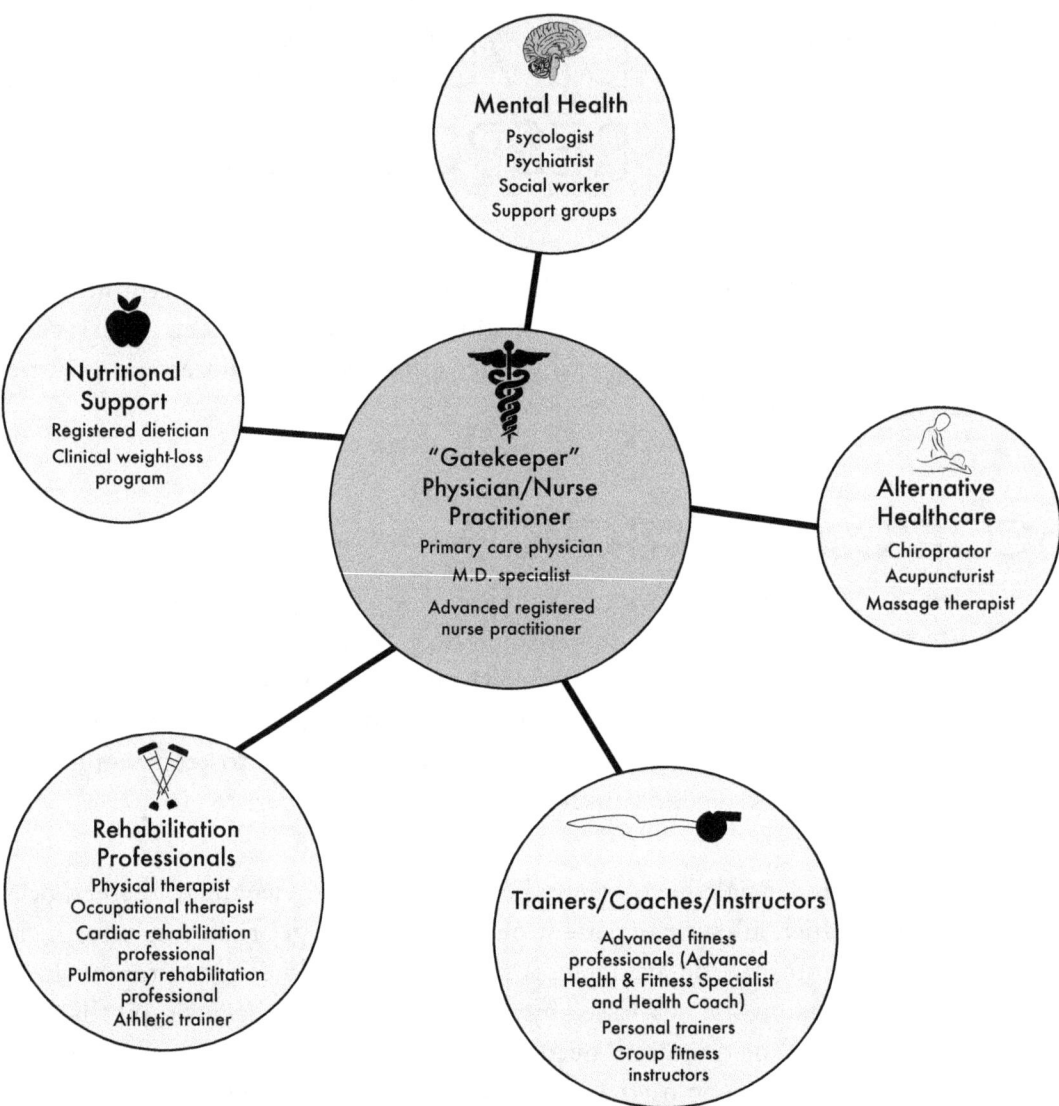

Figure 8.1. Allied Healthcare Continuum

Personal trainers must be very careful to not go beyond their scope of practice, which can be difficult, especially when a client asks about a meal plan or diet recommendations to accompany her fitness routine. Certified personal trainers can offer only general nutrition guidelines or refer a client to the federal dietary guidelines on Health.gov.

If a client wants specific nutritional advice, dietary guidelines for specific diseases, or information on dietary supplements, unless the trainer holds an additional nutrition certification, the trainer must refer her to a certified nutritionist or registered dietician. If the trainer does not know of a specific nutritionist or dietitian, the trainer should advise the client to speak to her physician.

A certified personal trainer must also refer clients to physicians if clients express prolonged discomfort or pain while participating in the training sessions or if they become injured. A personal trainer should never diagnose an injury or its treatment.

Clients who have positive and trusting relationships with their trainers may begin to solicit their advice on personal matters, or may confide in them about depressed feelings, marital problems, or eating disorders. Caring, passionate, or knowledgeable fitness professionals can find it difficult not to give advice or lend an empathetic ear when asked by their clients. However, professionalism must come first, and the trainer must refer clients to other specialists and not go beyond the scope of practice for certified personal trainers. These parameters are meant to protect trainers from any legal issues and keep the client safe.

PRACTICE QUESTIONS

1. If asked about a specific dietary supplement recommendation, a fitness professional can respond if

   A) he feels like it.

   B) the personal trainer has personally taken the supplement and had positive results.

   C) the fitness professional has personally taken it and had negative results.

   D) the fitness professional has an additional nutrition certification.

Answers:

   A) Incorrect. The personal trainer's response must be to refer the client to a certified nutritionist or registered dietitian.

   B) Incorrect. Even if the trainer has direct knowledge of the product, unless certified in its use, he cannot discuss nutrition supplements with a client.

   C) Incorrect. Regardless of his personal experience with a dietary supplement, a trainer must not discuss supplements with a client unless the trainer has an additional nutrition certification.

   D) **Correct.** The personal trainer can respond only if he has a nutrition certification that expands his scope of practice.

CONTINUE

2. _____ together are considered the top tier of the allied healthcare continuum.

- **A)** Physicians and nurses
- **B)** Occupational and physical therapists
- **C)** Registered dieticians and certified nutritionists
- **D)** Personal trainers and health coaches

Answers:

- **A)** **Correct.** Physicians and nurses are considered the top tier of the continuum.
- B) Incorrect. Occupational and physical therapists are not the top tier of the continuum.
- C) Incorrect. Registered dieticians and certified nutritionists are not the top tier of the continuum.
- D) Incorrect. Personal trainers and health coaches are not the top tier of the continuum.

Professional Standards and Codes of Conduct

Certified personal trainers, like all other health professionals, must adhere to a set of standards or guidelines to maintain the integrity of their certifying agency and other certified personal trainers, group fitness instructors, and health and wellness coaches. Although each certifying organization, such as the National Academy of Sports Medicine (NASM), American Council on Exercise (ACE), and American College of Sports Medicine (ACSM), has specific codes of conduct, the organizations generally adhere to the same professional standards, codes of conduct, and codes of ethics.

Certified fitness professionals should adhere to the highest standards of professionalism, confidentiality, legality, ethics, and business practices. While these are discussed in brief below, chapter 6 covers these issues in greater detail.

Physical Appearance and Personal Behavior

Certified personal trainers should wear tasteful and modest attire appropriate for fitness training. Attire should not be too tight or too revealing, and should be appropriate for all clients. Trainers are expected to maintain a high standard of personal grooming and hygiene. Facial hair should be well groomed. Deodorant should always be worn, but strong perfumes and colognes should not, since clients may be sensitive or even allergic to fragrance. In keeping with the aims of the fitness industry, trainers should maintain healthy lifestyles: eat healthy, exercise regularly, and avoid smoking, alcohol, and substance abuse.

Out of respect for their clients' time, trainers should be punctual and should arrive at least ten minutes before a scheduled appointment.

Safety and Communication

A client's safety should be a trainer's number-one priority, and a trainer must never compromise a client's safety, health, or goals for personal or monetary gain. A trainer should always provide a clean, professional, and safe environment for the client's training. Training sessions with a client must not begin until the trainer has received a proper medical clearance signed by the client, a fitness assessment, and a physical activity readiness questionnaire (PAR-Q) signed by the client.

Trainers must also remain within their scope of practice. They must not diagnose or treat ailments, allergies, or injuries, unless they have obtained the proper licensure and are working in that capacity. In the event that a client suffers an injury or experiences a change in health status or medication, the trainer must refer the client to a qualified professional.

To further ensure safety, every trainer needs to stay up-to-date with current health and fitness research, and be certified in cardiopulmonary resuscitation (CPR) and automated external defibrillator (AED). It is also each trainer's responsibility to remain in good standing with their certifying agency by obtaining the necessary continuing education credits.

> Not all certifying agencies are created equal. Be sure to verify that the certifying agency is accredited by the National Commission for Certifying Agencies (NCCA) or the American National Standards Institute (ANSI).

Finally, trainers are expected to clearly communicate and provide instruction during the client's initial screening, fitness assessments, program design, and implementation. Trainers should always use appropriate and professional communication when speaking to clients.

Confidentiality and Ethics

In keeping with HIPAA standards, trainers must maintain the privacy of client information (see chapter 6 for more details). All client information, including assessments, PAR-Qs, medical information, and payment information must be kept secure to prevent the theft and unauthorized use of the information. Physical paper files should be kept under lock and key, and electronic files should be password protected on secure computers equipped with malware software or firewalls. Trainers must respect a client's right to privacy and refrain from gossip. Client conversations and information on a client's training progress should be kept between trainer and client.

All trainers are expected to keep accurate notes on each client. If a client seeks a specialization that his or her current trainer does not offer or is dissatisfied with training methods, the trainer should refer the client appropriately.

A trainer's focus must be on business, rather than personal relationships. It is imperative that trainers maintain proper physical and emotional boundaries with both clients and peers. Touching should be used only with permission, and only to instruct clients on proper form. Sexually provocative conversations and contact with clients and peers must be strictly avoided. If a client relationship crosses the boundaries, the trainer should refer the client to another trainer, speak to a supervisor, or terminate the relationship. Trainers should also carefully adhere to sexual harassment guidelines with both clients and peers. Finally, trainers should at all times reflect the integrity of their profession. This includes accepting responsibility for one's actions.

Business Practices

A trainer is expected to accurately represent his or her qualifications with regard to years of experience and certifications. A trainer's approach to pricing should be consistent and fair, appropriate for the trainer's experience, and comparable with other trainers in the same geographic area. When planning a client's training program, a trainer should always base the number of sessions on the client's need, not on personal monetary gain.

Trainers should not solicit business from other trainers' clients. If working for a gym, trainers need to respect that the members referred to them are the gym's clients first. All trainers should strive to maintain professional and supportive relationships with other trainers and vendors, and should always pay vendors in a timely manner. Certified professional trainers are expected to be honest and tasteful in their advertising and avoid using sexually suggestive images or language. Ads should allow the public to honestly assess the trainer's services without suggestion or exaggeration. Marketing must follow copyright law. And finally, a trainer must not advertise outside the scope of his or her practice. Trainers are expected to comply with state regulations and guidelines for certified fitness professionals, and are required to retain accurate business records for at least four years. For their protection, trainers should always obtain appropriate liability insurance. In the event of a disagreement with a client or peer, a trainer is expected to respond with tact and professionalism and refrain from slanderous or inflammatory remarks.

In all aspects of their business practices, trainers must not discriminate based on race, creed, gender, physical abilities, age, or sexual orientation.

PRACTICE QUESTIONS

1. Anyone interested in obtaining a personal training certification should make sure the certifying body is accredited by which organizations?

    A) HIPAA and the NCCA

    B) ANSI and NASM

    C) ACE and ACSM

    D) NCCA and ANSI

Answers:

A) Incorrect. This is only half correct; NCCA is an accreditation organization, but HIPAA is a patient health confidentiality act.

B) Incorrect. This is only half correct; NASM is a certifying body and not an accreditation organization.

C) Incorrect. ACE and ACSM are both certifying organizations, not accreditation organizations.

D) **Correct.** NCCA and ANSI are the accreditation organizations that hold certifying bodies to a certain educational standard.

2. Which of the following is NOT considered the proper standard for a personal trainer's business practices?

    A) Defend yourself with rude and slanderous remarks, should a disagreement arise with a peer or client.

    B) Comply with state regulations and guidelines for certified professionals.

    C) Be honest and tasteful with advertising.

    D) Maintain professional and supportive relationships with vendors and peers.

Answers:

A) Correct. Making rude and slanderous remarks is NOT the proper way for a personal trainer to handle a disagreement.

B) Incorrect. Complying with state regulations and guidelines is a fundamental part of a trainer's business practices.

C) Incorrect. Honest and tasteful advertising is to be expected in a trainer's business practices.

D) Incorrect. Maintaining professional and supportive relationships with vendors and peers is a standard part of a trainer's business practices.

Professional Development

Passing the personal training certification exam is just the beginning for a trainer in the dynamic fitness industry. A personal training certification typically provides trainers with a cumulative understanding and application of the latest in exercise science; this is a solid foundation on which to build a personal training philosophy and style. However, because of the high profile of the health and fitness industry in preventing disease and maintaining personal health, much more information is now available; furthermore, it is frequently changing. It is imperative that certified personal trainers keep updated on changing research and industry standards and how to apply these standards in exercise science.

One way that a trainer can find his or her place in this industry is to understand, research, and certify in a specific style of exercise. Training style specializations and certifications cover a broad range, such as general specializations in group fitness exercise instruction, bodyweight training, core and balance training, and cardio training. More specific certifications include high-intensity interval training (HIIT), the functional movement system, strength and conditioning, TRX or suspension training modalities, CrossFit coaching, power/Olympic lifting, running coaches, bootcamp training, yoga, Pilates, triathlon/Ironman/Strongman coaching, swimming, golf, football, basketball, soccer, swimming, cycling, mixed martial arts (MMA), and Russian kettlebell club (RKC). An exercise specialization can bring a trainer in contact with a whole different network of fitness professionals to collaborate with, and can also create a training niche and philosophy that can be useful in differentiating a trainer's skills.

Certifying fitness organizations, such as NASM, ACE, and ACSM, create a strong network of professional, passionate, and talented fitness professionals by ensuring strict quality control. That quality control comes in the form of recertification requirements every two years. To recertify, a personal trainer must complete continuing education credits (CECs) and update his or her CPR/AED certification. This is an ever-changing industry, and there are several ways to gain CECs.

While some in the industry may see CECs as a burden to comply with every two years, continuing education benefits trainers by providing opportunities for professional growth through structured learning. Continuing education courses are taught by qualified health professionals and are intended to be compatible with all fitness philosophies. While fitness industry specialists usually require CECs that provide expanded knowledge in exercise modalities, trainers have the opportunity to broaden their horizons in healthcare, especially focusing on individuals and nutrition.

Structured learning specializations are typically offered through accredited certification organizations and include certifications in courses for special populations, such as senior fitness, youth fitness, women's fitness, and prenatal fitness, as well as courses for those with cancer, diabetes, or heart disease. Other specializations provide in-depth knowledge in corrective exercise, strength and conditioning, and performance enhancement. Certifications in fitness nutrition, weight management, behavior change, or health coaching provide more substantial information on nutrition and food choices and allow a personal trainer to broaden his or her scope of practice.

In completing their CECs, personal trainers can receive more hands-on education and opportunities for networking by attending college courses, live workshops, or annual conferences. Conferences and workshops feature some of the most dynamic and influential contributors in exercise science, nutrition, education, and brand or business growth. They also provide ways to try the latest equipment and products on the market. A flat fee gives the fitness professional an opportunity to attend demonstrations and listen to keynote speakers. While small workshops usually offer only one day of information and earn trainers only a few points toward their CECs, a conference offers several days of events, classes, and talks. These live events are great ways to meet with fellow fitness pros, talk shop, and walk away with new ideas in both exercise design and business development.

> 🔍 Some popular fitness conferences are The Fit Expo, MANIA| SCW Fitness, IDEA Personal Training Institute (East/West), IDEA World Convention, Fitness & Wellness Conference & Expo, ACSM| Health & Fitness Summit & Exposition, and NASM Optima.

Professional growth can take many forms, not just in a classroom or educational setting with textbooks and computer-based learning. A trainer can learn a lot from observations, internships, or mentorships, all of which allow a new trainer to shadow an experienced trainer on the job. These opportunities are usually available in health clubs, country clubs, fitness centers, or gyms. While these are not typically paid positions, they allow a new trainer to learn the ins and outs of how to run a gym, the proper legal parameters one must follow, and how to connect and communicate with potential clients, lead small classes, do a fitness assessment or health screening, or talk one-on-one to clients. Application is the key to being an effective trainer, so watching a seasoned trainer in action can be invaluable. These mentorships may also lead a new trainer to her first job.

Authoring a fitness blog, study guide, or newsletter article also can help a trainer grow, since these types of opportunities allow trainers to expand their expertise while learning how to effectively communicate.

Trainers will continually be bombarded with questions about health news, so it is vital that they keep up with the latest information to ensure they know what is credible. While fitness blogs are loaded with opinions that one might find agreeable, blogs cannot be considered credible. Trainers should stick to scholarly fitness and health articles, which are typically found in journals such as the *Journal of Exercise Physiology* or the *Journal of Sports Science and Medicine*.

 To check website reliability, ask the following questions:
> 1. Does the website tell you who is responsible for the site?
> 2. Is the website trying to sell you something?
> 3. Is the information based on results from medical research?
> 4. Has the information been reviewed and approved by medical experts?
> 5. Does the health information seem unbiased, objective, and balanced?
> 6. Does the information seem reasonable and believable?

Finding credible sources on the internet can be tough. Hundreds of sites claim to be the most popular source for fitness information, but even if this were true, the most popular source is not necessarily the most reliable. When searching for a credible website, look for sites that end in .gov (government organizations), .edu (school or educational organizations), or .org (not-for-profit organizations), which often provide credible, helpful articles on fitness trends, workouts, equipment, and business development. These articles are written by personal trainers who have excelled in their areas of expertise, and the articles are useful for new trainers and those who don't specialize in certain areas. For example, these articles might be appropriate for a trainer who wants to find information on safety protocols for clients with diabetes.

PRACTICE QUESTIONS

1. When acquiring the required CECs, which of the following is NOT an acceptable option?

    A) workshops

    B) conferences

    C) exercise specialization certifications

    D) blog contributions

    Answers:

    A) Incorrect. Workshops are among the acceptable options to gain CECs.

    B) Incorrect. Conferences are acceptable ways to gain CECs.

    C) Incorrect. Among the acceptable CEC options are exercise specialization certifications.

    D) **Correct.** Blog contributions are not an acceptable way to acquire CECs.

2. Professional growth doesn't just happen in a classroom or educational setting with textbooks and computer-based modules. A trainer can learn a lot from _____, _____, or _____, which allow the new trainer to shadow an experienced trainer while on the job.

    A) mentorships, ownerships, observations

    B) observations, internships, mentorships

    C) internships, leaderships, ownerships

    D) mentorships, internships, leaderships

    Answers:

    A) Incorrect. Mentorships and observations are correct, but ownerships is not.

    B) **Correct.** Observations, internships, and mentorships are the three ways a new trainer can gain hands-on experience while on the job.

    C) Incorrect. Internships provide opportunities to gain knowledge and experience, but the other two methods, leaderships and ownerships, are not.

    D) Incorrect. Mentorships and internships are correct, but leaderships is not.

NINE: Practice Test

SCIENTIFIC FOUNDATIONS

READ THE QUESTION AND THEN CHOOSE THE MOST CORRECT ANSWER.

1. Which vitamins act as hormones that bind to cellular receptors and regulate cellular processes?
   A) vitamins A and D
   B) vitamins D and K
   C) vitamins C and E
   D) folate and B-12

2. Bones, ligaments, and cartilage are types of
   A) organs.
   B) connective tissues.
   C) cells.
   D) joints.

3. Where are posterior parts of the body positioned?
   A) on the front
   B) on the back
   C) on the top
   D) on the sides

4. The pulmonary vein carries
   A) deoxygenated blood from the body to the heart.
   B) air from the lungs to the blood.
   C) oxygenated blood from the lungs to the heart.
   D) deoxygenated blood from the heart to the lungs.

5. Ligaments adhere
   A) bone to bone.
   B) bone to muscle.
   C) muscle to muscle.
   D) cartilage to bone.

6. The pericardium is the
   A) innermost layer of the heart.
   B) middle layer of the heart.
   C) heart muscle.
   D) outermost layer of the heart.

7. The radius and ulna are bones found in which body part?
   A) the hand
   B) the forearm
   C) the leg
   D) the neck

8. Which joint allows for the most freedom of movement?
   A) ball-and-socket
   B) hinge
   C) saddle
   D) uniaxial

9. How many vertebrae does the spine have, excluding the coccygeal bones?
   A) 22
   B) 35
   C) 29
   D) 20

10. What does kyphosis of the spine mean?
    A) excessive anterior curvature
    B) excessive posterior curvature
    C) excessive lateral curvature
    D) excessive medial curvature

11. Lordosis is most commonly seen in which part of the spine?
    A) thoracic vertebrae
    B) sacral vertebrae
    C) coccygeal vertebrae
    D) lumbar vertebrae

12. Which of these is contained in the H-zone?
    A) myosin only
    B) actin only
    C) actin and myosin
    D) the Z-bands

13. Which exercise can improve bone mineral density?
    A) non-impact exercise
    B) swimming
    C) axial loading of the skeleton through weightlifting
    D) walking outside

14. What are the two contractile proteins found in sarcomeres?
    A) actin and myofibrils
    B) actin and motor units
    C) actin and myosin
    D) myosin and action potentials

15. What is the name of a single neuron and its associated skeletal muscle fibers that are innervated by that neuron?
    A) a muscle fiber
    B) the neuromuscular junction
    C) a sarcomere
    D) a motor unit

16. What are the three conditions that define the female athlete triad?
    A) bulimia nervosa, anemia, fatigue
    B) anorexia nervosa, anemia, dehydration
    C) disordered eating, amenorrhea, osteoporosis
    D) disordered eating, amenorrhea, anemia

17. Which of the following is represented by the volume of oxygen consumed during a particular activity measured in mL/kg body weight/minute?
    A) VO2 max
    B) exercise intensity
    C) VO2
    D) respiration rate

18. To maximize performance, a pre-exercise meal should be
    A) avoided, as it will weigh down the athlete.
    B) eaten just before competition to maximize available fuel.
    C) eaten one to six hours before competition.
    D) liquid in nature.

19. What is muscle hypertrophy?
    A) abnormally large muscle cells
    B) an increase in muscle cross section leading to increased strength
    C) excessively long muscle cells caused by anabolic steroids
    D) excessive muscle contractions leading to cramping

20. Anabolic steroids are illegal in competition and carry undesirable side effects and health risks. Which natural hormone do they mimic?
    A) testosterone
    B) estrogen
    C) aldosterone
    D) human growth hormone

21. What should older adults spend more time doing than younger adults in an exercise program?
    A) strength training
    B) power training
    C) high impact exercise
    D) warming up

22. What are the major mineral(s) in bone?
    A) calcium and zinc
    B) calcium, phosphate, and manganese
    C) calcium
    D) calcium, phosphate, and magnesium

23. Which best describes the process in the muscles during which the proteins actin and myosin form a connection to pull the thin actin filaments over the myosin, causing a shortening of the sarcomeres and a concomitant shortening of the muscles, known as muscular contraction?
    A) sliding myofibril theory
    B) sliding filament theory
    C) sliding muscle theory
    D) sliding motor unit theory

24. Which of the following is NOT a form of blood doping, which is illegal?
    A) transfusions
    B) erythropoietin
    C) synthetic oxygen carriers
    D) iron supplements

25. Which drugs are sometimes used by athletes attempting to conceal illegal drug use?
    A) peptide hormones
    B) diuretics
    C) beta blockers
    D) TNF-a inhibitors

26. Which mineral is a component of the thyroid hormone?
    A) selenium
    B) iodine
    C) magnesium
    D) cobalt

27. Delayed onset muscle soreness (DOMS) is caused by
    A) lactic acid buildup in the muscles.
    B) static stretching.
    C) micro-tears in the muscle fibers.
    D) a sedentary lifestyle.

28. Saturated fat should constitute no more than 10 percent of daily caloric intake.

For a 2,000 kcal daily intake, what is the maximum number of grams of saturated fat that should be consumed?

- **A)** 200 grams
- **B)** 22 grams
- **C)** 20 grams
- **D)** 2 grams

29. High blood LDL cholesterol is detrimental to cardiovascular health; soluble fiber can lower LDL cholesterol levels. Which of the following foods contain soluble fiber?

- **A)** oatmeal, fruits, and beans
- **B)** meat and dairy products
- **C)** whole wheat, brown rice, and seeds
- **D)** vegetable oils

30. Waist circumference is a measure of abdominal obesity. Measurements greater than which of the following are considered unhealthy for men and for women?

- **A)** 40 inches for men and 35 inches for women
- **B)** 40 inches for both men and women
- **C)** 45 inches for men and 40 inches for women
- **D)** 45 inches for both men and women

31. Which of these is a proprioceptor found within the musculotendinous junction that senses the amount of force being placed on the muscle and functions to prevent excessive forceful contractions of the muscle via autogenic inhibition?

- **A)** Golgi tendon organs
- **B)** muscle spindle fibers
- **C)** motor units
- **D)** action potentials

32. Ventral and anterior are similar terms because they both imply something positioned

- **A)** toward the back of the body.
- **B)** toward the front of the body.
- **C)** toward the sides of the body.
- **D)** toward the feet.

33. Which athlete will benefit from fast-twitch muscle fibers the most?

- **A)** marathoners
- **B)** 1500-meter swimmers
- **C)** Olympic sprinters
- **D)** cross-country cyclists

34. What do slow-twitch muscle fibers contain more of than fast-twitch muscle fibers?

- **A)** mitochondria
- **B)** anaerobic capacity
- **C)** force production capability
- **D)** types of fibers

35. Which two actions do the quadriceps muscles perform?

- **A)** knee flexion and hip flexion
- **B)** knee extension and hip flexion
- **C)** knee flexion and hip extension
- **D)** knee extension and hip extension

36. A phase during the neuromuscular stimulation process that involves myosin crossbridges attaching and pulling actin filaments closer together, resulting in a shortening of the sarcomeres and subsequent muscle fibers, refers to which phase of muscle contraction?

- **A)** the relaxation phase
- **B)** the contraction phase
- **C)** the recharge phase
- **D)** the eccentric phase

37. The triceps perform elbow extension in which plane?

- **A)** frontal
- **B)** transverse
- **C)** sagittal
- **D)** oblique

38. What is the action of the gastrocnemius muscle?

- **A)** ankle dorsiflexion
- **B)** ankle extension
- **C)** ankle plantar flexion
- **D)** ankle flexion

39. Which of the answer choices refers to a muscular contraction in which the resistance and force are even and no movement is taking place?

- **A)** concentric muscle contraction
- **B)** isotonic muscle contraction
- **C)** isokinetic muscle contraction
- **D)** isometric muscle contraction

40. Which term describes when a joint is decreasing its angle by muscular contraction?

- **A)** extension
- **B)** circumduction
- **C)** flexion
- **D)** rotation

41. An example of a muscular stabilizer during an exercise is

- **A)** the latissimus dorsi during a lat pulldown exercise.
- **B)** the gluteus medius during the box step-up exercise.
- **C)** the biceps brachii during the biceps curl exercise.
- **D)** the quadriceps during a squat exercise.

42. Collections of tissues throughout the body with a similar function are referred to as

- **A)** tissues.
- **B)** posterior.
- **C)** organ systems.
- **D)** organs.

43. Which of the following refers to the optimal muscular length at the level of the sarcomere for maximum force potential of the muscle?

- **A)** length-tension relationship
- **B)** force-couple relationship
- **C)** sliding filament theory
- **D)** motor unit recruitment

44. What is muscular hypertrophy?

- **A)** an increase in the number of muscle cells
- **B)** an increase in the size of the muscle cells
- **C)** a decrease in the size of the muscle cells
- **D)** an increase in the length of the muscle cells

45. Which of the following feeds the right atrium with deoxygenated blood from the body?

- **A)** the superior and inferior vena cava
- **B)** the carotid artery
- **C)** the aorta
- **D)** the lungs

46. Because of an increased Q-angle, female athletes are at a higher risk of medial knee injuries in which sport(s)?

- **A)** rock climbing
- **B)** basketball and volleyball
- **C)** ice hockey
- **D)** snowboarding

47. Distal means
    A) toward the axial skeleton.
    B) toward the skull.
    C) away from the axial skeleton.
    D) toward the midline of the body.

48. The trachea carries air to the
    A) bronchi.
    B) mouth.
    C) bronchioles.
    D) alveoli.

49. Which of the following is found in blood and aids in clotting?
    A) red blood cells
    B) platelets
    C) white blood cells
    D) water

50. Which of the following is a muscle that helps to create a pressure differential in the abdomen and chest, allowing air to flow into and out of the lungs when contracting and relaxing, respectively?
    A) abdominals
    B) pectoralis major
    C) pectoralis minor
    D) diaphragm

51. Where does digestion begin?
    A) stomach
    B) esophagus
    C) mouth
    D) small intestine

52. The central nervous system is made up of
    A) the brain and nerves.
    B) the brain and spinal cord.
    C) the brain and proprioceptors.
    D) the spinal cord and nerves.

53. What muscular action occurs as a limb is pulled toward the midline of the body?
    A) abduction
    B) extension
    C) pronation
    D) adduction

54. What is multiple sclerosis?
    A) a disease associated with memory loss and dementia that occurs later in life
    B) a disease affecting bone mineral density
    C) a disease that affects the myelin sheaths that surround axons on a neuron
    D) a disease that damages the nucleus of neurons

55. When the nervous system sends an impulse for muscular twitch and then immediately sends another before the muscle has time to relax, it is referred to as
    A) motor unit recruitment.
    B) neuromuscular adaptation.
    C) summation.
    D) a stimulus.

56. What are disordered heart rhythms called?
    A) arrhythmias
    B) amenorrhea
    C) hypertension
    D) atherosclerosis

57. What are the two important types of hormones associated with exercise?
    A) anabolic and testosterone
    B) anabolic and IGF
    C) anabolic and epinephrine
    D) anabolic and catabolic

58. Which of the following is an organ associated with controlling the release of chemical substances, known as hormones, for the regulation of metabolic processes, growth, development, sexual reproduction, and other bodily functions?

A) a hormone
B) the brain
C) testosterone
D) a gland

59. The hypothalamus controls

A) autonomic nervous system function and the connection between the central nervous system and endocrine system.
B) the peripheral nervous system and associated nerves.
C) the musculoskeletal system and voluntary skeletal muscle.
D) human growth and development.

60. Which of the following is the part of the uterus that passes nutrition and nourishment to the fetus from the mother via the umbilicus during pregnancy?

A) ovaries
B) placenta
C) testis
D) pineal gland

61. A force-time curve for an isometric exercise will likely

A) not indicate any increase on the axis of the force.
B) spike dramatically and then return to normal levels within a short time period.
C) increase and then stable out due to the exercise being held for time at a specific force.
D) have a short spike in force, a drop, and then a stabilization.

62. The BMI might NOT be an accurate indicator of a healthy weight

A) when the individual is tall.
B) when the individual is short.
C) if the individual is a strength trainer.
D) if the individual is sedentary.

63. The components of a lever system include

A) the force, the resistance, and the weight.
B) the muscles, the resistance, and the force.
C) the fulcrum, the resistance, and the weight.
D) the fulcrum, the resistance, and the force.

64. What is the most common type of lever system the human body uses?

A) a first-class lever
B) The body does not use levers.
C) a second-class lever
D) a third-class lever

65. Which of the following best describes Newton's second law of motion?

A) force = mass × power
B) force = mass × acceleration
C) Momentum and impulse are the same.
D) Power and work are the same.

66. What is the amount of muscular force (force) needed to move an object through a joint's angular range of motion (distance)?

A) rotational power
B) angular velocity
C) rotational work
D) momentum

67. Which of the following best describes the maximal rate at which lactic acid due to exercise can be buffered from the blood stream?

- **A)** the lactate threshold
- **B)** the Krebs cycle
- **C)** the phosphagen system
- **D)** the anaerobic energy system

68. Approximately how much caloric expenditure through exercise is recommended to lose about one pound per week?

- **A)** 500 kcal/week
- **B)** 1,000 kcal/week
- **C)** 1,500 kcal/week
- **D)** 2,000 kcal/week

69. How might a rock climber and figure skater vary in muscle mass?

- **A)** They should have similar distributions of muscle mass.
- **B)** The rock climber will have stronger abdominal muscles.
- **C)** The figure skater will likely have more lower body muscle mass.
- **D)** The figure skater will likely have more upper body muscle mass.

70. What are the dietary protein recommendations for sedentary individuals, those engaging in endurance exercise, and strength trainers?

- **A)** The RDA for protein intake is 0.8 g/kg body weight.
- **B)** 0.8 g/kg, 1.6 g/kg, and 2.2 g/kg, respectively
- **C)** 1.2 g/kg
- **D)** 0.8 – 0.9 g/kg, 1.2 – 1.4 g/kg, and 1.6 – 1.7 g/kg, respectively

71. How does lean body mass differ from fat-free mass?

- **A)** Lean body mass includes just muscle.
- **B)** Lean body mass does not include water.
- **C)** Fat-free mass includes the brain.
- **D)** Lean body mass includes some fatty organs/tissues—like the brain and spinal cord—while fat-free mass does not.

72. What are the three components of the female athlete triad?

- **A)** amenorrhea, muscle growth, and reduced bone mineral density
- **B)** amenorrhea, reduced bone mineral density, and fatigue
- **C)** fatigue, reduced bone mineral density, and disordered eating habits
- **D)** amenorrhea, reduced bone mineral density, and disordered eating habits

73. IGF-1 helps promote

- **A)** muscle maintenance and repair.
- **B)** muscle energy stores.
- **C)** peak strength output.
- **D)** the rate of muscular contraction.

74. Which is **not** a type of cartilage?

- **A)** hyaline
- **B)** fibrocartilage
- **C)** elastic
- **D)** ligaments

75. Which population has difficulty regulating body temperature?

- **A)** children
- **B)** women
- **C)** older adults
- **D)** men

76. Disordered eating in female athletes can lead to

A) reduced bone mineral density and loss of menstrual cycle.

B) improved health.

C) muscle mass development.

D) improved fitness performance.

77. The musculoskeletal system is comprised of levers to

A) digest food.

B) create red blood cells.

C) create movement.

D) conduct nervous impulses.

78. How does age influence the heart?

A) It increases cardiac output.

B) It increases blood pressure.

C) It decreases maximum heart rate.

D) It decreases resting heart rate.

79. How many different amino acids are involved in protein metabolism?

A) twenty

B) ten

C) eight

D) twenty-one

80. What is the difference between a macromineral and a micromineral?

A) Macrominerals are larger than microminerals.

B) Macrominerals are required in the diet in larger quantities than microminerals.

C) Macrominerals bind together to form large complexes.

D) Microminerals are derived from microbial organisms in the gut.

81. Which vitamin or vitamin precursor is NOT an antioxidant?

A) vitamin E

B) vitamin C

C) beta-carotene

D) vitamin K

82. Which is an example of a convergent muscle?

A) biceps brachii

B) extensor digitorum longus

C) rectus abdominis

D) pectoralis major

83. Deficiencies of which vitamins or minerals can cause megaloblastic anemia?

A) thiamine

B) folate and vitamin B-12

C) iron

D) copper

84. Which type of athletes are at risk for iron-deficiency anemia?

A) both strength and endurance athletes

B) male athletes

C) strength athletes, female athletes, and vegetarians

D) endurance athletes, female athletes, and vegetarians

85. Which of the following is true? Vibrating belts and electric stimulators

A) burn calories with little effort.

B) can be used to lose fat in specific body areas.

C) are a useful addition to exercise.

D) do not burn significant calories and are not capable of eliminating fat in specific body areas.

86. Which macronutrients are the major fuels for exercise?

- **A)** carbohydrates and fats
- **B)** protein and carbohydrates
- **C)** protein and fats
- **D)** carbohydrates, fats, and protein

87. What is glycemic index?

- **A)** a measure of the energy density of a food
- **B)** a measure of the rate of glycogen depletion during exercise
- **C)** a measure of the rise in blood glucose caused by a standard amount of a food
- **D)** a measure of the percentage of kcal from carbohydrates in a food

88. Which electrolytes are responsible for the transmission of electrical signals across nerve and muscle cell membranes?

- **A)** sodium and chloride
- **B)** potassium and chloride
- **C)** sodium and potassium
- **D)** sodium and magnesium

89. Which of the following refers to the larger heart chambers?

- **A)** atria
- **B)** ventricles
- **C)** veins
- **D)** valves

90. What does EPOC stand for?

- **A)** Excess Post-exercise Oxygen Creation
- **B)** Excess Post-exercise Oxygen Consumption
- **C)** Extreme Post-exercise Oxygen Consumption
- **D)** Excess Pre-exercise Oxygen Consumption

91. During exercise that lasts over one hour, how much fluid intake is recommended to maintain hydration?

- **A)** 20 – 36 oz. per hour
- **B)** 8 – 12 oz. per hour
- **C)** 10 – 15 oz. per hour
- **D)** 40 – 45 oz. per hour

92. Body composition in relation to a healthy weight

- **A)** is a measure of the relative proportions of carbohydrates, proteins, fat, and water in the body.
- **B)** is the percentage of fat-free mass versus fat mass in the body.
- **C)** is the percentage of bone versus soft tissue in the body.
- **D)** is the percentage of dry mass versus water in the body.

93. What is the function of saliva?

- **A)** hydration
- **B)** assist in the breakdown of food in the mouth
- **C)** nutrient absorption
- **D)** water absorption into the gut

94. The myelin sheath on axons helps

- **A)** speed up nervous transmission of electrical impulses.
- **B)** pass information to the dendrites.
- **C)** protect the nerve from damage caused by multiple sclerosis.
- **D)** prevent the onset of Alzheimer's disease.

95. Which of the following does NOT make weight loss more difficult?

- **A)** sleep deprivation
- **B)** type 2 diabetes
- **C)** certain antidepressants
- **D)** the drug metformin

PRACTICAL/APPLIED

READ THE QUESTION AND THEN CHOOSE THE MOST CORRECT ANSWER.

1. Which test is the most effective for assessing speed, agility, and quickness?
   A) Rockport walk test
   B) push-up test
   C) hexagon test
   D) twelve-minute run test

2. What are the regions that are measured during the three-site skinfold assessment with a female client?
   A) chest, biceps, thigh
   B) triceps, suprailium, thigh
   C) subscapular, thigh, suprailium
   D) biceps, thigh, suprailium

3. All of the following tests are used to measure speed, agility, and quickness EXCEPT
   A) the 300-yard shuttle test.
   B) the LEFT
   C) the pro-agility test.
   D) the *t*-test.

4. Based on the principle of specificity, the fact that football players run one hundred yards at most should tell the trainer not to implement
   A) short-distance sprint intervals in the training program.
   B) long-distance running into the training program.
   C) power exercises for improved speed in the training program.
   D) muscular endurance exercises into the training program.

5. Which cycle is the shortest of a periodization program?
   A) the mesocycle
   B) the macrocycle
   C) the microcycle
   D) the preparatory period

6. Which of the following is generally NOT part of a fitness assessment?
   A) flexibility assessment
   B) static posture assessment
   C) daily caloric intake assessment
   D) cardiorespiratory capacity assessment

7. Movement assessments are used to test
   A) maximal force.
   B) core strength.
   C) agility and speed.
   D) dynamic posture.

8. Why is it important that fitness professionals obtain certification through a leading organization in the fitness industry?
   A) Trainers who are certified can make more money.
   B) Clients will often research the fitness professional's expertise and certifications.
   C) Trainers can guarantee client results with their certification.
   D) Certification is proof of the trainer's education.

9. A static stretch is held for how many seconds?
   A) 20 seconds
   B) 60 seconds
   C) 30 seconds
   D) 10 seconds

10. The body's response mechanism to absorbing too much physical stress in too short a time is called
    A) hypertension.
    B) hyperventilation.
    C) delayed onset muscle soreness.
    D) overtraining.

11. What are the legal parameters in which all credentialed or licensed health professionals should work?
    A) scope of product
    B) legality of specialization
    C) scope of practice
    D) terms of work

12. A network of licensed, certified, or registered professionals who provide healthcare resources to the general population is called what?
    A) allied healthcare continuum
    B) training continuum
    C) health professionals
    D) health maintenance professionals

13. Which assessment would be most appropriate for a sixty-five-year-old client who wants to lower his or her blood pressure?
    A) bench press test
    B) hexagon test
    C) Rockport walk test
    D) three-hundred-yard shuttle test

14. If a client complains of experiencing pain or injury during a session, a trainer should refer the client to
    A) the client's physician.
    B) a friend.
    C) a massage therapist.
    D) no one.

15. During the BESS, which of the following actions does NOT result in error points being given?
    A) opening of the eyes
    B) remaining in the proper position for twenty seconds
    C) moving hands off of the hips
    D) lifting the ball or heel of the foot off of the testing surface

16. Which type of exercises typically activates smaller muscle groups and is used for rehabilitative purposes?
    A) core exercises
    B) open kinetic chain exercises
    C) PNF stretching
    D) assistance exercises

17. A lifestyle questionnaire should NOT include questions which pertain to which of the following?
    A) sleep
    B) stress
    C) friends
    D) smoking

18. Clients with arthritis may have decreased
    A) joint pain.
    B) motivation to exercise.
    C) joint range of motion.
    D) muscular atrophy.

19. The allied healthcare continuum (AHC) includes all the following professionals, EXCEPT

    A) a nurse.
    B) a psychologist.
    C) an occupational therapist.
    D) a psychic.

20. Which of the following is NOT a muscular strength, endurance, and power assessment?

    A) long jump test
    B) Margaria-Kalamen test
    C) star excursion test
    D) reactive strength index

21. A professional trainer would wear which of following?

    A) khaki pants or jeans
    B) tasteful athletic attire
    C) revealing athletic attire
    D) strong cologne or perfume

22. Which tool is used to manually assess blood pressure?

    A) handheld bioelectrical impedance device
    B) sphygmomanometer
    C) calipers
    D) scale

23. How should the trainer modify abdominal exercises, such as the crunch, for pregnant clients?

    A) No modification is necessary.
    B) Reduce the range of motion dramatically.
    C) Pregnant clients are not allowed to perform abdominal exercises.
    D) Have the client seated slightly upright.

24. The second transition period is a period of

    A) high-intensity training.
    B) sports-specific training.
    C) no physical activity at all.
    D) active recovery involving non-specific recreational activity.

25. Which test helps determine an individual's ability to change direction and stabilize the body at high speeds?

    A) hexagon test
    B) *t*-test
    C) pro-agility test
    D) vertical jump test

26. Core exercises are classified into two subcategories: structural and _____.

    A) open
    B) assistance
    C) power
    D) static

27. Performing _____ stretching in a circuit can be a cardio warm-up.

    A) static
    B) passive
    C) dynamic
    D) active

28. If a client has a muscle imbalance, what should she be directed to do in her warm-up?

    A) active stretching before static stretching
    B) SMR or foam roll before dynamic stretching
    C) static stretching before cardio warm-up
    D) SMR or foam roll before static stretching

29. A superset in a training program refers to

  A) performing an exercise and gradually increasing load, then decreasing load per set.

  B) performing multiple sets of a single exercise with intermittent rest periods.

  C) performing an exercise and then immediately performing another exercise utilizing the antagonist or opposite muscle groups.

  D) performing a series of different exercises in a row with a rest period at the end of the series.

30. High-volume and low-load muscular endurance training can cause fatigue and should be saved for the

  A) in-season.
  B) off-season.
  C) competitive period.
  D) second transition period.

31. Performing a specific number of repetitions through the full range of motion is called

  A) a workout.
  B) the load.
  C) overload.
  D) a set.

32. The last part of a warm-up should consist of what type of stretching?

  A) static stretching
  B) PNF stretching
  C) dynamic stretching
  D) SMR stretching

33. What is a regression for a push press?

  A) seated dumbbell shoulder press
  B) standing upright row
  C) low pulley row
  D) push-up

34. How many spotters are needed for a dumbbell shoulder press?

  A) none
  B) 2
  C) 3
  D) 1

35. What method can assist the fitness professional in determining if a client is potentially overtraining?

  A) ask the client if he thinks he is overtraining

  B) ask one of the client's relatives for an opinion on whether the client is overtraining

  C) keep detailed records of the client's training outcomes and responses to training

  D) send the client to another fitness professional

36. Which of the following refers to the degree to which a test or test item measures what is supposed to be measured?

  A) relativity
  B) honesty
  C) validity
  D) strength

37. A dynamic warm-up for a field hockey player should include these three things:
- **A)** static stretching, dynamic stretching, and cardiovascular exercise
- **B)** dynamic stretching, single-muscle group exercises, and plyometrics
- **C)** five minutes of aerobic exercise, dynamic stretching, and specific movement patterns of the workout
- **D)** dynamic stretching, PNF stretching, and foam rolling

38. What is the primary sensor in autogenic inhibition?
- **A)** muscle spindles
- **B)** Golgi tendon organ
- **C)** tendon
- **D)** ligaments

39. Loads of 90 percent of 1RM require a rest period of how long for proper recovery?
- **A)** thirty seconds or less
- **B)** ninety seconds or less
- **C)** one minute
- **D)** three minutes or more

40. A foam roller is used for what type of training?
- **A)** PNF stretching
- **B)** active stretching
- **C)** power training
- **D)** self-myofascial release

41. Which of the following is NOT a positive body language indicator?
- **A)** nodding slowly or quickly
- **B)** leaning forward
- **C)** wringing hands
- **D)** firm handshake

42. Resistance training programs for children and adolescents should focus on
- **A)** increasing weight lifted.
- **B)** specific and repetitive movements.
- **C)** high-intensity exercise.
- **D)** proper technique and form.

43. Which exercise may require a spotter?
- **A)** barbell deadlift
- **B)** medicine ball slam
- **C)** back-loaded squat
- **D)** walking lunges

44. When meeting with a client, the trainer should exude
- **A)** cockiness, enthusiasm, and joy.
- **B)** confidence, enthusiasm, and professionalism.
- **C)** confidence, assertiveness, and likeability.
- **D)** pride, love, and goodness.

45. Which of the following assessments does NOT measure body fat percentage?
- **A)** dual-energy x-ray absorptiometry (DEXA)
- **B)** body mass index (BMI)
- **C)** near-infrared interactance
- **D)** air displacement plethysmography (BOD POD)

46. A grip used primarily in parallel bar or dumbbell pushing and pulling movements where the thumbs stay up and the palms face each other is:
- **A)** supinated grip
- **B)** alternating grip
- **C)** false grip
- **D)** neutral grip

47. To ensure accuracy of the results, the resting heart rate should be taken at what time of the day?
- **A)** before a workout
- **B)** at the end of the work day
- **C)** upon rising in the morning
- **D)** while resting during a workout

48. Which grip is overhanded?
- **A)** alternated grip
- **B)** supinated grip
- **C)** pronated grip
- **D)** clean grip

49. When clients who are new to running start a running program, they may benefit from a jogging and walking work-to-rest ratio of what?
- **A)** 1:5
- **B)** 2:1
- **C)** 3:1
- **D)** 1:1

50. What joint motion would be used in the frontal plane of motion?
- **A)** abduction/adduction
- **B)** flexion/extension
- **C)** rotational
- **D)** vertical

51. A tuck jump is an example of what type of training?
- **A)** plyometrics training
- **B)** explosive training
- **C)** resistance training
- **D)** kettlebell training

52. In a standing or sitting position, a client should maintain which three points of contact?
- **A)** shoulders, calves, heels
- **B)** head, shoulders, glutes
- **C)** head, glutes, calves
- **D)** shoulders, glutes, heels

53. What type of aerobic exercise should be included in programs focused on general health benefits?
- **A)** running only
- **B)** cycling and swimming only
- **C)** all modes are beneficial
- **D)** general health benefits do not require aerobic exercise

54. The gastrocnemius is another name for what muscle?
- **A)** forearm
- **B)** thigh
- **C)** calf
- **D)** neck

55. Personal attributes, which can hinder exercise adherence, include all of the following, EXCEPT what?
- **A)** age
- **B)** accessibility
- **C)** time
- **D)** fitness level

56. A circuit-training program involving a careful selection of varying muscle groups to minimize rest periods is called
- **A)** horizontal loading.
- **B)** single set.
- **C)** interval training.
- **D)** vertical loading.

57. _____ is the body's ability to react to a cue that propels a change in direction.

- A) Agility
- B) Quickness
- C) Readiness
- D) Stabilization

58. Strength training should follow a progressive plan with three tiers, which are _____, _____, and _____.

- A) power, muscle, matter
- B) strength, power, hard
- C) stabilization, strength, power
- D) stabilization, body, strength

59. Which of the following is NOT true of the drawing-in maneuver?

- A) It aids in core activation.
- B) It maintains neutral posturing.
- C) It is used for all core exercises.
- D) It stretches the hip flexors.

60. Why might plyometrics not be advisable for individuals who are overweight or obese?

- A) They develop muscular power.
- B) They are not fun.
- C) They are too easy.
- D) They place excessive force on the joints.

61. How many points of contact should a client have when lying in a semi-supine position?

- A) 7
- B) 3
- C) 4
- D) 5

62. When exercising for weight loss, the mode of cardiovascular exercise

- A) is not important.
- B) should be specific.
- C) should be steady state.
- D) must be low impact.

63. Plyometrics training primarily focuses on explosive movement and full range of motion, while speed, agility, and quickness training keeps the exercises _____.

- A) compact
- B) slow
- C) painful
- D) controlled

64. A barbell deadlift or a rear loaded squat can be considered _____ exercises.

- A) structural
- B) power
- C) agility
- D) assistance

65. Which assessment is used to assess weight relative to height?

- A) waist-to-hip ratio
- B) air displacement plethysmography (BOD POD)
- C) body mass index
- D) skinfold measurements

66. What type of training uses controlled instability to increase proprioception?

- A) plyometrics
- B) cardio training
- C) free weight training
- D) core training

67. Ice skaters are used for what type of training?

- A) plyometrics
- B) stabilization
- C) free weight
- D) stretching

68. The 1RM test measures the client's

- A) ability to perform an exercise at the maximal effort of strength for a single repetition.
- B) weight utilized for all exercises in the program.
- C) target heart rate zone.
- D) ability to perform an exercise at submaximal efforts for multiple repetitions.

69. Treadmills, elliptical trainers, and rowing machines are used for what type of training?

- A) functional training
- B) resistance training
- C) power training
- D) aerobic training

70. A push jerk is what type of core exercise?

- A) structural exercise
- B) stability exercise
- C) power exercise
- D) standing exercise

71. Detraining occurs more rapidly

- A) in cardiovascular health.
- B) in muscular strength.
- C) in clients who have previously trained.
- D) in professional athletes.

72. Which of the following assessments are used as indicators of a client's general fitness and overall health?

- A) cardiorespiratory assessments
- B) movement assessments
- C) muscular endurance assessments
- D) physiological assessments

73. Which of the following is most likely to cause a muscular imbalance of the upper body?

- A) a training program that utilizes alternating push-and-pull exercises
- B) a bodyweight training program that includes exercises for the chest, back, core, and legs
- C) a well-balanced yoga routine with a trained instructor
- D) a unilateral training program emphasizing strengthening of the pectorals and anterior deltoids

74. A false grip is

- A) an underhanded grip.
- B) where the thumb is wrapped around the bar along with the fingers.
- C) where the thumb is wrapped around the bar on the opposite side of the fingers.
- D) where the thumb is facing the ceiling and the palms are toward the body.

75. When should static stretching be performed in a workout?

- A) prior to exercise
- B) before the plyometrics
- C) before the cardiovascular exercise
- D) at the end of the workout

76. A typical mesocycle may last
    A) six to twelve weeks.
    B) one week.
    C) an entire year.
    D) nearly two years.

77. A floor crunch is a regression for what core exercise?
    A) reverse crunch
    B) plank hold
    C) hip bridge
    D) ball crunch

78. Which of the following is NOT an example of relapse prevention and recovery plans?
    A) use the ABC model of behavior to identify triggers
    B) plan a weekly menu and shopping list to eliminate the need for a fast food meal
    C) do NOT focus on fault
    D) create a contingency plan for social outings

79. Which connect chain checkpoint compensation reveals lower crossed syndrome?
    A) shoulders
    B) foot and ankle
    C) head and cervical spine
    D) lumbo/pelvic/hip complex

80. The Karvonen formula is used to calculate
    A) maximum heart rate.
    B) target heart rate.
    C) resting heart rate.
    D) heart rate recovery.

81. Why should power exercises be performed prior to muscular endurance exercises?
    A) to promote flexibility
    B) power exercises are lower intensity and should be performed first
    C) muscular endurance exercises are higher intensity and should be performed last
    D) power exercises require high levels of technique, and muscular endurance exercises can cause fatigue and decreased performance quality

82. How might a goaltender's training program differ from that of any other position in soccer?
    A) The specific movements will involve more forward movement speed development.
    B) The goaltender will perform more steady-state cardiovascular exercise.
    C) The goaltender will perform more exercises to develop kicking and core power.
    D) The specific movements will involve more lateral movement speed development.

83. Developing a training program to achieve a specific goal determined by the trainer and client refers to what?
    A) progression
    B) regression
    C) detraining
    D) specificity

84. Free weight benches with barbells should accommodate

- A) at least two spotters.
- B) at least three spotters.
- C) at least one spotter.
- D) at least the person lifting the barbell.

85. Which answer describes why the following is NOT a SMART goal?

The client wants to lose twenty-five pounds in two months.

- A) The goal is not specific.
- B) The goal is not time-stamped.
- C) The goal is not realistic.
- D) The goal is not measurable.

86. What is an appropriate amount to increase cardiovascular training variables?

- A) 0.5 percent
- B) 10 percent
- C) 11 percent
- D) 15 percent

87. Once the body has detrained cardiovascularly in a trained individual, how long does it take to recover to the same fitness level?

- A) It can take several months.
- B) It takes only a few days.
- C) Cardiovascular detraining does not happen.
- D) It takes several years.

88. During a gait assessment, the personal trainer should use the lateral view to check which kinetic chain checkpoint?

- A) lumbo/pelvic/hip complex
- B) head, low back, and shoulders
- C) knees
- D) ankles/feet

89. A macrocycle includes

- A) only the in-season program.
- B) the entirety of a training periodization.
- C) only off-season training.
- D) only the preparatory period of training.

90. Detraining occurs more quickly in

- A) resistance training gains.
- B) cardiovascular training gains.
- C) men.
- D) women.

91. Excessive training frequency can cause

- A) rapid gains in fitness.
- B) stress reduction.
- C) increased training intensity.
- D) overuse injuries.

92. What type of aerobic endurance training is the 10-kilometer row?

- A) interval
- B) zone training
- C) anaerobic endurance
- D) steady state

93. What is the primary mover for a wrist curl?

- A) triceps
- B) forearm
- C) shoulder
- D) biceps

94. Which of the following is NOT an example of the self-monitoring behavior modification technique?

- A) diet journaling
- B) activity tracking
- C) rewarding completion of a goal
- D) incorporating weekly weigh-ins

95. With resistance training, the intensity increases as the

- **A)** weight decreases.
- **B)** volume increases.
- **C)** weight increases.
- **D)** repetitions increase.

96. How might the trainer progress an already difficult exercise, such as a single-leg squat?

- **A)** There is no further progression.
- **B)** Add a box to sit down on.
- **C)** Add weight with a vest or dumbbells.
- **D)** Pick a new exercise to perform.

97. How long should the rest period be between sets of deadlifts at five repetitions and heavy loads?

- **A)** one minute
- **B)** less than thirty seconds
- **C)** three minutes
- **D)** six minutes

98. In which situation would a personal trainer need to immediately refer a client to a medical professional?

- **A)** a client complains of lower back pain
- **B)** a client complains of anterior knee pain
- **C)** a client has had recent complications with cardiac disease
- **D)** a client does not feel well

99. Which postural misalignment is characterized by rounded shoulders and a forward head position?

- **A)** lower crossed syndrome
- **B)** upper crossed syndrome
- **C)** pronation distortion
- **D)** knee valgus

100. Program design for weight management should include

- **A)** resistance training and nutrition.
- **B)** cardiovascular training and nutrition.
- **C)** nutrition only.
- **D)** warm-up, resistance training, cardiovascular training, nutrition, cooldown, and recovery methods.

101. To reduce the risk of liability in a potential lawsuit, fitness professionals should require that new clients complete which of the following?

- **A)** medical history forms, a liability waiver, informed consent to exercise, and a PAR-Q
- **B)** medical history forms, favorite hobbies, a bloodwork form, and a PAR-Q
- **C)** medical history forms, a liability waiver, informed consent, and a bloodwork form
- **D)** medical history forms, a liability waiver, a PAR-Q, and a fitness assessment

102. Which of the following is the strongest indicator of how a client's cardiorespiratory system is responding and adapting to exercise?

- **A)** resting heart rate
- **B)** 1.5-mile run
- **C)** body composition
- **D)** muscular strength test

103. Income is categorized as which type of barrier to exercise adherence?

- **A)** personal attribute
- **B)** environmental factor
- **C)** physical-activity factor
- **D)** core factor

104. Which compensations should the personal trainer look for at the foot and ankle while observing the client from the anterior view?

- **A)** not adducted or abducted
- **B)** not flattened or externally rotated
- **C)** not anteriorly or posteriorly rotated
- **D)** neither tilted nor rotated

105. Which test is most suitable to assess lower body strength?

- **A)** long jump
- **B)** barbell squat
- **C)** overhead squat
- **D)** hexagon

106. During the single-leg squat assessment, which of the following should NOT describe an individual's posture?

- **A)** The foot should be pointed straight ahead.
- **B)** The ankle, knee, and lumbo/pelvic/hip complex should remain in a neutral position.
- **C)** The shoulders should round forward, and the neck should rest on the chest.
- **D)** The knee should remain in line with the foot.

107. A personal trainer's attire should be

- **A)** tasteful and modest fitness clothing.
- **B)** jeans and a t-shirt.
- **C)** tight and revealing.
- **D)** sweaty and worn.

108. Verbal communication comprises only _____ of how we express ourselves.

- **A)** 7 percent
- **B)** 10 percent
- **C)** 55 percent
- **D)** 38 percent

109. What type of cardiovascular training is most specific to a golfer?

- **A)** sprint training
- **B)** a walking program with varying inclines
- **C)** spin classes
- **D)** long-distance steady-state jogging

110. Which of the following is NOT among the ways personal trainers can earn CECs?

- **A)** college courses
- **B)** industry specialization certification
- **C)** blog contributions
- **D)** structured learning modules from accredited programs

111. During clinical exercise testing protocols at a medical facility, it is the certified fitness professional's responsibility to

- **A)** administer testing procedures under the guidance of a physician.
- **B)** administer medical treatment and medical procedures to the client.
- **C)** diagnose the client's symptoms based on the exercise test.
- **D)** supervise the physician and staff during testing protocols.

112. Program design for clients with chronic back pain should emphasize

- **A)** upper body resistance training.
- **B)** core muscle endurance and flexibility training.
- **C)** lower body resistance training.
- **D)** avoiding the low back entirely.

113. Proper maintenance and routine checking of fitness equipment can help prevent

    A) client dissatisfaction.
    B) environmental emergencies.
    C) negligence lawsuits.
    D) overtraining injuries.

114. One major advantage of zone training in cardiovascular exercise programs is that

    A) it is always low intensity and safe.
    B) the mode does not change so it is easy to remember.
    C) it provides variety in cardiovascular training, which helps with program compliance.
    D) it takes less time than steady-state aerobic training.

115. Minimizing opportunities that trigger unwanted behavior in order to maximize desired behavior is called

    A) stimulus control.
    B) socio-ecological theory.
    C) self-monitoring.
    D) locus of control.

116. If a relapse occurs, using positive self-talk to acknowledge successes is an example of which behavioral change tool?

    A) cognitive coping
    B) social support
    C) relapse prevention
    D) time management

117. Which behavior change model focuses on understanding the relationship between a person and his or her environment?

    A) readiness-to-change model
    B) social cognitive theory model
    C) theory of planned behavior
    D) socio-ecological model

118. Which of the following is NOT a legal or ethical standard for personal trainers?

    A) denying culpability for personal actions
    B) maintaining accurate and honest notes for each client
    C) not discriminating based on race, gender, creed, age, ability, or sexual orientation
    D) complying with sexual harassment standards for both clients and peers

119. People who believe that life is controlled by things that happen to them have _____ locus of control.

    A) an internal
    B) an intrinsic
    C) an external
    D) a skewed

120. Low self-efficacy and external locus of control dominate people in the _____ phase; they believe their situations are hopeless and they would rather ignore them.

    A) preparation
    B) precontemplation
    C) action
    D) termination

121. In the relapse prevention and recovery plan techniques of behavior change, the ABC model of behavior helps to identify _____ for unwanted or desired activities.

- **A)** triggers
- **B)** obsessions
- **C)** irritants
- **D)** successes

122. Miscellaneous personal trainer's insurance covers which type of claims?

- **A)** defamation
- **B)** wrongful invasion of privacy
- **C)** wrongful termination
- **D)** bodily injury

123. Which term describes positive feedback emphasizing a specific aspect of an individual's behavior or task?

- **A)** kinesthetic feedback
- **B)** positive reinforcement
- **C)** targeted praise
- **D)** non-verbal communication

124. What percentage of 1RM should muscular power exercises be performed at?

- **A)** between 65 and 75%
- **B)** between 80 and 100%
- **C)** between 0 and 60%
- **D)** between 75 and 90%

125. Periods in a periodization follow this order:

- **A)** preparatory period, competitive period, first transition period, second transition period
- **B)** macrocycle, microcycle, mesocycle
- **C)** competitive period, first transition period, second transition period, preparatory period
- **D)** preparatory period, first transition period, competitive period, second transition period

SCIENTIFIC FOUNDATIONS ANSWER KEY

1. **A) Correct.** Vitamins A and D regulate a large variety of cellular processes as hormones.
   B) Incorrect. Vitamin K does not act as a hormone.
   C) Incorrect. Vitamins C and E are antioxidants, not hormones.
   D) Incorrect. Folate and B-12 are not hormones.

2. A) Incorrect. These are types of tissues, not organs.
   B) Correct. These are types of connective tissues.
   C) Incorrect. The terms listed in the question are known as tissues and are a collection of cells with a similar function.
   D) Incorrect. The three tissues listed in the question help make up the structure of joints, but they are only components.

3. A) Incorrect. This describes the position of anterior parts of the body.
   B) Correct. This is the correct position of posterior parts of the body.
   C) Incorrect. This describes the position of superior parts of the body.
   D) Incorrect. This is referring to the position of lateral parts of the body.

4. A) Incorrect. The pulmonary vein does not carry deoxygenated blood.
   B) Incorrect. The pulmonary vein does not oxygenate blood.
   C) Correct. The pulmonary vein carries oxygenated blood from the lungs to the heart.
   D) Incorrect. The pulmonary vein does not carry deoxygenated blood.

5. **A) Correct.** Ligaments adhere bone to bone.
   B) Incorrect. This refers to tendons.
   C) Incorrect. This is not the function of ligaments.
   D) Incorrect. This is not the function of ligaments.

6. A) Incorrect. This is the endocardium.
   B) Incorrect. This is the epicardium.
   C) Incorrect. This is myocardium.
   D) Correct. The pericardium is the outermost layer of the heart.

7. A) Incorrect. The carpals are the bones of the hand.
   B) Correct. The radius and ulna are the bones of the forearm.
   C) Incorrect. The femur, tibia, and fibula are found in the leg.
   D) Incorrect. The neck bones are the cervical vertebrae.

8. **A) Correct.** Ball-and-socket joints allow for the most freedom of movement.
   B) Incorrect. Hinge joints only allow for flexion and extension.
   C) Incorrect. Saddle joints do not allow rotation.
   D) Incorrect. Uniaxial joints only allow for movement through one plane of motion.

9. A) Incorrect. This is too few.
   B) Incorrect. This is too many.
   C) Correct. There are 29 vertebrae in the spine.
   D) Incorrect. This is too few.

10. A) Incorrect. This refers to lordosis.
    B) Correct. This is the definition of kyphosis.
    C) Incorrect. This refers to scoliosis.
    D) Incorrect. This does not refer to any of the discussed conditions.

11. A) Incorrect. Kyphosis is more common in the thoracic vertebrae.
    B) Incorrect. Lumbar is the most common area for lordosis.

C) Incorrect. This area is not common for lordosis.

D) **Correct.** The lumbar spine is the most common area for lordosis to occur.

12. A) **Correct.** The H-zone contains only thick myosin filaments.

    B) Incorrect. The H-zone does not contain actin.

    C) Incorrect. Actin is incorrect.

    D) Incorrect. The H-zone does not contain Z-bands.

13. A) Incorrect. Non-impact exercise does not load the skeleton to elicit improvement to bone mineral density.

    B) Incorrect. Swimming is a form of non-impact exercise.

    C) **Correct.** Axial loading of the skeleton through weight lifting improves and maintains bone mineral density.

    D) Incorrect. Though walking does involve impact, it is a relatively low-impact exercise.

14. A) Incorrect. Myofibrils is incorrect.

    B) Incorrect. Motor units is incorrect.

    C) **Correct.** Actin and myosin are contractile proteins in sarcomeres.

    D) Incorrect. Action potentials is incorrect.

15. A) Incorrect. The muscle fiber is only a portion of this definition.

    B) Incorrect. The neuromuscular junction is where the neuron and muscle fiber synapse.

    C) Incorrect. This is a single unit of the muscle fiber.

    D) **Correct.** This is the definition of a motor unit.

16. A) Incorrect. Although anemia is a risk for female athletes who do not eat much meat, it is not considered part of the female athlete triad, nor is fatigue part of the female athlete triad.

    B) Incorrect. Anemia and dehydration are not parts of the female athlete triad.

    C) **Correct.** Female athletes in many sports feel pressured to stay extremely thin, which can lead to disordered eating and low energy intake. Nutrient deficiencies and extremely low body fat can lead to the loss of normal estrogen secretion, amenorrhea, and osteoporosis.

    D) Incorrect. Anemia is not part of the female athlete triad.

17. A) Incorrect. This is the maximum rate of oxygen consumption an individual is capable of and improves with aerobic conditioning.

    B) Incorrect. VO2 increases with a rise in exercise intensity.

    C) **Correct.** VO2 is an abbreviation of the term volume of oxygen; it is defined as the volume of O2 consumed during any activity in mL/kg body weight/min.

    D) Incorrect. Respiration rate is breaths/minute.

18. A) Incorrect. A pre-exercise meal is important to maximize glycogen storage and supply blood glucose.

    B) Incorrect. This does not allow time for digestion and absorption of nutrients before the event.

    C) **Correct.** This will allow for digestion, absorption of nutrients, and the incorporation of glucose into muscle and liver glycogen.

    D) Incorrect. The meal does not need to be liquid in nature as there is time for digestion.

19. A) Incorrect. Hypertrophy is a normal increase in muscle size in response to exercise.

    B) **Correct.** Muscle hypertrophy is the normal increase in muscle cross section leading to increased strength stimulated by exercise.

    C) Incorrect. Hypertrophy is an increase in muscle cross section, not length.

    D) Incorrect. Hypertrophy has nothing to do with cramping.

20. **A) Correct.** Anabolic steroids are synthetic hormones that mimic the action of testosterone.
    B) Incorrect. Estrogen is a steroid hormone, but anabolic steroids mimic testosterone.
    C) Incorrect. Aldosterone is not involved in stimulating muscle growth.
    D) Incorrect. Human growth hormone is a peptide hormone, not a steroid hormone.

21. A) Incorrect. Spending more time strength training is safer in younger adults.
    B) Incorrect. Due to the high intensity of the exercise, excessive amounts of power training can be dangerous to an older adult.
    C) Incorrect. Some impact exercise is beneficial for older adults, but the higher the impact, the higher the risk of bone damage due to increased risk of osteoporosis with old age.
    D) Correct. As people age, they should spend more time warming up before an exercise program.

22. A) Incorrect. Zinc is present only in small quantities.
    B) Incorrect. There is no significant amount of manganese in bone.
    C) Incorrect. Calcium is not the only major mineral in bone.
    D) Correct. Calcium and phosphate are most abundant, but magnesium is present in significant quantities also.

23. A) Incorrect. Myofibril is incorrect.
    B) Correct. This is the definition of the sliding filament theory.
    C) Incorrect. Muscle is incorrect.
    D) Incorrect. Motor unit is incorrect.

24. A) Incorrect. Transfusing extra red blood cells is considered doping and is banned.
    B) Incorrect. Erythropoietin (EPO) stimulates red blood cell production and is banned. EPO is also dangerous since it thickens the blood and may lead to stroke or heart attack.
    C) Incorrect. Synthetic oxygen carriers could artificially increase the oxygen carrying capacity of the blood; they are banned.
    D) Correct. Iron is a normal nutrient needed by the body and may require supplementation in anemic individuals. Supplementation is legal, and excess iron is generally excreted.

25. A) Incorrect. Peptide hormones are used to enhance performance.
    B) Correct. Diuretics increase urinary excretion and may be used to try to flush out illegal drugs before testing.
    C) Incorrect. Beta blockers are used to enhance concentration and steady the hands.
    D) Incorrect. TNF-α inhibitors are immunosuppressants used to treat inflammatory diseases.

26. A) Incorrect. There are selenoproteins in the thyroid gland, but thyroid hormone does not contain selenium.
    B) Correct. Iodine is a component of thyroid hormone, which regulates metabolic rate.
    C) Incorrect. Magnesium is not a component of thyroid hormone.
    D) Incorrect. Cobalt is not a component of thyroid hormone.

27. A) Incorrect. Lactic acid does not cause DOMS.
    B) Incorrect. Static stretching does not cause DOMS.
    C) Correct. Micro-tears in the muscle fibers from resistance training cause DOMS.
    D) Incorrect. Fit individuals can also experience DOMS.

28. A) Incorrect. This is the amount of fat kcal, not grams.
    B) Correct. 2,000 kcal × 0.10 × 1 gram/9 kcal = 22 grams.

- C) Incorrect. Fat has 9 kcal per gram, not 10 kcal per gram.
- D) Incorrect. This is far less saturated fat than the maximum recommendation.

29.
- A) **Correct.** Oatmeal, fruits, and beans are sources of soluble fiber.
- B) Incorrect. Only plant foods contain fiber.
- C) Incorrect. Whole wheat, brown rice, and seeds are sources of insoluble fiber.
- D) Incorrect. Vegetable oils contain only fats.

30.
- A) **Correct.** Measurements over 40 inches for men and 35 inches for women are considered unhealthy.
- B) Incorrect. The measurements vary by sex.
- C) Incorrect. These thresholds are too high.
- D) Incorrect. The measurements vary by sex.

31.
- A) **Correct.** This is the definition of Golgi tendon organs.
- B) Incorrect. While this is a proprioceptor, it is not the correct proprioceptor.
- C) Incorrect. This is not a proprioceptor.
- D) Incorrect. This is not a proprioceptor.

32.
- A) Incorrect. This position describes the term dorsal (posterior).
- B) **Correct.** Both terms mean toward the front.
- C) Incorrect. This is referring to medial.
- D) Incorrect. This is referring to distal.

33.
- A) Incorrect. Marathoners benefit more from slow-twitch muscle fibers.
- B) Incorrect. Such swimmers benefit more from slow-twitch muscle fibers.
- C) **Correct.** Olympic sprinters require fast-twitch muscle fibers for improved performance.
- D) Incorrect. Cross-country cyclists benefit more from slow-twitch muscle fibers.

34.
- A) **Correct.** Slow-twitch muscle fibers contain more mitochondria than fast-twitch muscle fibers.
- B) Incorrect. Fast-twitch muscle fibers have a higher anaerobic capacity.
- C) Incorrect. Fast-twitch muscle fibers have a higher force production capability.
- D) Incorrect. Slow-twitch muscle fibers are referred to as type I, whereas fast-twitch muscle fibers are categorized into type IIa or IIb.

35.
- A) Incorrect. Knee flexion is incorrect.
- B) **Correct.** These are the two actions of the quadriceps muscles.
- C) Incorrect. Knee flexion and hip extension are both incorrect.
- D) Incorrect. Hip extension is incorrect.

36.
- A) Incorrect. This is the wrong phase.
- B) **Correct.** This refers to the contraction phase in muscle.
- C) Incorrect. This is the wrong phase.
- D) Incorrect. Although this is a portion of muscular contraction, it is not a phase during the neuromuscular stimulation process.

37.
- A) Incorrect. This plane of motion is not correct.
- B) Incorrect. This plane of motion is not correct.
- C) **Correct.** The elbow extends in the sagittal plane by the contraction of the triceps.
- D) Incorrect. This plane of motion is not correct.

38.
- A) Incorrect. This is the opposite muscle action of the gastrocnemius and is performed by a different muscle group.
- B) Incorrect. This is the wrong terminology for the muscular action of the gastrocnemius.
- C) **Correct.** This is the action of the gastrocnemius.
- D) Incorrect. This is the wrong terminology for the muscular action of the gastrocnemius.

39. A) Incorrect. This is the wrong type of muscle contraction.
B) Incorrect. This is the wrong type of muscle contraction.
C) Incorrect. This is the wrong type of muscle contraction.
D) Correct. This is the definition of isometric muscle contraction.

40. A) Incorrect. This is an increase in joint angle by muscular contraction.
B) Incorrect. This is a combination of many joint movements.
C) Correct. This definition refers to flexion.
D) Incorrect. This is when a joint moves in a circular pattern around an axis.

41. A) Incorrect. The latissimus dorsi is a prime mover in this exercise.
B) Correct. The gluteus medius stabilizes the hip joint during the box step-up.
C) Incorrect. The biceps brachii is a prime mover in this exercise.
D) Incorrect. The quadriceps are a prime mover in this exercise.

42. A) Incorrect. Organs are a collection of tissues.
B) Incorrect. This is an anatomical direction.
C) Incorrect. Organ systems are the next-largest on the biological hierarchy.
D) Correct. This definition refers to organs.

43. **A) Correct.** This is the definition of length-tension relationship.
B) Incorrect. This is the working of two muscle groups to perform the same joint movement.
C) Incorrect. This theory states the crossbridging of actin and myosin for muscle contraction.
D) Incorrect. This is the way in which muscle fibers are recruited with different exercise intensity.

44. A) Incorrect. This refers to hyperplasia.
B) Correct. This is the definition of muscular hypertrophy.
C) Incorrect. This refers to muscular atrophy.
D) Incorrect. This is not the definition of muscular hypertrophy.

45. **A) Correct.** These veins collect deoxygenated blood from the body and feed it into the right atrium.
B) Incorrect. The carotid artery feeds oxygenated blood to the head and face.
C) Incorrect. The aorta feeds oxygenated blood to much of the body.
D) Incorrect. The lungs are where deoxygenated blood goes for gas exchange after it exits the right ventricle.

46. A) Incorrect. Rock climbing does not necessarily increase the risk of medial knee injuries in female athletes.
B) Correct. Jumping increases the risk of medial knee injuries in female athletes with increased Q-angles.
C) Incorrect. Ice hockey does not necessarily increase the risk of medial knee injuries in female athletes.
D) Incorrect. Snowboarding does not necessarily increase the risk of medial knee injuries in female athletes.

47. A) Incorrect. This refers to proximal.
B) Incorrect. This refers to superior.
C) Correct. This is the definition of distal.
D) Incorrect. This refers to medial.

48. **A) Correct.** Air travels from the trachea to the bronchi.
B) Incorrect. The mouth is before the trachea.
C) Incorrect. Air flows from the bronchi to the bronchioles.
D) Incorrect. Air flows from the bronchioles to the alveoli for gas exchange.

49. A) Incorrect. The red blood cells carry oxygen to the tissues.

- B) **Correct.** The platelets found in blood aid in clotting.
- C) Incorrect. White blood cells aid in fighting infection.
- D) Incorrect. Water helps blood viscous move through the circulatory system.

50.
- A) Incorrect. This is not the function of the abdominals.
- B) Incorrect. This is not the function of the pectoralis major.
- C) Incorrect. This is not the function of the pectoralis minor.
- D) **Correct.** The diaphragm helps create a pressure differential in the lungs to aid in respiration.

51.
- A) Incorrect. This digestion location comes after the esophagus.
- B) Incorrect. This digestion location comes after the mouth.
- C) **Correct.** Digestion begins in the mouth.
- D) Incorrect. This digestion location comes after the stomach.

52.
- A) Incorrect. The nerves are part of the peripheral nervous system.
- B) **Correct.** The central nervous system is made up of the brain and spinal cord.
- C) Incorrect. The proprioceptors are found in the muscles.
- D) Incorrect. The nerves are part of the peripheral nervous system.

53.
- A) Incorrect. This occurs when a limb is pulled away from the midline of the body.
- B) Incorrect. This occurs as a joint angle increases with muscle contraction.
- C) Incorrect. This occurs as the hand is rotated so the palm faces toward the ground.
- D) **Correct.** This muscular action refers to adduction.

54.
- A) Incorrect. This refers to Alzheimer's disease.
- B) Incorrect. This refers to osteoporosis.
- C) **Correct.** Multiple sclerosis affects the myelin sheaths on axons.
- D) Incorrect. Multiple sclerosis affects the myelin sheaths rather than the nucleus.

55.
- A) Incorrect. This is the process by which the body recruits more motor units to perform the same task.
- B) Incorrect. This occurs after several weeks of resistance training.
- C) **Correct.** This is the definition of summation.
- D) Incorrect. This refers to a single environmental stressor.

56.
- A) **Correct.** Abnormal or disordered heart rhythms are known as arrhythmias.
- B) Incorrect. This is part of the female athlete triad.
- C) Incorrect. This is abnormally high blood pressure.
- D) Incorrect. This is a hardening of the arteries.

57.
- A) Incorrect. Testosterone is a type of anabolic hormone.
- B) Incorrect. IGF is a type of anabolic hormone.
- C) Incorrect. Epinephrine is a type of hormone associated with environmental stressors.
- D) **Correct.** The two hormone types associated with exercise are anabolic and catabolic.

58.
- A) Incorrect. Hormones are what an organ secretes, but they are not the organ itself.
- B) Incorrect. The brain contains glands, but it is not a gland itself.
- C) Incorrect. This is a hormone that is secreted by a gland.
- D) **Correct.** This is the definition of a gland.

59.
- A) **Correct.** The hypothalamus controls the autonomic nervous system and the connection of the central nervous and endocrine systems.

B) Incorrect. The hypothalamus does not control the peripheral nervous system and associated nerves.

C) Incorrect. The musculoskeletal system and voluntary skeletal muscle is not controlled by the hypothalamus.

D) Incorrect. This is regulated by the pituitary gland.

60. A) Incorrect. This is the female reproductive organ, but it does not carry these responsibilities.

B) Correct. The placenta is an organ that nourishes the fetus during pregnancy.

C) Incorrect. This is the male reproductive organ.

D) Incorrect. This is found in the brain and is responsible for the release of melatonin for sleep regulation.

61. A) Incorrect. The muscles apply force during an isometric movement, and this would be indicated on a force-time curve.

B) Incorrect. This would indicate force being applied quickly but not held isometrically—for example, a single vertical jump.

C) Correct. The force-time curve would indicate an increase and then a stabilization of force.

D) Incorrect. This would indicate an exercise where a high force is applied and followed by a lower force isometric movement. For example, a jump with a static hold at the bottom.

62. A) Incorrect. The BMI formula takes height into account.

B) Incorrect. The BMI formula takes height into account.

C) Correct. Strength training builds lean muscle mass, which is a healthy kind of excess weight.

D) Incorrect. For a sedentary individual, excess weight would likely be unhealthy fat, and BMI would be a measure of that.

63. A) Incorrect. The resistance and the weight are the same thing.

B) Incorrect. The muscles and the force are the same thing.

C) Incorrect. The resistance and the weight are the same thing.

D) Correct. A lever system is comprised of the fulcrum, the resistance, and the force.

64. A) Incorrect. This is the least common type of lever on the body.

B) Incorrect. The body uses all three types of lever systems.

C) Incorrect. This is not the most common type of lever system on the body.

D) Correct. This is the most common type of lever system the human body uses.

65. A) Incorrect. This is not Newton's second law of motion.

B) Correct. Newton's second law of motion states that force = mass × acceleration.

C) Incorrect. This statement is false.

D) Incorrect. This statement is false.

66. A) Incorrect. This is the amount of work being done by the muscles (work) at a joint divided by the rate at which they are applied (time).

B) Incorrect. This is the rate at which a muscle produces movement through full range of motion at a joint.

C) Correct. This is the definition of rotational work.

D) Incorrect. Momentum is the mass of an object times the velocity at which it is traveling.

67. **A) Correct.** This is the definition of the lactate threshold.

B) Incorrect. This is the aerobic process of creating ATP for energy.

C) Incorrect. This is the energy system utilized by the body for high-intensity short duration exercise of ten seconds or less.

D) Incorrect. This refers to the body's ability to use either creatine phosphate or muscle glycogen for energy production during exercise.

Answer Key 333

68.
- A) Incorrect. This is not a significant exercise expenditure.
- B) Incorrect. This caloric expenditure through exercise leaves a 2,500 kcal deficit to be obtained through diet, which could be difficult to maintain.
- C) Incorrect. This is a bit less than the optimum caloric expenditure through exercise.
- D) **Correct.** A caloric expenditure of at least 2,000 kcal/week in exercise, combined with a dietary caloric deficit of at least 1,500 kcal/week is recommended to lose at least a pound per week. A sustainable weight loss target is 1 – 2 lb./week.

69.
- A) Incorrect. There will likely be variations in the distribution of muscle mass between athletes.
- B) Incorrect. The two may not have a difference in abdominal muscle strength as both sports require strong abdominal muscles.
- C) **Correct.** The figure skater will likely have more lower body muscle mass as this is the primary mode of movement in this sport.
- D) Incorrect. The rock climber will likely have more upper body muscle mass as this is the primary mode of movement in this sport.

70.
- A) Incorrect. This is the RDA for sedentary nonvegetarians. Active individuals require more protein.
- B) Incorrect. An excess of 1.7 g/kg has not been shown to have any performance advantage, regardless of the type of exercise.
- C) Incorrect. Protein recommendations vary with activity.
- D) **Correct.** The protein recommendations for each of these categories of people is: 0.8 g/kg (meat eaters) – 0.9 g/kg (vegetarians) for sedentary individuals, 1.2 – 1.4 g/kg for those engaging regularly in endurance activities, and 1.6 – 1.7 g/kg for strength trainers.

71.
- A) Incorrect. Lean body mass also includes bone, tissues, and organs.
- B) Incorrect. Lean body mass contains significant water.
- C) Incorrect. The brain contains a lot of fat and contributes to fat mass.
- D) **Correct.** The brain and spinal cord are part of lean body mass but not fat-free mass.

72.
- A) Incorrect. Muscle growth is incorrect.
- B) Incorrect. Fatigue is incorrect.
- C) Incorrect. Fatigue is incorrect.
- D) **Correct.** These are the three components of the female athlete triad.

73.
- A) **Correct.** This is the function of IGF-1 as a neuroendocrine response to high-intensity exercise.
- B) Incorrect. This is the function of catecholamine.
- C) Incorrect. This is the function of testosterone.
- D) Incorrect. This is the function of catecholamine.

74.
- A) Incorrect. Hyaline is a type of cartilage.
- B) Incorrect. Fibrocartilage is a type of cartilage.
- C) Incorrect. Elastic is a type of cartilage.
- D) **Correct.** Ligaments are not a type of cartilage.

75.
- A) **Correct.** Children tend to have difficulty regulating body temperature.
- B) Incorrect. This is not a common issue among all women.
- C) Incorrect. This is not a common issue among older adults.
- D) Incorrect. This is not a common issue among men.

76.
- A) **Correct.** Disordered eating is one of the components of the female athlete triad and can lead to the other two components: reduced bone mineral density and loss of menstrual cycle.
- B) Incorrect. Disordered eating does not lead to improved health.

- C) Incorrect. Disordered eating can negatively affect muscle mass development.
- D) Incorrect. Disordered eating does not help improve fitness performance.

77.
- A) Incorrect. This is the job of the digestive system.
- B) Incorrect. The bones create red blood cells, but not the muscles.
- **C) Correct.** The levers of the musculoskeletal system are used for human movement.
- D) Incorrect. This is the job of the nervous system.

78.
- A) Incorrect. Cardiac output can be the same at various ages depending on training status and stroke volume of an individual.
- B) Incorrect. Age does not necessarily affect blood pressure; younger individuals can have hypertension, and older individuals can have normal values of blood pressure.
- **C) Correct.** Age decreases maximum heart rate.
- D) Incorrect. Age does not necessarily affect resting heart rate.

79.
- **A) Correct.** Twenty amino acids make up proteins.
- B) Incorrect. Eight to ten amino acids are considered essential to the diet, but several more can be synthesized by the body and are the building blocks of proteins.
- C) Incorrect. Eight to ten amino acids are considered essential to the diet, but several more can be synthesized by the body and are the building blocks of proteins.
- D) Incorrect. Taurine is an additional amino acid to the standard twenty; it is present in the body but is not incorporated into protein.

80.
- A) Incorrect. The size of the mineral atom has nothing to do with the naming.
- **B) Correct.** Macrominerals are typically present in the body in larger quantities and have larger dietary requirements.
- C) Incorrect. Macrominerals do not bind together.
- D) Incorrect. Minerals are obtained from the diet.

81.
- A) Incorrect. Vitamin E is an antioxidant that protects membrane lipids from oxidation.
- B) Incorrect. Vitamin C is an antioxidant that protects against free radicals formed from aerobic metabolism.
- C) Incorrect. Beta-carotene is a weak antioxidant.
- **D) Correct.** Vitamin K is involved in blood clotting and bone formation. Vitamins E, C, and beta-carotene are antioxidants, although beta-carotene is a relatively weak antioxidant.

82.
- A) Incorrect. The biceps brachii is a fusiform muscle.
- B) Incorrect. The extensor digitorum longus is a unipennate muscle.
- C) Incorrect. The rectus abdominis is a parallel muscle.
- **D) Correct.** The pectoralis major is a convergent muscle.

83.
- A) Incorrect. Thiamine plays no role in anemia.
- **B) Correct.** Folate and vitamin B-12 are critical to the synthesis of nucleotides, which are the building blocks of DNA. When DNA synthesis is impaired, red blood cells cannot divide fast enough and instead grow large.
- C) Incorrect. The type of anemia caused by iron deficiency is characterized by a lack of hemoglobin, which is needed to carry sufficient oxygen.
- D) Incorrect. Copper deficiency can lead to iron-deficiency anemia because it is involved in iron transport, not megaloblastic anemia.

84.
- A) Incorrect. The lengthy aerobic demands as well as increased sweat losses associated with endurance exercise are

more likely to cause an iron deficiency than strength training.

B) Incorrect. Male athletes are at lower risk than female athletes for iron deficiency since they tend to eat more meat and do not have menstrual iron losses.

C) Incorrect. As described in answer choice A, strength athletes are not at a high risk for iron-deficiency anemia.

D) **Correct.** Endurance athletes have higher iron requirements as well as higher iron losses. Female athletes have menstrual losses and also tend to consume less calories and meat than males; these can contribute to iron-deficiency anemia. Since iron from meat is the most bioavailable form, vegetarians are also at risk for iron-deficiency anemia, especially vegetarian endurance athletes.

85. A) Incorrect. These devices do not burn significant calories.

B) Incorrect. It is not possible to target specific body areas for fat loss; fat loss with exercise is distributed throughout body fat stores.

C) Incorrect. These devices do not produce significant weight loss.

D) **Correct.** These devices do not burn fat, and specific areas cannot be targeted effectively for fat loss.

86. A) **Correct.** Carbohydrates in the form of muscle glycogen and possibly liver glycogen, along with blood glucose, muscle triglycerides, blood fatty acids, and lipoproteins are the major fuels for exercise.

B) Incorrect. Although protein can provide fuel for exercise, its contribution is minor compared to that of carbohydrates and fat.

C) Incorrect. Contributions from protein to fuel exercise are minor compared to the contributions made by carbohydrates.

D) Incorrect. The contributions proteins make to fueling exercise are minor; carbohydrates and fat are the main fuels for exercise.

87. A) Incorrect. The glycemic index is more specific than energy density.

B) Incorrect. The glycemic index has nothing to do with glycogen depletion during exercise.

C) **Correct.** The glycemic index is the area under the blood glucose curve (AUC) over a two-hour time period following ingestion of the food, divided by the AUC of a standard food (usually white bread) times 100.

D) Incorrect. There are factors other than just the percentage of carbohydrates that affect blood glucose response to a food, such as the type of carbohydrate and the amount of fiber in the food.

88. A. Incorrect. While sodium is responsible for the transmission of electrical signals across nerve and muscle cell membranes, chloride is not.

B. Incorrect. While potassium is responsible for the transmission of electrical signals across nerve and muscle cell membranes, chloride is not.

C) **Correct.** The changes in membrane potentials that transmit electrical signals are caused by the flow of sodium and potassium ions across the membrane.

D. Incorrect. While sodium is responsible for the transmission of electrical signals across nerve and muscle cell membranes, magnesium is not.

89. A) Incorrect. These are the smaller heart chambers.

B) **Correct.** The ventricles are the larger heart chambers.

C) Incorrect. These carry deoxygenated blood to the heart.

D) Incorrect. These separate the chambers of the heart.

90. A) Incorrect. The word creation is incorrect.

B) **Correct.** This is the correct acronym.

C) Incorrect. The word extreme is incorrect.

D) Incorrect. The word pre-exercise is incorrect.

91. **A)** **Correct.** To maintain hydration, it is recommended to consume 20 – 36 oz. of fluid, preferably a sport drink with electrolytes, and ideally spread out at 15 – 20 minute intervals.

B) Incorrect. A fluid intake of 8 – 12 oz. per hour is not enough to maintain hydration during periods of prolonged exercise.

C) Incorrect. A fluid intake of 10 – 15 oz. per hour is not enough to maintain hydration during prolonged exercise.

D) Incorrect. It would be difficult to consume 40 – 45 oz. of fluid per hour, and such a quantity is more than necessary to maintain hydration.

92. A) Incorrect. Body composition does not divide out carbohydrates, protein, or water.

B) **Correct.** Body composition refers to the relative percentage of fat versus everything else: muscle, soft tissues, organs, and bone.

C) Incorrect. Both bone and soft tissues contribute to fat-free mass.

D) Incorrect. There is water associated with both the fat mass and fat-free mass.

93. A) Incorrect. Saliva primarily helps break down food in the mouth.

B) **Correct.** This is the function of saliva.

C) Incorrect. Nutrient absorption primarily occurs in the small intestine.

D) Incorrect. Water absorption primarily occurs in the large intestine.

94. **A)** **Correct.** The myelin sheath helps speed up nervous transmission of electrical impulses.

B) Incorrect. Impulses travel away from the dendrites (and soma) along the axon on a neuron.

C) Incorrect. The myelin sheaths do not protect against multiple sclerosis; they are damaged by it.

D) Incorrect. The myelin sheaths do not prevent Alzheimer's disease, and there is no known cure.

95. A) Incorrect. Sleep deprivation can lead to overeating and poor food choices.

B) Incorrect. In type 2 diabetes, tissues are less responsive to the stimulation of glucose uptake by insulin, which leads to high blood glucose. Taking insulin to treat diabetes can also stimulate the storage of glucose as fat. Exercise can help burn excess glucose, lowering the need for insulin and helping to prevent weight gain.

C) Incorrect. Certain antidepressants tend to cause weight gain.

D) **Correct.** The drug metformin is used to increase insulin sensitivity and decrease glucose production by the liver in type 2 diabetics. It does not lead to weight gain and may assist somewhat in weight loss.

PRACTICAL/APPLIED ANSWER KEY

1.
   A) Incorrect. The Rockport walk test assesses cardiorespiratory endurance.
   B) Incorrect. The push-up test is a muscular endurance test.
   C) **Correct.** The hexagon test is used to assess speed, agility, and quickness.
   D) Incorrect. The twelve-minute run test is used to assess cardiorespiratory endurance.

2.
   A) Incorrect. With female clients, the thigh is measured, but the biceps and chest are not.
   B) **Correct.** The triceps, suprailium, and thigh are the three sites measured on female clients.
   C) Incorrect. The thigh and suprailium are measured, but the subscapular is not measured on female clients.
   D) Incorrect. The suprailium and thigh are measured on female clients; the biceps are not.

3.
   A) **Correct.** The 300-yard shuttle test is used to measure anaerobic capacity.
   B) Incorrect. The LEFT is used to measure agility in the sagittal and frontal plane.
   C) Incorrect. The pro-agility test measures lateral speed and agility.
   D) Incorrect. The *t*-test is used to assess overall agility while moving forward, laterally, and backward.

4.
   A) Incorrect. Short-distance sprints will help football players since the longest distance they run is one hundred yards.
   B) **Correct.** Long-distance running does not follow the principle of specificity when it comes to football.
   C) Incorrect. Power exercises that develop speed will improve football players' one-hundred-yard yard sprint time.
   D) Incorrect. Muscular endurance exercises will help to benefit short-distance sprints.

5.
   A) Incorrect. A mesocycle typically includes multiple microcycles.
   B) Incorrect. A macrocycle includes the entire periodization.
   C) **Correct.** A microcycle is the shortest cycle in a periodization.
   D) Incorrect. The preparatory period typically involves mesocycles and microcycles.

6.
   A) Incorrect. A flexibility assessment is generally included in a fitness assessment.
   B) Incorrect. A static postural assessment is generally included in a fitness assessment.
   C) **Correct.** An assessment of daily caloric intake is generally not included during a fitness assessment.
   D) Incorrect. A cardiorespiratory capacity assessment is generally not included in a fitness assessment.

7.
   A) Incorrect. Movement assessments do not test maximal force.
   B) Incorrect. Movement assessments do not test core strength.
   C) Incorrect. Movement assessments do not test agility and speed.
   D) **Correct.** Movement assessments are used to test dynamic posture.

8.
   A) Incorrect. Certification through leading organizations does not guarantee more money.
   B) **Correct.** Clients who are thorough will research a fitness professional to make sure he or she has expertise in the field.
   C) Incorrect. Certifications cannot guarantee client results.
   D) Incorrect. Fitness certifications are not necessarily proof of higher education or training, although certified professionals have often obtained both.

9.
   A) Incorrect. Twenty seconds is shorter than the recommended time.
   B) Incorrect. Sixty seconds is longer than the recommended time.

	C)	**Correct.** Thirty seconds is the recommended time for static stretching.
	D)	Incorrect. Ten seconds is shorter than the recommended time.
10.	A)	Incorrect. Hypertension refers to high blood pressure.
	B)	Incorrect. Hyperventilation is an increased respiration rate.
	C)	Incorrect. Delayed onset muscle soreness is the normal physiological response related to micro-tears in the muscle fibers, causing acute muscular soreness.
	D)	**Correct.** The definition provided describes overtraining.
11.	A)	Incorrect. The legal parameters are not called scope of product.
	B)	Incorrect. Legality of specialization is not the proper name for the legal parameters.
	C)	**Correct.** Scope of practice is the term that describes the legal parameters within which credentialed or licensed health professionals must work.
	D)	Incorrect. Terms of work is not the proper name.
12.	**A)**	**Correct.** This network is called the allied healthcare continuum.
	B)	Incorrect. The term training continuum describes a progressive system in exercise technique.
	C)	Incorrect. While those in the network are considered health professionals, this is not the proper name of the network.
	D)	Incorrect. The term health maintenance professionals is not correct.
13.	A)	Incorrect. The bench press test would not be appropriate for this goal.
	B)	Incorrect. The hexagon test would not be appropriate for this goal.
	C)	**Correct.** The Rockport walk test would be the most appropriate test for the goal of lowering a client's blood pressure.
	D)	Incorrect. The three-hundred-yard shuttle test would not be appropriate for this goal.
14.	**A)**	**Correct.** A trainer should tell a client complaining of pain to visit his or her physician.
	B)	Incorrect. A trainer should not refer a client to see a friend.
	C)	Incorrect. A trainer should not refer this client to a massage therapist because the trainer does not know the scope of the injury or why the pain is occurring.
	D)	Incorrect. A trainer should always express interest in helping a client relieve his or her pain.
15.	A)	Incorrect. Error points are given for this deviation.
	B)	**Correct.** This is not a deviation.
	C)	Incorrect. Error points are given for this deviation.
	D)	Incorrect. Error points are given for this deviation.
16.	A)	Incorrect. Core exercises typically recruit large muscle groups and have multiple joint motions.
	B)	Incorrect. Open kinetic chain exercises do activate smaller muscle groups, but they are not used for just rehabilitative purposes.
	C)	Incorrect. PNF stretching is stretching used for rehabilitative purposes and typically requires assistance from another person.
	D)	**Correct.** Assistance exercises are used for rehabilitative purposes; they isolate a specific, smaller muscle group.
17.	A)	Incorrect. Questions pertaining to a client's sleep patterns should be included on a lifestyle questionnaire.
	B)	Incorrect. Questions pertaining to a client's stressors should be included on a lifestyle questionnaire.
	C)	**Correct.** Questions pertaining to a client's friends are not necessary on a lifestyle questionnaire.

18.
- D) Incorrect. Questions pertaining to a client's smoking habits should be included on a lifestyle questionnaire.

18.
- A) Incorrect. Arthritis typically causes INCREASED joint pain.
- B) Incorrect. Arthritis will not necessarily affect the motivation level of the client.
- **C) Correct.** Joint range of motion can be decreased due to arthritis.
- D) Incorrect. Muscular atrophy typically increases around an arthritic joint.

19.
- A) Incorrect. Nurses are part of the AHC.
- B) Incorrect. Psychologists are part of the AHC.
- C) Incorrect. Occupational therapists are part of the AHC.
- **D) Correct.** Psychics are not part of the AHC.

20.
- A) Incorrect. The long jump test is used to assess horizontal bilateral power.
- B) Incorrect. The Margaria-Kalamen test is used to assess lower body power.
- **C) Correct.** The star excursion test is used to assess dynamic balance.
- D) Incorrect. The reactive strength index is used to assess the body's ability to perform plyometric activities.

21.
- A) Incorrect. A professional trainer would NOT wear khaki pants or jeans.
- **B) Correct.** Tasteful athletic attire is appropriate for a professional trainer.
- C) Incorrect. Revealing athletic attire is NOT appropriate for a professional trainer to wear.
- D) Incorrect. Strong cologne or perfume is NOT appropriate for a professional trainer.

22.
- A) Incorrect. The handheld bioelectrical impedance device is used to measure body fat.
- **B) Correct.** The sphygmomanometer is used to assess blood pressure.
- C) Incorrect. Calipers are used to assess body fat percentage.
- D) Incorrect. The scale is used to measure weight.

23.
- A) Incorrect. The client should be seated slightly upright.
- B) Incorrect. Range of motion may be reduced by the client's physical changes; however, it does not need to be reduced dramatically.
- C) Incorrect. Abdominal exercises should be encouraged for pregnant clients.
- **D) Correct.** The client should be seated slightly upright.

24.
- A) Incorrect. The second transition is a recovery period.
- B) Incorrect. Sports-specific training occurs during the other three periods.
- C) Incorrect. The athlete should still participate in physical activity in the second transition period.
- **D) Correct.** The second transition period should involve active rest that includes non-specific recreational activities not related to the athlete's competition.

25.
- **A) Correct.** This test measures one's ability to change directions and stabilize the body at high speeds.
- B) Incorrect. This test measures an individual's agility while moving laterally, forward, and backward.
- C) Incorrect. This test measures lateral speed and agility.
- D) Incorrect. This test is used to measure total body bilateral power.

26.
- A) Incorrect. This is not a subcategory of core exercises.
- B) Incorrect. This is the main classification of core exercises, not a subcategory.
- **C) Correct.** Power exercises use multiple muscle groups and joint motions, but are not load-bearing, like structural.
- D) Incorrect. This is a form of stretching.

27.
- A) Incorrect. Static stretching is a technique that uses an implement to hold the leg in place.

- B) Incorrect. Passive stretching is not a cardio warm-up.
- C) **Correct.** Dynamic stretching includes stretches that are more intense and utilize full range of motion, so when they are performed in a circuit, they could be a challenging cardio warm-up.
- D) Incorrect. Active stretching is indeed a type of stretching that uses slow and controlled movements to increase range of motion, but it would not be challenging for a cardio warm-up.

28.
- A) Incorrect. General warm-up and SMR should come before static stretching.
- B) Incorrect. Dynamic stretching should be after static stretching.
- C) Incorrect. Cardio warm-up should come before static stretching.
- D) **Correct.** SMR is ideal to do before static stretching to ensure the loosening of muscle knots.

29.
- A) Incorrect. This is the definition of a pyramid set.
- B) Incorrect. This is the definition of a multiple set program.
- C) **Correct.** This is the definition of a superset.
- D) Incorrect. This is the definition of circuit training.

30.
- A) Incorrect. The excessive fatigue associated with this volume and load range can negate performance during the season.
- B) **Correct.** The off-season should include a period of muscular endurance development because athletic performance will not be hindered during competition.
- C) Incorrect. Excessive fatigue from muscular endurance training should be avoided during the competitive period because it can cause deleterious effects on performance.
- D) Incorrect. The second transition period should involve recreational activities and a break from resistance training protocols.

31.
- A) Incorrect. A workout is the complete dynamic warm-up, training stimulus, cooldown, and stretching.
- B) Incorrect. The load refers to the amount of weight being lifted in a set.
- C) Incorrect. Overload is the principle that increases to training variables stimulates the muscle to adapt.
- D) **Correct.** This is the definition of a set.

32.
- A) Incorrect. Static stretching should happen in the middle of the warm-up.
- B) Incorrect. PNF stretching should come in the middle of the warm-up, in lieu of static stretching if rehab is needed.
- C) **Correct.** Dynamic stretching should be done at the end of the warm-up to target the muscle groups that will be worked during a workout.
- D) Incorrect. SMR stretching is done after the general cardio warm-up if needed.

33.
- A) **Correct.** A push press is an explosive, standing shoulder press, which is an advanced shoulder press.
- B) Incorrect. While the primary movers are shoulders, the standing upright row is a pulling move, not a pushing move.
- C) Incorrect. The primary movers for a low row are the latissimus dorsi and the erector spinae.
- D) Incorrect. The primary mover for the push-up is the pectorals.

34.
- A) Incorrect. Spotting requires at least one person.
- B) Incorrect. A dumbbell shoulder press requires one spotter.
- C) Incorrect. A dumbbell shoulder press requires one spotter.
- D) **Correct.** One spotter is required behind the lifter, supporting the wrists.

35.
- A) Incorrect. The client may not know the signs and symptoms of overtraining, or may give an inaccurate response.
- B) Incorrect. The client's relatives may not know the signs and symptoms of overtraining.

36.
- C) **Correct.** Keeping accurate records of the client's progress means the trainer can consult data to determine whether the client is overtraining. There are often physiological and psychological symptoms associated with overtraining.
- D) Incorrect. Another fitness professional meeting the client for the first time might consider the client's abilities normal.

36.
- A) Incorrect. Relativity refers to a theory in physics.
- B) Incorrect. Honesty refers to the principle of personal values.
- C) **Correct.** This term describes the degree to which a test or test item measures what is supposed to be measured.
- D) Incorrect. This is part of an assessment.

37.
- A) Incorrect. Static stretching should not be part of the warm-up.
- B) Incorrect. Single-muscle group exercises and plyometrics should not be performed until after the warm-up is complete.
- C) **Correct.** These three items should always be included in the warm-up process for ideal preparation.
- D) Incorrect. Although dynamic stretching and foam rolling may be beneficial to the field hockey player, PNF stretching may inhibit the player's performance during the workout.

38.
- A) Incorrect. The Golgi tendon organ is in the muscle spindles.
- **B) Correct.** The Golgi tendon organ is the primary stimulator in autogenic inhibition.
- C) Incorrect. The tendons are not in the muscles; they are connectors between the muscles and bones.
- D) Incorrect. Ligaments are tissues that connect bones to each other.

39.
- A) Incorrect. This rest period is too short.
- B) Incorrect. This rest period is too short.
- C) Incorrect. This rest period is too short.
- D) **Correct.** Heavier loads require longer rest periods, and 90 percent of 1RM requires a full three-minute rest period for adequate recovery.

40.
- A) Incorrect. A stretching partner is used in PNF stretching.
- B) Incorrect. Active stretching uses bodyweight only.
- C) Incorrect. Boxes and medicine balls are used for power training.
- D) **Correct.** SMR utilizes gravity and a foam roller to ease muscle tension.

41.
- A) Incorrect. Nodding indicates positive body language.
- B) Incorrect. Leaning forward is another way to indicate a positive body language.
- C) **Correct.** Wringing hands is a negative body language indicator.
- D) Incorrect. A firm handshake also indicates positive body language.

42.
- A) Incorrect. This should not be the main focus of a resistance training program for children and adolescents.
- B) Incorrect. Specific and repetitive movements can cause overuse injuries even in children.
- C) Incorrect. High-intensity exercise may be part of the sport they participate in, but technique and form are more important in their training programs.
- D) **Correct.** Proper technique and form development should be the goal of child and adolescent resistance training programs.

43.
- A) Incorrect. A spotter cannot be used in a hip hinge motion.
- B) Incorrect. Medicine ball slams are explosive exercises and therefore cannot use a spotter; the weight is not heavy enough.
- C) **Correct.** Back-loaded squats can use up to three spotters to ensure proper form.

- D) Incorrect. Walking lunges are characterized by forward motion and cannot use a spotter.

44.
- A) Incorrect. Enthusiasm is the only one of the three attributes described correctly.
- **B) Correct.** Confidence, enthusiasm, and professionalism are the three attributes a trainer should personify when meeting with a client.
- C) Incorrect. Confidence is the only one of the three attributes described correctly.
- D) Incorrect. None of these are among the three attributes described in the text.

45.
- A) Incorrect. The DEXA scan is used to measure body fat percentage.
- **B) Correct.** Body mass index measurements do not measure body fat but determine if an individual's weight is appropriate for his or her height.
- C) Incorrect. Near-infrared interactance is used to measure body fat percentage.
- D) Incorrect. Air displacement plethysmography is used to measure body fat percentage.

46.
- A) Incorrect. The palms are facing up on a supinated grip.
- B) Incorrect. In an alternating grip, one palm is up and the other is down.
- C) Incorrect. In a false grip, the palms facing are down.
- **D) Correct.** The palms are facing each other in a neutral grip.

47.
- A) Incorrect. A heart rate taken before a workout would be considered a preworkout heart rate.
- B) Incorrect. A heart rate taken at the end of the day may be affected by factors such as stress, food, or beverages consumed.
- **C) Correct.** The best time to measure resting heart rate is upon rising in the morning for three consecutive days.
- D) Incorrect. Taking heart rate measurements during a workout would alter the heart rate due to the activity level.

48.
- A) Incorrect. Alternated grips are both underhanded and overhanded.
- B) Incorrect. Supinated grips are underhanded.
- **C) Correct.** A pronated grip is also known as an overhanded grip.
- D) Incorrect. A clean grip requires wrist flexion: the palms are facing the ceiling and the fingers are supporting a barbell at the shoulders.

49.
- A) Incorrect. 1:5 allows too long a recovery period to elicit an overload effect for cardiovascular training when the activity is as light as jogging.
- B) Incorrect. This ratio may be too difficult for individuals who are just starting.
- C) Incorrect. This ratio will likely be too difficult for individuals new to running.
- **D) Correct.** A 1:1 work-to-rest ratio of jogging and walking should be enough for most individuals who are new to running programs.

50.
- **A) Correct.** Motions from side to side cross the plane that bisects the body into anterior and posterior halves.
- B) Incorrect. Motions from front to back cross the plane that bisects the body into left and right haves—the sagittal plane.
- C) Incorrect. Twisting motions cross the plane that bisects the body into superior and inferior halves—the transverse plane.
- D) Incorrect. This is not a plane of motion.

51.
- **A) Correct.** A tuck jump is a plyometrics exercise.
- B) Incorrect. A tuck jump uses explosive force, but explosive training is not a training classification.
- C) Incorrect: A tuck jump is a bodyweight exercise and therefore not considered resistance training.
- D) Incorrect: Kettlebells are not used while doing a tuck jump.

52. A) Incorrect. Only the shoulders are a point of contact in a standing or sitting position.
    B) **Correct.** These are the three parts of the body that should maintain points of contact with the wall or dowel.
    C) Incorrect. The calves are not a point of contact in a standing or sitting position.
    D) Incorrect. The heels are not a point of contact in a standing or sitting position.

53. A) Incorrect. The client can benefit from other modes of aerobic exercise including running.
    B) Incorrect. The client can benefit from other modes of aerobic exercise including these two.
    C) **Correct.** For general health benefits, the mode of aerobic exercise does not matter and whatever modes the client prefers should be implemented.
    D) Incorrect. For improvements to cardiovascular and respiratory fitness, which are important general health benefits, aerobic exercise is required.

54. A) Incorrect. Another name for a forearm muscle is extensor carpi.
    B) Incorrect. Another name for a thigh muscle is the quadriceps.
    C) **Correct.** The gastrocnemius is the power producing muscle of the calf.
    D) Incorrect. The trapezius is a stabilizing muscle in the neck.

55. A) Incorrect. Age is a personal attribute.
    B) **Correct.** Accessibility is an environmental factor.
    C) Incorrect. Time is a personal attribute.
    D) Incorrect. Fitness level is a personal attribute.

56. A) Incorrect. Horizontal loading refers to performing multiple sets of a single exercise with intermittent rest periods.
    B) Incorrect. Single set refers to performing one set of each exercise during a workout.
    C) Incorrect. Interval training refers to using a timer to determine the work-to-rest ratio rather than repetitions.
    D) **Correct.** Vertical loading is a form of circuit training that loads different muscles per exercise to minimize rest.

57. A) Incorrect. While quickness and agility are connected, agility is the body's ability to accelerate and decelerate more so than reacting to a direction change.
    B) **Correct.** Quickness is the body's ability to react to changing direction.
    C) Incorrect. Readiness is not a term that describes an exercise function.
    D) Incorrect. Stabilization is the body's ability to utilize the core efficiently.

58. A) Incorrect. The terms power, muscle, and matter do not represent progressive fitness levels.
    B) Incorrect. Hard is not a fitness level.
    C) **Correct.** The terms stabilization, strength, and power represent three fitness levels.
    D) Incorrect. Body is not correct.

59. A) Incorrect. The drawing-in maneuver does activate the core.
    B) Incorrect. The drawing-in maneuver maintains neutral posturing.
    C) Incorrect. The drawing-in maneuver is used for all core exercises.
    D) **Correct.** The drawing-in maneuver does not stretch the hips.

60. A) Incorrect. Though plyometrics do increase muscular power, they may place dangerous forces on the already overstressed joints of overweight individuals.
    B) Incorrect. This is an opinion of the client and not relevant to the question.
    C) Incorrect. They are in the category of higher intensity exercises and can be difficult for many people.
    D) **Correct.** The force from landing after a plyometric jump exercise places excessive stress on the joints of the

ankles, knees, and hips, and may be dangerous for individuals who are overweight or obese.

61. A) Incorrect. Seven points of contact is appropriate for a supine position and would include the right calf and left calf.

B) Incorrect. Three points of contact refers to a neutral standing position—the head, mid-back, and glutes would touch the wall.

C) Incorrect. There are no body positions that require four points of contact.

D) Correct. The five points of contact in a semi-supine position are at the head, shoulders, glutes, right foot, and left foot.

62. A) Correct. The mode of cardiovascular exercise for weight loss is not important.

B) Incorrect. Variety in cardio activities is beneficial for weight-loss clients because it keeps programs from becoming stale.

C) Incorrect. The mode should vary in the energy systems used to prevent program staleness.

D) Incorrect. If the client is cleared for physical activity and has no restrictions detailed by a physician, the client can participate in cardio that has impact.

63. A) Correct. Plyometric moves are compact to aid in footwork focus and aerodynamics.

B) Incorrect. SAQ exercises should be fast, not slow.

C) Incorrect. No exercise should be painful—only challenging.

D) Incorrect. Here, controlled is synonymous with slow.

64. A) Correct. Structural exercises load the spine, the main postural component of the body to increase strength.

B) Incorrect. Power exercises are core exercises, but they are not load bearing and typically utilize reactive motions to increase force production.

C) Incorrect. Agility exercises typically do not use any weight and focus on agility through footwork and deceleration.

D) Incorrect. Assistance exercises are not core exercises and recruit single joint action and small muscle groups.

65. A) Incorrect. The waist-to-hip ratio correlates chronic diseases and fat stored in the midsection.

B) Incorrect. Air displacement plethysmography (BOD POD) is used to assess body composition.

C) Correct. Body mass index is used to assess weight relative to height.

D) Incorrect. Skinfold measurements are used to assess body composition.

66. A) Incorrect. Plyometrics training increases force production.

B) Incorrect. Cardio training increases aerobic endurance.

C) Incorrect. Free weight training increases prime mover and joint strength.

D) Correct. Core training increases core strength with balance.

67. A) Correct. Ice skaters utilize full range of motion and lateral explosive repetitions.

B) Incorrect. Ice skaters require balance, but the abdominals are not the prime movers, and the repetitions are not slow and steady.

C) Incorrect. This is a bodyweight move.

D) Incorrect. There is no focus on muscle lengthening in ice skaters.

68. A) Correct. The 1RM is single repetition maximum to determine the client's maximal effort of strength for one repetition of an exercise.

B) Incorrect. The 1RM determines strength for a single exercise, not all exercises.

C) Incorrect. Target heart rate zone is determined by the Karvonen formula.

D) Incorrect. Although estimates can be made from the 1RM for submaximal efforts, the 1RM test is for a single repetition.

69.
- **A)** Incorrect. Sandbags, resistance tubes, and stability balls are used for functional training.
- **B)** Incorrect. Free weights, functional equipment, and weight machines are used for resistance training.
- **C)** Incorrect. Bodyweight, medicine balls, and boxes are used for power training.
- **D) Correct.** Treadmills, elliptical trainers, and rowing machines are used for aerobic training.

70.
- **A)** Incorrect. Push jerks are explosive moves, while structural exercises are controlled.
- **B)** Incorrect. Stability exercises focus on core strength and controlled repetitions.
- **C) Correct.** Push jerks incorporate multiple muscle groups and challenge force production while building strength through explosive motions.
- **D)** Incorrect. While the lifter is standing, this does not classify any exercise; it is too generalized.

71.
- **A) Correct.** Detraining occurs more rapidly in the aspects of a cardiovascular training program.
- **B)** Incorrect. There is a more gradual detraining in muscular strength and some is retained following a short period of exercise cessation.
- **C)** Incorrect. Previously trained clients will retain some of their strength following cessation of a training program.
- **D)** Incorrect. This will depend on the type of professional athlete, and any muscular strength training will be retained slightly.

72.
- **A)** Incorrect. Cardiorespiratory assessments are used to help personal trainers identify safe and effective exercise intensities for cardiorespiratory exercise.
- **B)** Incorrect. Movement assessments are used to observe dynamic posture.
- **C)** Incorrect. Muscular endurance assessments are used to determine muscular endurance capacity.
- **D) Correct.** Physiological assessments, such as resting heart rate and blood pressure measurements, are indicators of an individual's general fitness and overall health.

73.
- **A)** Incorrect. Push-and-pull routines use a variety of large muscle groups on opposing sides of the body, limiting the risk of muscular imbalances.
- **B)** Incorrect. The bodyweight training program described includes exercises for both chest and back muscles, reducing the chance of one-dimensional training.
- **C)** Incorrect. A trained yoga instructor will incorporate exercises to increase flexibility and utilize all the major muscle groups, reducing the risk of muscular imbalances.
- **D) Correct.** Unilateral training programs have a high risk of causing muscular imbalances. A program focusing on the chest and anterior deltoids specifically can cause rounding of the shoulders and muscular imbalances of the upper body.

74.
- **A)** Incorrect. This is a supinated grip.
- **B) Correct.** The thumb wraps around the same side as the fingers.
- **C)** Incorrect. This is a hook grip.
- **D)** Incorrect. This is the same as a supinated grip.

75.
- **A)** Incorrect. Static stretching can limit strength and power output, causing poor performance and potential injury.
- **B)** Incorrect. Static stretching can harm power exercise performance such as plyometrics.
- **C)** Incorrect. Cardiovascular exercise should follow the same warm-up protocol as resistance training.
- **D) Correct.** Static stretching should be implemented in a flexibility program after the muscles have been warmed up and exercised to elongate the muscles.

76. **A) Correct.** Typical mesocycles include multiple microcycles and last around six to twelve weeks.
    B) Incorrect. This time period is too short.
    C) Incorrect. This time period is too long and is more likely for a macrocycle.
    D) Incorrect. This time period is far too long for a single mesocycle and the client will never reach peak performance.

77. A) Incorrect. The floor crunch lifts the head, neck, and shoulders, while the reverse crunch lifts the hip flexors and the pelvic floor; therefore the floor crunch is not the best regression for the reverse crunch.
    B) Incorrect. The floor crunch is performed in the semi-supine position, while the plank hold is performed in the prone position; therefore the floor crunch is not the best regression for the plank hold.
    C) Incorrect. The floor crunch lifts the head, neck, and shoulders, while the hip bridge lifts the glutes and the pelvic floor; therefore the floor crunch is not the best regression for the hip bridge.
    D) Correct. The floor crunch targets the same muscles and follows the same range of motion as the ball crunch; however the floor crunch allows for more stabilization than the ball crunch. Thus it is an ideal regression for a client who is not ready for the controlled instability a stability ball provides.

78. A) Incorrect. Using the ABC model of behavior to identify triggers is an example of relapse prevention and recovery plans.
    B) Correct. Planning a weekly menu and a shopping list is an example of time management, not relapse prevention and recovery plans.
    C) Incorrect. Not focusing on fault is an example of relapse prevention and recovery plans.
    D) Incorrect. Relapse prevention and recovery plans can include creating contingency plans.

79. A) Incorrect. The shoulders reveal upper crossed syndrome.
    B) Incorrect. The foot and ankle reveal pronation distortion syndrome.
    C) Incorrect. The head and cervical spine reveal upper crossed syndrome.
    D) Correct. The lumbo/pelvic/hip complex reveals lower crossed syndrome.

80. A) Incorrect. An estimated maximum heart rate is used in the formula.
    B) Correct. The formula is used to calculate the target heart rate for an activity.
    C) Incorrect. The client's resting heart rate is used in the formula.
    D) Incorrect. Heart rate recovery is determined using another method.

81. A) Incorrect. Flexibility is not greatly improved by either of these training techniques.
    B) Incorrect. Power exercises are high intensity.
    C) Incorrect. Muscular endurance exercises are lower intensity.
    D) Correct. Since technique is important with power exercises, they should be performed before the muscles suffer from fatigue and performance suffers.

82. A) Incorrect. Forward movement speed would be more important for the players moving up and down the field.
    B) Incorrect. Steady-state cardiovascular exercise will not benefit either position more.
    C) Incorrect. All positions in soccer will benefit from kicking and core power exercises.
    D) Correct. The lateral movement requirement for the goaltender is higher than for the players and therefore the goaltender will benefit more from specific movements in this plane.

83. A) Incorrect. Progression refers to a gradual increase in intensity throughout a training program.

ANSWER KEY 347

- B) Incorrect. Regression refers to a decrease in difficulty of exercise due to limitation or inability to perform the exercise.
- C) Incorrect. Detraining is the effect of cessation of a training program.
- **D) Correct.** This is the principle of specificity.

84.
- A) Incorrect. Two spotters is too few.
- **B) Correct.** There should be room for at least three spotters at a free weight barbell bench.
- C) Incorrect. One spotter is not enough for a free weight bench.
- D) Incorrect. There must be room for the lifter and at least three spotters.

85.
- A) Incorrect. The goal is specific in that the client wants to lose twenty-five pounds.
- B) Incorrect. The goal is time-stamped in that the client wants to lose the weight in two months.
- **C) Correct.** The goal is not realistic as this much weight loss is dangerous and unsustainable by healthy weight-loss methods.
- D) Incorrect. The goal is measurable in that the client's weight is the measurement.

86.
- A) Incorrect. This amount of training increase is too little to elicit an overload effect and training progression.
- **B) Correct.** The cardiovascular training variables should not be increased by more than 10% from workout to workout.
- C) Incorrect. This increase is too much and may cause overtraining.
- D) Incorrect. This increase is too much and may cause overtraining.

87.
- **A) Correct.** Cardiovascular retraining after a period of detraining can take several months to return to peak performance.
- B) Incorrect. The body does not recover cardiovascular fitness that quickly.
- C) Incorrect. Detraining does have an impact on cardiovascular fitness.
- D) Incorrect. With a healthy client, proper program design, and implementation it should not take several years.

88.
- A) Incorrect. The LPHC should be viewed posteriorly.
- **B) Correct.** These checkpoints should be viewed laterally.
- C) Incorrect. The knees should be viewed anteriorly.
- D) Incorrect. The ankles and feet should be viewed anteriorly.

89.
- A) Incorrect. A macrocycle includes off-season training as well.
- **B) Correct.** The macrocycle encompasses the entire training periodization.
- C) Incorrect. A macrocycle includes in-season training as well.
- D) Incorrect. A macrocycle includes all preparatory, transition, competition, and second transition periods.

90.
- A) Incorrect. Resistance training effects are retained longer than cardiovascular gains after stopping an exercise program.
- **B) Correct.** Cardiovascular gains are noticeably different only two weeks after training cessation.
- C) Incorrect. Gender does not make a significant difference in detraining effects.
- D) Incorrect. Gender does not make a significant difference in detraining effects.

91.
- A) Incorrect. Excessive frequency may not necessarily cause rapid gains because overuse injuries are more likely.
- B) Incorrect. Excessive frequency may cause added stress due to the body constantly being stressed through exercise.
- C) Incorrect. Training intensity and frequency are two different variables.
- **D) Correct.** Overuse injuries often occur due to excessive training frequency.

92.
- A) Incorrect. Interval training typically involves work-to-rest ratios and is not long distance.
- B) Incorrect. Zone training describes a method for increasing the intensity of aerobic conditioning, starting at long distance and working up to sprints at near-maximum heart rate.
- C) Incorrect. Anaerobic endurance is similar to interval training, in which rest periods are required for repeated high-intensity bouts of exercise.
- **D) Correct.** A 10-kilometer row is a steady-state aerobic exercise because a steady heart rate is maintained for the majority of the event, which has a long duration.

93.
- A) Incorrect. The triceps is a primary mover in a triceps extension.
- **B) Correct.** The forearm is a primary mover for a wrist curl.
- C) Incorrect. The shoulder is a primary mover for a lateral raise.
- D) Incorrect. The biceps is a synergist muscle for the wrist curl.

94.
- A) Incorrect. Diet journaling is a self-monitoring tool to modify behavior.
- B) Incorrect. Activity tracking is another example of a self-monitoring tool.
- **C) Correct.** This is an example of the rewarding technique for behavior modification.
- D) Incorrect. Incorporating weekly weigh-ins would be considered a self-monitoring tool.

95.
- A) Incorrect. Decrease in weight causes decrease in intensity.
- B) Incorrect. Increase in volume causes decrease in weight and therefore decrease in intensity.
- **C) Correct.** Increase in weight causes an increase in intensity.
- D) Incorrect. Increase in repetitions is similar to increase in volume, causing a decrease in intensity.

96.
- A) Incorrect. There are ways to progress a single-leg squat.
- B) Incorrect. This would be a regression of the same exercise.
- **C) Correct.** Adding weight to the exercise will increase the intensity and be a progression.
- D) Incorrect. A new exercise would not be a progression of the same exercise.

97.
- A) Incorrect. A one-minute rest period is insufficient for recovery.
- B) Incorrect. A rest period of less than thirty seconds is far too short for recovery.
- **C) Correct.** At heavy loads and low volumes, rest periods should be three minutes.
- D) Incorrect. Six minutes is too long a recovery period, and the muscles will start to cool down.

98.
- A) Incorrect. Lower back pain does not require a client to see a medical professional.
- B) Incorrect. Anterior knee pain does not require immediate medical attention.
- **C) Correct.** A client who has had a recent complication due to cardiac disease must be referred to a medical professional before the assessment may begin.
- D) Incorrect. A client who does not feel well generally does not need an immediate medical referral.

99.
- A) Incorrect. This is associated with misaligned lumbo/pelvic/hip complex.
- **B) Correct.** This is associated with misaligned neck, shoulders, and midback.
- C) Incorrect. This is associated with misalignment of the feet and ankles.
- D) Incorrect. This is associated with pronation distortion, causing the knees to internally rotate.

100.
- A) Incorrect. The program is incomplete and missing warm-up, cooldown, and cardiovascular training.

B) Incorrect. The program is incomplete and missing warm-up, cooldown, and resistance training.

C) Incorrect. The program is incomplete and missing warm-up, cooldown, resistance training, and cardiovascular training.

D) **Correct.** This program includes all of the major components of a workout.

101. **A)** **Correct.** These forms are used by fitness professionals to ensure they have taken all measures to improve client safety prior to exercise, to inform the client, and to ensure the trainer has the client's consent to begin training.

B) Incorrect. A client's hobbies may help in designing an exercise plan, but they will not minimize risk, and a bloodwork form is beyond the fitness professional's scope of practice.

C) Incorrect. The bloodwork form is beyond the fitness professional's scope of practice.

D) Incorrect. The fitness assessment should not be performed until all forms are completed and signed.

102. A) **Correct.** The resting heart rate is the strongest indicator of how the cardiorespiratory system is responding and adapting to exercise.

B) Incorrect. The 1.5-mile run is an assessment of cardiorespiratory fitness but does not provide a strong indicator of how the cardiorespiratory system responds to exercise.

C) Incorrect. Body composition is not an indicator of cardiorespiratory fitness.

D) Incorrect. Muscular strength is not an indicator of cardiorespiratory fitness.

103. A) **Correct.** Income is a personal attribute.

B) Incorrect. Income is not an environmental factor.

C) Incorrect. Income cannot be considered a physical-activity factor.

D) Incorrect. Income is not a core factor.

104. A) Incorrect. The compensation of the knees would be adducted or abducted.

B) **Correct.** The compensation of the feet from the anterior view is neither flattened nor externally rotated.

C) Incorrect. The compensation of the hips is anteriorly or posteriorly rotated.

D) Incorrect. The compensation of the head is tilted or rotated.

105. A) Incorrect. The long jump test is used to measure maximal jumping distance.

B) **Correct.** The barbell squat test is used to measure lower body strength.

C) Incorrect. The overhead squat assesses dynamic flexibility.

D) Incorrect. The hexagon test is used to measure agility.

106. A) Incorrect. This is a characteristic of correct posture.

B) Incorrect. This is a characteristic of correct posture.

C) **Correct.** The shoulders should remain neutral and in line with the LPHC; the head and neck should be straight, with eyes gazing forward.

D) Incorrect. This is a characteristic of correct posture.

107. A) **Correct.** A professional trainer should wear tasteful and modest attire that is representative of the fitness industry.

B) Incorrect. A professional trainer should wear attire appropriate for the fitness industry.

C) Incorrect. The attire of a professional trainer should be tasteful and modest.

D) Incorrect. A personal trainer's attire should be clean and appear professional to clients.

108. A) **Correct.** Only 7 percent of communication is through verbal communication.

B) Incorrect. The figure of 10 percent is not accurate.

C) Incorrect. Fifty-five percent of our communication is commonly attributed to our body language.

D) Incorrect. Vocal quality makes up 38 percent of our communication.

109. A) Incorrect. This is much higher intensity than the client will ever experience while golfing.
B) **Correct.** Walking at varying inclines on a treadmill may mimic the layout of the golf course.
C) Incorrect. Golfers do not typically ride bicycles on the course and this is a much higher-intensity activity than is typically seen in golf.
D) Incorrect. Golfing relies on kinesthetic control; long-distance cardiovascular activity is not a factor in a golf match.

110. A) Incorrect. It is possible to use college courses to earn CEC requirements.
B) Incorrect. Industry specialization certifications can be used to obtain CEC points.
C) **Correct.** Contributing to a scholarly article is an acceptable way to earn CECs, but contributing to a blog is not; blogs are not considered scholarly.
D) Incorrect. It is possible to apply accredited programs' learning modules to obtain CEC points.

111. A) **Correct.** The certified fitness professional may administer the test under the guidance of the physician supervising the clinical team.
B) Incorrect. Medical treatment and procedures are the responsibility of the supervising physician.
C) Incorrect. Diagnosing symptoms is the responsibility of the supervising physician.
D) Incorrect. The certified fitness professional does not supervise the physician during testing procedures.

112. A) Incorrect. A program that focuses mainly on the upper body will not help to reduce chronic back pain.
B) **Correct.** Core strengthening and improving flexibility (especially in the hamstrings) can help to limit chronic back pain and should be the focus of the training program.
C) Incorrect. Lower body resistance training will not reduce lower back pain.
D) Incorrect. Avoiding the problem all together will only weaken the client and could potentially make things worse.

113. A) Incorrect. Client dissatisfaction could be related to a number of issues.
B) Incorrect. Environmental emergencies typically are unavoidable, but emergency action plans can limit liability.
C) **Correct.** One potential source of negligence lawsuits is equipment breakdown and the resultant injuries. This risk can be reduced with routine equipment maintenance.
D) Incorrect. Overtraining injuries are not typically due to faulty equipment.

114. A) Incorrect. Zone training eventually increases in intensity as the client progresses.
B) Incorrect. The mode can change in zone training programs.
C) **Correct.** It provides exercise variance through different target heart rate zones and keeps the program interesting for the client.
D) Incorrect. It does not necessarily take less time than steady state and even starts by training the client in steady state.

115. A) **Correct.** Stimulus control is a behavior modification tool to facilitate a change of habits.
B) Incorrect. Socio-ecological theory is considered a behavioral change model.
C) Incorrect. Self-monitoring does not fit the description provided.
D) Incorrect. Locus of control is not a tool to bring about behavior change.

116. A) Incorrect. The activity as described is not an example of cognitive coping.

B) Incorrect. Self-talk is not part of social support.

C) **Correct.** Using positive self-talk to acknowledge successes is an example of the relapse prevention tool.

D) Incorrect. Time management does not include positive self-talk to acknowledge success.

117. A) Incorrect. The readiness-to-change model focuses on cultivating a person's self-efficacy to facilitate behavior change.

B) Incorrect. The social cognitive theory model focuses on one person's observing a change in someone else to motivate his or her own decisions.

C) Incorrect. While the theory of planned behavior is closely related to the description, it does not focus on the whole environment, no matter how removed, as a factor in behavior change.

D) **Correct.** This is the correct descriptor for the socio-ecological model.

118. A) **Correct.** Accepting responsibility for one's actions is not necessarily considered a legal or ethical issue, but it is a standard that a professional trainer should maintain.

B) Incorrect. Maintaining accurate notes on each client is an ethical standard for personal trainers.

C) Incorrect. This is a legal or ethical standard. Personal trainers must not discriminate based on race, gender, creed, age, ability, or sexual orientation.

D) Incorrect. Complying with sexual harassment standards is a legal or ethical standard for personal trainers.

119. A) Incorrect. An internal locus of control is the belief that a person has control over his or her own life.

B) Incorrect. Intrinsic characterizes motivation.

C) **Correct.** Those with an external locus of control believe that outside forces control their lives.

D) Incorrect. This is not a locus of control descriptor.

120. A) Incorrect. People in the preparation phase have a moderate self-efficacy but may still feel their locus of control is external.

B) **Correct.** People in the precontemplation phase have both a low self-efficacy and an external locus of control.

C) Incorrect. People in the action phase have grown their self-efficacy to a moderate level and are shifting from an external locus of control to an internal locus of control.

D) Incorrect. People in the termination phase have grown their self-efficacy maximally and have shifted into an internal locus of control.

121. A) **Correct.** The ABC model of behavior helps a person identify triggers for unwanted and desirable behaviors.

B) Incorrect. Obsessions are not a focus of this model.

C) Incorrect. Irritants can be considered a negative trigger, but not a positive one.

D) Incorrect. Successes can be considered a product of using this model.

122. A) Incorrect. Liability insurance covers defamation.

B) Incorrect. Liability insurance covers invasion of privacy.

C) Incorrect. Neither liability nor miscellaneous insurance covers wrongful termination.

D) **Correct.** Miscellaneous personal trainer's insurance covers bodily injury.

123. A) Incorrect. Kinesthetic feedback is not an actual type of feedback.

B) Incorrect. Positive reinforcement is not necessarily specific.

C) **Correct.** This is the correct description of targeted praise.

D) Incorrect. The description is not limited to just non-verbal communication.

124.
- A) Incorrect. This is too much resistance.
- B) Incorrect. This is too much resistance.
- **C) Correct.** Weights during muscular power exercises should be between 0 and 60% of 1RM for safe implementation.
- D) Incorrect. This is too much resistance.

125.
- A) Incorrect. The first transition period is between the preparatory period and competitive period.
- B) Incorrect. These are not the periods; they are the cycles.
- C) Incorrect. The order is incorrect.
- **D) Correct.** The preparatory period is first, followed by the first transition period, then the competitive period, and finally the second transition period.

Go to **ascenciatestprep.com/cscs-online-resources** to take your second CSCS practice test and to access other online study resources.

ANSWER KEY 353

www.ingramcontent.com/pod-product-compliance
Lightning Source LLC
Chambersburg PA
CBHW080724230426

43665CB00020B/2608